THE CORRESPONDENCE OF
H. G. WELLS

Volume 2 1904–1918

H G Wells and his mother, Spade House, 1903 (*H G Wells Papers, University of Illinois Library*).

THE CORRESPONDENCE OF H. G. WELLS

VOLUME 2

1904–1918

Edited by

DAVID C. SMITH

Consulting Editor

Patrick Parrinder

MUNDUS INTELLECTUALIS

LONDON
PICKERING & CHATTO
1998

Published by Pickering & Chatto (Publishers) Limited

21 Bloomsbury Way, London, WC1A 2TH

Old Post Road, Brookfield, Vermont 05036, USA

BRITISH LIBRARY CATALOGUING IN PUBLICATION DATA

Wells, H. G. (Herbert George), 1866–1946
The correspondence of H. G. Wells. – (The Pickering masters)
1. Wells, H. G. (Herbert George), 1866–1946 – Correspondence
2. Novelists, English – 20th century – Correspondence
I. Title II. Smith, David
823.9′12
Set ISBN 1 85196 173 9
This volume ISBN 1 85196 171 2

LIBRARY OF CONGRESS CATALOGING-IN-PUBLICATION DATA

Wells, H. G. (Herbert George), 1866–1946
(Correspondence)
The correspondence of H. G. Wells / edited by David Clayton Smith.
p. cm.
Includes index.
Contents: v. 1. 1880–1903 – – v. 2. 1904–1918 – – v. 3. 1919–1934 – – v. 4. 1935–1946.
ISBN 1–85196–173–9 (set : alk. paper). – – ISBN 1–85196–170–4 (v. 1 : alk. paper). – – ISBN 1–85196–171–2 (v. 2 : alk. paper). – – ISBN 1–85196–172–0 (v. 3 : alk. paper). – – ISBN 1–85196–158–5 (v. 4 : alk. paper).
Wells, H. G. (Herbert George), 1866–1946 – – Correspondence. 2. Novelists. English – – 20th century – – Correspondence. 3. Journalists – – Great Britain – – Correspondence. I. Smith, David C. (David Clayton), 1929– . II. Title.
PR5776.A4 1996
823′.912 – – dc20
[B] 96–31086
CIP

∞

This publication is printed on acid-free paper that conforms to the American National Standard for the Permanence of Paper for Printed Library Materials

Typeset by Waveney Typesetters
Wymondham, Norwich

Printed and bound in Great Britain by
Redwood Books, Trowbridge

CONTENTS

CHRONOLOGY

1903–4	Second son, Frank Wells born. Gissing dies. Publishes *Twelve Stories and a Dream* and his second political work, *Mankind in the Making*. Close friendship with Graham Wallas. Member of discussion group, The Co-efficients. Other friends include G. B. Shaw, E. Ray Lankester, Violet Paget ('Vernon Lee'), E. Nesbit, Henry Newbolt. *The Food of the Gods* appears.
1905	Writing steadily. Wide correspondence, growing circle of both literary and political friends. *Kipps* and *A Modern Utopia* appear.
1906	[Letters 612–655] Visits USA, and writes *The Future in America*. Publishes *In the Days of the Comet*. Falls in love with Amber Reeves. Publishes *Socialism and the Family*.
1907	Becomes centre of a political storm over future government of England and place of Socialism, throughout much of 1907. Breaks with Fabians. Publishes *This Misery of Boots*.
1908	Third major political statement, *New Worlds for Old*, is published as is his personal philosophical statement, *First and Last Things*. *The War in the Air* also published.
1909–10	Anna-Jane, daughter of Wells and Amber Reeves Blanco-White is born. Great period of literary production. *Ann Veronica*, *The History of Mr. Polly* and *Tono-Bungay* are published. Moves to 17 Church Row, Hampstead.
1911	Spends from June to September in France at Maison du Canal, Pont de l'Arche, Eure.
1911–13	His collection of short fiction, *The Country of the Blind* appears. Begins Friendship with Frank Swinnerton. Moves to Little Easton Rectory, Dunmow, Essex. Publishes *Floor Games*, for children, *The New Machiavelli*, for adults. His talk, 'The Contemporary Novel', published. Brief love affair with Elizabeth von Arnim. Meets Rebecca West. Publishes *Marriage, Little Wars* and *The Passionate Friends*.

1914 First visit to Russia (January 1914). Rebecca West's son, Anthony, born in August 1914. First World War breaks out. Publishes *The World Set Free*, *An Englishman Looks at the World* and *The Wife of Sir Isaac Harman*. His collection of newspaper pieces from the beginning of the war, *The War That Will End War*, has strong impact on public opinion. When in London he lives at 52 St James's Court, Buckingham Gate.

1915 Publishes *Bealby*, *The Research Magnificent* and *Boon*. This last leads to a break with Henry James, and with many pursuers of 'Art for Art's Sake'. Little Easton Rectory now renamed Easton Glebe after remodelling.

1916–17 Publishes *Mr Britling Sees it Through* and *The Elements of Reconstruction* and *What is Coming?*. Tours battle fronts in France and Italy in August 1916, and writes *War and the Future*. Publishes a statement of unitarian-like belief, later renounced, *God the Invisible King*, with related novel, *The Soul of a Bishop*.

1918 Works at Crewe House on war propaganda. Secretary to League of Nations committee, a private group. Strong friendships with Americans, especially Walter Lippmann. *Joan and Peter* and *In the Fourth Year* appear.

NOTE

A full chronology of Wells's life, 1866–1946, appears in volume 1, pp. xliv–l.

The Correspondence of H. G. Wells 1904–1918

491. To Henry Landers[1]

Illinois, ACCS

Spade House
Sandgate

Jan 1, 04.

Dear Sir:

Very many thanks indeed for your sympathetic letter. Gissing was indeed one of the most agreeable of companions & the most lovable of men. The best portrait I know of Gissing was published by Grant Richards. It was [from] a sketch by Rothenstein.[2]

Yours sincerely,
H.G. Wells

Also a very good one, photography, of Elliott & Fry published in a supplement to Literature.

---

[1] Landers, from Acton, had sent him a letter of sympathy after Gissing's death.

[2] The well-known portrait artist William Rothenstein, had lived in the same neighbourhood as the Wellses and knew Gissing quite well.

492. To W. Baxter[1]

Bromley, ALS

Spade House
Sandgate, Kent

12. 1. 04

My dear Baxter,

I've had the most disturbed and melancholy Christmas – I spent Christmas day by poor Gissing's death bed in the Pyrenees – & I've failed to write & thank you for that most interesting souvenir of old Morley's home. It's rather sad, that poor eyeless broken skull of a home that was once so vehemently alive.

A very Happy New Year to you,
Yours ever,
H.G. Wells[2]

[1] Baxter was a local historian who lived in Bromley. Wells and Baxter's wife were students together at Mrs Knott's infant school in Bromley in 1873–4. There are a number of letters from Baxter to Wells, asking for details about his early life. Baxter did write a few articles about Wells and Bromley, but never finished the biography of Wells he talked of all his life. Eventually Wells grew tired of responding, often to the same question or a variant, and Jane took over replying to Baxter's queries.

[2] Morley was Wells's second teacher, who ran a small private school. Although Wells was often harshly critical of his early education, he never lampooned or attacked Morley. Part of the shell of the school, used as a retaining wall for another building, could still be seen at the top of the High Street in Bromley in the late 1960s and early 1970s. Wells had been called to George Gissing's bedside by Gissing's wife, and he did see him, but had been misinformed about the real state of his health, and left before he died. This misconception continued to distress Wells throughout his life. Morley Roberts, who witnessed the death and the funeral, wrote and described the scenes for him.

493. To Elizabeth Healey

Illinois, ALS

Spade House
Sandgate, Kent 18 – 1 – 04

Dear Miss Healey,

You will be interested to hear that Isabel has been married for a year or more. Financial considerations induced her to keep this secret from me for a time, but she has recently informed me of the new state of affairs & we have arranged to set aside the order for alimony on terms satisfactory to her. So, this remarkable false step of my youth comes to a decent end. But I am rather anxious about one little matter. I have recently been seeing very much of poor Gissing's affairs – I spent Christmas day by his death bed at St. Jean Pied de Port – & I'm very much unprepared by the ghoulish side of my fellow men. Frankly, have you any old letters of mine? I know that they are safe in your hands, but one never quite knows how these scraps of paper may not presently fly about. Do you mind making a little holocaust of anything you have if it could be you <u>have</u> kept anything. It might save my widow someday something highly disagreeable.[1]

Yours ever,
H.G. Wells

[1] It was at this time that Wells had a number of letters burned. As in virtually all such cases however not all of the letters were destroyed. He was angered by the news of the secret marriage and tore up Isabel's pictures when he heard the news. Miss Healey came to his rescue when the *Autobiography* was published and supplied him with her own photographs of Isabel. Wells was later disturbed by the extent of his emotion in this case.

494. To Elizabeth Healey

Illinois, ALS

National Liberal Club
Whitehall Place, S.W.

21 . 1 . 04

My dear Miss Healey,

I think if you've kept my letters to you, that on the whole I'd like you to go on keeping them. I know you'll consider my pure feelings in the particular matter I've raised, and for the rest I'd rather, if I may, put my trust in you than have them back.

I'm rather sick in the particular matter I referred to. I think Isabel has been just a little bit base in the matter of her marriage. I've always meant to give her a decent wedding present and it has rather disappointed me to find she didn't count on fair treatment from me. Instead of which she has stuck to the careless wording of the order of the court to which I consented and has insisted that her alimony keeps on after the marriage. No man of course would stand that & after a miserable wrangle, she has compounded for her expectations of alimony for just £50 less than the gift we had always designed for her – which is a dismal end so far as I am concerned.

I'm tremendously glad that you think well of my wife. She's really my biggest fluke & I conceal with difficulty a pretty abject gratitude to her for being what she is to me. There's a sort of sturdy loyalty your sex seems to find its happiness in giving (barring such cases as I.M.W. who after all has probably only transferred herself in a rather stupid manner) that seems to me the most gorgeous & thank-heaven-for an aspect of a Universe that is frequently in other directions by no means above criticism. I'll give the photographs to A.C.W. when I get home.

Yours ever,
H.G.

495. To Elizabeth Healey

Illinois, ACCS

Spade House
Sandgate, Kent 22. 1. 04

Dear Miss Healey.

I strongly repudiate my own request and leave all this business in your hands. I return these letters again & pray you at your discretion to destroy all that there is from first to last that gives information about the particular affair I would obliterate.[1] The rest – if you value it enough to keep it – I can only thank you for valuing. Jane sends her warmest thanks for your photograph & you're right in what you say of her.

Yours ever,
H.G.

[1] Whatever affair it was – whether the courtship of Isabel, or another person – Healey followed his directions, and the excerpts quoted earlier in this work represent what remains. Even here, it is not always obvious that her cuts may also involve some small rewriting when the transcribed excerpts were made. A great many of her letters from him ended on the antiquarian document market and are now in the Harry Ransom Library at the University of Texas. They appear elsewhere in this volume.

496. To A. T. Simmons

Illinois, ALS

Sandgate Jan. 22/04

Dearest old Tommie,

I've been through the documents, I've found one or two that most wounded my vanity and here are the rest. If I'd had the thought of a self respecting Pig, I'd have asked you to act for me in this weeding, & I only hope you'll forgive me.[1]It is really a wonderful thing to find that you have kept so much of me that I've come near forgetting. There was that foolish affair at Holt that I suppose I've never turned over in my mind for the last six years & more.

They're outpourings – & to a certain extent I can already sit in judgment on the young man who wrote them. Why, I wonder, doesn't he write so fully now to his old crony? I think that's the greatest question I've found in reading them. I don't think indeed that he cares for his old Crony less, & for a time I was doubtful whether perhaps the man growing ever busy with a little fuss of success hadn't neglected one of the best things in life in letting a kind of distance grow between these his fellow students. But I hope it's not so bad as that. It is true, though, that the letters & their answers were written by two very lonely young men & now, if you & I get a thing to say into our heads, we have our newer receptacles. I'm tremendously impressed by this fact, – so evident in these letters that if ever a concerted a....

[*letter breaks off here*]

---

[1] Wells asked several of his closest friends to return letters he had sent to them so that he might vet them. He destroyed a few letters, mainly, one suspects, dealing with Isabel, but most were then returned to their recipients. In this case, he apparently destroyed only one or two that had been written to Simmons.

497. Morley Roberts[1] to H. G. Wells

Illinois, APCS

Switzerland 2/2/04

My Dear Prophet of Sandgate,

Many thanks for your highly illegible letter, so full of genial insults. The symbolism of R.M. is altogether beyond you as I feared it would be. That is why I didn't send it to you at first. Cheer up, oh prophet, but don't rely too much on your logical prayer-wheel, else one will actually have to ask you to read your Carlyle and be a youth again. Do you really think that certain other books are not equally part of the mental fabric of the time? Bless you, you are a youth still, after all. If certain truths be hidden from us (as they doubtless are) who is wholly right? I hoped there were suggestions in the book even for you, my child. There is no phallicism in it, not a single phallus properly understood. But alas, what shall any poor artist do when his most respected fellows can't see for wind? Aleikorum Salaam, Effendi of the Shrine on the Hill of Pisgah.[2]

Yours ever,

Morley Roberts

---

[1] One of the more important of Wells's early literary friends was Morley Roberts, author of a

number of novels of adventure. He is virtually unknown today. Both he and Wells were close friends of Gissing. Roberts attended Gissing's funeral and provided Wells with a description of it. He was a bit uneasy with Wells and his talent, as the correspondence shows. We provide one postcard from Roberts to Wells in order to indicate the tone of their relationship. It is couched in an artificial eastern address, filled with homage. R.M. refers to Roberts's novel, *Rachel Marr* (London, 1903).

[2] The last phrase might be rendered 'To the highest Guardian of the shrine on top Mount Pisgah', probably meaning the world of belles-lettres. Mount Pisgah is another name for Mount Nebo, from which Moses viewed the Promised Land, Deuteronomy 3:27.

498. To Ralph Mudie-Smith[1]

Hofstra, ALS

[Sandgate?] 6 – ii – 04

Dear Mudie-Smith,

Thank you very warmly for your thought in sending me your most interesting book. – a valuable sociological contribution. I hope you are going to help with the new sociological society we are trying to get together. Have you heard of our little movement?[2] If not, I shall be glad indeed to give you the fullest information of our aims, which include a Sociological Review to which you must contribute. About your book I'd rather talk than write, because it raises so many points of interest. I shall be in London on the 18th. Would you care to lunch with me at the National Liberal Club? I should really like a gossip.

Yours sincerely
H.G. Wells

---

[1] Mudie-Smith was a young radical writer on sociological questions.

[2] The Sociological Society was formed but its activities tended to be more in the publication of papers than anything else. Three volumes of *Sociological Papers* were published in 1904, 1905 and 1906. One of the papers was by Wells, in which he refuted the claims of eugenics (1904) pp. 58–60. Under the lead of Francis Galton, the society debated many aspects of eugenic thinking in its papers. Wells was heavily involved with several such groups at this time; the Fabians and the Coefficients are other examples, and he frequently corresponded with such like-minded people. The intellectual activity which this created played a prominent role in developing the thought patterns in his books *A Modern Utopia* (1905), *New Worlds For Old* (1908) and *First and Last Things* (1908) as well as in a great many analytical pieces in the press on these matters. There are twenty-six articles on these subjects by H. G. Wells published from 1904 to 1906.

499. To Ralph Mudie-Smith[1]

Hofstra, ACCS

[Sandgate?] 6 – ii – 04

My dear Mudie-Smith,

I book you Feb 18th. National Liberal Club 1:30.

Yours ever,
H.G. Wells

[1] Wells is in the process of making Mudie-Smith's acquaintance in these first letters. This is apparently their first meeting. Later Mudie-Smith becomes an important ally in the Fabian imbroglio. Their relationship occurred after a discussion of the preaching of Dr Clifford, about to resign from the Fabians over the issues of taxation for religious schools.

500. To Frederic Harrison[1]

LSE, ALS

Spade House
Sandgate 6. ii. 04.

Dear Mr. Harrison,

I know Gissing was a private tutor and I knew he had known you, but either he never put the two things together or the connexion has slipped my memory. For the rest I think now that I knew his life pretty completely. On the whole I don't think that it is a bad thing that all these 'young lives' as you call them, should be moving in a fine ignorance & causing the less distress. All that is written about literature nowadays is such careless & slovenly nonsense, that it seems better for them to slop about with legends rather than with facts. They'd make a worse lie of the facts.

You know perhaps that Gissing left two boys. Don't you think that something might be done for their education? His brother Algernon, his executor, tells me there is an estate of about £600 & one third of that goes to the wife. I have been trying to interest people in this matter with an eye to the civil list, but I find this business rather beyond my scope & power.

Yours very sincerely,
H.G. Wells

[1] Harrison was a positivist and had known Gissing as a boy.

501. To the Rt Hon. George Wyndham[1]

Boston, ALS

Spade House
Sandgate 6. ii. 04

Dear Mr. Wyndham,

I am very much concerned about the children (two sons) of George Gissing, the novelist, who died this last Christmas & for whose education there is left only the scantiest sum (two-thirds of about £600). I do not know how you appreciate his work, but to many of us he seems among the greatest as well as the most disinterested of contemporary writers. (His 'By the Ionian Sea' pleased Henley very greatly and will I know appeal to you, whatever you think of the bulk of his early novels) and it seemed to me not altogether unreasonable to look to public resources for some help at least in this case. You will remember that a Civil List pension of £50 a year is paid for the education of Bob Stevenson's son, though there was an estate of over £7000, and I have thought that something of the same kind might be a not inappropriate tribute to the memory of another of the dwindling band that did not write for gain. I've ventured to bother you with this matter in spite of your great public preoccupations, because I live very much out of the world of affairs, & I do not know how to set about this sort of thing. Do you think anything can be done in this matter.

Yours very sincerely,
H.G. Wells

[1] George Wyndham was a wealthy, prominent Conservative Member of Parliament. The previous year he had resigned as Irish Secretary from Balfour's government over the question of devolution.

502. To Janet Achurch Charrington

Hofstra, ALS

Spade House
Sandgate
Feb. 20 04

Dear Miss Charrington,[1]

I wish indeed I had that play & were it in the least degree possible I should only be too ready to grasp your opportunity. I don't need to ask Shaw who you are. But indeed I've never written a play. I've helped with suggestions once or twice & now I have a poor beginning in hand. But this playwriting is clearly a difficult enterprise, and I think it must be unwise for me to be tempted to hurry this to a conclusion. I'm very sorry the play wasn't begun a while sooner. It's very delightful just at this point to find you think of me as a possible dramatist & later perhaps – when you won't want it – I shall appear blushing & with a red ruled type written document.

Yours very sincerely
H. G. Wells

---

[1] Janet Achurch was an actress, the wife of Charles Charrington a theatre manager in Manchester. She played Cleopatra in 1897 to good reviews. Wells dabbled with the stage, but, as Shaw told him, the amount of work it took to do well enough was not an economic use of his time. Interestingly, Wells's novel, *The First Men in the Moon*, opens with a discussion of writing a failed play.

503. To Ralph Mudie-Smith

Hofstra, TLS

Spade House
Sandgate
21 2 04

My dear Mudie-Smith,

I have not answered your letter before because I have been in bed and out of action myself for the last few days. I had at the last moment to wire and cancel all my remaining engagements for Thursday and Friday. I do hope your week at Brighton has done you all the good in the world, and that our gossip has been deffered only for a little while. Can I book you for the 21st. of March? At same time and place.

Yours ever
H.G. Wells

[*in another hand*]
N.L.C.[1] one p.m.

[1] The National Liberal Club, which Wells frequented at that time.

504. To the Editor, *Daily Mail*[1]

Hofstra, ALS

[Spade House
Sandgate]
March 5/04

Dear Mr. Mee,

Proofs herewith.

I think now I've begun I'll run off the dozen articles I've contracted for.[2] Don't be in any hurry to begin 'em. Then when they do come, you can begin with three or four within a measurable distance of each other.

Yours ever,
H.G. Wells

[1] The editor was Arthur Mee (1875–1943), who was also a writer on a wide variety of subjects. In particular he is known for his books for children.

[2] There is a slight mystery about these articles. Wells contracted to write a dozen, of which six appeared on 14 and 24 March, 9, 20 and 28 April and 19 May 1904. The first and the last have never been reprinted. These articles appeared under the general title, 'From a Study Fireside'. A year later five more articles appeared under the general title 'Utopias'. These have never been reprinted. They appeared on 18 and 30 March, 18 and 20 April, 25 May and 7 June 1905. Another article on censorship also appeared much later in this year, but it was not connected to these two series, both of which are important pieces in the development of his thought.

505. To E.R. Pease [1]

LSE,[2] ALS

Spade House
Sandgate, Kent 17. 3. 04

My dear Pease,

Your letter reminds me of an intention I have been ripening, to resign my membership of The Fabian Society. I have now given up my flat in London and rare as were my attendances were last year I am afraid that were my membership to continue they would have to be still more infrequent in the future. This alone would not justify my abandoning the privilege & honour of calling myself a Fabian. But I find also that I am by no means in sympathy with the attitude adopted by the society toward various contemporary political issues. Neither the matter nor the manner of the recent tract upon "Free Trade" for example, is to my taste. Were I able to attend the meetings with any regularity I would do my poor best to establish my views & methods against the prevailing influence, in spite of my distinguished ineptitude in debate. As things are however I do not see what service I can do the society by remaining in it.[3]

Yours very sincerely
H.G. Wells

---

[1] Pease was a founder of the Fabian Society, one of the 'Old Gang'. He served as long time secretary to the society and as editor of *Fabian News*.
[2] Also read in manuscript at Bromley.
[3] This letter marks an early occasion on which Wells wanted to leave the Fabians because of the conservatism of their approach. Shaw, in particular, was well on his way to becoming an advocate for the Empire. The 'Old Gang' were able to persuade him to reconsider.

506. To Messrs Constable and Co.

Milwaukee, ALS

Spade House
Sandgate 20. iii. 04

Messrs Constable & Co.

Dear Sirs,

I am sending by the post the introduction to Gissing's "Veranilda." The past draft was submitted to his brother Algernon, Mrs. Gissing, Morley Roberts, an old school friend, Mr. Edward Clodd & Mr. Frederick Harrisson, and they have made various suggestions. I have done what I could to incorporate these, but in the case of Mrs. Gissing I am afraid nothing but gross praise would be satisfactory. I sympathise acutely with her feelings on the matter, but on the whole I think it advisable to maintain my tone of critical description.

Mr. Algernon Gissing will I believe make himself responsible for the correction of the proofs. But after his first revise, I think it might be well if you sent me duplicate proofs. Mr. Harrisson, who knows the period well, has offered to go through a proof & I think it will be a double guarantee of a correct text if we avail ourselves of his offer.

Yours very sincerely,
H.G. Wells

The typewritten copy of "Veranilda" was done by someone grossly ignorant of even the commonest names of the period. Totila[1] is spelt Irtila throughout & so on. Apart from such errors the copy is good. A.G. ought to write very carefully a full list of the dramatis personae I think to guide the printer.[2]

---

[1] Totila (d. 552) was the last king of the Ostrogoths. He controlled for a time central and southern Italy, until he was killed in battle against an army sent from Byzantium by Justinian.

[2] Even these changes were not enough for the Gissing family. Frederic Harrison finally wrote an 'acceptable' preface to the edition. Many in the literary world were disgusted with this turn of events, feeling that the removal of Wells's name cost the Gissing estate too much. Wells's proposed preface was later printed in *Monthly Review* as 'George Gissing: An Impression' (August 1904), pp. 160–72. It was also printed in a shorter version in *Living Age* and the *Eclectic Magazine*.

507. To Frederic Harrison

LSE, ALS

Spade House
Sandgate 20. iii. 04

Dear Mr. Harrison,

I'm very greatly obliged to you for your letter about Gissing and I very eagerly accept your offer to run through the proofs. I am almost magnificently ignorant of classical history, Algernon Gissing who is the responsible editor impresses me as rather careless & not by any means very learned, and the typewritten copy was never revised. I did, as a matter of fact, know all about the errata to which you refer but I find an easy charity in my heart for that crime, at any rate.

I hope too that we may have a meeting someday – it will certainly be a very interesting one for me.

Yours very sincerely,
H.G. Wells

508. To 'Vernon Lee'[1]

Colby, ALS

National Liberal Club
Whitehall Place, S.W.
(Please address me always
Spade House, Sandgate, Kent) 20 – iii – 04

Dear Miss Paget,

I was very glad indeed to have your letter and to learn that you read my books & find them interesting. I know your work very well indeed and it is a very pleasant surprise for me to find that with your nice sense of finish you can stand my crude & floundering efforts to reason out my difficulties. The preparation of bibliographies & guides on the lines I suggested is being done rather well in America by the Libermus (?) Association(?) under the influence of P.P. Wells & Geo Iles (?), but there is no doubt room for many workers in the field. Do you think of a translation of the guides of the Countess Paolini[?] into English or do you propose to use them simply as an example of what may be done? If the latter is the case, or even if the former is the case, I think I could interest Messrs. Macmillan in a project of the sort. Let me know your idea more fully & I will do what I can in the matter.

Do you know the work of the late George Gissing? I think you would find his By the Ionian Sea very much to your liking. If you do not know that, you will be rather surprised to hear that he has left a singularly fine romance of the time of Totila, complete except for the last three chapters. It is the sort of book that every visitor to Rome or Naples ought to read & I do hope you won't miss it.[2]

Yours very sincerely,
H.G. Wells

Do you ever come to England by way of Folkestone? We live not a mile from the pier & we shall be very glad if you will give us a chance of intercepting you with supper & a bed as you go or come.

---

[1] 'Vernon Lee' was the nom de plume of the early feminist author, Violet Paget (1856–1935). She wrote more than thirty books in her career. She was attracted to Wells's work and their correspondence was extensive, until they quarrelled over England's role in the First World War. The estrangement however did not last and they saw each other again in the 1920s and 1930s, although fewer letters exist from the latter period. Paget was an extremely good early critic of Wells's writing and he took notice of her criticisms. She was a confidante at the time of Amber Reeves's pregnancy.

[2] Wells is referring to Gissing's novel, *Veranilda.*

509. To Henry Newbolt

Hofstra, ALS

National Liberal Club
Whitehall Place, S.W. 21 – iii – 1904

My Dear Newbolt:

You are to be asked to join a Club called the Coefficients to which Reeves and I & such less important persons as Grey & Haldane belong. I hope you will consent to join our 13. We have no poet, and only one very second-rate literary man.[1] And also, how about the Society for the Visitation of Wells? Will it – in the persons of Reeves & you, meet for the week end, April 9th to 11th? I and Mrs. Wells will be very glad if it will.

Yours ever
H.G. Wells

[1] These letters to Sir Henry Newbolt (1862–1938) mark the strengthening of their friendship, which had begun earlier in the decade, see volume 1. The Coefficients were a dining and discussion club begun by Sidney Webb and Wells. It met on a monthly basis to discuss a paper presented by one of the members, who included Leo Amery, H. W. Massingham, Bertrand Russell, Pember Reeves (who is mentioned in this letter), R. B. Haldane, Sir Edward Grey, Halford Mackinder, Leo Maxse, James L. Garvin, Sydney Olivier and Lord Milner. The group met from December 1902 to late in1906. Wells spoke before the group on 'The Proper Shape of Municipal Organization', on 14 December 1903; 'The Future of the Coloured Races', on 16 January 1905, and 'The Higher Stage in Education', on 19 February 1906. He acted as rapporteur for Sidney Webb, on 'The Future Revolution in England's Local Government', on 17 April 1905. There were at least twenty-three meetings of the group and occasional guests were present; a summary of each meeting was published for members. This is another example of Wells's detractors failing to read the appropriate literature. There is no racism in 'The Future of the Coloured Races'; in fact it is an open invitation for everyone, regardless of race or colour,to accomplish whatever was possible .

510. To Edward Clodd[1]

Leeds, ALS

[Spade House
Sandgate, Kent] 25/ 3/ 04

My dear Clodd,

Very many thanks for your notes. I had sent the copy of the preface to Constables before your letter came but I shall try to weave in one or two of the Quotations. I think it will be very unwise for Gabrielle Gissing to come to England at this juncture. I have been promised – I may tell you in confidence – a small pension for their two children, but I really do not see how that project will get on if she advertises her existence just now. Can't you advise her to delay her visit? To us she has written nothing about it.

Yours very sincerely,
H.G. Wells[2]

[1] These letters to Edward Clodd (1840–1930) now form part of the Brotherton Collection at Leeds University, who have graciously granted permission to print. Gissing may have introduced them at the Omar Khayyam Club in the early 1890s.

[2] The issues between Gissing's literary executors and his family are very murky. Most biographers deal with his work, rather than his life. These letters, never before published, may help somewhat in aiding the understanding of these problems. Clodd was another singular writer, editor and observer of the literary scene. He and Wells were the Gissing literary executors. The Wells-Clodd relationship was stormy at times, especially over Henry James. The question at hand here is the legitimacy or illegitimacy of the Gissing children.

511. To Edward Clodd

Leeds, ALS

[Spade House
Sandgate]

[undated, but at virtually the same time as the previous and following letters]

Dear Clodd,

I didn't care after the hideous fuss made by the Gissing family about my obituary notice to incur fresh hostility & being mixed up in any further Gissing-ism. And it's doubtful after all, the Literary committee & so on at Manchester, if my name would not be rather a detriment to the subscription – list people than otherwise. Also [his] brother hasn't written [to] me. But its a good idea. You support it to make them at any rate get the name of the highest living authority on Gissing, – Thomas Seccombe. [1]

Yours ever,
H.G. Wells

[1] In the event the family did not choose Wells, Morley Roberts, Clodd or Seccombe, any of whom could have done a good job, but selected Frederic Harrison. These letters are very difficult to read because Wells's strong emotions apparently cause his handwriting to be quite illegible, and very small, which is frequently the case in a time of stress prior to the 1920s, when his handwriting stabilizes to the form known best. Letters to Seccombe and Roberts relating to this matter are included elsewhere in this volume.

512. To Edward Clodd

Leeds, ALS

[London] 30 -iii – 04

My dear Clodd,

So far as the pensions go it's all right – they're granted – £37 for each boy. But I do think it is silly for Miss Collet to bring Gabrielle over now.[1] Cannot Miss Collet be calmed in some way? If she begins to ventilate this romantic affair & generally to stir up the curiosity about Gissing that is now happily subsiding, there'll be the dance & all to pay! There are things – Harrisson knows them – that must not come out. Miss Collet probably knows nothing of the vehement reasons for letting everything personal subside. Cannot you suppress her? At any rate I think it would be well if you wrote to Gabrielle suggesting that she defer her visit to England for at least a year in order to end the risk of notoriety.

Yours sincerely,
H.G. Wells

[*Enclosed in this letter is a draft copy of Clodd's letter to Gabrielle, dated 30/3/04.*]

H.G.W. sent me a few days ago a draft of a preface wh he will contribute to the posthumous novel, & in sending it, I referred to yr coming to England.

He writes to me this morning to say that he thinks it important in the interests of the family that you shd postpone your visit. He is engaged in an effort to provide a pension for the 2 boys, & if any gossip which your coming over might cause to be set in motion, the scheme for the children's benefit may, indeed, will be imperilled.

He says. & of course it is so, that there is much curiosity afloat wh. it is important to suppress, & hence begs me to veto this suggestion, the only one wh. will further interest & wh. we all have at heart. E.C.

---

[1] Gabrielle Fleury was Gissing's common-law wife. Collet had similar claims on him. Gissings's marital situation was never a routine matter, and Wells and Clodd felt that this might damage the pension possibilities.

513. To Beatrice Webb

Illinois, ALS

Spade House
Sandgate
21[?] iii. 04

Dear Mrs. Webb,

I've not read the Prisons draft yet because I've been working fairly hard at the Utopia, so I'm writing to tell you as much & ask if it matters if I don't read it for three or four days more. Last night in bed I composed a long & insolent letter to you, the great part of which flew before daylight. It was first of all quite a lot of intricate thinking about these Webbs. The gist of the attack was to accuse you of being a "faceted" person – as distinguished from Webb who isn't. In these mechanical meditations I figured minds as of three classes, those which were of the nature of flames in which all facts are to be brought into relation (these are scientific & philosophical minds); those which are happy & amorphous, to these which have facets. Well you have a large main facet toward social & political inquiry, but every now & then you turn up another side. And here comes the story: – You were accused of having a Chestertonian facet, a G.K. Chestertonian facet. You like to take up some palpable absurdity such as the monarchy or the established church, produce beautiful upside-down reasons for regarding it as the most perfect of human institutions. There was much in this line, but this is all I can recall clearly of that lost epistle.

Yours very sincerely,
H.G. Wells

514. To E.R. Pease

LSE, ALS[1]

Spade House
Sandgate, Kent

8 – iv – 04

My dear Pease,

I haven't the heart to hold out against the Remonstrance of the Executive Committee. What's good enough for Dr. Clifford is good enough for me. I disapprove highly of the Fabian Society, withdraw my resignation, & am,

Yours very fraternally,
H.G. Wells

---

[1] Read in photocopy at Bromley.

515. To 'Vernon Lee'

Colby, ALS

Spade House
Sandgate

11 – 4 – 04

Dear Miss Paget,

My first inspection leaves me delighted with these beautifully printed little Guides.[1] I am perhaps handy more in the English rather than you at Florence – perhaps less so – but now & again opportunity comes to my door, & I may find the proper target for these convincing little books. Don't forget that we wait at Folkestone for birds of passage as the Capri people do with their nets.

Your admirer
H.G. Wells

---

[1] Paget had apparently sent Wells guides to Florence written in Italian. Individual cities in Italy often produced guides of their own, illustrated to accompany the Baedecker guides. The English and Italian language differences were occasionally quite great which probably accounts for Wells's comment. She may have asked Wells to consider rewriting them, or providing a market for them. The context is unclear.

516. To Henry Newbolt

Hofstra, ALS

[Spade House] 11 – 4 . 04

My dear Newbolt,

We had Prayers for you on Sunday night, & you were ever in our minds & hearts. We are a little doubtful of our influence up there & we shall be glad to hear you are better. Next time you must come dead or alive.

Yours,
H.G.

517. To Edward Clodd

Leeds, ALS

[Spade House,
Sandgate, Kent] 14. 4. 04

My dear Clodd,

Gabrielle Gissing has written to Miss Collet & she is too ill to come to England. I'm sorry to think of that poor woman ill, but I do think it is well for her & everyone that she should not come just now. Later on, when curiosity has quieted down, it will be different.

I shall be overjoyed and a little abashed to meet Meredith. He is so opulent that I have always had a certain terror of him. He's a Prince & his invitation is a command. For the 9th of May I am booked, but the 8th & 10th are clear. The 10th will suit me particularly well because I am in London on the night of the 9th.

Yours sincerely
H.G. Wells[1]

[1] George Meredith (1828–1909) was a late Victorian novelist, many of whose works Wells liked and some of which he reviewed in the *Saturday Review*. He is probably best known for *The Ordeal of Richard Feverel* (1859) and *Diana of the Crossways* (1885). He received the Order of Merit in 1905.

518. To Alex M. Thompson[1]

Bromley, Photocopy, ALS

Spade House
Sandgate, Kent

15 – iv – 04

Dear Mr. Thompson,

I'll be very glad to add a little more to the proof when it comes & I'm obliged to you for sending it. I'm constrained to think you had articles hastily done & superficial & a little vicious in temper, but I've done exactly the same sort of review myself & I know specifically how that sort of irritation comes about. If you really do devour my work greedily, how is it you accuse me of not discussing the means of changing inefficient to efficient after Mankind in the Making?

I'm afraid I can't hope to write anything for the Clarion. I want to do a little as well as I can – I think it's bad for a man & his subject & a sort of blacklegging to be all over the place & doing everything in a hurry. So that I have to exact a higher price for what I do – as Morris[2] had to do for his chairs & tables – and I get the best by giving virtual[?] monopolies and a period to things like the Strand (for stories) & the Daily Mail (for short articles.)

Yours very sincerely,
H. G. Wells

---

[1] Thompson was co-founder of the *Clarion*, a weekly newspaper of the Socialist left, who was apparently hoping that Wells would write regularly for the journal. He did write for it, but not on a regular basis. The other co-founder was Robert Blatchford, journalist, Socialist theorist and writer. Thompson was usually called 'Dangle'. What proof is being discussed is not known.

[2] William Morris, (1834–1896) the Socialist poet, and novelist, was prominent in the Arts and Crafts Movement, designing furniture and wallpaper. He was strongly associated with the Pre-Raphaelites Brotherhood. He is probably best known today for *The Well at the World's End* (1896) (which Wells reviewed), and *News From Nowhere* (1890). Wells met him once or twice and wrote a charming little essay on the occasion of the publication of *The Well at the World's End*; see *Saturday Review*, 17 October 1896, 'The Well at The World's End'.

519. To Henry Newbolt

Hofstra, ALS

[Spade House
Sandgate]
[? April 1904]

Sir,

I have read your honourable letter and I like the Poems. Clifton Chapel is admirable & antagonistic & helps me to understand things. I am depicted above awaiting your verdick.

Yours
H.G.

---

[1] Three letters from Wells to Newbolt appeared originally in Margaret Newbolt, ed., *The Later Life and Letters of Sir Henry Newbolt* (London: Faber and Faber, 1942). The originals are at Hofstra University. I read the last word in the letter as 'verdick', while the printed version gives it as 'suicide'. Wells and Newbolt had taken a long walk during this weekend and had argued about the beauty of Canterbury Cathedral. Newbolt sent Wells his book of poems, some of which were written at the cathedral. The book Newbolt sent may have been *The Island Race* (London: Elkin Matthews, 1898), but more probably it was an early version of *Clifton Chapel*.

520. To Beatrice Webb

LSE, ALS

National Liberal Club
Whitehall Place, S.W.

29. iv. 04

Dear Mrs. Webb,[1]

I read 'Prisons' before I came up yesterday, and Jane shall return it on Monday. My first impression is a profound regret that the public should get such admirable & thorough work done for nothing. Who is going to pay £1000 a year to research professors when you had turned out the best of work for nothing? I want to urge you strongly first of all to give all your private fortune to the Sch of Economics & then take all the income again as your salary. It's people like Darwin & yourselves who black leg research. You are all exactly in the position of the married woman who makes sweated shirts & ready made clothing. You make it nearly an impossible industry for unsupported persons like myself, & knock all the stuffing out of the arguments that might find a chair of sociology for me – not Kidd, not Geddes, not that flimsy thing Westermarck, but me to fill.[2] Then when I do put in a bit of fancy & affect a certain amount of manner & try & get a little easy money with the Sea Lady – Lord! But the disdain of you! But these are personal aspects of a great question that has nothing to do with 'prisons.'

About that I have first praise – which I pass over – & then to endorse what Shaw says about correlating a little more definitely the standard of comfort & so forth in the prisons with the social conditions outside. Was the mindless indecency, filthiness & violence in the prisons much lower than they were at the social level of the average person outside?[3] There is a risk that the reader will scale the eighteenth century prison against our contemporary standard of life & misapprehend the whole thing. I'm in sympathy with Shaw too in regarding the reformed prisons of the new type as far more horrible than the dirty display of humanity of the old school.

The range of your work[4] is necessarily restrictive in time. It throws a lot of light upon the psychology of authorities, workers & so forth under conditions that permitted private profits running out of control, but none upon the psychology under conditions that forbid such humanizing traffic.[5] Had you brought your work in to the present time, & made inquiries into American prisons, you would I think have found less disorder, perhaps, but more cruelty. You get glimpses of the sort of thing I mean in Marcus Clarke[6] , where rather dull minded, insolently bored gaol governors & warders are left under instruction astonishingly by that 'cant' with instruments of discipline & no other amusements at hand.[7] All actual prison results are special cases of the general psychology of authority. Similar groupings give similar results & quite [*illegible word*] prisons altogether. You will find the policemen & women of ill fame in the west end now, have quite similar relations to those existing between the turnkeys & women prisoners in old Newgate.I am inclined to say that where any class of people have relations of authorities over any other class, then any abuse of the first fair propositions of that relation that can be imagined, will presently be found in being. I think that in your summary you might point out that whatever arrangements are made for prisons in the future, the practical adminstration of the details of the business have to be entrusted to rather low common men. If only that fact is firmly grasped, a great multitude of well meaning projects for individual reformation, for profitable disciplinary treatment & so on, that might otherwise beget abuses may be powerfully knocked in the head. Prisons will always be heavy clumsy contrivances & all intervention with liberty in the nature of restraints are to be regarded as temporary expedients to be reduced to a minimum. Every possible device should be attempted before people are sent to prison. Then when you've got to the irreducible minimum, do them well.

I saw Branford here yesterday in a state of some depression about the S.S. I told him I thought the thing was on the running[?] lines, that it didn't seem likely to stand alone & that therefore it ought to lean up against other & stronger institutions. I said that he had lost the confidence of you people & that you were the people to whom he ought to have gone. I asked him why he hadn't come to you for advice & he said he didn't know you personally, which seems a stupid sort of reason under the circumstances. But why shouldn't the Scl of Economics annex the movement & employ Branford's activity & Kidd's aspirations[8] & Joyce & all the rest of the trimmings to some purpose.

Yours very sincerely
H.G. Wells

---

[1] This long letter, twelve pages in the original holograph, is somewhat difficult to read. Catherine and Wells had been guests at a dinner party on 20 April at the Webb's Grosvenor Street home. Other guests were the Prime Minister A. J. Balfour, the Bishop of Stepney, the Shaws, Mrs Pember Reeves and Wilfred Thesiger. In Beatrice Webb's diary for this date she says, 'There is always method in our social adventures and, at my instigation, Sidney after we left [the women retired], backed up by the Bishop and Wells and Shaw, gave an elaborate argument in favour of our half-time scheme for boys.' (This scheme involved a partial work, partial school life for boys who were not living at home.) She also described the party in a letter to her sister of 22 April 1904. This letter from Wells is in response to that conversation, and to a manuscript on prisons, probably a draft of material later used in the Webbs's *English Local Government* (London, 1906–22), which was sent to him for comment by Beatrice; see Norman and Jeanne MacKenzie, eds, *All the Good Things of Life: The Diary of Beatrice Webb*, vol. II, 1892–1906, pp. 320–1. Her response to Wells was written on 29 April 1904. She did not discuss his remarks on the funding of research.

[2] Professor Edward Westermarck (1862–1939) was Professor of Sociology at the London School of Economics 1907–30. The spring of 1904 was a time when Wells was actively seeking a university position, teaching and researching sociology and social theory. This phrase suggests that the Webbs may have known of his hope, although no correspondence exists about it with them as far as I can determine, nor is there anything in Beatrice Webb's published diary on this subject. Wells is saying that he had rather do the sort of thinking shown in this letter and at the dinner party than his fiction. He is assuming that the Webbs would not have read his fiction. The projected professorship is an elusive idea. Wells gave several public lectures at this time, including one at the Student's Union of the London School of Economics on 2 March 1903. Beatrice Webb took the chair at this talk; the subject was 'Local Administration', a subject to which he devoted a significant amount of time. He also spoke on the subject to the Coefficients.

The LSE talk to the Fabians was reprinted as an appendix to *Mankind in the Making* (London, 1903), pp. 399–417. He might have given thought, or have been encouraged to think, that these lectures were a sort of preliminary step to the professorship for which he hoped. In *Mankind in the Making* he has a section, pp. 341–4, on research professorships as a needed change in higher education. It is clearly a matter of importance to him at this stage, and eventually turned into his request for appointment to Balfour, see letter 586. Patrick Geddes was active in the creation of various sociological positions at precisely this time. He and Wells had a brief exchange at a meeting of the Sociological Society later over precision of detail.

[3] Wells is comparing the prison population discussed in the manuscript with that of the time of his writing.

[4] Wells is referring to their work on the Poor Law and the general status of persons in the lowest classes.

[5] Wells is being ironic, as he asks Beatrice (and Sidney) to describe how their reforms were going to ameliorate matters.

[6] Marcus Clarke (1846–81) was a novelist and journalist in Australia, to which he emigrated in 1864. His best known novel deals with the convict settlements, *For the Term of His Natural Life* (1874).

[7] Wells says that he believes that prison warders, left alone, will be as sadistic and horrifying as in earlier times, even in model prisons of the day. I imagine he is referring to the use of chain gangs working on roads as well as such 'new' establishments as the Idaho and Illinois state prisons, which were created to the specifications of 'modern' prison theory at about this time.

[8] Victor Branford was a disciple of Patrick Geddes. They, and others, using money given by Bernard Bosanquet, hoped to set up a School of Ethics and Social Philosophy to teach the new discipline of sociology. Eventually such as were able to survive did join the LSE. This is probably where Wells hoped to hold his professorship, as chairs named after the Bosanquet bequest, as well as one from Martin White given earlier, did exist. Wells's lecture at the LSE was part of the series set up to fill these bequests; see Ralf Dahrendorf, *LSE: A History of the London School of Economics and Political Science 1895–1995* (London: Oxford University Press, 1995), pp. 94–8.

521. To Henry Newbolt

Hofstra, ALS

Spade House
Sandgate

9. v. 04

My Dear Newbolt,

Your anthem is quite beautiful & after my heart, but when you give me only the part of the Boys, you arrogate to yourself years. Have I not been sick at heart & near to death, & do you fancy that I have never walked with God in beautiful places? You think because you have the gift of expression in beautiful forms that I have no sense of beauty because I don't say it so. And I think you are inclined to confuse a constant reference of things to the future, with a passion for the new. I do think many of the things upon which men waste loyalty & love, our Kingdom for example, drabbish tawdry street-walking ideals, & I grieve over such devotions as one might grieve over the generous foolish passion of a son. You find the devotion a sort of glorification of the object – it fills me with sombre rage. I am a poet whose medium is a lean prose, but so far as my poor power goes, I mean some men here & there shall glimpse a worthier mistress to dream about than the 'old school,' or Victoria R & I. You come so near to the spirit of the thing I mean at times – in 'Commemoration,' for example, & then you yaw away again. You believe in the 'Great Age' in rare moments, but your heart is with Clifton & the accidents of your own life. It's you that is careless of beauty, not I, You care for associations, your thought is thick woven with associations, with all the mellow, homely, sturdy, gallant things that stir the heart. This is a vision of beauty that makes me careless of all those dear old things.

Yours ever,

H.G. Wells

522. To Beatrice Webb

LSE, ALS

Spade House
Sandgate [*c.* May 1904]

Dear Mrs. Webb,

I got your letter when it was already too late either to [go to] lunch or reply. The question of [*illegible word*] & authority arrangements [in prisons] is very interesting to me & the solutions obviously are gratuitous adjustment as you say. I stand somewhere behind your public, which I suspect to be too much[1] – The direction[?] of creating & starting authority, and the position of a sentimental radical who trusts no government & yet, afraid of enough, thinks lawfully of man. I admit that nothing is satisfying for the mentally & physically able & I believe few people will escape the terrible sweep of that perspective, but precious few of these people are mentally sound enough to be trusted with prisons of the district. The remedy – it was discerned before our time – lies in creating & securing something impersonal called the law, which makes sentiment impersonal. The danger for all capable, intelligent, educated people is that in their desire to get things over, they should acquiesce too easily to the substitution of [*illegible word*] & regulations, and that they should fail to imagine what terrible instruments apparently good slight persons may become in the hands of more illiberal & greater persons than themselves. I think this ought to be pointed out very distinctly in your summary because it is so beautifully illustrated in your matter. These points have to be adjusted to the character & capacity of the people who will examine them, and currently[?] being included in affairs. You can see the consequences of that directly in the professional working of muncipal prisons, public prisons, [*illegible word*], prisons, everywhere.

You say nothing of the decadent[?] Branford.

Yours very sincerely,
H.G. Wells

---

[1] This letter is a continuation of the discussion with Beatrice Webb over prisons, and especially how prisons are to be run. Wells, as he sometimes does, leaves out words which he assumes she will supply as she reads. Wells did not 'compose' these intense letters.

523. To William Dean Howells[1]

Harvard, Transcription

[London] May 10th, 04

Dear Mr. Howells,

I am delighted to hear from you at such close range. I have long hoped to meet you, but I have always regarded it as a thing only to be achieved after a perilous pilgrimage, oceans & continents. I am in London with my wife for two nights but we shall be home on Thursday & then I shall come at once to call upon you.

---

[1] Howells (1837–1920) was a critic and novelist. He established new critical ideas which had an impact on Edith Wharton, Mark Twain and Henry James. The best known of his novels is probably *A Hazard of New Fortunes* (1890).

524. To William Dean Howells

Harvard, Transcription

[Sandgate] [12 or 13 May 1904]

Dear Mr. Howells,

I came up here today at 3:30 in the hope of carrying you off to tea both of you, but Lympne has done that it seems. Can you come & dine with us tomorrow at 7:30. We do hope you can. We are terribly afraid of your sands running out before we have had a session with you.

Yours very sincerely
H. G. Wells

This note has the incoherence of disappointment. If I may I will call up here tomorrow at seven & guide you both down. It is pleasanter to walk & so please don't dress.

525. To William Dean Howells

Harvard, Transcription

[Spade House
Sandgate] 14 – v – 04

My dear Howells

Your pleasant company released me for a while from the trammels of the Time Garment, & I discover with horror that not only have I invited you to lunch & tea on Monday but also that I have to make a speech at the London Sociological Society which meets at 4:30 in the city & afterwards dine with some politicians. But we cannot let you go without another gossip. The happy thing would be for you to stay over Tuesday & give us that day from 1:30 onward. That would be delightful for us. (Then you could do your neglected duty to Lympne Castle on Monday. — you can go in a boat from Hythe & walk up the hill) But if that is impossible then you must come down directly after your tea with Van de Poorten Schwarz tomorrow & share our Sabbath supper — a cold meal but with warm hearts — & there shall be fires alright. I dont ask you to lunch tomorrow because Van de P. Ss are coming & six would be so much more of an exhausting party for Miss Howells than four.

Yours ever
H.G. Wells

526. To William Dean Howells

Harvard, Transcription

Spade House
Sandgate
14. v. 04

My dear Howells,

Bang! You always pursue a retreat with shrapnel if you can & so here I discharge at you. I imagine you fleeing amidst these flying fragments. Your terror of more is only too well founded. The ammunition train hurries even now, & then I shall load & fire at Miss Howells a sort of pom-pom shell, The Wonderful Visit.

Yours very sincerely,
H.G. Wells

527. To William Dean Howells

Harvard, Transcription

Spade House
Sandgate
14 – v. 04

My dear Howells,

By some accident the note that should have accompanied these books got itself sent off to you separately. What you will make of the allusion in it to shrapnel & flying fragments passes my imagination. But this parcel is the fragment referred to.

Yours

H.G. Wells

528. To Mr Dawson[1]

Illinois, ALS

Spade House
Sandgate

May. 17. 04

My dear Dawson,

I am shocked to find this story in the midst of a heap of letters I have been holding over. It's a fine idea, but roughly done – it's a new game for you, and I don't think you've matured the thing enough. As it is it is quite unprintable – the percentage of the half breed for example – is just as revolting as drainage. I shall take this idea if I want to – I shall certainly do it quite differently from you.

Yours ever,

H.G. Wells

Thanks for the sight of the enclosed letter.

[1] Dawson, a young writer seeking advice, is otherwise unknown.

529. To William Dean Howells

Harvard, Transcription

[Spade House,
Sandgate]

26. v. 04

My dear Howells

'The Undiscovered Country' is a delightful addition to my knowledge of you. — & the Shakers. It's the nearest thing (I know of yours) to to a form I dream of, a novel in which the leading character so to speak is a topic. I think of something more living & eventful than Peacock & Mallock, but less dependant on the 'story' even than this. I like the figures of the wandering Boyntons best, the preoccupation of the Doctor, that perplexed good girl, the fading vanishing guest, the snow, the strange people.[1]

Yours very sincerely
H.G. Wells

---

[1] This is strong praise from Wells, but it is one of the reasons other authors enjoyed his company and his letters, for he read the books he received as gifts carefully and made useful comments. The book is virtually unknown today, as both *The Rise of Silas Lapham* and *A Hazard of New Fortunes* take precedence. Thomas Love Peacock (1785–1866) produced half a dozen satirical novels based on group conversation; the best known are *Headlong Hall* (1816), *Melincourt* (1817) and *Nightmare Abbey* (1818). William Hurrell Mallock (1849–1923) was much more of a philosopher and wrote many books on such matters as human equality. Wells is probably thinking here, however, of his novel, *The New Republic, or Culture, Faith and Philosophy in an English Country House* (London: Chatto and Windus, 1877).

530. To A.T. Simmons

Illinois, ANS

Spade House
Sandgate

29. v. 04

My dear Tommy

Thursday quite knocked me up & I've given up the next lecture. I've been working too hard & I'm quite done up. We think of going off to the Alps next week. Hope it won't put you out. – Tell old Giggleorums.[1]

Yours ever,
H.G.

---

[1] Another nick name for Richard A. Gregory.

531. To Henry Newbolt

Hofstra, ALS

[Spade House
Sandgate]   1 – vi – 04

My dear Newbolt,

Have you very extensively arranged for me & Bridges. I hope not. I'm ill. I've got a small actual illness – to be perfectly frank and open, an ulcer or some malignant growth inside my rectal sphincter – & I'm suddenly I find exhausted by work. My head won't work, my nerves flap like washing in a gale. Thank God all my books, three books, stand done – but I'm done too for a time. We are going to Switzerland tomorrow or next day, if the Channel permits, & then we shall go high, when Romecke ceases from trembling.

Yours ever,
H.G.

532. To William Dean Howells

Harvard, Transcription

[Spade House,
Sandgate]   [23 June 04]

My dear Howells

This I find on my return to Switzerland where we have been exercising our poor little legs & resting our poor little heads for a week or so. It was Colvin gave me your address as Eaton Terrace.

Yours ever,
H. G. Wells

533. To William Dean Howells

Harvard, Transcription

Spade House
Sandgate

June 25, 04

My dear Howells

I am delighted at your good word for Love & Mr. Lewisham, more than delighted, for there's no ones approval I'd value more highly. But your continent, Sir, wouldn't look at it. And against serializing its successor, a rather larger & wider portrait of a simpleton that has taken me no end of labour to do, your continent sets its face like a flint.[1] At times I blame your continent; at times I doubt my agent's savoir faire. But there it is!

How is Miss Howells [*illegible word*] & how do your movements go? Will you visit the continent (our continent) before you go back to America? If so the best & quietest route is via Folkestone and the Hotel Wells is eager to catch you going & coming for a nights rest.

Our warmest regards to you both,

Yours very sincerely,
H.G. Wells

---

[1] This is probably *Kipps*, although the time of writing the letter makes that somewhat problematical. It was serialized in 1905 in the *Pall Mall Magazine* but it was not serialized in the United States. It might be *The Wonderful Visit*, but he had already presented a copy of it to Miss Howells, or at least he had promised one to her, see letter 526.

534. To Edward Clodd

Leeds, ALS

[Spade House
Sandgate, Kent]

June. 26 1904

My dear Clodd,

Nothing could be more agreeable than your invitation & I very gladly anticipate a development of my pleasant acquaintance with you. We will arrive at Liverpool Street at 5 on Friday the 22nd July.

Yours very sincerely
H.G. Wells

535. To Edmund Gosse

Leeds, ACCS

Spade House
Sandgate, Kent

7. 1. 04[1]

Dear Gosse,

The earlier books were in most cases sold outright & the sale of them is slow & small. I don't know about the widow payments, but I shd think Gissing made them through someone in England. The elder boy's name is <u>Walter</u> but I'm asking Miss Come to tell you that. He's the cleverer of the two.

Yours ever
H.G. Wells

I shall be in London Monday week to Wednesday. Shall I try & catch you for ten minutes talk at the B. of T[2] . If so, tell me your best times please.

N.B. If this should come to anything the proper person to control these youngsters' education are the two Miss Gissings of Wakefield I think.

---

[1] Wells occasionally reverted to this American method of dating from time to time. This letter must go here however rather than in January 1904.

[2] Gosse worked as a civil servant at the Board of Trade much of his life, in addition to his work as editor and critic. The standard life is Ann Thwaite, *Edmund Gosse: A Literary Landscape 1849–1928* (London, 1984).

536. To Henry Newbolt

Hofstra, ALS

Spade House
Sandgate

8 – vii – 04

My dear Newbolt,

Do you care for this in the Monthly? If [so] I shall be very glad if you will use it & send me such recompense as is seemly. If not please return it at once. This was written & set up as a preface to the book it deals with, but for reasons that are too complicated to write it has aroused the fury of one of his two executors – a lady.[1] She has very generously sacrificed £150 of their two little orphans' small property to extinguish it. Constable's would have paid £300 for it with this preface & will pay only £150 without it. I don't intend to have the document suppressed & so here it is.

Yours ever
H.G. Wells

[1] This is the proposed preface for Gissing's novel, *Veranilda*, finally rejected by the Gissing family. Wells referred to Gissing's rather raffish life, living with prostitutes. His legal wife objected to a discussion of Gissing in anything but glowing terms. Newbolt took the piece for the *Monthly Review*, 'George Gissing: An Impression', which appeared in August 1904, pp. 160–72. Wells, Newbolt and others such as Clement Shorter, editor of *The Sphere*, were all very annoyed by this apparent cost to the children, for whom Wells and Clodd were literary executors. The *New York Times* paid some attention to the discussion over the preface as well, so perhaps Gissing's children benefited from the publicity and Wells's fees, to the extent to which the intervention had cost. *The Sphere* referred to the problem at least four times that summer.

537. To Edmund Gosse

Leeds, ACCS

Spade House
Sandgate. Kent 8. 7. 04

My dear Gosse,

I am afraid it is quite impossible for me to work with Miss Collet, but I shall be very glad if Mr. Balfour will relieve me from my Trusteeship. In his lifetime Gissing entrusted his children to Miss Come & his sisters respectively, & I had prepared to continue that arrangement & act simply as a paymaster to them. I think they ought to be consulted before things are placed too unreservedly in Miss Collet's hands.[1]

Yours very sincerely,
H.G. Wells

Could not Miss Come be associated with Miss Collet as co-trustees?

[1] Although Wells served on the trusteeship committee and signed their cheques, he never met the boys nor did he ever receive any recognition from the Gissing family for his efforts on their behalf.

538. To Henry Newbolt

Hofstra, ALS

[Spade House,
Sandgate] 9 – vii – 04

My Dear Newbolt,

We are back in a much more living state than when we went away & I'm at work again. I hear from Pinker that you have seen my 'Kipps'[1] but that you can't use it because I can't let Murray have the book? If that is so I'm very sorry indeed.I went round the publishers some time ago offering all my books to anyone who would take them & Murray never gave a sign he wanted to touch 'em. Now I've promised Macmillan all my fiction. I should have dearly liked a serial in the Monthly, and I think it a great pity that the matter cannot be arranged.

Yours ever,
H.G. Wells

[1] *Kipps* was serialised in *Pall Mall Magazine* (January-December 1905).

539. To Edmund Gosse

Leeds, ACCS

Spade House
Sandgate, Kent

19. vii. 04

My dear Gosse,

George Whale[1] ought to do very well. He's a decent little man, a mighty Johnsonian & he made Gissing's will for him & kept it. I can't act with any ladies & I dread Miss C. if I am left alone, but if Mr. Balfour does not know him & it will end this bother for Whale to be associated with me, I should be very pleased. I send you a letter I had from Pinker. I taxed him with the matter of Conrad after I saw you on Saturday. Frankly, I think there has been a lot of very shoddy lying about J.C.'s distresses. I approve very highly of Civil List pensions for all worthy writers of anything indeed that lifts us out of our accursed servitude to sales, but I do not see why Conrad's agent & all his unfortunate friends should be blackened in the process.[2]

Yours ever,
H.G. Wells

[1] Whale was a critic and writer, friend of literature and an old acquaintance of Wells. Wells wrote an obituary notice for a remembrance book when Whale died: Edward Clodd, C. K. Shorter and Winifred Stephens Whale, eds, *George Whale 1849–1925* (London: Cape, 1926). Wells' contribution is on pp. 39–46.

[2] Conrad was also granted a pension. As Prime Minister, Balfour named the trustees for gifts from the Royal Literary Fund to minors, such as the Gissing children.

540. To Edmund Gosse

Leeds, ACCS

Spade House
Sandgate, Kent 20 – vii. 04

My dear Gosse,

Probably you've directed that letter to Miss Collet. Our prayers are with you.

Yours ever,
H.G. Wells

541. To 'Vernon Lee'

Colby, ALS

Spade House
Sandgate 6 – viii – 04

Dear Miss Paget,

I'm glad of your letter & your excellent criticisms, though I'm sorry you cannot forgive the opening of The Sea Lady for the end. All that you say of The Time Machine is after my heart. But that book like all my earlier work was written against time, amidst a frantic output of 'humorous' journalistic matter. It took perhaps three weeks. It's only in quite recent years I've had any leisure to think, & I still can't afford time to read & the idea of any sort of travel – except to recuperate for fresh work – is beyond dreaming. Consequently you will always miss in me certain qualities that you particularly admire. I shall send you a little work called "Love & Mr. Lewisham" in a few days' time.

Yours very sincerely,
H.G. Wells

542. To A.J. Balfour[1]

British Library,
Add. Mss. 49856, ALS

[London] Aug. 26 1904

[Dear Mr. Balfour]

I have read your address to the British Association for the Advancement of Science which you kindly sent. I cannot resist the temptation to express my very keen intellectual sympathy with the predominant note of your thought.I sent you a few weeks since the reprint from Mind[2] of a little paper I read to some people in Oxford & in that you will find the same train of reasoning you follow in the second portion of your paper. I had previously used it, so long ago as 1893, in a little paper contributed to the Fortnightly Review, in which I said that the human brain was no more to be assumed to be an instrument for the discovery of truth than the snout of a hog. Both were the products of the process whose end seemed to be survival & whose means, [*illegible word*] & [*illegible word*]. So that your statement that though your train of thought has long interested you, 'it never seems to have interested anyone else' is [accurate] to the extent of at least one exception.

My paper in Mind leads to an ultimate scepticism as thorough as yours, but through an analysis of the chief assumptions of the commonly accepted logic. I have been trying to work out the conception of a modern Utopia in harmony with this fundamental incertitude and I shall inflict it upon you in due course.

I do not know if you have given any attention to the reception of your Address by the newspapers. There seems to me a curious failure to grasp what you are after, a positive disinclination in fact to do so.The ideas are too new & strange & they take refuge in not taking you seriously. You have [*illegible word*] so in 'paradox', you have been up to an intellectual spree. To be capable of doing anything else in the world is to taint one's philosophical reputation hopelessly. That is where the strength of Herbert Spencer's system lies.[3]

Yours sincerely,
H.G. Wells

---

[1] Balfour (1848–1930), was Prime Minister at the time of this letter. He and Wells had met at a famous dinner party given by Beatrice and Sidney Webb to honour Wells's contributions in *Anticipations*, *New Worlds For Old* and other contemporary work of the time; see letter 520.

[2] The original address was given at the Oxford Philosophical Society on 8 November 1903. It appears as 'The Scepticism of the Instrument' in *Mind* (n.s.) no. 51 and somewhat revised as an appendix in *A Modern Utopia* (1905).
[3] My friend Leon Stover first brought my attention to these letters to Balfour and supplied me with the transcriptions.

543. To Grant Allen[1]

Illinois, ACCS

Spade House
Sandgate 26. viii. 04

My dear Grant Allen,

I think perhaps I better get the play nearer written before seeing Welch. So I'll defer that Seccombe until later.

Yours ever
H.G.

---

[1] This cannot be the novelist Grant Allen as he died in 1899. Who it may be is unknown.

544. To Beatrice Webb

LSE, ALS

Spade House
Sandgate 29. – viii. 04

Dear Mrs. Webb,

We were glad of your letter & its fine plans of vigorous exertions. We came back greatly invigorated from nearly three weeks in Switzerland, but we're running down again. I've finished A Modern Utopia & it will begin in October in the Fortnightly. It's queer stuff in places, but it's all I can do under my present circumstances.[1] Just now I'm writing a play – not an old stage success play – but a lucrative play. I presume that there's no hope of an endowment for me unless I get it myself, & sociology will have to be considered in suspense with me until I've got a war chest. But it's infernally silly that I should have to interest myself in this way, with my limited energies.

We're all very jolly & Popham[2] carries his cancer as a gentleman should. I think the Pophams will live then write with us.

Our warmest regards to you both. I hope you'll be able to spend a weekend with us in October.

Yours ever,
H.G. Wells

[1] Wells is making another oblique reference to his hope for a university chair where he can be relieved from the pressure of funds to write mainly fiction. He presumed that his theoretical political and economic work would be of better quality with more time to work on it. He clearly felt the Webbs might have influence here, and this may account for his somewhat skittish approach in these letters to Beatrice Webb. The idea of the Sociological Society and its role in extending education in London was being discussed in substantial ways at this time. Could it have been that the famous dinner party discussed such a move?

[2] A. F. Popham and his family were close friends with the Wells family. Popham died just as he was beginning to make a career of writing at about this time. His wife Florence, whose children's books were fairly well known, also died early. A few letters exist, but their whereabouts are unknown at the time of writing, and since their sale at Sotheby's in 1972; see the Introduction to this work.

545. To George Alexander

British Theatre Museum, ALS

Spade House
Sandgate

6. ix. 04

[*in another hand*] – 4.0 clock
14th Pont St.

Dear Mr. Alexander,

I do intend to try my luck in the stage during the next three or four years & I should be very glad to talk to you.[1] I've little or nothing done but I have one or two projects playing loose in my mind & I've discussed a rather promising idea with Fenn. I've written a play on commission for Welch & that's my all, so far. I don't think much of writing plays at large, and I should be delighted to learn what sort of thing would be most likely to fall in with your ideas.

Yours very sincerely,

H.G. Wells

I shall be in London & free on the afternoon of the 14th & the 19th.

---

[1] George Alexander, a prominent play producer and impresario, had apparently written to Wells about the possibility of his writing a play. Wells played about with the idea of the stage for a long time – three different versions of *The Wonderful Visit* were proposed. Another effort to dramatize *The Wheels of Chance*, called 'Mr. Hoopdriver's Holiday', was never performed. Wells and Bennett also attempted a play together, but the work was dropped. Wells's novel *The First Men in the Moon* opens with a discussion of a failed play. The most successful adaptation of a Wells play was the musical 'Half a Sixpence', based on *Kipps*, which played both Broadway and the West End in the post Second World War period. This letter to a great impresario indicates the extent to which Wells was attracted to, and was involved in, the stage.

546. To Morley Roberts

Illinois, ALS

Spade House
Sandgate

13 – ix – 04

My dear Roberts,

Do, for God's sake, abstain from any more Slanting! You <u>did</u> endow the document in a greatly flattering manner. You applauded the Balzac comparison, what is the particular object made by that female lunatic who is solely in all of his mss. – Generally your helper let me in for this loathsome dance among the remains. I won't send you with your letter or your endowed draft – you, A.G. & Harrisson (particularly) have all gone away from your original standpoint and lent yourselves to my discredit – but if you want, I'll send you copies. But the whole thing is vain, troublesome, silly & detestible. I can only defend myself by quitting [*word blacked out*] & playing down to the pettiness of the attack. You know perfectly well my hands are clean in the matter.

Yours ever

H.G.

I'm very glad you're writing G.G. – if you do him fully & frankly it ought to be altogether fine. Perhaps I may share the privilege of friendship & read it when it is done. You see H.G. wanted to see (discuss) my book when done. Here.[1]

---

[1] This letter relates to the problems over the preface to *Veranilda*. Both Roberts and Frank Swinnerton planned biographies of Gissing. Swinnerton wrote his, and this led to his friendship with Wells; Roberts's work did not appear for some years, and then as a novel. Wells reviewed both books. The meaning of this postscript is obscure. A.G. is Algernon Gissing; H.G. may be another Gissing relative.

547. To Morley Roberts

Illinois, ALS

Spade House
Sandgate
15 ix 04

My dear Roberts,

Why not make G.G. into a novel? Or is it to be too documentary for that. I'm glad you're for endorsing that despicable little ——————. . I'm sorry I used the phrase "endorsed with enthusiasm," but I suppose you write "Mr Wells is mistaken in saying I endorsed his criticism with enthusiasm greatly as I admire it" etc.

Then that literary disease spot Dr. Roberston Nocils will write:

"Mr. Morley Roberts' comments serve from some resolutions about Mr. Gissing on the part of ————————."

Mr. Whitten of the Globe will follow with:

"I am pleased to find Mr. Morley Roberts repudiating any sympathy with the very firmly rejected practice of ————————."

And the Stick in the Mud Gazette issue:

"It is pleasing to find one more friend of the George Gissing display its device[?] against the callous libel of Mr. H. G. Wells. Mr Morely Roberts —— ————————."

You see?

I'll send you some press cuttings if you think this is a caricature.[1]

Yours ever,
H.G.

[1] Although this letter is virtually illegible, the effort to reconstruct it was necessary because it is an indication of how deeply Wells was hurt by the long controversy over Gissing's death, and the proposed preface. Nicol and Whitten were literary critics of the time and persons who did not like the sort of work that Wells was producing. He would satirize them in passing in his *Boon.* The unused illustrations for that book, which provide caricatures of these critics of the day and others, are quite powerful.

548. To R. N. Johnson

Illinois, ALS

Spade House
Sandgate 18 – ix – 04

Dear Sir,

I am obliged to you for your offer to consider my next work as a serial for the Century. I have recently drafted the outline of what I suppose you would call a scientific fantasy, which I shall probably finish in the course of the next year or so – but I cannot make you any promise of the first refusal at the present time. As I see the story now [it] should make an entirely suitable serial for your magazine. It will be novel, eventful & sympathetic – I think I may promise you that. If you really want my work in the Century I would suggest that you should make an offer for the serial now to be delivered January 1st 1906. I should be quite willing to make an agreement that should you be dissatisfied with the story when you get it, you should have the option either of using it or paying a reselling fine of £100 to be released from your bargain. The agreement would have to cover English & American serial rights only & would not touch book rights.

Yours very sincerely
H. G. Wells

549. To R. N. Johnson

Illinois, ALS

Spade House
Sandgate

18 – ix – 04

Dear Sir.

This letter will probably reach you by the same mail as my previous one – in which case I beg you to read that one first. In that I give you no particulars of the story to which I refer. It will perhaps make your reply easier if I tell you briefly the idea of that story. (I hope however you will consider this is a very confidential communication). The prospective title is The Trail of the Comet & the narrative centers about a commonplace man who paints on china in the potteries.I have chosen this position for him because the English pottery country presents very striking picturesque constrasts between country & a lurid industrialism. The Duchess of Sutherlands place at Trentham is within two mins. walk of Hanley's horrible coal pits, the sunsets are particularly fine & so forth. (The railway is a sort of British social compendium). The story opens with this man telling a friend of certain complications – he has lost his situation & he is in a state of violent jealousy about a coquettish girl. His friend dabbles in opera glass astronomy & stands at the open window listening with his attention distracted by his desire to make out a newly reported comet, which is just visible as a faint speck of light near Aldeberan. Now this comet is destined to sweep close to the earth, to mingle the gas of its tail with the atmosphere, & to revolutionize the whole of human life. The particular way in which the revolution is effected is the essential invention of the story. The story creeps up toward catastrophe & breaks abruptly into sunshine. That's the idea.[1]

Yours very sincerely,
H.G. Wells

Length I suppose from 60,000 to 80,000.

---

[1] This is the first bloom of what would become his famous and controversial novel, *In The Days of the Comet* (London: Macmillan, 1906). It may have been triggered by the imminent (1910) return of Halley's comet which has played some superstitious roles in English history. For instance it appeared in 1066 on one of its periodic trips. The book was serialized in the United States in *Cosmopolitan Magazine* from December 1905 to October 1906. It was also serialized in England in the *Daily Chronicle* in 1906. The controversy over this book and its reception provides many of the letters in 1907 and 1908 in this volume.

550. To George Sterling[1]

Bancroft, ALS

Spade House
Sandgate 23 – ix – 04

Esteemed Fellow Socialist,

On the principle that dog does not eat dog I return your pound note & I'm sending you a copy I chance to have of the Monthly which please accept, with the Gissing article therein. I've published little lately but A Modern Utopia will begin in the Fortnightly in October. None of your confounded American magazines will look at it (my agent tells me) & my publishers, Scribners, are put to the expense of printing it for copyright. I think it's the best thing I've done.

Please present my best respects to "Jack London" whose a great swell to hear of as reading me. [2]

Yours very sincerely
H.G. Wells

The "wine of brigandy" seems an excellent vintage.

---

[1] Sterling (1869–1926) from Piedmont, California, exchanged several notes with Wells on the subject of Socialism. He had sent Wells money for membership in a Socialist society which did not exist. He also had sent 'Jack London's' regards to Wells in the letter. Sterling wrote a play, *Truth*, (1923) and apparently was associated with Mills College in California

[2] Although they moved in the same circles, I know of no occasion when Wells and London might have met. 'London' was a pseudonym for John Griffith Chaney, (1876–1916); his best known English title is *In the Abyss*.

551. To Arnold Bennett

Texas, ALS

Spade House
Sandgate 30-ix-04

Dear E.A.B.,

The Savile Club has no bedrooms. The Arts has got 10. Otherwise the Arts is very much like the Savile, & these two visit when cleaning & so on.[1]

The Royal Societies is a very good little club indeed with about 25 or 30 bedrooms. These two are more in your lines. I belong only to the Savile & the N.L.C., but when I've got some money I want to belong to the Garrick & Reform.[2]

I won't comment on your next book[3] if you don't want me to, but I'd like to see it. You're no judge of your own work & often what you think is poor is good. Odd! Seeing you're a very good judge of other people.

Yours,
H.G.

---

[1] The two clubs acted as host for the other when undergoing cleaning or for other necessary closings.

[2] In the event both Wells and Bennett joined the Reform Club and frequented it for the rest of their lives. Wells also belonged for a time to the Whitefriars Club.

[3] Bennett's next book, perhaps his weakest, was *Teresa of Watling Street* (London, 1904).

552. To Henry Newbolt

Hofstra, ALS

Spade House
Sandgate

2. x. 04

My dear Newbolt,

What you say about my style is most comforting & timely. I have been reduced to such a state of nerves that I erased the word "innumerable" yesterday because there were such a lot of repetitions of liquids in it & what I am to call a hippopotamus, I don't know. – three 'p's in one word!

I'm glad you like my book – I doubted if you would.

I hope to see you on hand & in London. We're just off for a little walk about Maggiore & Como before the fine weather ends.[1]

Yours ever,
H.G

---

[1] H. G. Wells and Catherine took frequent holidays in the Alps (in this case on the Italian side), until Wells's lungs began to give him problems at altitude. Jane continued to ski in the Alps until her health prevented such journeys.

553. To Violet Hunt[1]

Cornell, Typed Transcription

Spade House
Sandgate [1904?]

Dear Suffragette

No, he hasn't dropped you and it's like your cheek to go proclaiming an innocent friendly soul a Shelley to such as you shouldn't.

Yours ever
H.G.

P.T.O.

Tired of Wedderism V'la toot [2]

H.G.

[1] Violet Hunt, a poet and novelist, was the longtime consort of Ford Madox Hueffer (later Ford); Hunt and Wells were close friends as well. Hunt and Ford maintained a famous literary house and salon, South Lodge. Wells contemplated moving in to South Lodge for a time during the turmoil of the Free Love controversy.

[2] What Wedderism was is not known. Wells occasionally ended such light notes with this fractured French remark, 'That's all'.

554. To Violet Hunt

Cornell, Transcription of APCS

Luino
Piazza Risorgimento
Lago Maggiore [postmarked 13 October 1904]
[Italy]

We are taking our impulsive holiday about these lakes but will be back by the 29th.

The Wellses

[*This was re-addressed from Chapman and Hall.*]

555. To an unknown addressee

Illinois, APCS

Rota, [Italy] Oct. 16/04

Dear Sir,

Your letter has only just reached me here. I doubt if any grant of the book rights of my 1906 book is possible now & I cannot promise you an offer of the serial. I will let you see it if I can but you won't come first.

Yours very sincerely
H. G. Wells

556. To Beatrice Webb

LSE, ALS

Hotel Mottarone
Stresa, Italy October 19th, 1904

Dear Mrs. Webb,

Your letter was delightful – we got it at Berta[?] – but I doubt you go too far in this crusade against food. Could it even, in cases of weakness, [*illegible word*] a month. I have known food to act as a temporary stimulant of great efficacy. God is a coarse creature – a large part of civilizations consists in man's strenuous efforts to correct the improprieties of Mr. Balfour & your Divinity – & I think the steady practice of abstinence from all forms of eating likely to produce some gross form of retaliation upon God's part. My own experience of G at any rate points to that expectation. Besides what is your advantage? Refinement doesn't tempt me. Intellectually I am already far too refined as it is. I would rather be after G's pattern, grave, varied, fecund & comprehensive, inexact & continually unexpected, than disciplined, theological, determinate, inadaptable and expert. Forgive me if I seem to be writing incoherently; I have been taking food.

You know, it is quite dreadful to hear from him that Webb would have suppressed The Food of the Gods. It' shows how fearfully far you two have gone in pursuit of administrative efficiency. If I were a more authoritative person I should speak to you very seriously. I should implore you both not to think about government for six months. I should prescribe a course of philosophy, sentiment & indulgence. I should hand you off to Mrs. Wallas to learn how to cook. Really & truly it is just as absurd to give yourself up so minutely & frankly to government experiment as it would be to give yourself up to cooking. You get in my mind. I have already done a large lump of my Modern Utopia to a careful analysis of the differences between public people (you) & poetic people (me) but if you don't mind I shall do a whole huge chunk[?] about your husband and I shall call it The Anatomy of Sidney Webb. It will be exhaustive. I will explain you to yourself quite finally.

We are having a jolly time here. There are practically no English people about at all. We are walking up & down valleys & our mountains & things & entering every village that comes in our way. We did a hundred miles in seven days which isn't bad for Jane. We can get more grapes than we two can eat & we eat a greedy amount for twenty centimes anywhere; we stop at albergos & rotinas of the simplest descriptions & the beds are invariably clean. This is almost the only respectable hotel we have taken up – hence writing fewer letters.

Please salute Webb from us both & believe me

Yours always,

H.G. Wells[1]

---

[1] This is an intriguing letter. There is a flirtatious air about the text which Wells occasionally adopted with strong willed women. The mention of Beatrice Webb's eating difficulties is unusual. Catherine and Wells had chosen the Italian side of the Alps for their walking holiday and he is comparing it with his walking tour with Wallas. The letter appears in small calligraphy as often happened when Wells was under personal stress. *The New Machiavelli* (London: John Lane, 1911) is the closest he came to writing about the Webbs and their work.

557. To Violet Hunt

Cornell, Typed Transcription

Spade House
Sandgate, Kent

Oct. 23. 04

Dear Miss Hunt,

We're most unfortunate to miss you. We got back here this afternoon and found your two letters. We've been away from letters, pedestrianating, and so these complicated misses and miss fires. Our times are in your hands. When can you come?

Yours ever,
The H.G. Wellses

558. To an unknown addressee

Illinois, ANS

Spade House
Sandgate 24 – x – 04

Dear Sir,

I thought that fighting, things in the key of the earlier part of the book, was a discord in the conclusion, where my aim has been the role of symbolism strong.[1]

Yours sincerely,
H. G. Wells

[1] Wells is responding to a query and criticism of the recently published, *The Food of the Gods* (London: Macmillan, 1904).

559. To Mr Rook[1]

Boston, ALS

Spade House
Sandgate 26 – X – 04

My dear Rook,

You always say kind things about my books. Everybody else writes either cursing the first part of the Foogods heartily or else the second. So that if it weren't for you I'd hide & run with the damn thing.

Mrs. Rook's invitations are commands & I will be in London on

Wednesday next & at her disposal to meet anyone [*three or four words are crossed out here with the word 'censored' in Wells's hand above them*] at the Lyceum. Wot 'our?

Yours trampled wormishly
H.G.

[*The third page of this letter is a sketch of a distraught person in a robe, labelled, 'God' under several objects (which surround God). The sketch has an overall caption, 'The globular objects are suns & worlds'.*]

---

[1] Clarence Rook was the author of *Hooligan Nights* (London, 1899).

560. To Morley Roberts

Illinois, ACCS

Spade House
Sandgate 30 – x – 04

My dear Roberts,

I've just seen your article in the Albany & I'd like to say that I think you're much more right about Veranilda than I am in my preface. You see the thing was written as a preface & for purposes not critical but seductive. You're much in evidence in the Albany which seem to me as bright a beginning as I've seen for some time. I wish you'd go on to your Gissing book now. Only silly scruples prevent you, you know.

Yours ever,
H.G. Wells

561. To Edward Clodd

Leeds, ALS

[Spade House
Sandgate, Kent] 2-xi-04

My dear Clodd,

We have been larking about for a little while in Italy & since we came back we have been complicated by these poor Pophams[1] – Popham is the man who wrote those insults in my hat the day he knew he had cancer & he's all wrong again & going in for a second operation – but now some dates are clear & there is still sunshine in the land. When is your week end to be, yours and Miss Larners's? We have the 10th & 17th & 31st of Dec. & all the January ones. Dec. is safer than Jan for blue clear weather.

Yours ever
H.G. Wells

[1] A. F. Popham and his wife, Florence, were friends of Catherine and Wells from 1898 to 1905. Both died young, leaving one child, Doris. A lot of thirty-two letters to the Popham family members was sold at Sotheby's in 1972. Where the letters are now is not known. The Sotheby description of the letters appears as an introduction to this work. No more is known of the incident of the hat. For Wells's relationship with Edward Clodd see letters 510–12 and 517.

563. To Charles Didier[1]

Bromley, ALS

Spade House
Sandgate, Kent 6 Nov. 1904

Monsieur Chas. Didier,

Dear Sir

I have read with very great interest your letter and the numbers of Le Cottage you have sent with it & I am particularly delighted with your project for the exhibition in Liège. Your idea of "units" is quite new to me and I should imagine it would prove of the utmost practical utility. I am rather a dreamer than a practical man, my function in life is to popularize general ideas rather than to succeed in their detailed realization, but I shall feel greatly honoured to be consulted upon the details of your experimental building. I will make it my business to see it at Liège in 1905 & I hope that before then I may have the pleasure of seeing & talking with you.

Yours very sincerely,
H.G. Wells

---

[1] Didier was a French architect. He may have learned of Wells from his article in *The Strand*, in which he discussed his dream house of the future; see 'The English House of the Future', *The Strand*, vol. 26 (November, 1903), pp. 679–80. This article emerged from Wells's relationship with C. F. A. Voysey, the Edwardian architect, who built Spade House.

563. To Sidney Low

Illinois, Typed Transcription

Spade House
Sandgate

6. 11. 04

My dear Low,

Your book comes to hand on one of my bad days. I'm in bed & out of conceit with myself and the Universe. I have no doubt I shall read it later with the interest & sympathy I always find for what you have to say. At present I can only see that you don't mention my work at all in these high discussions and I 've got no philosophy at hand for that emergency.[1]

Yours very sincerely
H. G. Wells

---

[1] The book which Low had sent him was *The Governance of England*.

564. To William Rothenstein[1]

Illinois, Typed Transcription

Spade House
Sandgate 9. xi. 04

My dear Rothenstein,

There's no need for you to be hardened this time. We both like the portrait enormously. You have penetrated the mere superficialities of my personal appearance & shown me how I should like to look. And my wife, who displays that very human resentment of wives when the camera with its facty emphasis brings home to them, with all the indisputableness & wrongness of statistics, what it is they have centred their poor dear lives upon – my wife I saw approves of it too.

Here at any rate it is a success, & it will go far to efface the painful memories of Max Beerbohm's little joke.

Yours ever
H.G. Wells

---

[1] William Rothenstein (1872–1945) was a portrait artist who lived just two houses away from the Wells family before they moved to Sandgate. They were good friends and shared many activities over several years. Rothenstein had done one drawing of Wells but was dissatisfied. He wished to do another. Wells responded with this letter. The drawing eventually appeared in Rothenstein, *Twenty-four Portraits* (1920). The volume consists of twenty-four portraits of famous writers and artists of the day, each with a one page essay on the person being portrayed. Arnold Bennett wrote the appreciative sketch about Wells for this work. This letter appears in Rothenstein's autobiography, *Men and Memories*, vol. II (1922), p. 64, and in *The Atlantic Monthly* where the book was serialized in part. Wells probably wrote the essay on Bennett in the same volume.

565. To Edmund Gosse

Leeds, ALS

[London] Nov. 26, 04

My dear Gosse,

I am in a state of vehement discontent with all my American publishers, agents, numerous critics. Do you know anything of that marvellous disorderly continent? Are there any respectable people there at all, although I admire Howells & William James? I want to get in touch with the American literary world (if any). I want an intelligent American publisher as an outcome of these enquiries. I want to be done properly. Who is it knows about these things? To whom might I to go? I've left these things to Pinker too long & I perceive something has to be done. I think even of going to America. But who are the people I ought to see? I hurl these impassioned enquiries to you with a sort of abandoned confidence in your good nature.

Yours ever

H.G. Wells

566. To Morley Roberts

Illinois, ALS

Spade House
Sandgate 2 – xii. 04

My dear Roberts,

Say no more of Veranilda. We are at peace & the right is with you. Anyhow you'd heard of my reaction from my speech of praise. You have I think gone some paces further in the direction of condemnation than you might otherwise have done. The book we are finally agreed about is By The Ionian Sea.[1] Veranilda ought not to have been a romance – that's the mischief of it all.

Pegram cannot possibly know my undistinguished head. He has probably seen Rothenstein's lithograph & Charles's illusions. I think if he had a quiet walk round my kopf, he'd drop the idea. It's my personal appearance & my slovenliness in writing joining with my chaste ideals of style, that stand in the way of my real greatness being recognized. Wait till I'm dead & translated!

But I wander from Pegram.

You put it to him.

What do you think of Conrad? I began the chorus of praise ten years ago, but I'm cooling off considerable. Short stories is his game. Nostromo is desiccated[?] conglomerate. And what do you think of Rachel Mear? How's your health?

Yours ever,

H.G.

[1] Even with all the excellent efforts of the contemporary discussion and editing of Pierre Coustillas and his associates, Gissing is not widely read today. Those who know his work, however, regard *By The Ionian Sea* as a wonderful book. Pegram specialised in sculpting busts.

567. To E.V. Lucas

Illinois, ALS

Spade House
Sandgate 15. xii. 04

My dear Lucas,

[*A flourish sketch of a head appears on half of the first page of this letter.*]

You encourage me very greatly to go on being quiet. I like Kipps myself, but Gawd bless you! the public won't.

Any chance of your coming here for a windy weekend, breezy but

[*The second page of this letter, with his closing is missing.*]

568. To E. Nesbit[1]

Illinois, ALS

Spade House
Sandgate, Kent 17. 12. 04

'Steamed Lady,

I never told you how we liked the Phoenix and the Carpet and how extraordinary more, than the late Mrs. Ewing who was once first we now esteem you.[2] The Phoenix is a great creation; he is the best character you ever invented – or anybody ever invented in this line. It is the best larking I ever saw. Your destiny is plain. You go on every Xmas never missing an Xmas, with a book like this, and you will become a British institution in six years from now. Nothing can stop it. Every self respecting family will buy you automatically and you will be rich beyond the dreams of avarice, and I knock my forehead on the ground at your feet in the vigour of my admiration of your easy artistry.

Our best wishes to you all for a picturesque and various Xmas

Yours ever,

H.G. Wells

---

[1] This letter appears in Doris Langley Moore, *E. Nesbit, A Biography* (London, 1932), pp. 192–3.

[2] Mrs Julia Ewing (1841–85) wrote many books for children.

569. To Violet Hunt

Cornell, ALS

Spade House
Sandgate, 30. 12. 04.

Dear Violet Hunt,

Jane's thus[1] — the nurse having decided to take her Xmas this week. So I'm writing.

We get Jacobses from the 6th to the 9th.

I wish indeed we or one of us (me) could have come.

Why isn't your mother in the Royal Kent? We've been hoping she would be, so as to get you incidentally. But we took you on the wrong walk, and you're set against the place.

Yours truly,

H.G. Wells

---

[1] A small sketch of Catherine Wells appears after these words.

570. To Mr Swinden[1]

Boston, ALS

Spade House
Sandgate

[*c.* 1904]

My dear Swinden

If not week ends then week middles? It's all the same to me. I wish I could come to Blackburn but my game is writing & a meeting to me, with me as part of the show, is more & more terrible. And you know I am an infernal muff on a platform.

Yours ever,
H. G. Wells

[1] Swinden is unknown to me.

571. To A. T. Simmons

Illinois, ACCS

Spade House,
Sandgate

[*c.* 1904]

Dear Tommy,

I shall be in London Thursday night & going down to Liss[1] Friday morning by the 11:15 train from Waterloo. Will you & Gregory come & brekfus at the National Liberal Club at 9. or 9.30?

Yours ever,
H. G.

Ask Gregory – thare's a dear.
Answer to the N.L.C.

[1] Wells's family had been moved to a house in Liss, which Wells purchased for them.

572. To Methuen

Illinois, ALS

Spade House,
Sandgate [*c.* 1904]

My dear Methuen,

I see you have terminated our agreement over the Sea Lady by remaindering copies. I propose therefore to make arrangements for its publication elsewhere. I wish you would offer the rest of the remainder, 1978 copies, to Macmillans & I could probably arrange with them for its continued sale.

Very sincerely yours,
H. G. Wells

573. To Edmund Gosse

Leeds, ANS

[Spade House,
Sandgate] [*c.* 1904]

My dear Gosse,

I've been extraordinarily delighted with some praise I've found over your signature. I do really value your good opinion of my work.

Very many thanks,
Yours ever,
H.G. Wells

574. To the Editor, *Nature*

PLS

[Spade House] [? January 1905]

[Dear Sir],

I addressed a letter to the editor of Nature replying to what I allege to be misrepresentations and misstatements in a review of three of my books by "F. W. H." (December 29, 1904, p. 193).[1] After a delay of some weeks, due to the absence of "F.W.H." abroad, the editor of Nature has written to ask me to modify and shorten my protest.

"F.W.H.' told the readers of Nature that my "Food of the Gods" claimed to forecast the future. This was untrue, and I said so.

"F.W.H." mixed up my discusson of probabilities in "Anticipations"with my general review of educational influences in "Mankind in the Making," and presented this as my ideals. I pointed out that this was an unsound method of criticism.

"F.W.H." presented the following as my opinions: – "Germany will be cowed by the combined English and American Navies, and Anglo-Saxonism will eventually triumph. There remains the Yellow Races. Their star, too, will pale before that of the Anglo-Saxons." I repudiated this balderdash with some asperity. It is violently unlike my views.

He wrote of me, "he seems unaware of the part in the national life that is played by the lower stratum of society, the 'stagnant' masses as he would call them." I denied that I should, and pointed out that no one does know what part is played by any stratum of society in national reproduction. It is a field of unrecorded facts. I commented on "F.W.H.'s" assumption that he was in possession of special knowledge.

He wrote of "the fact that this stratum is an absolute necessity." This is *not* a fact. It may or may not be true. I commented on this use of the word "fact" in view of "F. W. H's" professorial sneer at my "imagination unclogged by knowledge."

He declared that I want to "get rid of the reckless classes, and depend solely on the careful classes," a statement which has not an atom of justification. He not only "guys"my suggestions, but foists an absolutely uncongenial phraseology upon me.

Finally, he wrote, "we are to introduce careful parentage, *that is*, put a stop to natural selection." I quoted this in view of his statement that I had "no very thorough grasp of the principles of evolution." I discussed what appeared to be his ideas on evolution. They appeared to me to be crude and dull, and I regret I cannot condense my criticisms to my present limits.

I expressed some irritation at his method of misstatement followed by reply, and hinted a doubt whether my own style of inquiry – in spite of the fact that romances blacken my reputation – was not really more scientific that his.[2]

H. G. Wells

---

[1] The reviewer was undoubtedly the well-known scientist, F. W. Hirst. In fact, his article about Wells's novels is a positive piece, and is also one of the first long analyses of his work from a scientist.

[2] F. W. H. and Wells are referring, in the main, to the last few pages of *Anticipations*. They are heavily ironic, and other readers after F. W. H. have also found the words difficult, or, at least, the ironic presentation difficult. Much contemporary criticism of these works, and *In The Days of the Comet*, published at about this same time, takes the views presented in Wells's fiction to correspond exactly to his own ideas. This letter originally appeared in *Nature*, 2 February 1905, p. 319, and should be read in the light of the furore over establishing a Sociological School in London, as well as Francis Galton's views on eugenics then being debated.

575. To Fred Wells

Illinois, ALS

Spade House
Sandgate 29. 1. 05

Dear old Fred,

I will look up the Rosemeath people soon, but it is very difficult to do very much to alter affairs there.[1] When one tries to persuade the old lady to have a servant she gets angry or cries. All that I can do to keep them comfortable is done, you may rely on that. Things go on very evenly & uneventfully here. We all keep well & the children grow more & more interesting every day.

I hope things go on well with your land speculation & so forth.

Your ever affectionately

HG Wells

---

[1] Rosemeath was the name of the cottage at Liss which Wells had purchased for his family. Fred had returned to South Africa after his long visit in 1902.

576. To Henry Newbolt

Hofstra, ACCS

Spade House
Sandgate

28 – ii – 05

Honoured Sir & Unique Newbolt,

Will you be my guest at the Whitefriars Club at 6:30 on Friday March 31. The club guest is Welldon, the Chairman is C. Arthur Pearson & the topic is Public School Training.[1] The orgie will do you no end of good.

Yours ever
H.G.

[1] There were two Welldon's, one was Bishop of Manchester and the other was a master at Rugby School. Which person gave the main address is not known, but the latter is more likely. Pearson (1866–1921) was a publisher in London, and founded the *Daily Express.* Wells was a member of the Whitefriars Club before he shifted his allegiance to the Reform Club.

577. To Robert Ross[1]

Illinois, Transcription

Spade House
Sandgate

18. 3. 05.

My dear Ross,

I'm very sorry you couldn't come here and still sorrier for the cause of your absence. I'd very much like a week end with you and gossip and meandering. Week ends here are full up until April 28th – with the doubtful exception of Easter, for which them as is arst asn't replied yet. Can I bag you for the 28th-29th, weekend.

Yours ever,
H.G. Wells

[1] Robert, 'Robby' Ross was a good friend and literary executor of Oscar Wilde. Wells was a very strong 'straight' friend of Ross, Vyvyan Holland (Wilde's son) and others in the Wilde circle such as Reggie Turner. The Ross correspondence sheds more light on the late Edwardian literary scene.

578. To the Editor, *Outlook*[1]

Texas, ACCS

Spade House
Sandgate 23. iii. 05

My dear Sir,

Your telegram came to my hands too late for me to wire reply. I'm very sorry that my contract with the Daily Mail prevents my writing you any article at present. As far as Jules Verne goes, I think I shouldn't like to in any case. A good deal of injustice has been done the old man in comparison with me. I don't like the idea of muscling into the circle of attention about him with officious comments or opinions eulogy. I've let the time when I might have punished him decently go by.[2]

Yours very sincerely,
H.G. Wells

---

[1] The editor was J. L. Garvin.

[2] Although Wells did not care for having his work compared with that of Verne, and denied any influence from that source, he always refused, as here, the opportunity to attack Verne or Verne's science, as he felt they were writing for different audiences. At this time in France, many critics hoped that Wells would attack Verne, for their own purpose, but he did not rise to the bait, and within three or four years the comparison was no longer made except to have it denied in a perfunctory way by virtually everyone concerned. In fact, the standard comparison in France was to Poe.

579. To the Editor, *Century Magazine*

Illinois, ALS

Spade House
Sandgate 12. iv. 05

Dear Sir

We had some time since a brief correspondence about my next book. I forgot how things were left, but I am posting you tomorrow a typewritten copy of what is practically the finished story. I shall be obliged if you will read this & keep it by you until I write further as to the disposal — whatever the outcome of this correspondence may be. I am sending it you in the supposition that you will make me an offer for all the English American & colonial serial rights & I will keep any offer I may have open until a month from this date. I have made arrangements for both English & American book rights. Something was said in your previous letter of the book rights following the serial in America. I believe that possibly this might be managed by discreet negotiation, but it will be far more convenient for me to deal separately with the two things.[1]

Yours very sincerely
H.G. Wells

---

[1] Nothing came of these negotiations, and it was not until 1914 that the *Century Magazine* did one of his serials, *The World Set Free*.

580. To the Editor, *Outlook*

Texas, ALS

Spade House
Sandgate 18 – iv – 05

My dear Sir,

It was only when I got home here this evening when I heard of your pursuit of me. I wrote you on Saturday, asking if I could see you yesterday (Tuesday) & as I didn't hear from you, I concluded you weren't in town. So I didn't call. The project I had in mind was a sort of serial of a new season[?] I'm discussing it now in another quarter but very probably that is only a temporary. I'd prefer for my manuscript [to go] in your direction. I think I've invented a form that will serialize in weekly papers – a new thing altogether.

Yours very sincerely,
H.G. Wells

So new that Anatole France has been doing practically the same thing in France for years.

581. To J. L. Garvin

Texas, ALS

Spade House
Sandgate 19. iv. 05

Dear Mr. Garvin,

Your letter comes to hand just as I have posted one to you – which does to a certain extent undercut my project. But I'm a little embarrassed at having now suggested the thing in another quarter. There's many a slip, however, between the author of an idea & the proprietor who has to pay for it & I don't see that there's any harm in asking what you think you'd be prepared to go to, for a feature of about 3,000 words weekly (I can't do the thing I want to do shorter than that) for 25 weeks. Anatole France, A Modern Utopia, Tristram Shandy, & O.W. Holmes will suggest something of the form & method if you think confusedly of them all together & the subject is our literature in some aspects.[1]

Yours very sincerely,
H.G. Wells

I won't use your office, you understand, to haggle with in the other quarter, because there a price has been named.

---

[1] A rather provocative description. Anatole France, about sixty at this juncture was a French literary critic and writer, Lawrence Sterne's *Tristram Shandy* is a remarkable eighteenth-century novel and Oliver Wendell Holmes was a well known essayist and poet in Massachusetts. His best known book, a set of critical essays, is called *The Autocrat of the Breakfast Table*. Wells is providing a good description, in fact, of some of his pieces collected in *An Englishman Looks at the World* which appeared in 1914.

582. To Edward Garnett

Texas, ALS

Spade House
Sandgate

20 – iv. 05

I want to read Tarde.[1]

Dear Garnett,

You're a man of prejudices & prior assumptions. You are a tense critic & the ideal critic relaxes & lets himself go at times (see Marie Corelli's last preface). Fancy reading my Utopia from the middle onward in order to see if your totally inadequate views of things are denied or confused. Wait till I've got you here! Then I'll talk to you.

Yours ever,
H.G.

[1] Gabriel Tarde (1843–1904) was a French municipal functionary and philosopher. He began to write fiction about the future in middle age, and spent the remainder of his life in writing. Wells wrote a preface to his work, *Fragment d'histoire future* (Paris, 1904), translated as *Underground Man* (London, 1905), pp. 1–19. They met once and I believe that a few pieces of correspondence exist in private hands in Paris.

583. To the Director, Natural History Museum

Boston, ALS

Spade House
Sandgate

30 – iv. 05

Dear Sir,

I very much regret that I shall be prevented from attending your very interesting ceremony on May 12th.

Yours very faithfully,
H.G. Wells[1]

[1] The director was E. Ray Lankester. He and Wells were close friends until Lankester's death in the mid 1920s. What the ceremony might have been is not now known.

584. To Robert Ross

Illinois, Typed Transcription

Spade House
Sandgate 5.5.05.

My dear Ross,

I have been reading this sumptuous book – not a bit too splendidly apparelled in its crimson binding – with very great pleasure and sympathy.[1] It is extraordinarily mine in many ways. Did I send you my Modern Utopia? If not I will do so. – I meant to do it – and then you will see how in a curious way Wilde and I interweave.

I wrote a paper in 1891 (see my Modern Utopia, p. 378) which Harris printed in the Fortnightly and which I think must have come in Wilde's way. I wrote not fully grasping, I have only recently come to understand, the extraordinary importance of the thing I wrote. But it found Wilde on the same road. In the 1895 book of his he says things quite clearly that show he was exactly where I have arrived in 1905.[2]

Yours ever,
H.G. Wells

[1] Wells was reading *De Profundis* which had just been published in a new, complete edition. Wells had received one of the specially bound fifteen presentation copies. The success of the republication was remarkable, five new editions within a year, and the success led to the first collected edition of Wilde's work, edited by Ross, and to the beginnings of the revival of interest in Wilde's writing. In 1908 a group of Ross's friends gave a dinner in his honour and recognition of his work on behalf of Oscar Wilde. Two hundred people were in attendance at the Savoy Hotel: Wells and William Rothenstein proposed Ross's health.

[2] Although Wells never met Wilde, except perhaps once in passing in the offices of *The Yellow Book*, he felt that Wilde had been badly treated and punished for his intelligence. When Wilde went to Reading Gaol, Ross took books to him, one of which was *Select Conversations with An Uncle*. Wells was also active on Wilde's behalf, playing an important role in raising the funds to have the Epstein statue placed on Wilde's grave in the Père Lachaise cemetery in Paris.

585. To the Century Co., N.Y.

Illinois, ACCS

Spade House
Sandgate 5. v. 05

Dear Sirs -

Are you making an offer for my 'In The Days of the Comet'? If so, please hold the M.S. until negociations are concluded, but, if not, would you oblige me by sending it on to the F.A. Munsey Co. 111 Fifth Avenue, New York[1]

Yours very sincerely
H.G. Wells

[1] *Cosmopolitan*, a Munsey magazine, published the serial in North America.

586. To A. J. Balfour

British Library, Typed Transcription[1]
Add Mss. 49857 208-213

[London] 10 May 1905

[Dear Mr. Balfour]

I recall that when we met at Mrs. Webb's some time ago, you spoke of the problems of endowing people who have made original contributions to thought. I want to ask you whether you think it might not be desirable to endow me. Now I do not want you to think that I am what is called "needy" as things are or that this is in any way an appeal in that key. I speak about £1000. I save money over and above that & my life is insured for a reasonably large sum. To a large extent I write the sort of thing I ought to write.The only flaw indeed in my position is that in order to keep it stable & independent I have to turn out about two books a year & that even at that I have to devote a lot of intellectual energy to negotiations with editors & publishers & the <u>ingenious adjustment of what I have to say to what the reading public supposes it wants.</u>

I believe I could do something more worthy of the name of literature if I could disregard these adjustments. At present I have three books more or less complete and it is interesting to go from one to the other & [revise] this & that in a leisurely way. But I shall be obliged to foreclose with one of these soon & finish it, with a sort of violence, to sell. And I have one or two projects that under existing conditions it would be too adventurous for me to undertake because it might be difficult to cast them into a form that would sell, but which nevertheless are projects of some literary value. I have thought, for example, of a text-book of Sociology that I venture would be a seminal sort of work. There's a good deal of activity in the directions of sociology and a certain amount of irregular disorganized endowment & I believe if I could be let loose in this field for a time I could give things a trend.If I could be placed in some position that would leave my time free & relieve me from the obligation of earning at most more than five or six hundred pounds a year I believe I could do better and more significant work than under existing conditions.

I feel a sort of ingratitude to Fortune in even making this suggestion. I do have now a very good prosperous time & there are a great number of better men than myself hampered & limited by considerations, that make my own concessions to necessity most trivial. On the other hand there are endowments, there are academic positions, and, assuming that I do signify, it is not altogether right that my intellectual process should go on under the perpetual fog & pressure of the market-place.

My publisher will have sent you my Modern Utopia. Everything down to the meretricious illustration has been done to make that saleable & it sells. But you can scarcely open it at any point without discovering vistas along which it is hopeless to attempt to lure the general book- hungry public & from which I have, very reluctantly, to turn.

Don't let this letter bother you at all. I've blown it off at the end of a lot of troublesome explaining & expostulating with my American publisher. It is a passing remark, an aspiration. I thought I would let you know how things stand with me. As things are, I get on very well, you understand.

[Sincerely yours]
H. G. Wells

P.S. I mean, you know, to get my work done in any case. But I suggest I should do it better in serenity than in active competition for subsistence like Miss Marie Corelli[2] .I think too, unless my pretensions are vain, it would be well if instead of being an intellectual free lance I was brought into relation with the organized thought & the university system of the country. I think there ought to be some sort of post or fellowship for me in that system, that I merit a certain standing & security. I know of no other great political leader, I can imagine none as probable to whom I should write as I am writing now to you. But your stand is curiously alone in your double relation to ideas & practical statesmanship, that I have ventured upon this step.[3]

---

[1] These transcriptions mark the end of the Sociological Society effort to establish a chair either at London University or the LSE; see also letter 542.

[2] This was the pseudonym of Mary Mackay (1855–1924) who wrote several romantic novels during her career.

[3] Balfour asked his Private Parliamentary Secretary, Ramsay, to comment on the Wells request. In a memorandum dated 12 June 1905, Ramsay told Balfour that Wells had presented a good case, but he was not sure that Wells was a true genius, that sociology was not an exact science, and because Wells made over £1000 annually, such an appointment would raise an outcry. Ramsay reported a distillation of these views to Wells. Balfour, who resigned this month, did not respond to the request.

587. To Mr Ramsay

British Museum, Transcription
Add. Mss. 49857 208-213

[London] 6 – 12 – 1905

I am greatly obliged to you for your letter. The suggestion I threw out to Mr. Balfour was one quite casually made & one I should have been amazed to find productive of any positive result in my case. But I am very glad that he considered it, because I think that this problem of unremunerated or not immediately remunerative literary work is altogether too little regarded at present & unlikely to be at all adequately dealt with by any one but him. I trust you will convey my acknowledgement to him.

H.G. Wells

588. To James Garvin

Texas, ALS

[London] 21 – v -05

Dear Mr. Garvin,

My contributions to the Outlook, I hope are only deferred, but after all that other negociation I'd conclude in a bargain & for the time I am 'elsewhere'.

Yours very sincerely,
H.G. Wells

589. To Frank Wells

Korn, APCS

St. Moritz, Switzerland 1 – 6 – 05

Please reply to Sandgate.
Love to everyone.
Dashed ugly postcard. Try & get everything in order & we'll come along Wednesday next – to agree with whatever you have settled.[1] Please write Spade House & say what it is you have done.

H.G.

[1] This probably concerns decisions concerning the care of his mother in her last days of her life (see letters 592 and 593) and whether Frank and Joseph were to live on in Liss. That was what was eventually decided.

590. To the Editor, *Grand Magazine*[1]

PLS

[Spade House,
Sandgate, Kent] [late Winter 1905]

I find it extremely difficult to judge among the stories I have written and say which I think best. My stories vary a good deal in type; some are written for one sort of effect and some for another. I am, perhaps, least dissatisfied with "The Star," but find it very hard to say why. I think almost equally well of at least ten or eleven of the stories I have done, and the others hardly count at all. This is rather like making a choice between one's hob-nailed boots and one's slippers, or discussing whether one prefers daffodils or cheese. If they are good of their kind, each is best at the proper time. If they fail, they fail altogether. I don't like discussing precedence between one work of art and another. Either a work of art has something unique and incommensurable or it is nothing. "The Star" seems to satisfy more people than any other story I have written, and so, with these reservations, I pick it out for the editors of "The Grand Magazine" to reprint.

H.G. Wells

[1] Wells was often asked which of his short stories was his favourite. After 1925 he always said "The Pearl of Love." Prior to that time he said "The Country of the Blind," but before it was written, his favourite was "The Star." A new magazine, *The Grand Magazine*, was begun in 1905. They asked Wells for his opinions and he responded with this letter, vol. 1, no. 3 (April, 1905, pp. 353–61). They published the story as well as his letter.

591. To Edgar Jepson

Hofstra, ALS

Spade House
Sandgate 5. vi. 05

Dear Jepson,

We are just back from Switzerland. Your letter has no address and I've dropped your envelope into the W.P.B.[1] but I guess you are at Dymchurch & I'm addressing there, to say we lunch at 1. & will be very glad to see you (bring your sister) any day next week or next after. This week is complicated with engagements. Till then

Yours very sincerely,
H.G. Wells

[*In the corner of the paper it reads, 'address to D church'.*]

[1] Waste Paper Basket.

592. To Mrs Burgess

Bromley, ALS

Liss[1]
Spade House
Sandgate
Kent

17. vi. 05

Dear Mrs. Burgess,[2]

My father is in bed with his foot rather painful today & he asked me to answer your very kind & touching letter and to tell you something of my poor dear mother's last days. You know I think that since last October her mind has been very feeble, though her health remained good. She stopped writing letters even to Fred and seemed to like nothing but to be left alone. Last Easter Monday she had, I am sorry to say, a very serious accident. She fell down stairs as she was going to bed & broke her ankle. Everything was done at once that could be done to make her comfortable, we got a nurse into the house, & made everything ready for what we expected to be a long illness. She suffered hardly any pain at all but it now seems there was some injury to the spine that the doctor did not at first detect & which hastened her end. She lay, and for a time she seemed clearer & brighter in her head than she had been for some months, until Whitsuntide & then she began to sink very rapidly. I was mostly here in the Saturday & on Whit Monday I was called to her again & arrived just too late to see her alive once more. She died very peacefully & lay with a look of childish tranquillity on her dear innocent old face. She will leave a great void in the life of my father & Frank. Frank has been wonderfully good to her in these years, while I & Fred have been away, just writing her letters & sending her money; Frank has had the harder task of waiting on her day by day. She was very independent, she would not have a servant, try as we would to induce her to do so and the result is that all the housework & waiting on her has fallen on my brother. My father's feet have become very painful & of course the trouble of the last few months has kept him up & about when he ought to have been lying up, but I hope now with care & attention that things may be made easier for him. He joins with me & Frank in warmest regards.

Your very affectionate cousin,
Bertie Wells

[1] When Sarah finally left her employment at Up Park, she came to a cottage in Liss, which Wells purchased for her. Frank also lived in the cottage. This letter is marked '1st letter' on the envelope and the following letter is marked '2cd letter'.

[2] This letter is to Wells's cousin, on the occasion of his mother's final illness and death on 12 June 1905. It was written on behalf of his father, who was unwell.

593. To Mrs Burgess

Bromley, ALS

Liss.
Spade House
Sandgate, Kent[1] [postmarked 14 July 1905]

Dear Mrs. Burgess,

I am sending you a last sad little reminder of my poor dear Mother.[2]

Yours very sincerely.
H. G. Wells

Do you know I have two little sons now?

[1] The Bromley files indicate that this letter is postmarked 14 July 1905. I find it most difficult to read. They were clearly sent at different times, although they are marked '1st letter' and '2cd letter'.

[2] Wells sent two photographs of his mother after her death, which he had probably taken himself. They are now in the Wells Collection at Bromley.

594. To Henry Newbolt

Hofstra University, ALS

Spade House
Sandgate 30 – vi – 05

My Dear Newbolt,

I'm returning the proof of your fine article on my unworthy work. I don't know how to thank so generous a friend & critic. So, I won't thank you. But I do think the thing is most admirably done. Your use of quotation in particular most happy, & all your criticisms neat & right. If I might venture one comment it is why have you made no mention of Plato's fine Laws?

I've been much disturbed these last weeks by the death of my mother & I'm afraid I cut a poor figure when you opened the other night at the Coefficients & so to speak called me.

Yours ever,
H.G

595. To Henry Newbolt

Hofstra, ALS

Spade House
Sandgate [probably early 1905]

Dear Mr. Newbolt,

If you have finished with the numbers of the Fortnightly, could you let us have them back? The book has to go to press, & I think HG has some corrections. [1]

Sincerely yours,
Catherine Wells

[1] Probably the serial parts of *A Modern Utopia*, which appeared in the *Fortnightly Review* from October 1904 to April 1905.

596. To the Editor, *Fortnightly Review*[1]

PLS

[Spade House
Sandgate, Kent] [*c.* September 1905]

Sir, – My attention has been called to an article by Dr. Crozier in the September FORTNIGHTLY REVIEW upon my sociological work. He appears to have written this article under the sting of some extremely mild depreciation of his books, and of Mr. Kidd's kindred efforts, which occurred in a little essay of mine originally published in the Independent Review. This dodging from review to review will be a little perplexing to some of your readers, who will not have had access to my paper in the latter publication, and I may perhaps, therefore, invade your space with a word or two upon the greater issue which underlies Dr. Crozier's attack. His more personal challenges I will notice only briefly. He asks me, in the length of a page or so, what I have added to the Science of Sociology, and I will answer at once and finally, I hope and believe – nothing; mere scavenger's work has been mine. He seems, moreover, to be worried by some fancied claim I make to consideration as a sociologist, and I would at once eagerly repudiate so disastrous a claim. He declares I am in extraordinary error, and that he has said it all before, in some essay called "God or Force," of which I now hear for the first time. I leave these delicate questions of priority to anyone sufficiently interested to read the matter concerned, though what either God or Force has to do with a question of logical method appeals to one's curiosity. The decent path of sociological distinction is, however, not for my feet, nor academic laurels for my brow, and I do not care who believes that I have built up my mind upon a secret and insidious study of Dr. Beattie Crozier. Such matters of repute have become of scarcely more importance to me now than they are to the public. But I do care to maintain the thesis implicit in my Modern Utopia and explicitly given in my article in the Independent Review against – I cannot say the arguments, but the protests of Dr. Crozier. Which thesis is that the so-called Science of Sociology is not a science at all, that the large copious writings upon Sociology of Comte, of Herbert Spencer, of Mr. Kidd and of Dr. Crozier are interesting intellectual experiments of extraordinarily little permanent value, and the proper method of approach to sociological questions is the old, various and literary way, the Utopian way, of Plato, of More, of Bacon, and not the nineteenth century pneumatic style, nor by its constant invocation to biology and "scientific" history and its incessant unjustifiable pretension to exactitude and progress.

I say I am ready to maintain this thesis, but, indeed, I have very litle here to maintain it against! I stated my case in the Independent Review, and by way of reply, Dr. Crozier says chiefly that I speak disrespectfully of Comte and of Herbert Spencer.There is no denying I do that,and no doubt it will seem very shocking to some of your readers. *But it will not continue to be shocking*. Both these remarkable products of the nineteenth century justify me by example. They were ridiculously disdainful of Plato; and Herbert Spencer quite preposterously refuses to read Kant.The world at large has still to realise how wordy and shallow both these writers were and the sooner it is shocked into that realisation the better. I grew up in the atmosphere of their reputations, and I have had to overcome the prejudices of my type and class in repudiating them. But who could turn repeatedly, as I have had to do, from the lean pretentious emptiness of Spencer, to the concrete richness, the proliferating suggestions of Plato, and not be forced at last to that admission? I shall count myself fortunate if it is given me in any measure to help rescue sociological questions, the only questions that really interest adult human beings, from the sea of abstractions, from the seas of thinnest intellectual gruel, under which the nineteenth century, so busy and preoccupied about so many things, permitted them to be submerged.

The science of sociology is no real science, I assert, and I am eager to help drain the flow of it away. So I reiterate and emphasise my thesis. I will even expand it and enlarge my radiant area of offence. There is no science of sociology, there is no science of economics, but only an elaborate expansion of certain arbitrary and unjustifiable assumptions about property, social security, and human nature. There is also, if one may glance at the Fabian Society, no "scientific" socialism. Because writings upon any subject are recognisably not literature, it does not follow that they are scientific. Because a work or writer has imagination it does not, therefore, as Dr. Crozier seems to think, cease to be a contribution to thought. Quite the reverse. That was one of the peculiar weaknesses of the nineteenth century, to be capable of believing quite sincerely in the scientific possibilities of anything, of the possibility of treating any human affair almost, in a dull, slow, arithmetical superior abstract way called "scientific." In that dear old time, I remember, I once had my hair cut – and cut very badly – by a "scientific" hairdresser.

But to come now to Dr. Crozier's arguments, so far as they seem to effect my positions. Essentially, they consist in two misreadings of my case. He must have read my article in the Independent Review with the most extraordinary carelessness, and failed to run over it again when his own article was printed. He says I ignore the past, would not have men learn from that past, and by spelling it with a capital P, he gives it a sort of technical air,and gets an effect of really believing himself that my dismissal of the scientific claim of sociology is a refusal to use the material of history and anthropology. Absolutely the reverse is the case. I state in that article, with the utmost explicitness, that I would have sociology approached by the construction of Utopian schemes,which can then be criticised and tested through a cautious and analytical use of the stores of history, anthropology, psychology, and so forth. It is true I am wanting in respect for Comte and Herbert Spencer, and that a "constructive scheme of ways and means founded on evolution" seems to be me about as intelligible a phrase as "a constructive scheme of ways and means founded on devolution or involution or Chinese metaphysics," but this alleged disrespect for the "Past" is purely a dialectical invention of Dr. Crozier's.

Dismissing that, I come to his second misconception. My case against the scientific nature of sociology, as it was stated in my Independent Review article, rests on the fact that it is a subject with only one unique object for study – society. Dr. Crozier has muddled this up with the discussion of individual uniqueness in my Modern Utopia, and states that I base my objection to the scientific claims of sociology on the fact that every individual human being is unique. This is an absurd error. However, it enables him to say, what I have myself said at the Royal Institution,[2] that given a sufficiently innumerable multitude of cases the individual difference disappears. But I have altogether wider ideas than Dr. Crozier of the multitude necessary for the establishment of any laws of collective human action, and I do not see that he has helped his case at all, or confuted me upon any point by raising that. He goes on, with needless italics, to assert that "the problem of Sociology deals entirely with *men in the mass*." That answers me nothing; it only gives him back into my hands. If this alleged science of Sociology is dealing with masses of men, then clearly there are far fewer units than if the sociologist dealt with single men. A single mass of men is as unique and individualised a thing as a single man. A Grundenwald conference is a mass of men, the South African Chinese are a mass of men, London is a mass of men, the Russian army – are they not all individual and unique? You have a mass of men still alive in the Russian Empire, and a mass that has played the game right out in the Roman Empire; what light does the general fate of the latter throw upon the former? Will Dr. Crozier, "basing himself upon evolution," apply his knowledge of past masses to Russia,and tell us what must inevitably happen there in the next half century, what Sociological Law will be confirmed in that instance? I submit his masses do not serve him. I submit his instance and his Italics only confirm the thesis he has failed to grasp.

So much for Dr. Crozier. But having countered his attack, I may, perhaps, add a few sentences to still further underline my aggression upon the scientific claims of sociology. Please notice that I have been trailing my coattail for some time, loudly denying scientific authority to Sociology, emphatically disputing dignified and respected claims and asserting the rightness of the literary, poetical, and Utopian method of dealing with these things, and that Doctor Crozier is as yet my only reply. I have been disrespectful to Comte and Herbert Spencer, disrespectful to Mr. Benjamin Kidd; to all "scientific" sociologists, my gestures go to the very limits of permissible disrespectfulness. It is not, however, true that I disdain the Past. I sincerely hope there remains no ambiguity about my attitude in these matters.

H.G. Wells

[1] This letter, which appeared in the October 1905 issue, was an answer to Dr Crozier, who had written, 'Mr. Wells as A Sociologist' for the September issue. It is a sample of Wells at his best invective. It was entitled 'Is Sociology A Science?'.
[2] 'The Discovery of the Future', *Nature*, vol. lxv, p. 326 and the *Smithsonian Report* for 1902.

597. To Elizabeth Healey

Texas, AL

Spade House
Sandgate   Oct. 6 – 05

Dear Miss Healey,

Cheer up. The Lord deals mercifully with us, but fattening & things go on ! [*a sketch of the Wells family marching along in file*]. I shall send you Kipps A Novel in a week or so.

[*remainder of letter missing*]

[*Attached to the letter are two photographs, one of a skeleton of a human being, with an arm around Wells's neck, taken while at the Royal College of Science. This picture was probably taken at the same time as the more familiar one of the skeleton with a horse's head, again with its arm over Wells's shoulder. This photograph also appears in my H. G. Wells: Desperately Mortal, (London: Yale, 1986), p. 25. These spoof photographs had as their origin photographs taken of Huxley in the 1850s.*]

598. To Arnold Bennett

Texas, ALS

Spade House
Sandgate   5-11-05

Dear Bennett,

Next after 'A Great Man', which lies & ripens in my mind like sacred Wine in a cellar, I like these short things of yours. They are well & carefully done (which after all isn't anything) & are & above [all] they're authentic (which is everything) – at least most of them are. 'The Dog', the 'Feud', 'Phantom', the Hotel thing (except that you don't quite get the vulgarity of these places) (you seem, I mean, to feel their magnificence is magnificence) & Clarice I like best, & in about that order; but there is nothing I haven't read with interest & some approval. 'A Letter Home' is, as one might expect, least differentiated; it might have been [written] by half a dozen hands I could name; & Tiddy fol-lol is the weakest. I think you go on getting better, wider in your range, and finer and surer in your movements.

But I'm damned if I can stand your friend Phillpotts: His Secret Woman – the trite dawns, the laboriously done sunsets, the vast dyspeptic "tragedy" of these people, the perpetual petty, mediocre "freshness"[?] of the phrasing, the whole signifying nothing! In a measure I've told him as much.[1]

Yours ever
H.G.

[1] Eden Phillpotts (1862–1960) had a long literary collaboration with Arnold Bennett on novels and in the theatre. He wrote over two hundred books in his life time. Wells did not care for him.

599. To Bernard Shaw[1]

Illinois, ACCS

Spade House
Sandgate

5–11.05

My dear Shaw

In spite of your disgraceful caricature of me in Broadbent – even my slight tendency to embonpoint was brought in – I enjoyed John Bull's Other Island. There is some very dramatic gorgeous rhetoric, beautiful effects, much more serious Shaw than ever before, & I'd rather see it again than see anyone else's new play. All the same there's dreadful things in it. A fine speech by the daft priest for example is quite spoilt by the old Butlerism about the hellish so on. As a matter of fact Larry is just as much English as Irish. I can't distinguish him from Hamlet. And Broadbent looks like Redmond & becomes more like a Anglicized Dutch Jew of any people I ever met. None the less it's an admirable play and a picture of a politico-social system better in the P.O.W., a well-known person I'm told peeping at it.[2] Perhaps he learnt something – perhaps he is deeply impressed.

But really you know I don't want to hold Greyfriars[?] everywhere. The play has some cruelty of teaching children to read. And the dreadful pulling of the girl character is due to sheer laziness on your part, you needn't go over her again. Then of course the contrast of English & Irish is just late-Victorian sham – all the balderdash about the soul of a people & than I thought could be done on the stage.The priest is golly.

You're a great swell Shaw really – with something in your blend that ever & again breaks out into little blemishes of perversity. You have every element of greatness except a certain independence of your own intellectual eccentricity. You can't control your instinct & your love of larking. You ought to fill yourself with meat & you'd be vast.[3]

Yours ever
H.G.W.

[*First alternative text*]

Dear Shaw,

In spite of your disgusting caricature of me in Broadbent – even my slight tendency to embonpoint was brought it – I enjoyed John Bull's Other Island. There was something very dramatic in the P.O.W. A well known person, I'm told, peeping at it. Perhaps he learnt something. – perhaps he was deeply impressed.

But really you know I don't want to hear[?] of everywhere. The play has some really gorgeous rhetoric, beautiful effects, much more serious Shaw than ever before & I'd rather see it again than see anyone else's new play.

All the same there are dreadful things in it. A fine speech by the daft priest for example is quite spoilt by the old Butlerism about the hellish cruelty of teaching children to read, and the dreadful description of the girl's character was due to sheer laziness on your part. You should go over her again. Then, of course, the contrast of English and Irish is just late Victorian sham & all the balderdash about the people and so on. As a matter of fact Larry is just as much English as Irish. I can't distinguish him from Hamlet. And Broadbent looks like Redmond & behaves more like an Anglicized Dutch Jew of any people I have ever met. None the less its an admirable play & picture of a polite & social system better than I thought could be done on the stage. The priest is golly.

You're a great swell Shaw really – with something in your blood that ever and again breaks out in little blemishes of perversity. You have every element of greatness except a certain independence of your own intellectual excitability. You can't control your own wit & your love of larking. You ought to dull yourself with meat and then you'd be great.

Yours ever,

H.G.W.

---

[1] This letter exists in four forms. One, the original, is on three correspondence cards, written on both sides. The second copy is in pencil, a third is in pen, and the fourth is typed. All these later three copies have transposed paragraphs and changed wording from the original. The second and third transcriptions have only the one head sketch. Someone at Cornell thought Shaw made these changes, but for what reason it is difficult to say. The text from the correspondence cards is the one reprinted. The first alternative text follows the original.

[2] The Prince of Wales, later King George V, who is supposed to have attended incognito on the night Wells attended. The two heads, one crossed out partially, are supposed to represent the Prince.

[3] Shaw, of course was an Irishman (although of English ancestors) and a vegetarian which accounts for some of Wells's twits at Shaw and his play.

600. Israel Zangwill to H.G. Wells

Illinois, TLS

3, Hare Court
TEMPLE, E.C.

April 15th, 1905

Dear Mr. Wells,

I was very pleased to receive your new book, and I am taking it down into the country to study it at leisure. As a projector of Jewtopia your ideas interest me peculiarly. I expect many of your ideas will have been anticipated in the Talmud, as Eugenics was really invented by Moses, to the extent at least of excluding all physically imperfect persons "from the congregations of the Lord".

From a hurried glance over your appendix it seems to me not very much unlike the Kantian demonstration, by the Antigones of the imperfection of Reason, with the subsequent reconstruction of the shattered universe through the medium of the Practical Reason.

Congratulating you on many things, not the least of which is your extraordinary influence in France, I am,

Sincerely yours,

Israel Zangwill

601. Israel Zangwill to H.G. Wells

Illinois, TLS

Jewish Territorial Organization
15, Essex Street
Strand, W.C. November, 1905

Dear Mr. Wells,

I now have the pleasure of sending you a pamphlet from which you will be able to gather details as to the scheme about which you kindly promised me to write a brief opinion for publication. The scheme in a nutshell is to build up a autonomous Jewish state out of the refugees from Russian persecution a State which will likewise attract a number of prosperous and idealistic Jews. In our quest for a territory we wish, if possible, to take advantage of England's offer of a virgin soil under British suzerainty.

We have elements to offer England in return which are not to be disdained even by so mighty an Empire, since scattered over her dominions across the seas of thirteen million square miles she has only a white population of twelve millions which is less than one per square mile.

A flourishing settlement of one of the most potent white peoples on earth cannot but bring a gain of strength to any power that accords it a stretch of territory at present waste. But of course an independent territory is theoretically open to the organizations, – even Palestine, if it were attainable.

Thanking you in advance for the help your kind opinion will give me,

Yours sincerely,
Israel Zangwill

602. To Israel Zangwill

Central Zionist Archives, ALS
File A120/614

Spade House, Sandgate 11. xi. 05

My dear Zangwill,

The Jto[1] has my sympathy – in the abstract – & the project seems altogether sane & practicable. But it's not my doorstep, & I can offer you neither help nor advice. Your people are rich enough, able enough & patient enough to save themselves.

Yours ever
H.G. Wells

[1] This appears to be Wells's, and perhaps Zangwill's, abbreviation of Zangwill's word 'Jewtopia'; his name for a Palestine homeland.

603. To Winston Churchill

Churchill, ALS

Spade House
Sandgate 15–10–05

Dear Mr. Churchill

I'm very glad you liked my Utopia. You'd find it quite lively enough if you went there because it would be quite lively enough if you went there. I shall certainly hope some day to meet you again.

Yours very sincerely
H. G. Wells

604. To the Editor, *Cassell's Saturday Journal*[1]

ANS

[London] [before 15 November 1905]

The title was altered. I think I called it "Of an."

Yours ever,
H.G. Wells

[1] On 15 November 1905, *Cassell's Saturday Journal*, carried on page 241 a number of facsimle examples of handwriting. In addition to Wells's comment printed here, others on the page were contributed by Samuel Clemens, Hall Caine, Arthur Conan Doyle, G. B. Shaw, and Arthur Pinero.

605. To Victor Fisher[1]

Boston, ALS

Spade House
Sandgate

Nov. 29. 05.

Dear Mr. Fisher,

I like your pamphlet extremely. Why did not you offer it to the F.S. Can the Twentieth Century make so good & attractive pamphlet pay at a penny? Anyhow, good luck to it & a big sale. I see you have given up the idea of forming an organized Samurai, an abandonment quite in accordance with my views. We are I think developing a school of thought, a natural grouping of people round & about the old Fabian organization & these people will I feel sure work out a way of living, to which my Samurai & so forth will be just contribuing suggestions. Shelton is urgent to go on & I am dealing with him, but I do not see that his efforts are likely to give us more than a hard artificial rather barren group of ascetics.

Yours ever
H. G. Wells

[1] Fisher remained a Wells supporter and friend for many years. He was active on the left of the Labour Party and joined in attacking the I.L.P. stance on entrance into the First World War.

606. To Edward Clodd

Leeds, ALS

[Spade House
Sandgate, Kent]

10-XII-05

My Dear Clodd,

I wish I was in town next week. I'd certainly come. But I'm not.

And, I say, – I'm working very hard to buck up the Fabian Society and revive propaganda among the student class & so on in London. I think great things might be done in that direction now. I've written what is to be a tract –

it's in the Independent Review this month – & I want to get a series of such tracts, very clearly and simply written & widely distributed.[1] Does the game interest you at all? I wish it did, & if so I would ask you to come into the Fabian & lend me a hand. You ought to be a Fabian you know.

Yours ever,

H.G.

[1] The tract was 'This Misery of Boots' which became a Fabian tract later, and was also reprinted by the Independent Labour Party in the 1930s. The piece, with much autobiographical detail of Wells's life, was one of his most successful political articles of this period.

607. To L. Haden Guest[1]

LSE, ALS
[read at Bromley, photocopy]

Spade House
Sandgate

12. xii. 05

Dear ill treated Guest,

I'm having a go at the Fabians on Jan 12th. Mine's not a question of formulation but organization. I want to organize a canvass of the students, journalists, & middle class, especially in London, generally, get in more income through subscriptions, supplement Pease[2] with vigorous helpers & make things hum in a business-like way. We ought to have 7000 members, instead of 700 & everything to scale. I hope you'll be cooperating. There are hundreds of people in London willing to come under the Fabians for the asking. I shall be in London on the 18th. Would you care to lunch with me at the N.L.C.?

Yours ever,

H.G.

[1] Guest was a fellow Fabian and Wells is angling for support for his reform ideas.

[2] Pease was the long time secretary of the Society, and he was a person who liked attention and homage. Part of Wells's 'revolution' against the 'old gang' involved an opening of membership in the body as well as on the executive.

608. To Edgar Jepson

Hofstra, ANS

Spade House
Sandgate [unknown date, *c.* 1905]

Dear Jepson,
The article is off. Love to your lot.
Yours ever,
H.G.

609. To an unknown addressee

Korn, ALS

Spade House
Sandgate [*c.* 1905?]

Dear Sir,

This wasn't the origin of the title (which indeed was just a blunder). But you might get a paragraph as you suggest. I've no objection.[1]
Very sincerely yours,
H.G. Wells

You see the books get good notices in the Fortnightly and the Nineteenth Century.

---

[1] This may be about the letter printed in *Cassell's Saturday Magazine* to show Wells's handwriting; see letter 604.

610 To Edgar Jepson

Hofstra, ALS

Spade House
Sandgate

[*c.* 1905]

Dear Jepson,

Your note amazes me. I expected you to share Hubert Bland's opinions. I'm really very glad indeed that you liked the book.

Yours ever
H.G. Wells

611. To L. Haden Guest

Texas, ALS

[Spade House
Sandgate]

Saturday [*c.* 1905 – early 1906]

My dear Guest,

I have thought about the matter of an address & I have decided to ask Ball, Mrs. Reeves, Smith & Jackson to sign one with me. This will make us a group so that the Reform groups will be three, the Guest-Taylor, the [*illegible word*] & the Wells.[1]

Yours ever,
H.G.

[1] This is another letter in the development of the attempted reformation of the Fabian Society to reflect newer and younger interests.

612. To Fred Wells

Illinois, ALS

Spade House
Sandgate Jan 6. 06

My dear Fred,

I was glad to have your two letters & good wishes. I've been very busy this year end or I would have written before to reciprocate your greetings. I'm sorry to hear that things are still slumpish with your firm. It's bad for a man if the business he is in, doesn't move with the times. But I shall hope for better news in the new year.

With us things keep well, the children flourish & the work goes on. My last book has been distinctly a success[1] & has run to a sale of 12,000 copies – of which my share is 1/6 a copy. In March I hope to get over to America for a couple of months & I shall probably turn out a book upon it.

Frank seems going on all right with the Parent.[2] Frank himself & I had a day in London last month – went to a theatre & so on, & we were all very jolly & the memories of Godalming flew to & fro.

Love from my wife & the children

Yours ever
H.G.

---

[1] This book was *Kipps* (London: Macmillan, 1905) which was indeed a great success. The book has never been out of print since its publication as far as I can tell.

[2] Sarah Wells had recently died and Joseph and Frank were now living in the Liss cottage. Joseph Wells died suddenly in 1911, see letter 887.

613. To Henry James

Illinois, ALS

[Spade House
Sandgate] Jan. 25. 06

My dear James,

I have rented a cabin on the Germania for March 27th. Heaven knows when I shall return, & I am going to write loose large articles mingled with impressions of The Future in America (no less). I shall be very greatful if you can give me letters to any typical people. I suppose you know no one in Salt Lake City?. If I could get any insight into the social life of that place I might brave that long train journey from Chicago very willingly. I want to see something of the social effects of the varying divorce laws & there perhaps Miss Edith Wharton will talk to me – you must know her. I shall stay seven days in New York coming & going. I shall make a desperate attempt on your brother, spend a day or so in Boston & I'm resolved on Chicago & Washington. The rest is as God wills. I should be very glad if I could be put up as a temporary member of any New York club in which there are literary people to be met & perhaps you could think of a sponsor for me. Forgive these huge demands. I'm too greedy to see & hear to be modest. [1]

Yours ever,
H.G. Wells

A letter on the Golden Book impends. Three gross demands in the meanwhile.

[1] Wells did not go to Salt Lake City, but he did visit New York, Boston, Washington and Philadelphia on his tour. Henry James did introduce him to several people as did Graham Wallas. He met Edith Wharton and renewed his aquaintance with William Dean Howells. This was the first of a half dozen trips to the States for Wells.

614. To Moberly Bell

PLS

Spade House
Sandgate

Feb 1, 1906

Dear Mr. Moberly Bell,[1]

The Times Book Club issues a list of recent books, with no indication whatever that it is not a complete list of all books recently published, from which my "Kipps" is omitted. Practically the club professes to serve its subscribers, and then does its best to ignore the books that are published by Macmillans. The public does not understand this sort of secret-commission business at all. May I ask you, for the last time, to remedy this differential treatment for

"Kipps"? Otherwise I see nothing for it but to write a letter upon your Book Club, and send a copy to every paper in the three kingdoms.

Yours very truly,
H. G. Wells

[1] This letter is only one of a great many written to *The Times* in 1906. *The Times* had formed what it called a Book Club. The Club purchased books wholesale, described them as 'used' and resold them below the standard price. Authors were ambivalent about the scheme – their books sold, but they received a lower royalty. Although today we would think selection by a book club a good thing in general, such sales usually involve payment upon selection, rather than later royalties. This practice would have been unusual then and many publishers and authors refused to participate. Macmillan refused to recognize the book club idea and they published Wells's work. Moreover the Book Club did claim to have sold copies of *Kipps* but without any payment to Macmillan. Lower royalties for book club sales date from this time. This particular letter was located in a column in *The Times* summarizing the views of the editors and correspondents, 'Publishers and the Public', printed 14 November 1906. Moberly Bell was a subeditor of *The Times*.

615. To William Dean Howells

Harvard, Transcription

[London] 17. ii. 06

My dear Howells,

I shall be in New York early in April for a little while. Professor Albert Bushnell Hart[1] has put me up at the Century Club (7 West 43 St.) and I shall be very glad if I can find a chance of talking to you a little more about things American.

Yours very sincerely,
H.G. Wells

[1] Professor Albert Bushnell Hart conceived of the idea of the first multi-authored, multi-volume history of the United States, *The American Nation* (ff. 1904) and was the general editor.

616. To E. V. Lucas

Illinois, ALS

Spade House
Sandgate
22. ii. 06

My dear Lucas,

A little rook-shooting would do me just fine – the dress suit was not hired – oddly enough that wounds me most.[1]

I'm going to America March 27th on the Germania (D.V.) & poor dear Jane is to be left to mind the babies. It's just Rookery to say I've written my articles on America beforehand.[2]

Why don't you take a house in Sandgate where you'll get a chance of meeting civilized people like what we are? I do come to London but always I have been up to my ears lately in strawdinary intrigues to upset the Fabian Society like making buttered slides for an old lady, most amusing.

And the enclosed.

How is Mrs. Lucas? We often talk of you two as people like what we shall pal about with in Heaven. Perhaps we fix our hopes too high.

Anyway we don't meet you often, still

All the most warmly yours

H.G.

What's sure? What of Jan 21st or Feb. 4th. We don't see enough of you, really for our taste.

Yours ever,
H.G.

[1] I presume that this refers to a full dress dinner appearance, and that rook-shooting was a metaphor for such an occasion.

[2] Elsewhere Wells says he had written the introduction to his articles, which is much more likely.

617. To an unknown addressee

Hofstra, TLS[1]

[Spade House
Sandgate] [Spring 1906]

I am afraid that very little is to be done by "answering" Mr. Farrage. He seems to be almost completely ignorant of the thought of either Shaw or myself, and he just invents ideas for us. Why does he not either read us intelligently or leave us alone? Half at least of socialist literature is a discussion of social motives, which he declares it ignores. Because both Shaw and myself detest priestcraft and canting "piety", he supposes we are not "religious." Yet on Easter Monday I saw Shaw's "Major Barbara" which is as brilliant and penetrating an exposition of modern religion as can be. This is a free democracy and Mr. Farrage has a perfect right to be entirely ignorant of what religion and socialism mean, but he has no right to devise opinions for Shaw and myself out of that ignorance.

H. G. Wells

---

[1] This letter, possibly for the press, was probably written in spring 1906. *Major Barbara* opened on 22 November 1905.

618. To Fred Wells

Illinois, ALS

Spade House
Sandgate 5. iii. 06

My dear Fred,

Don't think I have delirium tremons. I'm writing this in the train, hence the shakiness. I was very sorry to hear of changes but I hope you'll find in the end it's a change for the better. I know you don't think much of my advice in your affairs but I do hope you won't set up in business in Johannesburg on £500. It won't keep you two years. I hardly know what to advise as to your future but on the whole unless you go to some small place & fly round I believe you'd have a better prospect for starting business in the old country.

Couldn't you come back & do something with Frank? Let me know how your plans go & with all good wishes.

Yours ever
The Busswhacker

Life & England very prosperous here. I am going to America next month for six weeks or a couple of months.

619. To Graham Wallas

LSE, ALS

Spade House
Sandgate

15. iv. 06

My dear Wallas,

I never see you now. Why don't you come back into the Fabian instead of leaving me to fight all the battles for righteousness alone?

Yours ever,
H.G.

Live 4 to 3.

620. To Catherine Wells

Illinois, ALS

The Union League Club
Chicago, Illinois

Sunday evening
May 6, 1906

Dearest of all Bits,

Where did I leave off?[1] I think it was at 7:30 on Saturday night. After that I had an eventful evening. The good Crane introduced me to a pleasant person called Doc Green – once a notorious gambler & now the chief vote organizer of the Republican party in the wards 'of jubious reputation' in Chicago – & off we went together. We went to a saloon kept by a notorious alderman of Chicago called Hinky-Dink who controls three thousand votes & described the world & life with him.[2] Afterward we went to his low class saloon full of the vilest ruffians I ever saw, drinking schooners of beer & smoking & then on to a Buddhist temple & an opium joint & the Chinese quarter. Thence we visited various saloons of high repute & the Pekin Theatre with a coloured company playing to a coloured audience. Thence to a low class saloon where a number of ladies in exiguous raiment came & sat on our knees & used endearments in vain. Thence to a most respectable house of ill fame where a most dignified parallel of Mrs Warren came & conversed. She wore diamonds & embraced me with effusion at parting, regretting deeply I found no charm in any of her gurrls. But I bought a bott of champagne [for] one young lady. – orful thing. Then along a street with highly lit houses on both sides with doors inscribed with engaging frankness, "Ella D'Arcy – Walk Right in." "Violet Hunt. Walk In" (N.B. The country can't stand Gorki's morals.) [3] Then to a dancing saloon to see people waltzing slowly to an excellent band. then to a Japanese house of vice – nother btl champagne. & then I felt I had seen enough of that side of this wonderful Chicago & got home to bed at 2. Then a morning of writing and at 1 to Hull House to lunch with Miss Addams[4] & a long table of people connected with settlement work. Agreeable afternoon in a circle of arm chairs & things round a big wood fire & talk about Fabian Society, Gorki, & socialist methods &c. – talked well. Tea talk combined with a number of Negroes & half breed people on how to behave in the circumstances that a violently race based play had come to Chicago.[5] Supper, ices, glorified by a Yiddish vaudeville entertainment & amateur dramatics at a Italian boys club – uptown to talk to Crane & the Hungarian consul & so to the letter & then to bed. So seepy.

B'lvd Binder

[1] Earlier letters from this trip no longer exist. Wells is in the midst of his first trip to the United States, later the subject of his book, *The Future in America* (London, 1906).

[2] See Lloyd Wendt and Herman Kogan, *Lords of the Levee: The Story of Bathhouse John and Hinky Dink* (Indianapolis: Bobbs Merrill, 1943) for an account of the lives of these gentry at the time of Wells's visit.

[3] Maxim Gorki, (1868–1936) a Russian novelist and writer was turned away at Customs in New York City as he was travelling with a woman who was not his wife. The incident was a *cause célèbre* of the time. Gorki's autobiography in three volumes is widely read, and his play, *The Lower Depths* (1902) has some of the characteristics of a classic.

[4] Jane Addams (1860–1935) founded the Chicago Settlement Center, Hull House, based on her

observations of Toynbee Hall in London. She was later president of the Women's International League for Peace and Freedom (1919–1935) and was awarded the Nobel Peace Prize in 1931.
[5] This was a play adapted from Thomas Dixon's novel, *The Clansman*, better known today as the source of D. W. Griffith's long film, *Birth of A Nation*, released in 1915 which discussed in detail the activities of the Ku Klux Klan.

621. To Catherine Wells

Illinois, ALS

Cosmos Club
Washington, D.C.

Saturday [12 May 1906]

Dear Heart,

I dined last night with Mrs. Canles. The Lodges were there & Alice & the Townleys.[1] Lady Townley reminded me in a public & peculiar manner of our organization[2] – & Secretary Root & Alice's husband, (new – not seen before) & a sister of Mrs. Lodge's (also fresh) and an additional note of novelty was given to the assembly by the absence of the Holmes.[3] I dine with the Holmes' s tonight & expect to meet the Townleys, the Lodges, Cowles's, the Longworth's ....[4] If any are absent I shall ask for them. I don't intend to be done out of my rights in the matter. One is led to expect the complete set & are here to insist upon the complete set. Which reminds me that I didn't see Miss Tuckerman last night. Why don't they produce Miss Tuckerman. Was it to save washing or what? There was a trumped up French ambassador & a nice wife who called H.G. Wells, in French, but that is no reason whatever why familiar faces should be omitted.

Well, dear, the great thing is we're through with 12 hours since I wrote last & there are 14 or 13 nights before us. I shall spend most of today writing & a typist is at work duplicating No. 1. It's very warm this morning & Washington is a pleasant orderly place & very shady & flowery after Chicago & Boston & New York.[5] But there is no Bits here & I feel the need of clagging & Bits & so

Warmly expectantly your Binds

Bins

Have you got Paradise perfeck? Is the moosic ready & the piano in tune? Is the garden study at attention & the turf all level & rolled? Is the sea there still

& will you remember me? My dear. Fink you a little man in green carrying a 'eavy overcoat & taking a ticket to New York.

---

[1] Probably Henry Cabot Lodge (1850–1924), US Senator from Massachusetts, and perhaps Alice Roosevelt, for whom the song 'Alice Blue Gown' was written to mark her debut at the White House. Townley was British Ambassador to the United States.

[2] He may be referring to the Neo-Malthusian League which was a major advocate of the availability of birth control for all.

[3] Elihu Root (1845–1937) was Secretary of State at the time. He was a major figure in developing peace treaties through arbitration using the Hague court. Alice's husband was Nicholas Longworth, Speaker of the House of Representatives. Oliver Wendell Holmes (1841–1935) was a justice of the U.S. Supreme Court. A dinner party of these individuals gives a strong indication of Wells's reputation.

[4] The Cowles family owned Washington newspapers.

[5] The irony in comparing the visits to Chicago and Washington D.C. did not escape Wells, or Catherine, one suspects. The differences were highlighted even more when Wells spent most of his Boston visit talking with the black educator, Booker T. Washington.

622. To Mr Boucher[1]

Texas, Typed Transcription

Spade House
Sandgate 25. v. 06

My dear Sir,

I've looked through the play you have done & I've given it to one or two people who know more about the sort of thing than I do, & the impression on the whole is an unfavourable one. On the whole. For my own part I think you've got the thing put together with very considerable ability. The real test I think might come from a manager, & to that I think you might put it. Let it be clearly understood that I remain uncommitted to any line of action in the matter, that I remain willing to discuss proposals & on that understanding take it to anyone you think proper. Get your manager in fact & then let us have a triangular discussion. In any case your name must appear as the sole responsible playwright basing the play on my novel.

Yours very sincerely,
H.G. Wells

[1] Despite the lack of evidence, it would seem that this letter was sent to Boucher, who was the second person to attempt a play based on *The Wonderful Visit*.

623. To Graham Wallas

LSE, ALS

Spade House
Sandgate

May 30. 06.

Dear Wallas,

Just home. But don't tell anyone. I want to get in a fortnight's work. Will you back this bill enclosed?

Yours ever,
H.G. Wells

Miles was a dear. I had a gorgeous time.[1]

[1] Wells had just returned from his first visit to America, which resulted in his book, *The Future in America*. Miles was an acqaintance of Wallas who lived in Philadelphia. At Wallas's suggestion Wells spent some days there, where he learned a great deal about the United States.

624. To Graham Wallas

LSE, ALS

Spade House
Sandgate

June 22. 06

My dear Wallas,

I'm immensely sorry to hear about May's eyes – & yours. I do hope your oculist is of the pessimistic school. But, anyhow it's a battle in which you have our sincerest sympathy.[1]

We're not in London much in this weather & next week I've got a brother here to keep my eye upon. What are Miles's movements? Give him my love.

Couldn't he run down here to lunch & idle through an afternoon? If he could please convey that invitation to him – for any day between Monday & Friday next week.

Jane's love to Mrs. Wallas,
Yours ever,
H.G.

---

[1] May Wallas was the daughter of Graham and Audrey Wallas. Both recovered from their eye ailments. May Wallas went on to follow her father as a lecturer at the LSE.

625. To Elizabeth Healey

Illinois, ALS

Spade House
Sandgate [*c.* August 1906]

Dear Miss Healey,

Miss Levitas was a great lark. Please don't let me know what she puts in the interview. My fortunate ignorance of German will serve me unless you translate. I detected in her romantic leanings of the most sinister description.

Poor dear Miss Calvert! Where is she now? Let us hope for the best. Earthquakes have no doubt their disagreeable side but I should think these form a fresh sort of break with the monotony of teaching. I imagine in a letter of application, "I then taught English in Valpariso until my class was swallowed up by a fissure or buried under the school buildings."

Love from Jane,
Yours ever,
Esencialmente filosophico
H.G.

Why aren't you a Fabian? I've sprained my knee & am in bed hence the abominable writing.

626. To Haden Guest[1]

Texas, ALS

Spade House
Sandgate

Sep. 15. 06

Dear Guest,

Coit's writing off & doesn't want to sign the report. Go & tame him for God's sake.

Yours ever,
H.G. Wells

[1] While Wells was in America, an unofficial truce occurred in the Fabian reform battle. This letter marks the return to that effort. His chief ally was Haden Guest. Guest had been an important Fabian for many years, so he was an ally of stature. He was married to Ivy Low's sister, and his and Wells's acquaintance went back to Wells's deep friendship with her father, Walter Low. Guest travelled widely and wrote about his travels. He remained a political associate of Wells long after the Fabian matters were over. A series of letters from Wells to Guest follows, some are given a date, but most are not. I have placed them in the order they seem to me to have been written, but others may disagree. The time of writing, however, is less important than the topics and methods discussed.

627. To Joseph Conrad[1]

ALS

Spade House
Sandgate

[1906]

My Dear Conrad,

I've been reading first in – and then through from beginning to end your delightful (it's the right word) talk of seas and winds and ships. It's talk, good talk, discursive yet not without point, admirably expressive without at any time becoming deliberately and consciously eloquent, full of all the admirable calm, a quality that never deserts you. A fine book...the sea under my eyes most wonderfully. I shall for all my life be the better for it. I see better as I go to and fro.

My many thanks. When are you coming to see us. I hope very soon. Come to lunch when you do, we'll wait an hour if needful.[2]

Yours ever,
H.G.

---

[1] This is the second of the two letters to Conrad which were saved by G. J. Aubry. The first (1896) appears in volume 1. This letter concerns Conrad's recent book, *The Mirror of the Sea* (1906).

[2] Conrad rather fulsomely dedicated his next book *The Secret Agent* (1906) to Wells:

To
H.G. Wells
The Chronicler of Mr. Lewisham's Love
The Biographer of Kipps
The Historian of the Ages to Come
This simple Tale of the XIXth century
Is Affectionately Transcribed.

628. To the Editor, *Times Literary Supplement*[1]

PL

[London] [*c.* 15 September 1906]

(With reference to the review of "In the Days of the Comet," in our issue of the 14th inst. Mr. H.G. Wells writes that the reviewer)

fails to see the artistic intention of the book; he reads it as seriously and as bitterly as an East-end audience hisses the villain. 'Socialistic men's wives, we gather,' he writes, 'are to be held in common, no less than their goods' – and so on with a sort of indignant gusto. Now, the intention of my book is to achieve an effect of contrast, to tell in dark and despairing tones, with an intensifying note of urgency, of the life of the present, and then to get an immense sense of release, of light coming, of dawn, freshness, freedom and purity. Probably I have failed to get that, but at any rate I sought it, and had I got it it would have been more beautiful, which is what a work of art is for. The

Socialism of the book is as incidental as the anatomy in Michael Angelo's Last Judgment, and the end is not Socialism at all, but a dream of human beings mentally and morally exalted. Given a great change of heart in human beings, and it is not my base imagination only, but an authority your reviewer would probably respect that assures the world there would be "no marrying nor giving in marriage." I stated, indeed, with punctilious clearness that I do not present unregenerate humanity in my second part. I wrote: – "He and these transfigured people – they were beautiful and noble people, like the people one sees in great pictures, like the gods of noble sculpture, but they had no nearer fellowship than these to men." Comparing small things to great; if your reviewer's method is legitimate with my book, it would be equally legitimate to write, let us say, of Beato Angelico as an "unpleasant" Italian dreamer who wishes us all to participate in ambiguous mixed entertainments in which ladies and gentlemen mingle together in night gowns – a pretty kettle of fish! or to describe Blake – but I hesitate at the encounter of your reviewer with Blake. Your reviewer, since he generalizes about my career, ought to be aware that in another book, 'A Modern Utopia,' I have set forth what I believe to be a possible Socialist State. If he knows of that book how can he accuse me of advocating Free Love? Well, the thing was not only bad criticism, which I am always willing to overlook, but injurious and annoying, and so, will you oblige me by publishing this explantion and disavowal?

---

[1] This letter, a rather dignified response, to the *Times Literary Supplement* review of his controversial novel, *In The Days of the Comet*, appeared in the *TLS* issue of 28 September 1906, p.330.

629. To the Editor, *Daily Express*[1]

PLS

Spade House
Sandgate, Kent
[*c.* 16 September 1906]

Will you please oblige me by publishing my emphatic contradiction of certain statements contained in the "Express" of September 15, and will you be so good as to give my contribution a prominence at least equal to that given to the libel of which I complain?

To say that it is my dictum that the ultimate goal of Socialism is free love is an outrageous lie. It is equally a lie that this theory is set forth in my book, "In the Days of the Comet". I cannot conceive how any respectable newspaper – even in the utmost rancour of anti-Socialist propaganda – can have brought itself to make so wanton and so mischievous a statement.

Your sole ground for this invention seems to be a remarkably unintelligent or remarkably dishonest review of my book in the "Times" in which the writer, guarding himself from positive statement by a judicious "we gather," says: "Socialistic men's wives, we gather, are no less than their goods, to be held in common," and goes on to impute to me all sorts of nonsense about "free love." The "Times" reviewer has gathered wrong. So have you.

You, then, it would appear, sent a representative to "draw" the Rev. Percy Dearmer, and he, judging my book on the "Times" report of it, falls in with your libel. The Rev. Lenthal Davids, too, has been, one gathers, caught in the same way, and subscribes to the growing snowball of falsehood about me. Why cannot these reverend gentlemen either read a book carefully, or avoid these hasty, foolish condemnations of what they do not understand?

My book presents the coming of a great change in the world, a great mental and moral exaltation that alters the whole of life. Human beings cease to be human beings with our present limitations. The narrow life of our present conditions disappears – is replaced by something wider and more splendid. That dream has no relation whatever to my Socialist proposals.

The people in this exalted world, in this kingdom of heaven on earth, become communists – as the early Christians did (what does the Rev. Percy Dearmer think of the early Christians?) – and, just as in the Christian Utopia, there is neither "marrying nor giving in marriage among them." If the suggestion in my book is "horrible" to the Rev. Lenthal Davids, equally "horrible" must be that teaching of the Founder of the religion he has undertaken to represent.

And what do you expect to do by smearing my reputation in this way? I'm in no way a representative of any Socialist organization – I'm merely a private, unorthodox, and rebellious member of the Fabian Society, and if I were a Public Scandal, it wouldn't cast the ghost of a shadow upon the Independent Labour Party.

H.G. Wells

---

[1] Wells's recent novel, *In the Days of the Comet*, created a firestorm over the meaning of Socialism. The *Daily Express* was among the most vehement opponents of Socialism. Wells wrote this letter to the paper, which appeared on 19 September 1906, p. 1, under the title 'The Fraud of Socialism'. Prior to his letter, the editor delivered himself of homilies on the fraud perpetrated

on working-men by M.P.s who were Socialists, and it printed a number of letters in opposition to Wells and Socialism on that page and on page 2. Wells's letter did get a sub-heading, 'A Vehement Denial from the Novelist'.

630. To the Editor, *Daily Express*[1]

PLS

Spade House
Sandgate,Kent [19 September 1906]

Sir, – I am amazed that in your leader of to-day you continue in your hopeless attempt to show that I want the ordinary human beings to-day to live in a state of promiscuous sexual intercourse. It is, I repeat, an outrageous libel on me. You take certain quotations from my book; you omit to state that they are supposed to be written by a character in the book, and not by myself; and so you seek to bolster up your case. I appeal to your readers! Here is a passage from the epilogue; does it not say distinctly and conclusively that my story is not what you are trying to make it out to be?

This was as much as this pleasant-looking, grey-haired man had written. I had been lost in his story throughout the earlier portions of it, forgetful of the writer and his gracious room, and the high tower in which he was sitting. But gradually, as I drew near the end, the sense of strangeness returned to me. It was more and more evident to me that this was a different humanity from any I had known, unreal, having different customs, different beliefs, different interpretations, diffferent emotions. It was no mere change in conditions and institutions the comet had wrought. It had made a change of heart and mind. In a manner it had dehumanised the world, robbed it of its spites, its little intense jealousies, its inconsistencies, its humour. . . He and these transfigured people – they were beautiful and noble people, like the people one saw in great pictures, like the gods of noble sculpture, but they had no nearer fellowship then these to men.

How any one can stick to it that the conditions represented in my book are a Socialist ideal or a Communist ideal or any other sort of ideal for this world after reading that beats me altogether!

And you read your own coarseness into the passage you quote. It runs: -

But we four from that time were very close, you understand. We were friends, helpers, personal lovers in a world of lovers.

Here are the words that follow immediately: -

"Four?"

"There was Verrall"

Then suddenly it came to me that the thoughts that stirred in my mind were sinister and base, that the queer suspicions, the coarseness and coarse jealousies of my old world were over and done for these three more finely living souls.

Who gets filth out of that must first put it in.

H. G. Wells[2]

---

[1] Neither Wells nor the newspaper was satisfied with the exchange. Wells wrote in response to the paper's editorial methods with his first letter. They put his second letter on the front page, 20 September 1906, again under the title 'The Fraud of Socialism'. In the subheads to this letter, the paper described the response as 'A Final Letter', saying that, 'We give it space merely as a matter of courtesy to a distinguished novelist, for our readers must certainly have judged Mr. Wells's letter of yesterday in its true proportions, wherefore further discussion does not seem to be necessary. We shall continue to print letters on the original subject of Socialism and the danger to which working men are exposed by the insidious propaganda of impracticable enthusiasts.'

[2] The *Daily Express* responded to Wells's letter with a long diatribe in a *tu quoque* style, countering his quotations with others. The long article ran over to another page. Little was actually settled, of course, for the novel and its story were of substantial importance for the next year and longer. The battle of the next year about Wells, Socialism and 'Free Love' had been clearly stated in this exchange.

631. To the Borough Librarian, Bromley

Bromley, ANS

Spade House
Sandgate, Kent

Sep. 19. 06

My dear Sir,

I regret extremely that my engagements this autumn forbid me what would have been the very great pleasure of visiting my native place & giving a lecture there.

Very sincerely yours,
H.G. Wells[1]

---

[1] Wells avoided such invitations from Bromley all his life. He had an ambivalent relationship with his home town. In fact, he later refused the honour of being made a freeman of Bromley, a refusal which is still often mentioned by Bromley natives. Wells's most powerful descriptions of Bromley occur in his novel *The New Machiavelli* (London: John Lane, 1911), but even more perhaps in an anonymous (although later acknowledged) essay, 'The Degeneration of the Ravensbourne – A Memory of Bromley, Kent', in *Pall Mall Gazette* 12 July 1894.

632. To Edgar Jepson

Hofstra, ACCS

Spade House
Sandgate

Sep 19. 06

Dear Jepson,

re trees – they are more likely to be elms or ash up there than oaks. I can't go & see for a bit as I have a sprained knee. The place is not "Caesar's Camp" but Startfall Castle. If you are doing something historical you can have what trees you like. There is a sort of rotation of crops in forestry.- & in natural woods too.

Yours ever
H.G. Wells

633. To S. S. McClure[1]

Indiana, ALS

Spade House
Sandgate, Kent

Sep. 25. 06

My dear Mr. McClure,

I've just heard from Pinker re the constructive articles you want. The intervention by Pinker puts me in an awkward position. You see I've instructed Perris & Casenove to make enquiries with a view to my producing a book to give a plain account of modern Socialism & its ideals. So far as I can gather that is quite the book you want as a serial.

I'm immensely sorry to have missed you under the circumstances. You'd better, if you really want to come in for these articles, see Perris & Casenove at once & discuss Pinker's position afterwards.[2]

Yours very sincerely
H.G. Wells

---

[1] McClure was proprietor of American magazines, in which Wells published several important pieces.

[2] Perris and Casenove were now acting as Wells's American agents. Eventually the *Independent* took several of Wells's pieces on Socialism in late 1906 and early 1907.

634. To Pinnie Robbins

Illinois, ALS

Spade House
Sandgate

Sep. 26. 06

My dear Pinnie[1]

I've sold your Japanese 4° & your B.G.Ts & this with £50 you gave me to invest makes £173. I've reinvested the money in New Zealand (National Bank) & Sao Paulo Railway with some of my own & in my name & I'm giving you my I.O.U. herewith.

Yours ever,
H.G. Wells

---

[1] Catherine Wells's mother.

635. To Henry Newbolt

Hofstra, ALS

[London] [October? 1906]

Dear Newbolt,

Very many thanks for your appreciation. I forgot – confound it! – about Lady Grey. But you know I never shall be a gentleman, so one more sin hardly matters.

The little fuss about Free Love has, I think, blown over – I had to bludgeon that ruffian in the Express at once or I should have been baited. I think it was better in that case to have that out in my own? The Times letter was a mere bye product of that squabble

I'm afraid that when one talks of polygamy, or monogamy or polyandry one gets among the incompatabilities of life. My impression is that the unregenerate man wants to have any woman he fancies & all the others to stand about ready if he calls, & that's about what the unregenerate woman does. I think women are less promiscuous than men; a priori they ought to be. For the rest these questions remain incurably individual & are only to be dealt with in novels.[1]

Yours ever,
H.G.

When does your novel come? Everybody is on the look out.[2]

---

[1] Wells had come under a great deal of criticism for his novel *In The Days of the Comet* which described three-cornered and even four-cornered relationships in his fanciful world. For his responses to the *Daily Express* about their review of 14 September 1906 and to *The Times Literary Supplement* see letters 628–30. Wells was very wrong about the free love issue blowing over, as it soon reemerged as a central part of the 1907 'War Against Socialism' campaign in the right wing papers of the time.

[2] Newbolt's new novel was *The Old Country* (London: Smith Elder, 1906).

636. To the Editor, *Daily Mail*[1]

PLS

[Spade House
Sandgate, Kent] [*c.* 10 October 1906]

Sir,- I have been doing my best so far to disregard this vexatious and threatening discussion, but on the whole perhaps it is as well that your innumerable readers should have as many points of view as possible to consider in this matter, and so I am giving you an answer.

Let me set aside any pretensions of modesty in this matter. I take myself very seriously as an author. I don't write to grow rich, I don't write to please great numbers of people; but I do seek, industriously and habitually, for the truth and beauty of things, and I try to the utmost limit of my ability to render it. My work is literature or nothing. But I have to live, and to write one's best, it is necessary to live free from an intolerable pressure of anxiety, with a certain leisureliness, a certain range of social experience, with events and a coming and going of other minds and a certain dignity. To secure these necessary conditions for sustained effectual work the modern author, however exalted his pretensions, is already obliged to make a lamentable diversion of his energy and attention to business affairs. He has to constantly leave his proper work (as I am doing this morning) to see to his welfare.

It is all nonsense to pretend that an author has only to write well to prosper. He will starve unless he is business man enough to secure an effectual sale of his work. If he isn't, although he writes not only admirably, but quite the most popular books imaginable, he will never escape poverty. The publisher and book seller are business men; they have, indeed, no other course open to them under present conditions other than to buy as cheaply and sell as dearly as possible. Beneath the proper intellectual life of a modern author, therefore, this irritating poisonous flow of business activity is necessarily going on. He is forced to attend shrewdly to business considerations of a more and more squalid sort, lest presently he should be forced to cease his writing altogether. He has to weigh the relative disadvantages of the publisher who can not write an advertisement against the publisher who can not write a cheque; he has to learn how the timid bookseller may be persuaded that even the works of writers with new ideas may conceivably be sold if they are stocked; he has to choose between the invasion of his privacy by paragraph and camera, on the one hand, and dignity and going into some alien business that will support him on the other.

[Here an editor has inserted a cross-head, THINGS GETTING WORSE. Nothing could have irritated Wells more than this. His strongest bêtes noires were the paraphraser and his assistant the subeditor. As the newspaper publication of Wells's is virtually always the best copy available, an editor is faced with a difficult decision. Where they are demonstrably not Wells's own words, it has been determined to delete them from this edition.]

In all these aspects, I think, things have been getting worse during the last few years. The methods of calling attention to new books have grown noisier, the factors of success more and more independent of literary quality, and the literature itself meretricious. The cheapening of fiction to a nominal six shillings has been of benefit only to writers with a wide popular appeal. I suppose that in every generation desperate men will be found to write occasional good books, but the material inducements and the opportunities to do so are fewer and fewer, and the chance of the public getting the good work that is done for it smaller and smaller.

Now the invasion of the book trade by these American advertisers of the "Times" Book Club, seems to me a quite murderous raid upon literature. I can compare it to nothing so aptly as a rush of wild asses into a garden. Before their coming the book trade was perhaps slow and sleepy, but it did permit a number of sincere producers of literature of a kind not vulgarly popular to reach and retain little supporting subjects for themselves.

Suddenly now they find themselves trampled under hoof in the wild scrimmages of a book war. These "Times" people seem to have no conception of any duty either to literature or their readers at all. The books of the publishers who concede the most favourable terms are, as Mr. Byles points out, shoved at their subscribers with a rude American vigour; the books of the publisher who stand out are relatively held back. A curious new sort of literature – the "Times" Book Club specialities – appears. The serene impartiality of Mudie's and the older subscription libraries – an impartiality touched only by a certain regard for decorum – is abandoned. I have been favoured with a foretaste of the new life for authors promised by the "Times" Book Club.

A year ago I wrote, with a certain passion and certain pleasure, "In the Days of the Comet," a book that you did me the honour to praise very highly. That book, apart from any merit it may or may not possess, goes down in this scrimmage. It was published by Messrs. Macmillan in September and Macmillans are "fighting" the "Times."It is omitted, therefore, from the October book list issued to the "Times" Book Club subscribers and from the lists of suggestions made to them; it is kept out of their sight. Moreover, in order to kill the trade in it at the 'booksellers' shops and to check the booksellers stocking and showing it, an advertisement promises it at greatly reduced terms in a month or so. It is a promise that will be difficult to fulfil – but it chills the spirit of the bookseller. And my publishers retort by discontinuing the advertisement of my book in the "Times."

Now, I want your readers to ask themselves how men of letters can go on writing if this sort of thing is to happen to their books. And the same things are, or will be, happening to Kipling's books, to Conrad's, to Jacobs's, to Henry James's – so that my argument holds good, even if your readers don't think much of me. Here in a drawer at my desk is a novel I am writing. (I wish I were working at it now instead of writing you about these disagreeable things.) It has been in hand, intermittently, since I finished my last novel, "Kipps," and I want it to be a larger and longer book of the same type.[2] There is a solid year of work in it, and I shall, I know now, have to spread it over several years. I had hoped to get it finished in 1907 by working straight on, but it is clear I must interrupt it to do some newspaper articles and things of that sort.

Just think of the added zest this kicking of my "In The Days of the Comet," into a corner must give to my work upon this new book. When it is done it will have to run the same gauntlet of these new rowdy trade methods, and quite possibly the general public may never get a fair chance to read it at all. It will have to be published, I suppose, at 10s[?], in the same format used for the work of prolific ladies who do six books a year and if it is lucky it will go on the same shelf with them. A few people who know me through my books will certainly take the opportunity to hunt it out there and buy it, the people who take the six-volume-a-year ladies won't think much of it, there will be one or two good reviews – my publishers may lose heart. . . . [*in original*]

I shall, I think, get it finished anyhow but if this particular book fails too, I think I shall be killed as a novelist. Moriturus te saluto.[3] I want very much to write novels; it is the best thing I think that I can do – at the outside I have, I suppose, fifteen years of intellectual activity left me before I slacken and decline – but really it is not in human nature to go on day after day in the face of impending bankruptcy, in the face, too, of remunerative special journalism, writing and publishing novels that in all probability will be shied into the waste-paper box in the course of some fresh and still more idiotic development of "book war."

That's the point I want to urge upon your attention. The long carefully-written novel is being killed amid these disorders of bookselling. That is, I think, something more than a personal disaster. Better men than I are bawled down and trampled in these noisy onslaughts upon public attention. . . . [*in original*] It isn't within my province to suggest methods of salvation, but I have no doubt whatever that the defeat of the "Times" Book Club in this present dispute will be a victory for all that remains decent and leisurely and fine in contemporary literary life.

I am, Sir, very truly yours,

H.G. Wells

---

[1] Although written at the same time as the fuss over the Times Book Club and the selling of books more cheaply than through the book shops, with little or no royalties for the author, this piece, entitled, 'Mr. Wells and Poverty. How the Author is to Escape it', is also related to a much-quoted article of the time, 'Ought Socialists to Live Poor?' in *The Labour Leader* 14 February 1908. The letter appeared in the issue of 12 October 1906, p. 5.

[2] Probably *Tono-Bungay* although the *War in the Air* preceded it in print. *Tono-Bungay* was certainly the novel to which he gave the most time. It was so important to Wells that its publication was delayed by the postponement of the first issue of the *English Review* which featured the book's serialization. Wells also referred to *The War in the Air* as a pot-boiler on occasion.

[3] A version of the gladiator's call at the beginning of the games in Ancient Rome – [Hail Caesar] We who are about to die, salute you.

637. To Ralph Mudie-Smith

Hofstra, ALS

[Sandgate] 15. 10. 06

Private

My dear Mudie-Smith,

Will you object to being put up for the Executive of the Fabian Society? I hope not. There will be an unique opportunity of bringing in fresh blood amidst the disturbances of this forthcoming Special Committees report & I want to get a really representative list of candidates. I know how overworked you are, but if you could possibly continue to help me in this I shall be very glad. I want new men, younger men, – then we'll get things done.

Yours ever,

H.G. Wells

638. To 'Vernon Lee'

Colby, ALS

Spade House
Sandgate 17 – 10 – 06

Dear Miss Paget,

I've got your delightful little book. I had not read the story[1] before & I read it with extraordinary delight & that feeling behind the eyes which is like a phantom self weeping. But why did you break the heart of my Arthur Watts who wanted to do you a picture about it, by never letting him know you were publishing it like this? He has, I think, done you a picture. It's good for him anyhow to have done it.

Yours ever,
H. G. Wells

Was the story published in America? If not, couldn't some agent sell it & my Watts's (widowed though unwed) picture together?

---

[1] *Sister Benvenuta and the Christ Child,* (London: Grant Richards, 1906). The story also appeared in *The Fortnightly Review* (1906).

639. To Ralph Mudie-Smith

Hofstra, ACCS

Spade House
Sandgate Monday – [October ? 1906]

My dear Mudie- Smith,

I want to make you an unparalleled proposal in the matter of the Fabian Society. I am in a very complicated position & I may have great difficulties in framing a "ticket" for the Executive election that may now occur at any moment. I may get too many names or not enough. May I nominate you or not as I find convenient? You will enormously oblige me if you will give me that large freedom. In any case I shall hope to nominate you for the Council so soon as we have fought our reforms through. But now we must fit together all sorts of interests & I may have to take on board one or two candidates I'm not particularly eager for. You see my position?

Yours ever,
H.G.

640. To Ralph Mudie-Smith

Hofstra, ALS

[Sandgate] 22nd October 1906

My dear Mudie-Smith,

Very many thanks for your letter of cooperation. I will certainly remember there is a very able man at large in the world. – I wish I had a paper. I'd sweat[?] you.

Yours ever
H.G. Wells

641. To Haden Guest

Texas, ALS

Spade House
Sandgate [late 1906 – early 1907]

Vry Conftl
Dear Guest,

Looking forward to seeing you. It's quite lamentable your people have decided for the 21 Executive. It means we shall either get Bland, Cecil & all that damned tail back or we shall have to put up 16 or 18 strong candidates. We haven't got them. Your men probably think they're making more room for reformers; they're only finding a muddled scramble. [*a sentence completely blacked out by Wells*] G.T. doesn't want to go up. Colegate is very good stuff indeed, he will have an admirable chance, on account of his Select Committee position, & I strongly urge he should be put up. (The executive are going to put up Clifford Sharp – but we may vote for him.) Lawson Dodd has to be saved & Aylmer Maude is, I tell you, indispensable for the publishing department.

How does the list stand now? [1]

Can't you get Philip Snowden or his wife to stand – his wife is pretty good stuff?

We might adopt Lawson Dodd, Stuart Headlam, Pease & Clifford Sharp for our ticket. Even that leaves 3 votes loose for fools to mess about with. We must recover Webb & Standing. (We are anti-Shaw) Mrs. Standing I've never heard of, but J.S. Middleton might do. We ought however to put Keir Hardie up. He'll fill a place & crowd out an antagonist for us. I'm getting more and more sick of the way he keeps out of this affair.

Calmer is a damned fool & I don't care what he thinks.

Yours ever,
H.G. Wells

By the bye, get Hamilton Fyfe on your committee – a very good man. How about old Richard Whiting?

Ticket mostly a rotten tail. – will let in Bland, Chesterton & all the rest of the old crew to a dead certainty.

1. Olivier }
2. Mrs. Reeves }
3. Wells } SAFE
4. Guest }
5. Coit ? Might be a risk.
6. Taylor ?? Must make a show
7. Alymer Maude – ought to be safe.
8. Muggeridge – good man but wants backing
The women don't like him.
9. Shalland – good ought to speak
10. Mrs. Townsend – good
Bad 11. Joseph Edwards ? 2 to 1 against his return
Bad 12. J. E. Matthews ?? Unknown to me

13. Mudie-Smith good, if sweaty. (Exhibition record
is most impres.)
Bad 14, Ensor Mediocre stuff
Very Bad, 15. Mrs. Phillimore absolutely [*illegible word*] Great friend of Webbs & Shaws.

---

[1] Although this letter may seem somewhat elliptic, Wells is handicapping the chances for a change in the Fabian executive. There were approximately three party groups involved, but membership varied from day to day. One, 'the so-called Old Guard', wished to remain in control of the Society, while still allowing some new ideas to seep in. Shaw seems to have led this group by default. A second group, headed by Haden Guest, with allies, wanted reform of the Fabian ideas and goals, but wished also to retain some aspects of the 'Old Guard' people, while Wells represented the real reformers. His constituency tended to be younger, more radical, and also tended to be people without much power. They wished to create an active executive, take on political action, and move to consolidate some Labour holdings in the Parliament. All of the goals were subject to some change as the time for the last debates and the election drew closer. Wells's proposed slate is more ephemeral than he thought, as he had not yet done his canvassing of all possible characters. Old animosities continued to exist and several potential supporters had resigned from the Fabian Society in earlier times, such as Keir Hardie; see, among other books, Norman and Jeanne Mackenzie, *The First Fabians* (London: Weidenfeld and Nicolson, 1977).

642. To Haden Guest

Texas, ALS

[London?] [end 1906, early 1907]

Dear Guest,

We must also "adopt" Granville Barker who is going to be put up by the Shaws. He's a pretty good reformer on the whole. Of your list I must scrub[?] Mrs. Townsend & J.E. Matthews. & I don't think Mrs. Snowden too new to stand. She's a jolly good name. Barbara Low I'd love to see on but it won't do this time. She must speak more. There's all the provincial members to consider. Ensor I'll accept anyhow.

I sent you the names yesterday. Miss D.M. Richardson, 140 Hurley Street – Mrs. Badley of Beedales Petersfield, T. Bryant Summers. Arthur Watts & old Hartland Marsten Watt, 2 Fitzroy Street Marsten 50 Orley Crescent, SW

Chelsea. Dr. & Mrs. T.K. Rise (Royal Mint E.) The President, Dr. Kenneth Mees, (Rylands, Caterham, Surrey.) ——- C.H. Ginsberg of the Woolwich Pioneer, reporter. Granted that may have escaped you.[1]

Yours ever,

H.G.

I may or may not turn up on Friday. I think the ticket is 16 & 2 adopted. Vita Brevis. & you seem to be getting along all right.

[1] This list indicates the breadth of Wells's support, but relatively few of these persons were very well known. Granville Barker was a playwrite, and commentator on the theatre. D.M. Richardson is Dorothy Richardson, later a significant novelist. She has given a brief description of these Fabian meetings in her *Dimple Hill*. Richardson was to become pregnant with Wells's child at about this time, but it was stillborn.

643. To Haden Guest

Texas, ALS

[London] [end 1906- early 1907]

Thoroughly Confidential. Mrs. Shaw had just sent me a copy of her answer to your card, with which I thoroughly agree. Make the new committee, a new thing, a Reform Committee. & please act with Mrs. R. & Olivier.

The S. committee is in & done.

Dear Guest,

Can you people come Jan. 19th? If so it will be very jolly for us. With regard to the F.S. I've been talking over things with Olivier who has been here. We think your idea of an enlarged Committee a good one – & it will, if properly done, do just what our cttee has failed to do, bring in the votes in consequence. Coit is a difficult person to deal with. If he wants to show, he must, but if he has any scruples about standing I don't see that we need crush them down. He's done very little except make trouble so far. Then any I.L.P. man who can speak and does speak in the next few meetings, will be good for us. In addition I've an idea that we might induce some of the larger groups to put up each a candidate & agree to support the other group candidates, e.g. there might be a nursery candidate, a Cambridge & a Croyden one also perhaps a west central one.

Each having the support of all the groups. In that case they'd have to be specific not as Report. Every vote not given to a Blandite or a hard shell executive is a vote to push that candidate down the list. The Blandites will, I expect, organize a short ticket & vote solid – "plumping" so to speak for four or five names & sacrificing Mrs. Shaw, Webb and so on. If so & our less ardent supporters dribble a few votes that way they may come in at the expense of Headlam, Standing & some of us.

Yours ever,

H.G.

(If they vote a full 15 they will count themselves out.)

644. To Mr Clarke[1]

Hofstra, ALS

Spade House
Sandgate

Oct 27th 06

Private

Dear Mr. Clarke,

I've got your bale of stuff from its custodian & I've looked through the m.s.s. My impression is that you stand no chance of getting a footing in literature at this present time. It's a world altogether more crowded than you can possibly imagine and to try to get in all at once with a novel is hopeless. You need to serve an apprenticeship at journalism & suchlike work. But I do think there is a certain emotional quality in your work & narrative force. Your defects are want of education – if you will forgive my frankness – & want of experience. Let me offer you this advice — and it is so far good advice that it is what I did myself. I began to write things when I was nineteen about – I messed up my last year at the Royal College of Science, writing stories & essays & I spent a year in doing what I can see you have been doing, sending them out & getting them refused. Then I found myself on the steep slope that leads to absolute pennilessness. I said, I will get a living anyhow first – & then try again. For a time I worked for a whole wage of £60 a year. I worked up in my profession teaching until I could afford leisure & then tried again &, as you know, have made a sort of success. Now you do the same. Stop this hopeless pursuit of editors & publishers & get some work. You write a good hand. Get any sort of job that utilizes that. You are a young man of intelligence & I'm quite satisfied after glancing through your documents that you are reasonably steady & "all right". I wish I could do something for you myself, but I have my little household organized. I'm not rich & I can't work you in. But show this letter to anyone who seems likely to give you work & it may do instead of a proper testimonial. You'll have to accept very low pay at first – you'll be lucky if you can get £1 a week. If I were you I'd take less than that. And work like anything to keep it when you get it. Do any sort of work that is given you & when you're a solvent citizen let me know again.

I am going to Italy next week for a short holiday. Your m.s.s. will, if you like, remain here. My secretary Mr. Horsnell[2] will be here every day from 10 to 11 & I've left a small sum with him for you.

Give up all thoughts of writing stories or novels or books at present – get any work you can.

And believe me
Your sincere well-wisher
H G Wells

Keep Mr. Horsnell aware of your address.

---

[1] Clarke is unknown. This letter is a sample of many Wells wrote to unknown prospective authors – virtually always with tolerance and good cheer for the recipient.
[2] Horace Horsnell, his secretary at the moment, became a very well known editor in the 1920s.

645. To Henry Newbolt

Hofstra, ALS

Spade House
Sandgate

[late October?]
Thursday, '06

My Dear Newbolt,

I've read the book[1] with immense interest and delight – and a good deal of technical curiosity. You've managed your magic superbly, I think. You've thrown just the right veil of indefiniteness over all that, a veil of moonshine and summer mists and sunlit distance, and you've certainly emerged with beauty of a very pearly and exquisite kind from the dip into fiction. It's the beauty of the book that strikes me at first, it leaves an effect that reminds me of that produced by Hudson's Crystal Age, except that you are more delicate and pellucid. Of Bulmer and your metaphysics I shall speak to you later.

Yours ever,

H.G. Wells

---

[1] *The Old Country*. This letter also appears in Margaret Newbolt (ed.), *The Later Life and Letters of Sir Henry Newbolt* (London, 1942), p. 39.

646. To the Editor, *The Times*[1]

PLS

Grand Hotel
Venice

[10? November 1906]

Sir, – I find you have quoted a long passage from my book, "Mankind in the Making," as though it supported *The Times* Book Club in its present dispute with publishers, and a little note at the end seems to intimate that you claim to find some inconsistency between this and my very present distinct hostility to your enterprise. It will clear up a certain ambiguity if I state as plainly as possible my grounds for that hostility. My position is that, as a matter of fact, your Book Club is not achieving and has never honestly attempted to acheive what in your more poetical moments you profess as an aim – the better organization of book distribution in this country; that – to be perfectly frank and simple with you – from the first you have been greedy for gain and unscrupulous in method. That is the real case against you, and it is well that you should be under no misapprehension as to the nature to your development. So far from introducing new and improved expedients from the trade in books, from the first you harked back to the uncivilized and inefficient devices of preferential dealing and the boycott. It is not sufficiently understood by your readers that it was the Book Club which began boycotting and not the publishers. More than a year ago, for example, you partially boycotted my novel, "Kipps," omitting it from your book list and buying as small a number of copies as you dared. I protested and your manager then explained clearly to me that this was done to force my publishers to undertake to spend a certain *minimum* of advertisement in your columns. He invited me to quarrel with them and to bring pressure upon them to induce them to yield to his terms. He boasted of the large number of copies he could "shove" if it was made worth the Book Club's while, and he anticipated all subsequent display in your columns. The result of that conversation was to convince me for good and all that, apart from any question of public duty on the part of *The Times*, your Book Club was conducted without either the impartiality, restraint or dignity necessary for its permanent success as a book-distributing concern, and, that, in fact, it was mere caricature of the honourable and quasi public book-distributing organization I had foreshadowed. That remains my conviction today. My friend Mr. Bernard Shaw entirely ignores any question of your Book Club management – which is surely to any reasonable person an essential question. One may be entirely in favour of the monarchy and still disposed to fight with great vigour against a casual person with more energy than deliberation who sees fit to snatch at the crown, and in the same way, one may still hope for better methods of publishing and bookselling while regarding your Book Club with distrust and sincere dislike. It is the boycotting, and the withholding of book that you have not been specially paid to push, and the "shoving" of your new type of book, this heavily advertised book, The Times Book Club special line, to which I object.

H. G. Wells

---

[1] This letter appeared in *The Times* on 14 November 1906, as part of the year long battle over *The Times* Book Club. It was printed as part of a news story, rather than appearing in the correspondence columns.

647. To Victor Fisher

Boston, ALS

Spade House
Sandgate Nov 29, 06

Dear Mr. Fisher,

I couldn't get a chance of talking to you last night but I want you to be sure to turn up on Dec 7th. Practically all the old Executive has committed suicide. It has brought formal proposals to found a separate middle-class Socialist party, – a really genteel Socialism platform independent of everything. Webb is either mad or riding for a fall. Shaw is spring-heeled Jack, his favourite part, & the rest are – the Fabian Executive.

Yours ever,
H.G. Wells

Are you disposed to put in work in the future for the Fabians if a revolution can be brought off.

648. To Victor Fisher

Boston, ACCS

Spade House
Sandgate

Dec. 3, 06

Dear Mr. Fisher,

Thanks for your letter. I'm not in town before the 7th & on that day as I shall have to speak. I'd not want much attentive talking beforehand. The Fabian women are forming a sort of temporary reform committee to push for their ends. The Croyden, Camberfeld[?], West Central & Nursery groups are discussing concerted action. Taylor & Guest are also writing and also working among others. It would be helpful if you could get any Fabian reform people together.I hope that after we have settled the Revolutions on the 7th & 14th to resolve the meeting into a discussion of subsequent activities. We have got to put up a new Executive & my plan is to get the reform elements in the groups to nominate each one or two names & so make a strong reform ticket. The Reform ticket will stand for "the spirit & purpose" (but not for the details) of the Special Committee report as against the Civil Report.[1]

Yours ever,
H.G. Wells

[1] These letters and others suggest that this episode in the history of the Fabian Society could benefit from more work. Wells and his followers had planned better than is usually thought.

649. To Violet Paget

Colby College, ALS

[Sandgate] Sunday
[probably December 1906]

Dear Vernon Lee,

I've read your Open Letter with immense interest & pleasure & whenever, in your delightful & flattering way you differ from H.G.W., I'm right on your side.[1] One derives one's schemes & efforts through a world of infinite possibility through sheer incapacity of apprehension as a child makes a cubby house out of Bibles & great books. It's the only use its capacity can make of them. I fully appreciate your point. Perhaps I am in some obscure way learning to read. Meanwhile I build my cubby house, and put my order of Samurai in it & decline to take on grown-up manners before my time. All this month I have been fighting Shaw for the Fabian Society as though it mattered. Well, it does matter for a little chap like me.

Yours Ever Fraternally
H. G. Wells

---

[1] 'Vernon Lee' wrote an 'Open Letter' to Wells, about his work, and especially about *A Modern Utopia*, 'Vernon Lee', 'Modern Utopias: An Open Letter to H. G. Wells', *The Fortnightly Review* (December 1906), pp. 1123–37.

650. To Violet Hunt

Cornell, Typed Transcription

Spade House
Sandgate [date unknown, but
perhaps in 1906]

Dear V.H.

I like the new end of White Rose of Weary Leaf very much though in a sort of way it lacks the vigour and realism of the earlier ending. But it's odd rather in the fact that it's by a different V.H. than the one who wrote the earlier part. It's got a different attitude, fresh ideas. I believe the suffrage has changed you. Amy I like more than ever, and the man is more of a man (though some of his speeches are really short addresses. He orates.) Go on to the next one. I think its altogether the most interesting book you've done and the most probable success. But you're still growing. If you go on you will be a credit to the Fabian Society. I'm quite sure you're ripe now to join, bless you. But you weren't a year ago.

Yours,
H.G.

651. To Violet Hunt

Cornell, Typed Transcription

National Liberal Club
Whitehall Place [possibly 1905 or perhaps 1906]

Dear V.H.

Bless your heart! I may be at loose ends on Tuesday but I shan't have hot coppers. Do you know of any convenient place for sin in Kensington? If so, write it here and tell me and I'll wire you if I can get away. But I am so tired of Wedde.

Yours ever,
H.G.

652. To Violet Hunt

Cornell, Typed Transcription

Spade House
Sandgate [undated, *c.* 1906]

Poor dear,

Shall I come and read to you? Here is a letter to Brentano anyhow – and you got a letter from me yesterday, and I wish I had a new book to send you, which I haven't.

My knee gets better every day, and I shall soon be troublesome to the world again. What's been up with you? Why is your poor stummick all swimming with fluid things. You poor dear!

Some day we shall meet again.

Why not ask Jane to come to lunch on your way to Paris. Come down by the 10 boat train from Charing X and go on by the 4 p.m. boat?

Yours,
plethoric, over-eaten, under-
exercised, panting, but entirely
sympathetic
H.G.

If B's letter isn't what you want – I'll do another.

653. To Miss Franklin

Texas, ALS

Grand Hotel
Saas-Fee Valley
Suisse [*c.* mid-September 1906?]

Dear Miss Franklin,

I am a disgrace to the Utopians – you will have to expel me. I'm afraid I can't promise to come to that meeting of Maude's. I am here in weather that no Utopian dialect could describe waiting for a gleam of sunlight to go up there.[1], & then to go on over the Monte Meso to Italy & all the hotels are closing & snow up the valley is falling & Mrs. Wells has a visitor & Heaven knows when I shall see my home again. – but it may not be until October – second week.

Commend me to the Utopians. I shall think of you in your nice warm meeting & believe me,

Yours ever,
H.G. Wells

[1] An arrow drawn to a letterhead showing the foot of the glacier where the hotel is located. Miss Franklin is unknown.

654. To Edward Garnett

Texas, APCS

Grand Hotel
Wildstrubel
Adelbogen

[*c*. mid-September 06?]

Delighted with your letter. I had some doubts about your notoriously severe judgments – I'm nose in air just now but God is always just.

Yours ever,
H.G.[1]

---

[1] This post card could have been sent as early as 1905, or even as late as 1911, and which book of Wells Garnett liked is difficult to know.

655. To Henri Davray

Indiana, ACCS

Spade House, Sandgate

Sunday [December 1906]

My dear Davray

Forgive my silence. I have been very busy with a little political development over here. It will be quite out of the question for me to prepare & deliver two lectures in Paris in 1907. – my time is already far too mortgaged. I will write about the old things in a few days time.

Yours ever most amicably
H. G. Wells

656. To Henri Davray

Indiana, ACCS

Spade House, Sandgate　　　　Dece. 13. 06

My dear Davray

It is all very inviting but; you cannot put a quart into a pint bottle & my pint bottle is full up for the spring of 1907.

Yours ever
H.G. Wells

657. To the Editor, *The Bookman*[1]

PLS

[Spade House,
Sandgate, Kent]　　　　[early January 1907]

[Sir, -] Pardon the telegraphic style. No single dominant book this year, but a shower of admirable ones – "Joseph Vance" struck me as a book that would have made a great reputation in Victorian times – "The Old Country" (Newbolt) I found charming – I re-read Hudson's "Crystal Age" with zest – "Sir Nigel" (Doyle) a ripping good story with a delightful clear brightness of detail – Some of Conrad's best – "The Mirror of the Sea" – "The House of Islam," a happy recovery of Pickthall – the early part of "The Workaday Woman," is the best I've read of Miss Hunt. I was interested by the unconscious verity of Bennett's "Whom God Hath Joined" – and there were lots more.

P.S. Was "The Golden Bowl" (James) in 1906? If so, I put it first of all.

H.G. Wells

---

[1] This letter appeared, with others, under the title 'The Book of 1906 Which Interested Me Most', in the January issue of the magazine, p. 103.

658. To Violet Hunt

Cornell, Typed Transcription

Spade House
Sandgate

16. 1. 07

Dear V.H.

God bless you! I'm delighted to come to your lunch on Tuesday next, but I shall have to catch the 5 at Victoria home. Is it at South Lodge? I am presuming that's so.

Yours,
H.G.

659. To Haden Guest

Texas, ALS
[London]

17 – 1 – 07

Dear Guest,

Miss Hutchins isn't our sort. (Let her show her quality first.) We've got nearly enough names, haven't we? Still it's not a bad idea to get the list too long & prune it, if by so doing, you don't give offense. If Barker can keep on our list – he's all right. We ought to 'adopt' him & Sharp & Dodd, anyhow. I'm dining with Barker at six on Friday.

Given people we don't know who are for Reform in the Sy. but a little resentful at being out of it. I doubt about having a formal ticket but I think it might be well if you could arrange for the candidates to have indicated after their names, in the F.N. – 'Supports Select Ctte Report on the whole. – Supports Exec. Report.' I think your men on whom the bulk of the work will fall should frame the informal ticket & I think it might very well be as long as twelve. It must include Olivier, Mrs. P.R., Alymer Maude, you & me – that's 5 & we shall be safe for election. – so that's five present executives dead. It will also have to include Taylor who so far hasn't shone in the meetings & as such is doubtful bait for a Counter Report candidates, but as "Croydon group candidate" etc.

This is merely a suggestion. As for the two names I mentioned, they need not trouble you if you can get a good ticket without them. M.S. has very generously put himself entirely in my hands, & G.T. is not keen.[1] But we are dealing with a very queer mixed constituency, with a lot of women & young members. They will vote first of all for the six or seven names they know. Then they will vote for names that are clearly indicated for them to vote for – e.g., by the words "supports R of S.C." Then I am afraid they will splash votes about rather than <u>not use them.</u> I want a "basket" candidate or so to get in such votes, besides. But I've no doubt your Ctte will do all right.

Yours ever,
H.G.

---

[1] M.S. is Mudie-Smith. G.T. is George R. S. Taylor who was on the executive already. He supplied Wells with documents, draft documents, and a precis of their meetings throughout the imbroglio. In fact there was a discussion of censuring him for breach of 'executive silence' after the fact; see chapter 4 of my *Desperately Mortal*, 'Falling Among the Fabians'.

660. To Haden Guest

Texas, TLS

[London] [early 1907?]

My dear Guest,

Here is the completed draft report. You will, I trust, consider that it has been compacted from a rather cumbersome mass of material. I hope you will find that on the whole it hangs together to your satisfaction. I have added, you will see, certain suggestions for reconstructions that were, when we dispersed, only very vaguely adumbrated. If you are not in perfect agreement, will you write in any amendments you would like to make, and will you please say when it will be possible to get you at a meeting in London to discuss the whole conclusively.

Yours very sincerely,
H.G. Wells

[*in pen*] Note especially page X.

661. To Ralph Mudie-Smith

Hofstra, ANS

Spade House
Sandgate. 5. ii. 07

My dear Mudie-Smith.

I'm first rate glad – though I hope it won't be long before you go in to something much better.

Yours ever
H. G.

662. To an unknown addressee

Boston, ALS

Spade House
Sandgate 5. ii. 07

Dear Sir

My father's date of death is still unsettled. If you would write to him at Rosemeath Liss Hants he might be able to throw some light on the matter.

Seriously I wish you'd send him a line about the books – he's nearly eighty and mentally pretty vigorous but a good deal tormented by gout or some such vile thing which worries him in the broken leg & ankle that terminated his cricketing career in the seventies. I hope you do justice to his feat at Brighton.[1]

Who is publishing the official history? I would like an early copy to go to him.[2]

Very sincerely yours
H.G. Wells

---

[1] Joseph Wells took four wickets in consecutive balls, but not in the same over, in a match between Kent and Sussex.

[2] Whether an official history of Kent cricket was published is not known. I have never seen one.

663. To Haden Guest

Texas, ALS

Spade House
Sandgate 6. ii. 07

Dear Guest,

Will you try & get the ticket chosen for the Reform Assn as soon as possible? I suggest we should have 15 names including one more woman, & that we should do no fancy work in the way of rigging votes, but try & get the Assn to vote the straight ticket & nothing else. Or failing this vote all 15 & any six others they fancy. A solid block of a hundred odd voters will carry in all 15 – rest assured I want the names settled finally before I go my rounds. We must have Coit on the ticket – if only one reason there are 30 odd votes at Cambridge that will be shaken to pieces by a row with Coit. Do bear in mind that our job now is to get in votes, not to define exact positions. Pending the association action, I shall preach the ticket we chose; Sharp & Barker & Dodd must take care of themselves. Don't explain so fully as you want to do that I am a fool, incompetent, untrustworthy, & don't "stick to my guns." & so on. All that may wait. The job at hand is to get a reform executive elected & quarrelling among ourselves will do no good at all. Shut it.

When the ticket is chosen – as I hope it will be this week – then what are you doing to advise members of it? Have you got envelopes addressed to all the members? If not, why don't you get some of the women to do it fortuitously? It will take a week to do. This is your job you know. I've left things very much in your hands & so far you've (Keep Calm) done nothing except get up a difficult vote-losing row in Taylor's I.L.P. obsession & then underline the trouble by losing your temper last Friday. Do pull things together now & get the ticket & the circular envelopes ready.

Yours very sincerely,
H.G. Wells

Warmest affection (when he cares to admit it.)

664. To Violet Hunt

Cornell, Typed Transcription

Spade House
Sandgate,

Feb. 12, 1907?
[*in another hand*]

Dear V.H.

Be nice to a very melancholy man on Tuesday please. Come and Torino at one. I'm rather down, cross, feeble. If you can't, please leave a note at the N.L.C.

No afternoon appointments.

Yours ever,
H.G.

665. To Ralph Mudie-Smith

Hofstra, ALS

Spade House[1]
Sandgate

20. ii. 07

My dear Mudie-Smith,

We got to the breaking point last Friday & there will be no Reform Associated Manifesto & – no ticket. Instead I want to arrange that you & I, & as many more of our way of thinking as possible shall sign the enclosed joint address. I hope you'll see your way to sign it anyhow & be done up in a bundle with me. United we stand, divided we fall.

Yours ever
H.G. Wells

[1] This letter is written on stationery of the National Liberal Club, which is crossed out and 'Spade House, Sandgate' added in Wells's hand.

666. To Ralph Mudie-Smith

Hofstra, ALS

[Sandgate] 21. ii. 07

My dear Mudie-Smith,

The situation waggles about. I'm sorry to bother you again but we've fixed up a sort of compromise for the Reform movement. We are to have several separate election addresses, the Guest-Taylorites, the Ensorrites, & my especial lot & I want you to join these. They will be you, if you will, Mrs. Reeves, I & Bull & perhaps Holbrook Jackson. So will you sign this draft & will you send me a wire to say you do.

In addition to these election addresses, the F. Ref. Association will issue a Manifesto, as arranged on Wednesday, naming 14 names of all these groups & asking for a fair vote for all 14.

Yours ever,
H.G.Wells

p.s. I since note that Tuesday is the last day for sending in manuscript addresses so will you please wire your reply.

667. To Haden Guest

Texas, ALS

[London] Saturday.
[probably 23 February 1907]

My dear Guest,

I have thought over the matter of our address & I have decided to ask Ball, Mrs. Reeves, Smith & Jackson to sign [it] and only me. This will make us a group so that the Reform groups will be three, The Guest-Taylor, the Ensorite & the Wells.

Yours ever,
H.G. Wells [1]

[1] It has been the received wisdom that Wells did not know how to play the political game with the Fabians. In fact, he knew the rules well and used them to his advantage. This letter is part of the strategy which was a divide-and-conquer strategy. In the end, he simply did not have the votes.

668. To Haden Guest

Texas, TLS

[London] February 25th, 1907.

Dear Mr. Guest,

Mr Wells thinks it would be advisable for you to have the manifesto of the Reform Committee set up at once so as to have proof to discuss when we meet on Thursday because it is most important that the address should precede by half a day or so the voting papers and the election addresses.

Holbrook Jackson wires that his name may appear, but a letter is following, so put his name on provisionally.

Yours sincerely,
Horace Horsnell[1]

[1] This letter signed by his then secretary, deals with the nuts and bolts of the effort to reform the Fabian Society, just prior to the final discussion and vote.

669. To Ralph Mudie-Smith

Hofstra, TTY

Sandgate

Fe. 25 07

Mudie-Smith
80 Warrington Crescent
Maida Vale
London

Please fill that form for Pease mention particularly sweating Exhibition
Wells.[1]

[1] Wells is asking Mudie-Smith to reserve a speaking position at the Fabian meeting with the secretary, E. R. Pease, who was in charge of the agenda for the discussion.

670. To Miss Dawson[1]

Texas, ALS

Spade House
Sandgate 25. ii. 07

Dear Miss Dawson,

Very many thanks for your letter to my wife. There have been many tribulations in the 'Reform' movement since we met you, but there will emerge a list that will be sent out together with the 'Manifesto' of the Reform Association at the end of this month. We are alas! poor in women's names. It will be a list of 14; that will leave you seven votes for desirables not on the list, Shaw & Webb I hope, Granville Barker, Mrs. Shaw & the rest I leave up to you. Hobson is a 'separate middle-class Socialist party man' & not to be encouraged.

Very sincerely yours
H.G. Wells

[1] She is unknown.

671. To George F. McCleary

Illinois, ANS

[London] Feb. 27, 1907

Amber Reeves is on your track at my instigation. She's doing what I firmly believe is an epoch making thesis on motive in Social Service and she wants to be put onto the motives & views of ... officers of health.[1]

Yours sincerely,
H. G. Wells

[1] There are a series of drafts and notes to George McCleary in 1907, They mainly involve a proposed series of republished classic books, including the first one, Plato's *Republic*, which Wells was to sign. The series was to be offered to the Fabian Society, but after the defeat of Wells and the Reform efforts, the plans were abandoned. Reeves was in her last term at Cambridge this Spring. Reeves may have been working on one of these republications.

672. To W. Baxter

Bromley ALS

North Western Hotel
Liverpool   Feb. 28th, 1907

My dear Baxter,

I can't possibly make any more engagements just at present or I would certainly promise your Reading man. But now that the Fabian fight is about over I must do some writing. And I find I can't write between meetings except upon Socialism and things like that.

It's very delightful to think your wife was my oldest schoolfellow. I do wish I could remember her name, but I do not as a matter of fact recall any of the children's names. I used to be under Miss Salmon; was she?[1] I remember slates on a table in the corner & how I used to try to get top of that little class in order to fret more of the wall paper off the wall & more; it was a sort of obsession with me.

Yours ever,
H.G. Wells

---

[1] Miss Salmon was the infant teacher, in the first primary school he attended. She was the daughter of the proprietor, Mrs Knott.

673. To John Galsworthy

PLS

[Spade House
Sandgate]   March, 1907

Dear Galsworthy,

I've read The Country House and I spent the better part of last week-end going over it with Barker,[1] who'd just read it too. I wish life were long enough to write down the effect of it to you. You know that we begin by assuming you're a considerable person and the book a notable novel, but after that become unfavourable again. I think you are much better as a playwright than as a novelist because you paint into the corners so and have no illuminating omissions. And your range is narrow. You seem to look at things from the point of view of a very limited class indeed, and I miss your irony — I see where it comes in, but I don't feel it in any way — just as one misses domestic satire in the members of a family. Pendyce is good and the hard riding husband and so is the parson. George is a stick, and you don't seem quite to feel and get his woodenness. Mrs. Pendyce is curious. I see clearly a personality and that you are drawing it —but in all the trip to London her moods are somehow not got, and the Totteridge explanation of her is all nonsense. There are moments when she is ladylike — and you didn't mean that. The bad woman you've seen across a room.

But you know The Silver Box was real good.

Yours ever,
H.G. Wells

[1] This letter appears in H. V. Marrot's *The Life and Letters of John Galsworthy* (New York: Scribner, 1930), p. 206. Criticism similar to this formed a *cause célèbre* in the late 1920's until Wells was able to deny saying the remarks; see volume 3. Barker is Granville-Barker the director and playwright, who added the hyphen to his name in 1918.

674. To an unknown addressee

Korn, ALS

Spade House
Sandgate 6. iii. 07

My dear Sir,

I hope by this time you see that getting moderate adventurers elected by splitting the votes of public spirited men isn't the way to advance Socialism or get it respected by the average common sense person. I am not against the Socialist vote splitting for all I'm worth. If he takes Capitalist money, he's a knave & if he doesn't he's a fool, for nothing could so effectively play the game for financial adventure as to make a break between Socialists & Socialist Programmes & Liberals

Yours very sincerely,
H.G. Wells

675. To Violet Hunt

Cornell, Typed Transcription

The Reform Club
[London] [postmarked 9 Mar. 07.]

Dear V.H.

Did I ever say I couldn't come that day to meet Mrs. Farley. If I didn't, please forgive me. And I have a Pure Flame for Rosamund who is the Most — Quite![1]

Yours ever,
H.G.

[1] Rosamund is probably Rosamund Bland, with whom Wells was having a short fling; see volume 3.

676. To Beatrice Webb

LSE, ALS

Stanway[1]
Winchcombe [*c.* Mar 1907]

Dear Mrs Webb,

Enclosed is a little effort by my elder brother, who knows I have been doing something "about Socialism" & isn't clear just what.

Yours ever,
H.G.

[1] Stanway was the country home of Lady Elcho who was Wells's *entrée* into upper class society. He spent several weekends there at the time of the Fabian affair and later.

677. To the Editor, *Daily News*[1]

PLS

Spade House
Sandgate c. March 11, 1907

Sir, – There seems to be considerable misconception as to the relation of Fabian Socialism to Mr. Shaw on the one hand, and Liberalism on the other. Mr. Shaw is not the Fabian Society and his habit of speaking as though he was is a misleading one; his exposition of the irreconcilable gulf between Liberalism and the Fabian Society is just an intellectual freak for which we are not responsible. There is no such gulf. There are the closest links in sympathy and personality between the Liberal left and the Fabian Society. Dr. Clifford, for instance, is a Fabian.

Yours, etc.,
H.G. Wells

[1] This letter to the press was published on 13 March 1907 under the title 'Liberalism and the Fabian Society'. A letter from Shaw on the subject was published on 11 March which led to Wells's comment.

678. To John Gregory[1]

PLS

[Spade House
Sandgate, Kent] [early in 1907]

Dear Mr. Gregory,

You will, I hope, forgive my writing to you to tell you how much I like and value your book of poems. Your son has just given it to me and I have been reading in its contents a constantly increasing delight and surprise. He had often told me that you wrote verse but he had given me no idea of the simple, curiously straightforward graciousness of your songs. They come I think most appropriately with this spring time; they have so much in common with the bright freshness of primrose and aubrietia and all the daffodils and narcissuses with which the garden is singing. I have been reminded of Blake and

Herrick and of all that is most truly English as I read. R.A.G. is one of my earliest friends – I didn't expect at this date to find a quite new reason for liking and respecting him – in such a book as this.

I am myself a sort of literary man though I've never risen to either verse or science. That must be my excuse for bothering you with these praises.

Yours very sincerely,
H.G. Wells

---

[1] Gregory was the father of Sir Richard A. Gregory who had sent Wells a copy of his father's poetry, and the letter resulted. It appeared in *Nature*, 13 June 1953, p. 1040 in an article by Sir Harold Hartley. Its whereabouts is not known. John Hammond kindly brought this letter to my attention.

679. To Henry James

Illinois, ALS

Spade House
Sandgate

20, iii. 07

My dear James,

I've read the American Scene & again I've read in the American Scene & I've reread Richmond (which is one of the most wonderful things you have done) & Baltimore several times and – I found very little to say to you except something in the way of a more respectful salutation than even I've made before on these occasions.

The things are so completely done, the atmospheres return[?] elucidated; once again I have visited Washington & the White House. You take the thing (as you said) at the opposite pole to my attack, you make it a criticism of life & manners – things I have had only incidental dealings with – you take the whole thing as an ineffectual civilization & judge it with so temperate & informed decisiveness. But I wish there was a public worthy of you – & me. After the book is closed & I have gloated again in the still almost incredible marvel of a cover "uniform" with mine, I do get this gleam of discontent.[1] How much will they get out of what you have got in?

Yours ever
H. G. Wells

[1] This is almost precisely the time when Wells began to think of and to write the first parts of what became his novel parodying James's style, *Boon,* which was published in 1915. Two of the chapters in that book were offered to publishers in 1908, but were then withdrawn.

680. To Violet Hunt

Cornell, Typed Transcription

Stanway
Winchcombe
℅ Canon Greenwell
Durham [postmarked 30 March 07.]

Tragic our separation! When will you be back? I shall be in London on the 10th of April.

Yours ever,
H.G.

681. To Mr Making

Korn, ALS

Spade House
Sandgate 30. iii. 07

My dear Making,

No! – you're wrong. You write as if Socialism was a fundamentally different thing from Progressive Liberalism. Shaw does the same thing. But it is not, nor is it true that there is one orthodox Socialism, one & indivisible. I've been trying for some months to give a clear account of Socialism in a book.[1] It has involved working out things pretty clearly, & if one thing comes out since this analysis it is the fact that these qualities of the strength of Socialism lie outside the Socialist organization & parties. We want an open door towards Progressivism & liberty because we do not want to start them out from our synthesis.

Yours very sincerely,
H.G. Wells

---

[1] The book, the fourth of his efforts to provide a guide towards the future at this time, is *New Worlds For Old* (London: Constable, 1908). The first half of the book was serialized in *The Grand Magazine*, see letter 689. This cogitation also produced a statement of his private philosophy, *First and Last Things: A Confession of Faith and Rule of Life* (London: Constable, 1908). With these publications the private battle over Socialism, that with the Fabian Society, was over. The public battle, carried out in the press mainly, is a feature of much of the correspondence printed in the next sixty or so pages.

682. To the Editor, *The Nation* (U.K.)[1]

PLS

Sandgate — March 30, 1907

Sir, – Your interesting article upon the Fabian Society will, I hope, do much to induce those Socialist and Socialistic thinkers who constitute the left wing of the Liberal party to consider very seriously the advisability of joining us in our work. You state clearly the need for some association a little apart from immediate political organisations in which the constructive scheme that must underlie and determine progressive activity may be elaborated, and by which the new generation may be educated in broad political conceptions, and you make a very handsome acknowledgement of the use and possibilities of our society in this respect, but you complicate your case, by your criticism of two important members, whom it would seem you regard as vitiating very gravely the great work the Fabian Society has done, and is still doing, in developing and maintaining a co-ordinating theoretical basis for social effort. You attach too much importance, I think, to these two personalities, and to the incidental utterances of their more immediate supporters, and you do not sufficiently appeciate how necessarily the spirit and idea of Socialism must override the eccentricities and inconsistencies of which you complain. In particular you object to the way in which the idea of opportunism has been brought into the Fabian atmosphere. It is, of course, the very antithesis of the Socialism idea – the idea, that is, of a comprehensive scheme of systematic social reconstruction – but for that very reason one need not trouble, I think, if some forgetful exponent lapses for a time into the "hand to mouth" method. His Socialism will right him automatically sooner or later. The proper thing to do for the broad-minded observer is surely not to fling out into undiscriminating opposition to the Fabian Society and all its works, because a meeting or so in London makes a muddle-headed vote under the influence of Mr. Bernard Shaw's gift for lucid inversion and the terror of losing his bright presence, but rather to do the utmost to diminish such regrettable incidents by coming in to redress our balance.

And, as one who has worked intimately with Mr. Shaw and Mr. Webb, I must protest against your treatment of either them as – sinister. They are the least diabolical of men. To regard Webb, for example, as a Machiavellian statesman is ridiculous. He has a mind, it is true, of immense activity, and he is a glutton for work; he has a real enthusiasm for social organization, and in particular for education, and his peculiar freedom from rhetorical habits of mind, his distrust of vague enthusiasms, have been of immense value as corrective and chastening influences upon British Socialism. He has, it is true, certain weaknesses. He is almost timidly averse to wrangling disputations and politic in disposition, and he has adopted latterly a pose of self-satisfaction in his own dexterity that arouses unworthy resentment and makes colleagues and opponents alike unduly suspicious of him. But that little weakness really only humanises his very real intellectual greatness, and the wise will love him none the less on this account. Over the internal educational work of the Fabian Society it throws a pleasant, and, I think, quite harmless tinge of innocent artifice, that may perhaps neutralise our immediate political influence, but that hampers not at all our work of study and discussion and the slow building up of our great constructive project.

Mr. Shaw is, I think, a much more inconvenient personality in the development of Socialism. He is inconvenient, but he is certainly not evil. He has a nimble and vagrant mind which rejects no conception, and is wholly subject to none. After years of talking round and about and over and under Socialism, for example, one finds him apropos of the "Times" Book Club, falling back upon *laissez faire* and a simple faith in competition ultimately righting everything. With that I – who had somewhat clung to him – gave him up as being any sort of intellectual vertebrate. But his gifts are unique. Surely no man could ever so effectually confuse and disorder the issue before a meeting as he. He is able to do it because he first confuses himself because he has no end to serve except the cheerful interest of the confusion. Under his solemn absurdities, his erratic profundities of bathos, his lapses into impassioned personality, the London Fabian meetings fall into incalcuable mental states, and hold up wavering hands, – astonishingly. Life is an uncertain thing, and it is perhaps for one's ultimate good that Shaw should be at hand to keep one in mind of that. That he should be taken seriously as an evil influence is quite another matter. Shaw is a kindly man, a profoundly well-meaning man, a sentimentalist at heart, a man of catholic temperance, a *good* man, to the ultimate implications of that phrase. He gives no evil bias to the mind, no incurable perversion of thought or attitude; he implants no weed-like ideas. In turn he resonates to all ideas, and stands for none. So that he leaves no really harmful after-effects, and many pleasant memories. And on the positive side he arouses curiosity, he draws attention to Socialism. He is a constant reminder, too, of forgotten and neglected aspects of questions now grown trite.

Neither Mr. Webb nor Mr. Shaw stand for Fabianism. May I in conclusion reiterate that. You do a number of obscure workers much injustice, and you weaken and hamper the new spirit in the renascent society when you lend your columns to that suggestion. Mr. Shaw sometimes speaks as thought he were the appointed mouthpiece of the society, but that is a form of humour that must be conceded him. And the more that constructive and progressive thinkers and workers come into the Fabian Society, the larger will be its scope and activities and the less these two distinguished personalities (long may they work with us!) will dominate its work and reputation.

Yours, etc., H.G.Wells[2]

---

[1] Another of Wells's responses to newspaper commentary on the Fabian Society. It appeared on 6 April 1907 under the title, 'On the Alleged Diabolical Interests in the Fabian Society'.

[2] The editor responded at the end of the article with, 'We imputed nothing "sinister" to Mr. Shaw or Mr. Webb. What we deprecated was the later developments of their genius for politics and social and economic analysis. We think Mr. Wells underestimates their importance.'

683. To George Meek[1]

Illinois, ALS

Spade House
Sandgate

April 6 '07

Dear Meek,

My movements are very uncertain but I hope to go down to Eastbourne [?] in April – after I've read the M.S.

Yours ever
H.G. Wells

[1] Meek was one of the more unusual of Wells's friends and protégés. He made his living by pushing a bathchair, a large wicker chair on wheels, on the beaches of southern England. In that era, the elderly, or those taking the waters, were trundled about in this fashion. Meek, fancied himself as something like W. H. Davies who had written, *The Autobiography of a Super Tramp*. Wells encouraged Meek to write, and his autobiographical account, *George Meek Bathchairman, by Himself*, appeared in 1910, with a Wells introduction.

684. To Lewis Browne[1]

Illinois, ALS

Spade House
Sandgate 30. iv. 07

Dear Mr. Browne.

I've taken a week to consider your letter.[2] Well first I'm a thoroughly immoral person – not "non moral" or anything like that but just discursive, experimental and fluctuating & I have no organizing energy & very little organizing capacity. I am interested in discipline, I try over all sorts of things, I have presented the idea of the Samurai & I shall probably return to it & kindred problems again. But I couldn't create any 'order'. I think an 'order' could be created by a man or group of men of the right sort now upon the lines of my Samurai, but I am the last man to do it. They ought to devise a rule, try it, reconstruct it – finding first a sort of body, but only as committee of enquiry. I don't think I would mind a talk with your little group; about practicality. Would Wednesday the eighth of May be of any use to you? – in the afternoon?

Yours ever,
H.G. Wells

[1] Browne was a supporter of Wells in the Fabian imbroglio. He later moved to the United States and there are a few letters to him after the move; see volume 4.

[2] Browne was offering comment on Wells's ideas as well as on a significant conference discussing the possibilities of a Samurai Society, held at the New Reform Club under the auspices of the Fabian Arts Society on 11 April 1907. Participants were Wells, Beatrice Webb, Haden Guest, Dr Lake of Leyden, Aylmer Maude, Edward Carpenter, and Mr Montifiore. Shaw attended and attacked the goals of the meeting after the initial discussion. The meeting was described in detail by *The New Age*, 2 May 1907, pp. 9–11. The new magazine began a major discussion of Socialism in this issue, which was welcomed by many of the left. See the next letter in this volume.

685. To the Editor, *The New Age*[1]

PLS

[Spade House
Sandgate,Kent] [April 1907]

You are going to make a most valuable, interesting, difficult, and, I think I may venture to add, successful experiment. Socialism in England has long stood in need of what you propose to give it – a Review which, without being official, shall be representative, and which shall direct itself primarily, not to propaganda nor to politics, but the development of Socialist thought. Particularly attractive, I think, should be your handling of contemporary literature and art, not, as in the ordinary Press, from vague, unspecified standpoints, but from a definitely Socialist position. Your enterprise will, I am sure, be of the utmost help and value to the new movement in the Fabian Society; it will do with the freedom and vigour of irresponsibility what it would have been almost impossible under existing conditions to do officially – supply a co-ordinating and educational link for the new members who are now coming in, and give fresh scope to the many young and vigorous minds in the Society who are now seeking (and needing) the discipline of written expression. My warmest good wishes.

H.G. Wells

[1] This letter from Wells is a welcome to the new Socialist paper, and to its editor, A. R. Orage. Published with many others under the title, 'Letters From the Front,' in the issue of 2 May 1907, p. 3, Wells was joined by, among others, Prince Kropotkin, Granville Barker, E.R. Pease, Sidney Webb, Hubert Bland, Cecil Chesterton, Sydney Olivier, E. Nesbit and Canon Holland.

686. To Beatrice Webb; Francis Galton et al.

LSE, TCCS
With a Typed Enclosure

Spade House,
Sandgate, Kent May 15, 1907

My dear Mrs, Webb,

Can you see your way to sign the enclosed? If you can, I hope very earnestly that you will do so. It does, I think, speak for itself. The document is to be sent in the first place to Mr. Pease to be read to the committees concerned, and if that fails to arrest the very considerable forces which are pushing the Society in the direction of a new Socialist party, I then propose to all the members for signature. If you approve, will you please not only sign it yourself, but obtain also the signatures of any other members in sympathy who are accessible to you?

Yours very sincerely,
H.G. Wells

We, the undersigned, consider that the chief value of the Fabian Society lies in its development of socialist theory and social method, and in its work of propaganda and education in the country and we deprecate any action which is likely to hamper or restrict these, its paramount, activities. Particularly do we desire that in the future, even more than in the past, it should be a common meeting-ground, a field for frank discussion, and whenever practicable a means of reconciliation and concerted action for Socialists of every party and type, however diverse their ideas of the political action necessary for the attainment of their common social and economic ideals. Such a comprehensiveness is compatible with the most unrestricted treatment of socialist differences in debate, with the fullest discussion of political situations, and with the political freedom of every member, but it is not compatible with definite political interventions on the part of the Society as a whole, nor with resolutions of a definite political nature on the part of the London or other meetings which speak in the name of the Society. It is our earnest wish that the Society as a whole should not commit itself further than it is already committed in this direction; that, if anything, it should abandon rather than increase its present limited intervention in the direction of the Labour Party, and it should abstain from any share whatever in the development of any fresh political socialist organization. For the sake of unity and the intellectual vigour of Socialism, we want the Fabian Society, as a society, to keep out of the chances, tactics, and personalities of faction altogether, and to remain a factory of ideas and suggestions; and we want its members, and particularly its more promising members who do intervene in the party arena, to do their utmost to disentangle the name and reputation of our Society from their personal and sectional views.[1]

We feel very strongly on this issue. If an energetic (but we believe a small) party of our members persist in their attempts to associate our Society with a definite aggressive Fabian political policy at the present time, we shall be forced into an extremely undesirable position. Many of us are not London members, many who are, are too busily engaged in special work of our own to bicker in a series of committee meetings and evening meetings on behalf of our views. We cannot always be on our guard against snatch votes and emergency resolutions. We may be easily out-manoeuvered. We are forced, therefore, to put it to our fellow members that unless this conception of the party neutrality of the Fabian Society is sustained, a situation becomes almost inevitable in which the only alternative to the association of our names with embarrassing political resolutions will be resignation. We ask them very earnestly therefore, not to allow party zeal to blind them to the inconveniences of any attempts to force the hand or use the name of the Society for purposes of political faction which may endanger the unity of the Society and with it the whole future of the Socialist propaganda in Great Britain and America.

[1] Although this manifesto is Wells's last significant attempt to remodel the Fabian Society, it is also a fairly strong attack on the tendency for some Labour members of Parliament, as well as G. B. Shaw, to become expansionist protagonists with regard to the British Empire.

687. To Lewis Browne

Illinois, ALS

Spade House
Sandgate

June 3. 07.

Dear Sir,

Very many thanks for your prospectus. It's an entirely original idea for a method of publication & I like it. About my dream of the Samurai, I have you know a certain diffidence. The higher one climbs the steeper the cliff & there are moments when I feel with Chesterton about Wells & his confounded Samurai. They chase that great fat man rolling through his dreams with stern relentless pertinacity.

Your format would be a delightful one for a short story – if it deserved it. I can see one or two of Henry James done like this, a volume of the two perfect things of Chesterton's, the knight and his game of Croquet, my 'Country of the Blind'; a story or so of Vernon Lee.

I'm very curious to know what your First Book of the Samurai is to be & curious to read Songs of Exile & Toward the Isles.

Yours very sincerely
H.G. Wells

688. To Francis Galton; Beatrice Webb et al.[1]

LSE, TLS

Spade House
Sandgate, KENT 15th June, 1907

Dear Sir,

I am greatly obliged to you for your reply to my circular of the 15th May last. The document was sent altogether to 72 members picked out hastily from the general list and constituting on the whole, I think, a fairly representative sample of the Society. Of these 32 have signed or agreed to sign the document as it stands now and 12 more are in pretty complete agreement but think action at the present time premature or object to the suggestion of a possible resignation. Three of the remainder are in partial agreement and 16 have not replied. I take it therefore that there is a strong body of opinion in the Society opposed to any attempt to force collective political action upon us. May I take the opportunity of pointing out that I have opened what I hope will be an elucidatory discussion of this important question in the current number of the New Age – and again thanking you for your kindness to my circular, remain

Yours very sincerely,
H. G. Wells
sgd. Horace Horsnell

---

[1] Copies of the round robin letter occur in the papers of Beatrice Webb, and Francis Galton at the LSE. Galton responded saying that he agreed with Wells but could not sign it because of the threat of resignation. Wells's response is in the Galton papers. This, of course, is really Wells's last effort to reform or revolutionize the Fabians. I am unable to explain the discrepancy in numbers provided by Wells. Beatrice Webb agreed as to interference in electoral politics, and told him she accepted the 'spirit of your memo'; Beatrice Webb to H. G. Wells, 25 May 1907.

689. To the Editor, *The Grand Magazine*[1]

PLS

[Spade House,
Sandgate, Kent] [*c.* mid June 1907]

At present, when education is fast levelling up the entire population of the civilised world and is brushing aside all artificial distinctions, there remains the wide spread conviction that there is at hand a time when there may be a radical readjustment of the class divisions into which society is now split up, and of the privileges which each class considers its due. Whether the change, which all foresee – some with dread, some with elation – will be effected by violent or by peaceful methods, the future alone can say. Meanwhile, the upper and middle classes, so-called, are distinctly uneasy at the innumerable vague theories with which the air is filled, all of which in their eyes tend more or less to spoilition, pure and simple, and which they contemptuously lump together under one label – "Socialism."

What, precisely, is this new doctrine? Thousands of people are asking this every day without being able to obtain any satisfactory answer. It seems, indeed, to be almost a case of Quot homines, tot sententiae, and it is high time, therefore, that some sort of a definite schema should be put before the world.

H. G. Wells

---

[1] In July 1907 *The Grand Magazine* began a nine part serial publication of Wells's book, *New Worlds For Old*. The serialization was presented with a boxed lead of this letter by Wells as to the purpose of the book. The rubric appears before nearly all serial parts. There is some minor difference from one to another, but this appears to be a consequence of available space rather than anything else.

690. To the Editor, *The New Age*[1]

PLS

[Spade House
Sandgate, Kent] [late June 1907]

I hesitate to understand the controversial standards of Mr. Chesterton. He has written an article in which he does not so much discuss this proposed new

Socialist party as seek to ascribe wanton inconsistency to me. I do not think his method of doing so a justifiable one. He puts together clipped quotations from my article in your issue of June 13th which was addressed to convinced Socialists and concerned party politics only, with passages, from my propaganda tract, "This Misery of Boots," addressed to the unconverted, he twists the necessary difference of tone between these two into an apparent contradiction and works his way laboriously to the imputation of bad sense and bad faith. He accuses me of going over, "bag and baggage" to permeation, and he does this in the face of an article in which, as plainly if not as rhetorically as I do in my tract upon the supreme need of outspoken statement and open confession of our Socialist faith, and in which there occurs such a statement as this -

Now you may say this is the old doctrine of permeation, I do not think so. The conception of permeation carries with it to my mind, and I think to many other minds, a flavour of insidious substitution, a suggestion of wire pulling and trickery, and what I suppose is the open triumph and imposition of ideas.

I ask your readers, what do they make of Mr. Chesterton's device of avoiding this passage altogether in his reply to my article? The whole of his argument against me is in fact a strained attempt to make out that my exhortation to all those who acquiesce in the general theory of Socialism to call themselves Socialists, was an exhortation to separatism in party politics. I find it hard to believe, that Mr. Chesterton is capable of such extreme clumsiness of apprehension.

But his clumsiness of apprehension becomes still more difficult to credit when he drags in my book, "In The Days of the Comet," as a book advocating polygamy. That issue had been discussed I had hoped sufficiently fully, and I find it difficult to suppose that Mr. Chesterton is unaware of that discussion. But he must be unaware of it or otherwise this new attack would be just wanton and unjustifiable mud-throwing. I imagined when I published "In the Days of the Comet," that even without discussion no intelligent person could mistake the idealized of my comet-struck world for a definite Socialist proposal. But Mr. Chesterton, Mr. Shaw, and the Anti-Socialist expert of the "Daily Express" disillusioned me. Let me, therefore, repeat that not only is this confusion made without any countenance from me, but after I have been at great pains and trouble, to insist upon what I had once imagined were the obvious facts of the case. I cannot, of course, supply Mr. Chesterton with general understanding, but I may, at any rate, do my best to deprive him of the excuse of ignorance for any further offense in this direction. The comet-changed world of "In the Days of the Comer" has not and never was intended to have any closer relation to what I regarded as practicable and desirable in the sexual institutions of contemporary human beings than has Mr. Coburn's[2] recent photograph of "The Thinker" to what he and his sitter consider a desirable costume for a Socialist soirée. There are very definite limits on conduct, costume and so forth, in the actual practical world, that have no value in the world of imaginative art. For example, I think myself that the idealized nude human form is nearly the most beautiful thing in the whole imagination of man, but that does not mean that I would incite Mr. Chesterton and his associations of the Anti-Puritan League to dance along the Strand in their native buff. Mr. Chesterton must really try to grasp this very simple and generally understood distinction, and when he does so thorougly, then he will go on to realise that this particular controversial device is incompatible with his self-respect.

There gleams, too, in Mr. Chesterton's paper a third and more excusable – what shall I call it? – controversial indistinctness. It will, I think, be plain, to everyone who read my paper in your issue of the 13th, with an unprejudiced mind, that I was writing of Fabian *collective* political activity and using the word "political" not in its etymological sense which would make "politics" nearly an equivalent of "sociology," but in its common accepted English sense as an affair of party organisation and electioneering. It will be quite easy – but I think it will be rather silly – for anyone to pretend that I want to disavow any attempts whatever to secure Socialist legislation, and to seem to score a brilliant victory on that misunderstanding.

H.G. Wells

---

[1] The long debates and discussions over Socialism, its methods, and its goals led to a number of efforts to establish a basis for new societies. One of these was offered by the author, Cecil Chesterton, brother of G. K. Chesterton. Wells responded to it, and its rather *ad hominem* remarks about Wells in *The New Age*, 27 June 1907, p. 143, as 'A Note on Methods of Controversy'.

[2] Wells's friend, Alvin Langdon Coburn, (1882–1966) whose photography was influenced by the Pre-Raphaelite school of painting. He illustrated a de luxe edition of *The Door in the Wall* with photographs, and Wells wrote an introduction to his photographic study of *New York*.

691. To the Editor, *Magazine of Commerce*[1]

PLS

Spade House
Sandgate, Kent

August 5, 1907

My Dear Sir,

I wish very much I could reply at adequate length to your very admirably framed question. The constant stream of abuse and of almost imbecile misrepresentations of Socialism in the Press, has no doubt served to distort the idea of our movement in the minds of a large proportion of busy men, and filled them with an unfounded dread of social insecurity. If it were possible to allay that by an epigrammatic programme, "Socialism in a nutshell," so to speak, I would do my best. But the economic and trading system of a modern State is not only a vast and complex tangle of organisations, but at present an uncharted tangle, and necessarily the methods of transition from the limited individualism of our present condition to the scientifically organised State, which is the Socialist ideal, must be gradual, tentative and various.

To build up a body of social and economic science, to develop a class of trained administrators, to re-arrange local government areas, to educate the whole community in "the sense of State," are necessary parts of the Socialist scheme. You must try and induce your readers to recognize that when Socialism finds such supporters as Professors Oliver Lodge and Karl Pearson; as William Morris (who revolutionised the furniture trade); as Granville Barker (who is revolutionising the London stage); as Mr. George Cadbury and Mr. Fels (whose names are not unknown in the world of advertisement); as Mr. Allan (of the Allan Line); as Mr. George Bernard Shaw; Mrs. Shaw; Mr. and Mrs. Sidney Webb; and Sir Sydney Olivier, the present Governor of Jamaica; all of them fairly comfortable and independent people, practically acquainted with the business of investment and affairs generally, and quite alive to the present relations of property to the civilised life – the suggestion that it is a raid of the ignorant Have-nots on the possessions of the wise and good Haves cannot be a very intelligent one, nor addressed to intelligent people. Essentially, Socialism is the scientifically organised State, as distinguished from the haphazard, wasteful, blundering, child-sweating State of the eighteenth century. It is the systemisation of present tendency. Necessarily, its method of transition will be progressively scientific and humane.

So far as your specifics go, I do not think there could possibly be anything in the nature of "compulsory profit-sharing" if a Socialist Government came into office. There is, at present, a compulsory profit-sharing in the form of an income-tax, but that tax does not appeal to the Socialist as a particularly scientific one. The advent of a strongly Socialistic Government to power would mean no immediate revolutionary changes at all. There would be, no doubt, a vigorous acceleration of the educational movement to increase the economic value and productivity of the average citizen of the next generation, and legislation upon the lines laid down by the principle of the "minimum wage" to check the waste of our natural resources by the "destructive employment," also a systematic shifting of the burthen of taxation from enterprise to rent would begin. But nothing convulsive would occur.

The means of transit and communication of the country (both internal and external), and especially the railways and canals (which are now rapidly falling into inefficiency through the exhaustion of their capital upon excessive dividends in the past), would probably be transferred from competitive private to organised public control, a transfer that would certainly be enormously stimulating to business generally. (There would be no "robbery"; the former shareholders would become stock or annuity holders.)

A Socialist Government would certainly also acquire the coal mines and the coal trade, and relieve industry from the inconveniences due to the manipulation of the supply of this vitally important factor, and it would accelerate the obvious tendency of the present time to bring the milk trade, the drink trade, slaughtering, local traffic, lighting and power supply into public hands. But none of this is the destruction of property, but only its organisation and standardization. Such a State organisation of public services is, I submit, enough to keep a Socialist Government busy for some few years, and makes not only for social progress, but social stability.

And does an honest and capable business man stand to lose or gain by the coming of such a Socialist Government? I submit that, on the whole, he stands to gain. Let me put down the essential points in his outlook as I conceive them.

Under a Socialist legislation:-

He will be restricted from methods of production and sale that are socially mischievous.

He will pay higher wages.

He will pay a larger proportion of his rate-rent outgoings to the State and municipality and less to the landlord.

These items in his outlook the businessman may contemplate with doubt, but, on the other hand,

He will get better educated, better fed, and better trained workers.

He will get a regular, safe, cheap supply of power and material. He will get cheaper and more efficient internal and external transit.

He will be under an organised scientific State, which will naturally pursue a vigorous scientific policy in support of the national trade.

He will be less of an adventurer and more of a citizen.

But the men of affairs who read the Magazine of Commerce will naturally go to original sources for a more detailed statement of the Socialist idea. Mr. J. Ramsay Macdonald's little shilling book, published by the I.L.P. , "Socialism and the State," is a good authoritative contemporary rendering of the Socialist case, and I hope to publish next spring a complete general statement of the modern Socialist position under the title "New Worlds For Old," in which I shall dispose of a mass of popular errors about Socialism, and sketch the Socialist conception of economic organisation more fully than I can do here.

"Fabian Essays" (1s), published by the Fabian Society (3, Clement's Inn, W.C.), dates from the eighties, but is still very informing upon Socialist ideas, and the same Society publishes a bound volume of its tracts for 5s., which deals in detail, soberly and scientifically, with the land, transit, food, drink and similar problems.

The man of affairs will begin to realise, after he has turned over the pages of the latter volume, that much of this panic talk about Socialism, in the more adventurous section of our Press, is really no more and no less than a rather cruel joke at the expense of the timid investor – and his esteemed self.

Very sincerely yours,
H.G. Wells

[1] A letter to the *Magazine of Commerce* published under the title, 'Socialism and The Business World' (August, 1907), pp. 9–11. I have deleted the cross-heads in the published version.

692. To George Meek

Illinois, ANS

Spade House
Sandgate
Aug. 23. 07

Dear Meek,

I'm sympathetic, but no more Committees for me!

Yours ever,
H.G. Wells[1]

[1] What this committee could be is unknown. Meek was a Socialist, of rudimentary views, and this is why he had sought out Wells initially. Wells's views on committees was jaundiced by his Fabian experience.

693. To George Meek

Illinois, ACCS

Spade House
Sandgate [August 1907]

Dear Mr. Meek,

Many thanks for your letter. I shall look in at Tunbridge Wells if I can [*illegible word*] it. I return copy of your New Age letter. I'm not against Socialists going into politics but I am against the Socialist movement being made a mere political campaign.

Very sincerely yours,
H.G. Wells

694. To Joseph Wells

Korn, APCS

[Switzerland] 4 – ix – 07

This is a bit of our walks last week. We have been all over the Monte Miro Pass into Italy & back by the Simplon tunnel here.

Love to you both,
Bertie

695. To Harold Monro[1]

Illinois, ACC

Spade House
Sandgate 29 Sep. 07

Dear Mr. Monro.

I've just got your letter here on my return from a long walk of three weeks with my wife in the Alps. I'm ashamed to say I've got no credo ready though I've drafted notes for 'What I Believe' for the Fabian Society. I can't promise you anything for a month, but may I

[*remainder of note missing*]

---

[1] Harold Monro ((1879–1932) was the founder of the Poetry Bookshop. He lived near Haslemere, where he founded the Samurai Press which published *Proposals for a Voluntary Nobility* (1907).

696. To George Meek

Illinois, ACCS

Spade House
Sandgate 30 ix. 07

Dear Meek,

I find your card unanswered on my return from Switzerland. Good luck to your writing. I shall read it with interest but don't imagine I can do anything to get it published or make it sweeter[? – *ink blot covers the word*]. That will depend entirely on its quality.

Yours ever
H.G. Wells

697. To Percy Redfern

Manchester, ALS
Local Studies Unit
MSP 091.5 Rel.[1]

[Spade House
Sandgate] 30. ix. 07

My dear Redfern,

I find your 'Tolstoy' here on my return from a Swiss holiday. Your mention of me in the preface to so good a little book honours me greatly.[1]

Yours ever
H.G. Wells

[1] When this collection was originally catalogued, and before its transmission to the Local Studies Unit, an undated post card was present from Wells to Redfern expressing sympathy with Redfern's ideas. It has gone missing, however. I rely on a description as I have not seen the original postcard.

698. To Frederick Macmillan[1]

Bromley (photocopy), ADLS

Spade House
Sandgate, Kent

Oct. 3. 07

Dear Mr. Macmillan,

Perhaps you are right and Nelson's £400 a giddy bore. Still it does seem to me that with the book doing practically nothing (vide account to hand) it was worthy [of] more consideration. Either Nelson has a public you don't touch or he is a philanthropist eager to give out £400.

I note your offer to relinquish my books. Well, that's not a matter to go into in a hurry. I like your firm in many ways. I don't think you advertise well and I think you're out of touch with the contemporary movement in literature. I don't think you have any idea of what could be done for me (but that you will of course you will attribute to the Vanity of Authors). But on the other hand you are solid & sound & sane.

I'll come and talk of these things later, if I think more of it – but I doubt if I shall unless you disappoint me horribly over Tono Bungay. I'm putting all I can into that & when the book comes I shall expect you to do the same.

Yours ever,
H.G. Wells

[1] Macmillan was the owner and proprietor of the famous publishing firm. His rival Nelson had obviously offered Wells a £400 advance for his next book. Macmillan published many of Wells's works but often attempted to modify Wells's descriptions of human relationships, while Wells offered advice on how best to market his books. This letter is a four page holograph, and it occurs also in a long draft of one foolscap page. They do not differ much and the text presented is the final draft. The originals of the Macmillan papers are in the British Library. Lovat Dickson photocopied most of the materials concerning Wells for his biography, *H. G. Wells: His Turbulent Life and Times* (London: Macmillan, 1969). These were deposited in Illinois, where I consulted them, and also in the New York Public Library.

699. To Percy Redfern

Manchester, APCS

Local Studes Unit
MSF 091.5 Rel.

Spade House
Sandgate   Oct. 9. 07

My dear Redfern.

Many thanks for your admirable little book. You will do more – I know.

Yours ever,
H.G. Wells

700. To the Editor, *The New Age*[1]

PLS

[Spade House
Sandgate, Kent]   [mid-October 1907]

Will you permit me to make a personal statement that may be of service to your readers who are actively engaged on the defensive side in the present Anti-Socialist campaign? My name is frequently given by the Anti-Socialists as an advocate of "free love," as one who wants to "take children from their parents," etc., etc., and sometimes these assertions are supported by [the] minutest rags of quotations from my writings. Now a great number of Socialists have never read any of my books, and probably none have read all – they have other things to do – and as I am not quite the ordinary type of Socialist writer, they don't precisely know what to do about me. Some accept the opponent's lie and disavow me, which is perhaps the silliest thing possible under the circumstances; others send the lie along to me, which is sensible of them but troublesome to me; some take a risk and disavow the alleged opinion as mine. Well, I want to say that they are quite safe in denying the lie. I have never advocated "free love," nor the destruction of the family. They may boldly challenge the opponent for evidence and then denounce him as a liar. There is nothing anywhere to support these statements, and there is a mass of my writings to prove the contrary.

Of course, I have written about the relation of Socialism to the family, and it is almost impossible to write upon such a topic without at times writing phrases that in unscrupulous hands and torn from their context may "look bad" in their discussion. I discuss these points in my "Modern Utopia," but there I really never made the ghost of a slip and it is never quoted, and in a pamphlet, 'Socialism and the Family" (Fifield, 6d.). In the latter I have to confess to careless writing. I speak once or twice of the "family" when I ought to have said the "patriarchal family," that is to say, the family in which the mother is regarded not as a citizen but as the property of the father. My meaning is perfectly clear, and only in such absolutely unscrupulous controversy as the present Anti-Socialist campaign will it have been distorted. If the pro-Socialist will bear that in mind and read "Socialism and the Family" before replying, he will have no difficulty in tackling the antagonist upon this particular point. It is all he need read of me for that purpose. But in my forthcoming book, "New Worlds for Old," now appearing in the "Grand Magazine," I believe I have got the Socialist position in these matters stated in absolutely unambiguous language, and the portion relating to the family is already available for quotation.

There is, however, a second point upon which attacks were made for which the pro-Socialist must be prepared. A romance by me called "In the Days of the Comet," presents the world as altered mentally and spiritually by a comet. The inhabitants of the earth become changed and exalted, they become "above the law"; like the early Christians, they have all their goods in common, and they develop towards a state which, as in the kingdom of Heaven, there is no marrying, nor giving in marriage. The book is dream, is intended to be a beautiful dream, and it ends with an epilogue, that makes that intention perfectly clear. If the book is immoral and indecent, then the New Testament is equally so. The story has just as much to do with current politics and ordinary social relations as Michael Angelo's Last Judgment or the well-known picture of "Love and Life." So far as I know, no one has been fool enough to say Mr. G. F. Watts wants young people who are not married to stand together in exposed situations without clothes because of that picture, and it is quite equally foolish to treat "In The Days of the Comet" as a Socialist tract. A fellow Fabian (bless him) saw fit in the course of heated controversy to treat this book as my Socialist Utopia, and the misrepresentation has been caught up by the Anti-Socialist writers. In the interests of Socialism I have done all I can to stop this mischievous and silly perversion. I have written letters to papers and articles, and I have dragged the point into everything I have since written about Socialism. It is quite possible, however, that those who are busily fighting "at the front" have not heard anything at all about that, and it may be useful to tell them what to say if "In the Days of the Comet" is suddenly flung in their faces.

Apart from these books, I do not think there is the minutest possibility of misrepresentation in my writings in relation to these matters.

I must apologise, Sirs, for the apparent egotism of this letter, but my daily bundle of Press cuttings makes it clear that Socialism is being frequently attacked through me upon these points, and my correspondence shows that our side finds these attacks at times extremely inconvenient to deal with. This letter may save one or two good men the bother of a hunt through my books.

H.G. Wells

---

[1] By mid-October 1907 Wells had been under strong attack for his views on Socialism and 'free love' for over a year. His books continued to sell well, but the campaign against him and Socialism was taking its toll. He continued to defend himself wherever the attacks appeared, but he also filed a manifesto of his views in an Open Letter in the hope that the discussion would move on to discuss the more important political issues of the day. In fact, the debate grew hotter. The Open Letter had as its immediate target speeches and comments by William Joynson-Hicks, (The *Manchester Courier*, 7, 12 October 1907), and a leaflet which reprinted much of his speech at Sale. The chronology of the correspondence that follows is as accurate as is possible, for letters were written, and published on different days, and while the public battle of the press continued, the private battle between Joynson-Hicks, Catherine and Wells was fought out in private letters.

This Open Letter appeared in *The New Age*, 17 October 1907, on p. 392, as 'Mr. Wells and Free Love; A Personal Statement,' in *Clarion* of 18 October 1907, p. 4 under the title of 'Mr. H.G. Wells, "Free Love" & The Family', and finally in a small single sheet double-sided hand out, published by A. C. Fifield, 44, Fleet St, E.C. It also appeared in *Justice* 19 October 1907, p. 9 under the title, 'H.G. Wells and Our Enemies'. I own a copy of the handout and there are other copies at Illinois. It also appeared, virtually intact, in the *Clarion* 12 October 1907 as it had appeared in the *Daily Mail* in their regular column, 'The Book Man's Burden', on 12 October 1907, tying the letters and the attacks on Wells expressly to the 'Book War'. They sub-titled the piece as 'Mr. Wells's Pathetic Confession.'

Although Wells may have thought that his Open Letter would end, or at least diminish the campaign against 'Free Love', and incidentally, Socialism, it was, in fact, the beginning of six weeks battle between Wells, the press, and J. H. Bottomley, Joynson-Hick's election agent.

Joynson-Hicks (usually called Jix) responded quickly to the letters he received from Wells and Catherine. On 17 October he wrote to Wells but said that he was responding to both letters. He sent them a copy of the correction to the first report in the *Manchester Courier*, and promised a fuller report in another paper. Joynson-Hicks said that he had not read Wells's books, but promised to do so, saying that he would not attack Wells 'when there are so many other Socialist writers that one can attack'. He followed this with another letter to Wells dated 22 October, saying he was 'innocent, at all events I have been till recently, of the idiosyncrasies of Socialist literature'. On the 29th, Jix said he had read the article in *The Spectator* and accepted their view of Wells's book, *In the Days of the Comet*. These letters are in the University of Illinois Rare Books Room, Wells Collection, in the file incoming from Jix to Wells. Wells and Jix served together on a commission to study air travel after the First World War. They became friends and in the 1930s visited each other while in their Riviera homes.

701. To William Joynson-Hicks[1]

Illinois, ALS

Spade House,
Sandgate
COPY

Joynson-Hicks Esq.
26a Bryanston Square, W. October 11, 1907

Dear Sir.

Are you correctly reported in the Daily Despatch as having said at Sale -

"In Mr. Wells' book it is clearly stated that wives no less than goods were to be held in "common" & "every infant would be taken away from the mother & father & put into a state- nursery." These statements about my husband are absolutely untrue, & very damaging to him, & if you have been correctly reported we shall be glad if you will make a prompt & complete public apology.

Yours faithfully
A. Catherine Wells

Joynson-Hicks, Esq.

[1] Sir William Joynson-Hicks (Jix) was to become Baldwin's Home Secretary in his second government of 1924.

702. To William Joynson-Hicks

Illinois, TLS

[London] Oct 12th 07

Dear Sir,

My wife I believe wrote to you a day or so ago with regard to your recent speech at Sale. I have since received a press cutting from The Manchester Courier in which there occur the words typewritten on the slip enclosed. Did you use these words or did you not? And if you did not say this what did you say? I want to be perfectly clear because I intend to follow up this speech of yours. One or two of your people may have got it into their heads that the law of libel does not apply to Socialists and that a Socialist will not bring an action for damages. I want to dispel this silly delusion.

Very sincerely yours,
(signed) H.G. Wells

703. To Fisher Unwin[1]

Illinois, ADLS

Spade House
Sandgate 17 October 1907

Private

My dear Fisher Unwin

You say you are disposed to speculate in futures. Very well, what will you give for all rights (serial & book) American, British & colonial of the version in English of a novel by me which I have in hand, more or less at the present time. It is to be called Ann Veronica. It is to be the love story of an energetic modern girl who goes suffragetting & quarrels with her parents. It is to be over 70,000 & under 90,000 words in length. It can be delivered in a state fit for negociation before the end of this year and it is to be published in book form between September 30th & December 25th 1909. Next as to the state of my books in the market. Kipps did just 10,000 at 6/- & has since yielded a handsome price from Nelson's for a 1/- edition. The Socialist book of the summer New Worlds For Old is about a 100 under 5,000 at 6/- (considerable colonial sales in addition). It stands high in British advanced circles. The novel is fairly advanced. It is also humorous & passionate. My last two books sold & forthcoming in America get £500 & £300 in advance of royalties respectively. Tauchnitz pays usually £40 sometimes £50. Ann Veronica I must warn you is not a particularly good serial. I have a book The War in the Air just coming from Bell which is bound to do well with the booksellers & my next novel form is to be the chief item of the new English Review which has a successful air about it & is to be published in book form by Mac. in the spring. Put up a firm offer of £1500 payable Oct. 1st 1909 & Ann Veronica is yours. 'We will eliminate the agent' [*two lines blackened out*] and you shall be absolutely unhampered by accounts & free to sublet rights to Nelsons for the shilling edition series or anything of that sort to any extent. No other new book by me shall appear between Sept. 1st & the end of the year 1909. And mark this, this text is sacred, all refunds must be submitted to me in proof for approval if not for corrections & not for serial or book use a line shall be added or taken from Ann Veronica. And this offer is made without prejudice to the negociations I am carrying on elsewhere. I shan't bind myself to keep it open for you.

Yours very sincerely
H.G. Wells

[1] This letter, although signed by Wells, is clearly in a draft form. There are balloons, interpellations, cross outs and no paragraphs. I presume that his secretary organized the letter into proper business form before it was sent, if it were sent; compare letter 707.

704. To William Joynson-Hicks

Illinois, TLS

Spade House
Sandgate, Kent

Oct. 18th. 07.

Dear Sir,

You really must be a very innocent person to flounder out with these reckless libels upon me on the strength of a "Book War" notice of my romance

"In the Days of the Comet," a notice which was followed by a disavowal which the Times with the quite characteristic shabbiness of your side in these matters printed as a paragraph without a heading a fortnight after the review. It is absurd that you should make such sweeping statements on so little. I really must insist upon you making an adequate apology & giving it an equal publicity with your previous comments upon me.

Yours very sincerely,

H. G. Wells

I enclose a cutting dealing with your second point. (enclo. letter in Lab. Leader.)

705. To the Editor, *Lancashire Daily Post*[1]

PLS

Spade House
Sandgate, Kent 19th October 1907

Sir, – Your readers will, I think, find the following series of incidents throw a vivid illumination of the methods of the present Anti-Socialist campaign.

At Sale, last Friday, Mr. Joynson-Hicks made the following comprehensive statements about me:

> He quoted Mr. H.G. Wells's book to the effect that 'wives, no less than goods, are to be held in common. No binding contract was to be necessary between men and women,while property in children should cease to exist; every infant, as soon as it came into the world, would be born to full citizenship, taken away from mother and father and put into state nurseries, and thus a new development of social life would take place, an association terminable at the notice of either party. This was Mr. Wells' explanation'.
>
> Manchester Courier, 12th October, 1907.

My wife who does the bulk of my correspondence wrote at once demanding an ample, prompt, and complete apology. Mr. Joynson-Hicks replies to me that *he has never read anything of mine at all,* and he then says, publicly —

> Mrs. Wells had written asking him to make an ample, prompt and

> complete apology for what he had said in his speech at Sale about Mr. Wells's opinions as expressed in his works on the subject of marriage under Socialism. He (Mr. Joynson-Hicks) would be the last person in the world to refuse an apology to a lady if he had done or said anything that was wrong. He should feel exceedingly annoyed if he had done anyone an injustice, a Socialist or anyone else. *He had therefore gone more deeply into these writings.* Now he had not read Mr. Wells's book, but he took his quotation from a statement in the *Times* in a review of Mr. Wells's book a year ago. If it was wrong he would make a most ample apology, but he had not seen the *Times* contradicted. Mr. Joynson-Hicks then quoted the *Times* criticism to the effect that "according to Mr. Wells" free love was to be the essence of the new social contract.
>
> Manchester Courier, 17th October, 1907

This notice was, as a matter of fact, contradicted at once, and the contradiction with a characteristic meagre word of apology (it was at the height of the Book War), published in the *Times* literary supplement a fortnight later. It is all apparently that Mr. Joynson-Hicks had to go upon in making his preposterous charge.

With regard to his second point: -

> Mr. Joynson-Hicks said that those who had studied Socialism knew that it was also of the very essence of it that all Ten Commandments should be swept away, and he quoted from Mr. Wells's book, "Socialism and the Family," that "not only must land and the means of production be liberated, but women and children just as men and things must cease to be owned."
>
> Manchester Courier, 17th October 1907.

Now this occurs in an explanation that the Socialist regards a woman as a citizen equally as with a man, and that he repudiates, as I suppose Mr Joynson-Hicks would repudiate, the old patriarchal idea of the family in which wife or wives and children were all slaves owned by the man. (Or are we to understand that the Conservatives stand for woman and child slavery.) But Mr. Joynson-Hicks cuts off this mean little scrap to make his audience believe that I would do away with all family faith and family union.

As a matter of fact, the opinions Mr. Joynson-Hicks puts upon me are almost diametrically opposed to those I advocate, as everyone may see who will consult my articles in the Grand Magazine (more particularly that in the October issue.)

But consider, sir, the reckless zeal this incident displays, the childish unveracity with which Mr. Joynson-Hicks insults the native intelligence of Lancashire.

He still has to apologize. Yours, etc.,

H.G. Wells

---

[1] The offending pamphlet was written for an election campaign in Lancaster, where Joynson-Hicks was standing as a Tory. His agent, J. H. Bottomley, had written the pamphlet. Wells responded to Joynson-Hicks and Bottomley in this newspaper, 23 October 1907, 'Anti-Socialist Campaign: Mr. H. G. Wells Denounces Methods Adopted', p. 4.

706. To the Editor, *Manchester Courier*[1]

PLS

[Spade House
Sandgate, Kent] October 22, 1907

Sir, – I am gratified to find Mr. J. H. Bottomley coming into this discussion of my opinions of the relations between Socialism and the family because I have a bone to pick with him as well as Mr. Joynson-Hicks. He is the author of an anti-Socialist pamphlet entitled, "Socialism, Atheism and Free Love," and published by the "St. Helens and Prescot Reporter," Limited, in which occurs this alleged quotaton from my works:

> Essentially the Socialist position is a denial of property in human beings; not only must land and the means of production be liberated, but women and children, just as men and things, must as men and things, must cease to be owned.
>
> *So, in future, it will be not my wife, or your wife, but our wife.*

Now it is a fact that the words italicized have been put into that by Mr. Bottomley. I never wrote them. It is a – what shall I say? – a gap in the truth so absolute that I do not see how even an anti-Socialist can evade this consequence. It is a forged quotation.

I must confess, that Mr. Bottomley made me feel more charitable to Mr.

Joynson-Hicks – who undertakes to tell an audience all I think and believe before he has read a line of my works on the strength of the sort of information Mr. Bottomley supplies. Apart from this issue there is little to answer to Mr. Bottomley's letter. No intelligent person who reads his letter through will consider the quotations he makes support Mr. Joynson-Hicks assertion that I advocate free love. It is manifest that I advocate marriage and fidelity. But I do think his method of dragging in the name of Oscar Wilde in this connection merits a word of comment. In the first place he quotes a passage from my article in the "Fortnightly Review" for November, 1906, in which I recommend a paper by Wilde as putting the attitude of the artist towards Socialism – not, you perceive, the Socialist attitude, but the attitude of the artist towards Socialism – quite admirably. Subsequently I re-read Wilde's article. I found much to alter my first impression, and cut out that paragraph when I reprinted that article in my "Socialism and the Family." And Mr. Bottomley thinks your readers such fools that they are going to hold me responsible for the very words that made me withdraw my recommendation. -

Yours, etc., H. G. Wells

---

[1] The *Manchester Courier* probably commanded a higher circulation in the areas where the Bottomley pamphlet had been distributed. Wells monitored this paper and its contents very closely. In this letter, published on 24 October 1907, and entitled, 'Mr. H.G. Wells and Family Life', Wells continues his discussion of the Bottomley pamphlet.

707. To William Joynson-Hicks

Illinois, Handwritten copy[1]

[Spade House
Sandgate, Kent] 23rd October 1907

Private (2 encs.)

Dear Sir,

Yes. It is well I think you should read me. Quite respectable people on your side do. I enclose copies of two letters, one I have just sent to the Spectator re the article of last Saturday, & one with regard to your friend Bottomley & his new & improved method of controverting Socialism by <u>forged</u> quotation. I shall be glad if you will read my <u>Anticipations</u> which interested

Mr. Balfour very much, and my Future in America inter alia. I think that when you have looked through these books, you will see you do your country & your side no service by running about the country representing me as a nasty-minded advocate of promiscuous copulation. You force me to throw every scrap of influence I can command into the scale against you and you estrange the decent minded people on your side. You do me no good of course for some mud sticks when mud is thrown. And frankly is this the way any man should treat another, whether it helps him or not?

Yours very sincerely,
H.G.W.

[1] The handwritten copy was not made by the principals in the matter – perhaps a fair copy by H. Horsnell.

708. To the Editor, *Lancashire Daily Post*[1]

PLS

Spade House
Sandgate, Kent 23rd October 1907

Sir, – From a paragraph that reaches me from your columns I gather that you object to my speaking of a certain type of anti-Socialist writer as a "liar" and of the campaign as "lying". These are, I admit, vigorous words, but can you suggest anything more suitable for the following passage. It is put in inverted commas, and over my signature in the current "monthly pamphlet" of the Birkenhead Workingman's Conservative Association, and it is also used in a pamphlet entitled Socialism, Atheism, and Free Love, by J.H. Bottomley and published by the St. Helens and Prescot Reporter, Limited.

> "Essentially the Socialist position is a denial of property in human beings; not only must land and its means of production be liberated, but women and children, just as men and things, must cease to be owned. *So in fuure it will be not my wife or your wife, but our wife.*"

I italicize the last sentence. These words are pure invention. What else can you call it?

Yours, etc.,
H.G. Wells

[1] Wells and the provincial newspapers were not done with each other. This brief letter appeared the next day, under the title, 'Mr. Wells and His Critics', p. 4. This same letter also appeared in the *Bristol Daily Mercury*, 25 October 1907. That editor remarked, 'We sympathise entirely with Mr. Wells and consider that he is quite entitled to call a spade a spade.' On the same page a report of a speech given by Mrs. Philip Snowden, who represented Blackburn in Parliament, was printed under the title 'Socialist and free Love', which repudiated the newspaper attacks on Wells, herself, and other Socialists. This speech was greeted with very loud applause.

709. To the Editor, *Spectator*[1]

PLS

Spade House
Sandgate, Kent

[between 21 and 24 October 1907]

Sir, – My attention has been called to your article on "Socialism and Sex Relations" in your issue of October 19th, in which you say -

> "For example, we find Mr. Wells, in his novel, making free love the dominant principle for the regulation of sexual ties in his regenerated State.The romantic difficulty as to which of the two lovers of the heroine is to be the happy man is solved by their both being accepted, Polyandry is 'the way out' in this case, as polygamy might be in another."

I know you will do me the justice to refer to that book again, and tell your readers whether or no you find any intimation that sexual relations occur between these two people to justify your use of the words "polygamy" and "polyandry" in this connexion; whether, in fact, there is anything more that what is understood among that large section of public which does not read Plato as "Platonic love." *Honi soit qui mal y pense.* You read more into the book than is there. There is nothing dishonourable nor dishonouring among these people; whatever is dishonourable is not there. On the other hand you do find this passage set at the end in the fullest anticipation of such a reading as that in your article.-

> I felt a subtle embarrassment in putting this question that perplexed me. And yet it seemed so material to me I had to put it.

'And did you—?' I asked. 'Were you – lovers?'
His eyebrows rose.
'Of course,' – 'But your wife-?'
It was manifest that he did not understand me.
I hesitated still more. I was perplexed by a conviction of baseness.
'But-' I began 'You remained lovers?' – 'Yes.'
I had grave doubts if I understood him. Or he me.
I made a still more courageous attempt.
'And had Nettie no other lovers?' -
' A beautiful woman like that! I know not how many loved beauty in her, nor what she found in others. But we four from that time were very close, you understand, we were friends, we were helpers, personal lovers in a world of lovers.' 'Four?' – 'There was Verrall.'

Then suddenly it came to me that the thoughts that stirred in my mind, the coarse jealousies of my old world were over and done for these more finely living souls.'

I trust to the traditions of fair play that have always distinguished the Spectator for a proper acknowledgement from you upon this point, and for the publication of this letter in full.

But even could your assertions be substantiated, the fact still remains that "In the Days of the Comet" represents, as *I wrote in that book, carefully and deliberately to prevent this misunderstanding*, "transfigured people – beautiful and noble people, like the people one sees in great pictures, like the gods of noble sculpture, they had no nearer fellowship than these to men."

"In the Days of the Comet" is no more a Socialist Utopia than the Velasquez "Venus" in the National Gallery is a Spanish Catholic's idea of a suitable costume for a young lady. It never was intended to be a Socialist Utopia, as these disavowals I quoted show. It is no more creditable or discreditable to the Socialist movement than the poetry of Herrick or the works of Dean Swift or the Rev. Lawrence Sterne are to the established Church.

May I add that if Miss Florence Farr represents the Socialist attitude toward prostitution, then, by the same method of reasoning, belief in Christianity involves the advocacy of polygamy by virtue of Milton, and all Individualists are free-lovers because of the views of the late Mr. Auberon Herbert? One inference is as fair as the other, –[2]

I am, Sir, etc.,
H.G. Wells

[1] Another of Wells's responses to the attacks on him and Socialism. Printed in the issue of 26

October 1907, it was titled, 'Socialism and Sex Relations'. The *Spectator* had a wider circulation than many of the other places where Wells repudiated the libellous attacks on his work. In addition it was widely read in literary circles where Wells hoped to find a sympathetic audience.

[2] The editor of the *Spectator* professed delight in Wells's letter, was proud to print it in full, and to say they had mistaken 'the intention of his novel'. He went on to say, with tongue-in-cheek, 'One is, we supposed, stopped from arguing as to what in the post-comet world would have come of the emotional labyrinth described by Mr. Wells, but one knows, unfortunately, only too well how such things end in real life. In any case, we owe Mr. Wells an apology and that apology we offer in all sincerity. He is the best exponent of the meaning of his own novel, and we have no right and no wish to assert the contrary.' Other letters on the subject were also printed in the *Spectator*. This entire issue was a part of a year long debate throughout the press of the United Kingdom on the meaning of the move toward Socialism which was so widely perceived. The issue needs discussion as a context in English history. It may also be worth noting that Wells and his book were being given, relatively free, large amounts of publicity. Where Wells drew the line on this is when those who commented did so through the use of misquotation, creative use of quotation marks, and attribution to him of words and ideas he did not hold.

710. To the Editor, *Daily Express*[1]

PLS

Spade House
Sandgate, Kent

[*c.* 22 October 1907]

Sir, I do not believe that the leaders of the Conservative party can realise for a moment the quality of the methods of the present anti-Socialist campaign in the country. I find today in the second edition of a pamphlet by J.H. Bottomley, M.N.S., and published by the "St. Helen's and Prescot Reporter", Limited, the following alleged extract from my writing.

> "Essentially the Socialist position is a denial of property in human beings; not only must man and the means of production be liberated, but women and children, just as men and things must cease to be owned. So in the future it will not be my wife or your wife, but our wife."

The last sentence has been added by Mr. Bottomley! This, as Americans say, is probably the "limit", but similar things of only slightly less enormity are happening daily. I am sending this letter to every leading Conservative and Tariff Reform morning paper in London because I am curious to see just how many of them will countenance by their silence this type of libel, and how many are prepared to publicly disavow the support of Mr. Bottomley and his like.

H.G. Wells

---

[1] An identical letter, dated 22 October, was sent to the *Daily Chronicle*, who published it on 24 October 1907, p. 4. It also appeared in *The Times* on this same date, p. 9 and was printed, up to the last paragraph, except the first line, which appeared in italics, in the *Yorkshire Evening Post*, on the same date. (The Yorkshire paper also carried significant quotations from Mrs. Snowden's speech on women's suffrage on this date.) The letter was also sent to the *Morning Post* and the *Euston Morning News*. A version of the letter, describing the Jix libel, and ending as does this letter, appeared in *The New York Times*, 10 October 1907. This suggests that there may have been an earlier publication in Britain as well.The *Daily Express* also carried an announcement of a London meeting of the London Municipal Society, a special agency of the Primrose League, to make 'War Against Socialism' according to their headline. Other articles were reports of a speech by Lord Rosebery (1847–1929) on the evils of Socialism, which described a man whose Socialism allowed him to 'let his wife go', and Mrs. Philip Snowden's speech in Blackburn where she remarked in response to a query as to whether she believed in Socialism, that, 'The advocacy of Free Love would be simple justification for any attempt to retard the progress of Socialism'. Snowden later became the first Labour Chancellor of the Exchequer. His career is well described in Howard Spring's novel *Fame as the Spur*.

711. To the Editor, *Daily Chronicle*[1]

PLS

[Spade House
Sandgate, kent] October 22, 1907

I see that Mr. Bottomley has written to prove his good faith in the matter of the forged quotation of which I complained. The forgery, he states, was due to an accidental displacement of the inverted commas. The value of his good faith, however, may be better gauged by my restoring the immediate context of his quotation.

> "Essentially the Socialist position is a denial of property in human beings; not only must land and the other means of production be liberated (from the multitude of little monarchs among whom they are distributed, to the general injury and inconvenience), but women and children, just as men and things, must cease to be owned. (Socialism indeed proposes to abolish altogether the patriarchal family amidst whose disintegrating ruins we live, and to raise women to an equal

> citizenship with men. It proposes to give man no more property in a woman than a woman has in a man. To stupid people who cannot see the difference between a woman and a thing, the abolition of the private ownership of women takes the form of having "wives in common", and suggests the Corroboree. It is obviously nothing of the sort. It is the recognition in theory of what in many classes is already the fact – the practical equality of men and women in a civilised state. It is quite compatible with a marriage contract of far greater stringency than that recognized throughout Christendom to-day.")

He cuts out the words in brackets, and then adds the comment that so unfortunately slipped inside the inverted commas – 'So in the future it will not be my wife or your wife, but our wife'. Originally the pamphlet was a speech, and I think there can be little misapprehension in the mind of any intelligent person that Mr. Bottomley's audience took those words as mine and shouted "Shame!" and were deeply moved against me.

I rejoice to see a writer in the "Saturday Review" and one or two Conservative speakers in the country are already dissociating themselves from this school of foul tactics. I believe, as I said in my first letter of complaint, that prominent Conservatives have no conception of these, shall we say, 'excesses of zeal' on the part of their associates of the Tory Democrat Anti-Socialist type, and I am glad of this confirmation of my views.

H. G. Wells

---

[1] Printed in the issue of 31 October 1907, p. 4. under the heading 'Anti-Socialist Campaign'. An identical letter also appeared on 7 November 1907, p. 38, in the *New Age* under the title, 'Mr. H.G. Wells And An Anti-Socialist Pamphlet'. The letter was also printed in *The Times* 31 October 1907. There the letter was dated 29 October 1907 and Christendom was substituted for Christianity.

712. To the Editor, *Labour Leader*[1]

PLS

Spade House
Sandgate, Kent

23rd October, 1907

Sir, — I am sorry to trouble you again about passages in my work, but the following quotation appears in the current "monthly pamphlet" of the Working

Men's Conservative Association, and in a pamphlet called Socialism, Atheism, and Free Love by J. H. Bottomley, and published by the St. Helens and Prescot Reporter, Limited: -

> "Essentially the Socialist postion
> is a denial of property in human
> beings; not only must land and the
> means of production be liberated,
> but women and children, just as men
> and things, must cease to be owned.
> *So in future it will be not my wife*
> *or your wife, but our wife.*
> H.G. Wells

The line in italics has been added! It is a simple bold lie. I am consulting my solicitor in the matter to see what remedy one has against a forged quotation, but in the meanwhile will comrades in the localities affected note the state of affairs.

H. G. Wells

[1] This letter was headed 'A Simple Bold Lie'. The newspaper urged readers who had information about the issue of 'free love' and Wells's published work, especially 'alleged quotations' to send the information to Wells. The names of printers, publishers and speakers were asked for as well. The notice, published with this letter on 1 November 1907, p. 298 of the paper, ended with: 'Any evidence from local booksellers or librarians tending to prove damages through the creation of a predjudice against his books will also be of the utmost use.' An identical letter also appeared in the issue of 31 October 1907, p. 19, of *The New Age*, under the title, "Mr. Wells and Free Love'. The same letter, and the same editorial emendation also appeared in *Justice*, 2 November 1907, p. 9. under the title 'Anti-Socialist Misrepresentation'.

713. To Captain Sykes[1]

Illinois, TL

SPADE HOUSE
SANDGATE, KENT October 24th, 1907

My dear Captain Sykes,

I need hardly say how highly I appreciate your admirable paper on the development of the countryside. It marches with all my ideas and I am sure with the ideas of every modern Socialist. It is remarkable how closely you and I are in accord, for not only upon this issue but upon that of Tariff Reform, that is to say a scientific State control of trade, we are in principle agreed. But once it comes from principle to politics I am afraid the mental quality of some of your fellow Conservatives comes between us. Frankly I distrust your party. A party that has no regard for the truth is going to display no great regard for the public welfare in framing a tariff. Well, the post before the one that brought me your letter brought me a bale of troublesome communications referring to the activities of a couple of speakers on your side in the Manchester district. They are engaged in what they call an Anti-Socialist campaign, and the vehement lying about myself appears to be an integral part of that campaign. They declare that I advocate "free love" which is absolutely untrue, and they support their case by forged quotation. I am forced at last to set aside my proper work in order to get up evidence for an action for libel. Apparently these outrages are part of an organized filth-throwing through which these gentlemen hope to advance (I don't quite see how) the cause of Tariff Reform. May I suggest that you and I have so much in common, you should do something to put your party straight in this matter with a public repudiation of these attacks.

Let me repeat my warm approval of your essay. As I have said before in writing to you, I hope very much that you will presently be able to state your opinions from the floor of the House of Commons. Please make any public use you like of this letter, provided you use it as a whole.

Very sincerely yours,

---

[1] Sykes is an otherwise unknown Tory who wrote to Wells.

714. To the Editor, *The Standard*[1]

PLS

Reform Club
Pall Mall, S.W.

[*c.* 26 October 1907]

Sir, – You publish in your issue of to-day (Saturday) a letter, signed H.R.S., in which I am directly challenged to state what I do mean about marriage and the family, and why Mr. Bottomley's false quotation is a libel. In view of this challenge, you will, perhaps, do me the favour of publishing this present letter in full. I make the request with some diffidence, since the pressure on your space prevented you from publishing my flat contradiction to the views you ascribed to me in your issue of the 10th.

In the first place, then, Mr. Bottomley's statement was a libel (for which H.R.S. will note he has still to express his regret) because it was grossly untrue and injurious. He said I expressed offensive ideas, whereas I did nothing of the sort.

In the second place, I do not and I never have proposed to abolish marriage, to separate parents from their children, or to arrange things upon some novel and inconceivable plan, in which "children will have no father and no mother belonging to them". But I do assert that a woman should be a citizen and a responsible person equally with a man, and that a wife is not to be regarded as her husband's "private property" any more than he is hers. In the barbaric past wives were slaves; until quite recently a husband might beat or indecently assault his wife with impunity, and all her property was his. Well, I deny that she is his own in that sense at all. Wives, I declare, cannot be private property, and equally do I deny that there can be private propery in children. I deny the right of either father or mother to under-feed, under-educate, or beat causelessly. Their children are not their own to do what they like with. I hold that their children are a trust they hold for the nation and humanity, that their children are also the nation's children, and that with double ownership necessarily cuts both ways. The parents are responsible to the State for the culture of their children, and, conversely, the State is also responsible to the parents for the support of their children. That millions of children should be growing up in this country in dirt and disease, also without proper nourishment or exercise or training, is a thing for which I hold the State responsible far more than the parents. And hence I get to the advocacy of free education, of free meals, of State aid of all sorts, in support of the home and the family, not as a charity, but as a right and patriotic thing.

This is what I set out in my "Socialism and the Family" and in my "New Worlds For Old", and, it is, I believe, the position of nearly all prominent modern Socialists. By playing upon the word "property," by clipping quotations and forging additions, it may be possible to produce in careless and nasty minds the delusion that I suggest "wives in common." I submit it is an outrageous method of political controversy, and one that must in the end hopelesly discredit the side that employs it. I believe, however, that you will see your way to repudiating these extreme and dishonourable expedients.

And while I am replying to this challenge you published, may I call the attention of H.R.S., and any other of your readers who are interested, to an apology in this week's "Spectator" upon the particular point arising out of my

"In The Days of the Comet", to which you referred in your issue of October 10, and against which I protested in the letter for which you could not find space?

I trust in the sense of fair play which always distinguished The Standard for the publication of this communication unabridged.

I am, Sir, your most obedient servant,

H. G. Wells

---

[1] Wells continued to monitor his treatment in the press as the fall-out from the anti-Socialist campaign and the attack on him continued. This piece was published in *The Standard* of 28 October 1907. The letter, with the exception of the first two paragraphs, one line of the next, and the last two paragraphs, minus the line just previous to this cut, also appeared in the *Yorkshire Evening Post*, 28 October 1907.

715. To the Editor, *The Times*[1]

PLS

Spade House
Sandgate, Kent

Oct. 29 [1907]

Sir, – I see that Mr. Bottomley has written to you to show his good faith in the matter of the forged quotation of which I complained. The forgery, he states, was due to the accidental displacement of the inverted commas. The value of his good faith, however, may be better gauged by my restoring the immediate context of his quotation :-

"Essentially the Socialist position is a denial of property in human beings; not only must land and the means of production be [liberated from the multitude of little monarchs among whom they are distributed to the general injury and inconvenience] , but women and children, just as men and things, must cease to be owned. [Socialism indeed proposes to abolish the patriarchal family amidst whose disintegrating ruins we live, and to raise women to an equal citizenship to men. It proposes to give a man no more property in a woman than a woman has in a man. To stupid people who cannot see the difference between a woman and a thing, the abolition of the private ownership of women takes the form of having 'wives in common', and suggests the Corroboree. It is obviously nothing of this sort. It is the recognition in theory of what in many classes is already the fact – the practical equality of men and women in a civilized state. It is quite compatible with a marriage contract of far greater stringency than that recognized throughout Christendom today.]

He cuts out the words in brackets, and then adds that comment that so unfortunately slipped inside the inverted commas – "So in the future, it will not be my wife, or your wife, but our wife." Originally the pamphlet was a speech, and I think there can be little misapprehension in the mind of any intelligent person that Mr. Bottomley's audience took those words as mine and shouted "Shame!" and were deeply moved against me.

I rejoice to see a writer in the *Saturday Review* and one or two Conservative speakers in the country are already disassociating themselves from this school of foul tactics. I believe, as I said in my letter of complaint, that prominent Conservatives have no conception of these shall we say "excesses of zeal" on the part of their associates of the Tory-Democratic Anti-Socialist type, and I am glad of this confirmation of my view.

Very sincerely yours,
H. G. Wells

---

[1] This letter appeared in *The Times* and the *Daily Chronicle* 31 October 1907. With publication of his responses to Bottomley in *The Times* and the other leading newspapers in the country, that part of the Anti-Socialist campaign directed towards Wells began to die down. It continued in the press in a general way for another month or so.

716. To Graham Wallas

LSE, ALS

Spade House
Sandgate

Oct. 31. 07.

My dear Wallas,

You promised (noble man!) to look through this – Shaw & Webb have seen all that concern them. It is as you well remember partly a propaganda & partly an adherent-educating book.

When is the Prolegomena coming.

Yours ever,
H.G.[1]

---

[1] Although it is probably the manuscript of *New Worlds for Old* which Wells is sending, it might be an earlier draft of *First and Last Things*. Wallas's book was published in 1908 under the title, *Human Nature in Politics*.

717. To the Editor, *Labour Leader*[1]

PLS

[Spade House
Sandgate, Kent] [*c.* 26-7 October 1907][2]

Newton-le-Willows November 5, 1907

Sir, – I see Mr. H.G. Wells calls attention to an error in my pamphlet on "Socialism, Atheism, and Free Love". He quotes the second edition (the only one where the mistake occurs, out of fifteen), and it has been explained locally by the printer, who takes the responsibility. In re-setting, a quotation mark got one line below where it ought to have appeared, and where it has been printed in most of the fifty thousand copies issued. I sent a copy of two of the editions to Mr. Wells, with an explanatory letter, and am amazed he has not the courtesy and manliness to acknowledge that. I proved there had been no attempt to make him appear as saying more than he did. – I am, sir, your obedient servant,

J. H. Bottomley
Conservative Agent

[*Wells to the editor*][3]

He cuts out the words I have put in brackets, and then adds the comment that so unfortunately slipped inside the inverted commas: 'So in the future it will be not my wife or your wife but our wife.'

Originally the pamphlet was a speech, and I think there can be little misapprehension in the mind of any intelligent person that Mr. Bottomley's audience took those words to be mine, and shouted, "Shame!" and were deeply moved against me.

I rejoice to see a writer in the 'Saturday Review' and one or two Conservative speakers in the country already disassociating themselves from this school of foul tactics. I believe, as I said in my first letter of complaint, that prominent Conservatives have no conception of these, shall we say, "extensions of zeal" on the part of their associates of the Tory-Democratic Anti-Socialist type, and I am glad of this confirmation of my view.

---

[1] After Bottomley's reply, Wells gave a full account of the context of the questioned quotation, which was not printed in the paper, The reply then went on with these and several continuing paragraphs. The reply appeared in the issue of 8 November 1907, p. 314, under the title, 'Mr. H.G. Wells and Socialism?'.

[2] A problem in this story is that letters were published when there was space and not necessarily in the order of their composition. I have followed the publication sequence rather than the dates of composition.
[3] The material printed is, of course, essentially the same material as the latter part of his letters to the *Daily Chronicle* of 31 October, and *The New Age* of 7 November 1907 as well as his letter to *The Times* of 31 October.

718. To the Editor, *Daily Chronicle* or *Labour Leader*[1]

Illinois, TL

Spade House
Sandgate, Kent

PRIVATE 31st October 1907

Dear Sir,

I do not know if Mr. Bottomley will reply to my letter in your current issue with his story of the dropped inverted commas. If so I think the enclosed will give you the material for a squashing footnote that ought to finish up this business – and Mr. Bottomley.

In a way this affair has been a bore, but I think the incident has been very useful in heartening the local speakers against Bottomleyism and discrediting the Anti-Socialist propaganda.

Yours very truly

[1] Possibly the former, probably the latter, although the actual addressee is not known.

719. Hamilton Fyfe to H.G. Wells

Boston, ALS

"The Daily Mail"
3, Carmelite House
Tallis Street
London, E.C.

27th October, 1907

My dear Wells,[1]

I want you, if you will, to contribute an article to a series I am arranging for the "Daily Mail" on "What Socialists Want". The articles will be by Ramsay MacDonald, George Bernard Shaw, Philip Snowden, Walter Crane, George Barnes, and others.[2]

The special branch of the subject I would suggest for you is, "Does Socialism Want to Change Human Nature?" with special reference to the idea which so many people have that every man's interest and every woman's is bound up with his or her family; that they are anxious to do the best they can for their sons and daughers, and that they don't care about anything or anybody else. This is a view which needs to be combated, and I am sure you would deal with it in a most interesting way.

I hope you will do this.The series would be incomplete without an article from you. Of course, the "Mail" intends to pay.

Believe me yours ever
H. Hamilton Fyfe

[*Wells comments:*]

I've said I'm interested but busy & that you'll communicate. I will do it for £30 (including America), but I'm not keen.

[1] This letter to Wells is included as Wells's marginal comments are useful, in demonstrating how he dealt with much of his smaller business correspondence.

[2] If Wells wrote the piece, I have not seen it.

720. To William Joynson-Hicks

Illinois, ALS

Spade House
Sandgate [*in another hand:* Oct. 28, 07]

Dear Mr. J.H.

May I remind you that on ———, according to the Daily Dispatch, you said;

Quote from Daily Disptach

I have placed in your hands the necessary documents & references for you to see that your statements were incorrect. I would also call your attention to the current issue of the Spectator & to Standard for today's date. I shall be very glad now to hear from you what course you mean to take with regard to these misstatements. Are you going to behave like a peer of the Bottomley type or are you going to make a fair & honourable & public retraction of these offensive charges you launched at me? It seems to me that the latter course is the only one open to a gentleman.

Very sincerely yours,
H. G. Wells

721. To the Editor, *The Times*

PLS

[London] [*c.* 29 October 1907]

To the Editor of The Times[1]

Sir, – The Prime Minister has consented to receive during next month a deputation from the following dramatic authors on the subject of the censorship of plays. In the meantime may these authors, through your columns, enter a formal protest against this office, which was instituted for political, and not for the so-called moral ends to which it is perverted – an office autocratic in procedure, opposed to the spirit of the Constitution, contrary to common justice and to common sense?

They protest against the power lodged in the hands of a single official – who judges without a public hearing and against whose dictum there is no appeal – to cast a slur, on the good name and destroy the means of livelihood of any member of an honourable calling.

They assert that the censorship has not been exercised in the interests of morality, but has tended to lower the dramatic tone by appearing to relieve the public of the duty of moral judgment.

They ask to be freed from the menace hanging over every dramatist of having his work and the proceeds of his work destroyed at a pen's stroke by the arbitrary action of a single official neither responsible to Parliament nor amenable to law.

They ask that their art be placed on the same footing as every other art.

They ask that they themselves be placed in the position enjoyed under the law by every other citizen.

To these ends they claim that the licensing of plays shall be abolished. The public is already sufficiently assured against managerial misconduct by the present yearly licensing of theatres, which remains untouched by the measure of justice here demanded.

[*Seventy-two names are appended to the letter.*]

---

[1] An issue of importance to writers was the problem of censorship, which was most noticeable in the theatre. A letter, signed by seventy-two authors and playwrights, including Wells, appeared in *The Times* on 29 October 1908 calling for an end to the Lord Chancellor's work in censorship. A long article 'From a Correspondent' surveying the history of recent censorship was printed along with the article. The plays which focussed the issue were Edward Garnett's play, *The Breaking Point* and Granville Barker's *Waste*. The latter play was not produced in London until the 1980s. A reading of the play for copyright purposes was undertaken by Catherine and Wells, Bernard and Charlotte Shaw, and Beatrice and Sidney Webb as well as other prominent individuals of the left in the autumn of 1907.

722. To the Editor, *The Standard*[1]

PLS

Spade House
Sandgate. Kent

October 31, 1907

Sir, – The letter in your issue of October 29, signed "Verax", has only just reached me (October 31) through my press cutting agency. Although above that letter you challenged me for a reply, you omitted to send me a copy of your issue containing it, and were it not for Messrs. Durrant, I might have missed seeing it altogether. In his letter "Verax" repeated the charges for which the "Spectator" has so honourably apologized, and I suppose that once more I must set myself to refute these charges. You give that attack extreme prominence, you endorse with the heading of "A Pertinent Reply", and I must ask you to give my reply to it an equal prominence and to print it in full. Then first, I have to deal with black untruths.

"Verax" says:

> All that he has written about the relations between the sexes and the bond of marriage, and the ties of family under a Socialist *regime* condemns him as an advocate of promiscuous sexual intercourse, and of the abolition of the contract of marriage and the responsibility of parents in anything like their present form. Many quotations have been made by writers in the present anti-Socialist controversy from serious works in which Mr. Wells professes to speak for his particular school of Socialism, and, analyze them as you will, they all are evidence against him.

Now, it is difficult to make any reply to that but one; that it is absolutely untrue. It flies in the face of fact. On the bookstalls, for example, at the present moment lies my "Socialism and the Family," with these words upon its cover, words that the contents abundantly justify, as anyone who reads it will agree: In this booklet Mr. Wells refutes the charge that Socialism tends to free love and states pretty completely the real attitude of modern Socialism to family life. In that booklet I state in the most unambiguous manner the Socialist case *for* marriage. Next he says:

> 'In the Days of the Comet" was meant to describe the advent of Socialism, and to give an attractive picture of the realations between the sexes in the new society.'

That also is absolutely untrue. Then "Verax" writes:

> 'I have set myself to write the story of the Great Change', Mr. Wells says in the first lines of the book, but in succeeding chapters he speaks of the Socialist movement, of the part played by Socialist leaders in "destroying" the domination of capitalism, and he even mentions the "Clarion" by name. There is not the smallest doubt

> about the author's intention, and he must be held responsible for the ideas the book sets forth.

This is the flat reverse of the truth. The book begins with a prologue in italics. "I saw a grey-haired man . . . sitting at a table and writing", it runs, and there is the clearest and most unambiguous dissociation of myself from the person who is supposed to tell this story. It is he who wrote, "I will tell the story of the Great Change". Then, with an air of absolute superiority and detachment, this old man tells the story of his youth, how he was an infidel and an evil-passioned, under-bred wretch – an"ill-conditioned, squalidly-bred lad", the author calls him in an interruption of the narrative (p. 41.) No doubt, to begin with, this man was a revolutionary Socialist of a now fast vanishing type. The Great Change altered all that. After the Great Change, Socialism, like war and mindless passion, vanishes from the story.These things are emphasized, and even underlined, and then "Verax" makes the above statement.

After some preliminary flourishes in the name of fact, "Verax" proceeds to give your readers a pretended summary of the story, a summary which is, as a matter of fact, a gross caricature. He cannot even, you will note, count the characters. He makes this statement:

> Running through the story is a love theme – the love of a woman for two (or was it four?) – and the love of a man for two women. There is no mistake about the nature of these loves; there is nothing platonic about them. They are just the primeval passion of male and female.

Now, not only is this not true, not only is this wanton perversion and degradation of the meaning of my book done without positive support in its pages, but it is done in the face of a calculated and deliberate statement to the contrary. Because, indeed, I foresaw "Verax" so far as his nature goes, even if I failed to anticipate his mental inpenetrability. I said to myself, if you will forgive me for putting it so plainly, "There are nasty-minded people in the world to whom love has only one meaning, and that a disgusting one. I will make it so clear that my meaning is not a disgusting one that even the very nastiest of them will be arrested and be made to realise that it his own dirt that has got into his eyes." And accordingly I wrote this passage:

> I felt a subtle embarrassment in putting the question which perplexed me. And yet it seemed so material to me I had to put it.
>
> "And did you —?" I asked. "Were you – lovers?"
>
> His eyebrows rose. "Of course."

> "But your wife —?"
> It was manifest he did not understand me. I hesitated still more. I was perplexed by a conviction of baseness.
> "But— " I began. "You remained lovers?"
> "Yes."
> I had grave doubts I understand him. Or he me...I made a still more courageous attempt.
> "And had Nettie no other lovers?"
> "A beautiful woman like that! I know not how many loved beauty in her, nor what she found in others. But we four from that time on were very close, you understand, we were friends, lovers, personal lovers in a world of lovers."
> "Four?"
> "There was Verrall."
> Then suddenly it came to me that the thoughts that stirred in my mind were sinister and base, that the queer suspicions, the coarseness and coarse jealousies of my old world, were over and done for these more finely living souls.

And a little further on I wrote:

> "How harshly I stood out among these fine, perfected things. I had a moment of rebellious detestation. I want to get out of all this. After all, this wasn't my style. I wanted intensely to say something that would bring him down a peg, make sure, as it were, of my suspicions by launching an offensive accusation."

I imagined that intimation of *Honi Soit Qui mal y Pense* " would stop anyone, but it could not I see, stop "Verax". "Nobody after reading his "In The Days of the Comet" will venture to doubt that its author has not advocated "free love."

He says this immediately after quoting a passage in which I distinctly state that Anna and the teller of the story were married by the "Council of our Group". What can you do with such methods of controversy?

It is absolutely untrue that the story of "In the Days of the Comet" is indecent or immoral, except to exceptionally foul-minded people. And to foul-minded people everything is indecent. Nothing in this world is pure enough for them. But if "In The Days of the Comet"is indecent and immoral, the exhortaton, "Love all men" is equally indecent and immoral. It is just as indecent as, and no more than, the word "Love".

But even were this communistic state I present, of a "world of lovers" in which people are not jealous nor jealously restrained from friendship and free movement, in any sense what "Verax" pretends it to be, the idea remains that it is not, the fact is that it is not, as I reiterate again and again in the book, a Socialist Utopia. It is a dream of a changed humanity. As I wrote in my book, as with any desire to be charitable, I cannot but believe "Verax", in his hunt for something he might touch and turn to filth against me must have read, these people were "transfigured people – beautiful and noble people, like the people one sees in great sculpture, but they had no nearer fellowship than those to men".

So that, firstly, the book is not indecent or immoral, and, secondly, if it were indecent and immoral, it still has nothing to do with Socialism generally, or the Socialism I advocate personally, and which I have been at great pains to set forth clearly and simply in my "Socialism and the Family," my "Modern Utopia" and my "New Worlds for Old."

Now, Sir, may I finally address a word to you? You printed the letter of "Verax", with commendations and endorsements. You then revived charges which your anti-Socialist specialist at least should have known had already been raised and rebutted in the "Times" and in the "Spectator", and which are flagrantly opposed to the tenor of my writings. In so large an enterprise as the conduct of The Standard, it is quite possible to be ill-advised upon the question of detail. The man who has never made a mistake has never made anything. Has that not happened to you in this case, and do you not owe me, in addition to the publication of this letter, some word of apology?[2]

I am, Sir, your obedient servant,

H.G. Wells

---

[1] As the campaign for and against Socialism increased in fervour, those newspapers which had attempted to sustain the charges against Wells found themselves the recipients of some very strong letters from him. He took the opportunity not only to correct the errors but also to provide publicity for his work. Such a letter is this second letter to *The Standard*, which appeared on 1 November 1907, under the heading 'Mr. Wells on His Defence', pp. 7–8.

[2] This is one of the longest letters written by Wells. It appears on pages 7 and 8 of the newspaper, and consists of a complete column on the first page, followed by three inches more of copy on the second, set in very small type.

723. To the Editor, *Lancashire Daily Post*[1]

PLS

Spade House
Sandgate, Kent

Nov. 4th, 1907

Sir, – I see that Mr. Bottomley has written to you to prove his good faith in the masses of inaccurate quotation of which I complained. The value of his good faith, however, may be better gauged by my recording the immediate context of his quotation:

"Essentially the Socialist position is a denial of property in human beings; not only must land and the means of production be liberated (from the multitude of little monarchs among whom they are distributed, to the general injury and inconvenience), but women and children, just as men and things must cease to be owned. (Socialism, indeed, proposes to abolish altogether the patriarchal family amidst whose disintegrating ruins we live, and to raise women to an equal citizenship with men. It proposes to give a man no more property in a woman than a woman has in a man. To stupid people who cannot see the difference between a woman and a thing, the abolition of the private ownership of women takes the form of "wives in common", and suggests the Corroboree. It is obviously nothing of the sort. It is the recognition in theory of what in many classes is already the fact – the practical equality of men and women in a civilized state. It is quite compatible with a marriage contract of far greater stringency than that recognized throughout Christendom today.)"

He cuts out the words I have put in brackets[2] then adds the comment that so unfortunately slipped inside the inverted commas, "So in future it will not be my wife, or your wife, but our wife." Obviously the pamphlet was a speech, and I think there can be little misapprehension in the mind of any intelligent person that Mr. Bottomley's audience took these words as mine and shouted "Shame!" and were deeply moved against me.

I rejoice to see a writer in the "Saturday Review", and one or two Conservative speakers in the country are already dissociating themselves from this school of foul tactics. I believe, as I said in my first letter of complaint, that prominent Conservatives have no conception of these, shall we say, "excesses of zeal"? on the part of their associates of the Tory-Democrat Anti-Socialist type, and I am glad of this confirmation of my view.

Yours, etc.,

H. G. Wells

[1] Wells continued to update the record as his opponents wrote letters, or provided explanations or excuses for their activities. This letter to an important northern newspaper was published on 5 November 1907, p. 4, under the title, "Mr. Wells and Mr. Bottomley". The letter shares strong affinities with his responses to *The Labour Leader, Daily Chronicle* and *New Age* of this same week. Most people who read newspapers (mainly the middle class) are likely to have read only one. It was therefore important that Wells issued his refutations in each newspaper as the story broke there. The majority of the book-buying public were also members of the middle class and people Wells hoped to win over to the Socialist cause. It has been suggested to me that the official formation of a Labour Party may have helped bring on these attacks as well.
[2] There are parentheses in the text, as here.

724. To the Editor, *The Standard*[1]

PLS

Spade House
Sandgate, Kent

November 5, 1907

Sir, – I see Mr. Bottomley has written to you again, and those who have read the previous correspondence about his pamphlet will be quite prepared to hear that he writes to make another misstatement in his entirely hopeless struggle against the truth of this case. He implies that I write to the Press to expose his misquotations after he has sent me a copy of the pamphlet he sent me proved no good faith; it merely cleared up the minor fact of misplaced quotation marks. The fact remains, and it will remain, although Mr. Bottomley continues to shower insults on me to the end of his days, that he took a quotation from my "Socialism and the Family", cut off certain words at the end, and added words with a diametrically opposite meaning.

For that trick he offers no apology, he simply roots about for some new possibilities of misrepresentation. His last feat in that direction is to couple my name in an ambiguous manner with that of the late Oscar Wilde, and to say that I "quote his views (unspecified) with approval" because I wrote in the "Fortnightly Review" that Wilde's "Soul of Man" was an admirable exposition of the attitude "of the artistic mind towards Socialism". Just think of the mental and moral quality of the man who can resort to that style of mud throwing!

Mr. Bottomley seeks to salve his self-respect among his associates by pretending that I am "furious" with him for this nasty attempt. No doubt he would like to have it on that footing. But one is not furious with Mr. Bottomley; at the worst, one is annoyed or disgusted. And I have written to the Press about Mr. Bottomley's feats of falsehood, not because I care a rap about Mr. Bottomley, but because I do want to make it clear to the Unionist gentlemen of the north of England just how victory is being organised by their agents.

I am, Sir, your obedient servant,

H. G. Wells

---

[1] The press continued to print Wells's correctives, but they gave little quarter in other ways. As an example, in the same issue, 7 November 1907, in which they printed another of his screeds, 'Mr. H.G. Wells and His Views', they also provided a very long exegesis of his book *New Worlds For Old*, with subheadings, 'Position of Mr. Wells', 'A Cure Worse Than the Disease', and 'Pigs Not to Be Shared'. The exegesis was continued on the next day as well. Letters of correction in such venues must have seemed of little use to Wells.

725. To Henry Newbolt

Hofstra, ACCS

Spade House
Sandgate
Nov. 28 07

Dear Newbolt

Bless you! Jane sends her best to Mrs. Newbolt.

Yours ever

H. G.

726. To Dr Saleeby

Illinois, AL copy[1]

Spade House
Sandgate
11. 30. 07

Dear Doctor Saleeby

What do you mean by the allusion to me in the Pall Mall Gazette for Nov. 28th?

On the face of it it seems stupid and ill-tempered. I have never written against marriage and as you ought to know – we have a number of friends in common – am quite happily married and with two jolly children. I don't think even the passion of the fluff preliminary of this new journalistic volume of yours quite excuses this breach of decent manners.

Yours very sincerely,
(signed) H. G. Wells

---

[1] Letter is a holograph copy, probably done by Horace Horsnell.

727. Ben C. Apps to H.G. Wells[1]

Dartford, Kent, ALS

(1 Albemarle Street,
London w. is crossed through) Dec. 2nd 1907

Dear Mr. Wells,

Perhaps you will pardon me for troubling you with this letter, but I have been much interested in reading some of your correspondence which has recently appeared in the London Press on the question of "Socialism". But I write first to explain who I am, as you may have difficulty in remembering after a lapse of so many years.

I had the privilege of being a fellow student of yours at the Midhurst Grammar School. I was one of the first Gilbert Hannan scholars when the school reopened in 1880. If I remember rightly you came some short time afterward & when I left at Xmas 1884 you were an assistant master. You may recall me by the fact that that I was chiefly known by the name of "Tubby" as I have a recollection of being caricatured as a "tub" in a sketch of yours which was exhibited in the School Room.

I have had a keen struggle since I left school in gaining a position. There is always a prejudice against the "poor" man, particularly if a profession is embraced. But I had no choice. My father was very very poor & I had to take what came my way. I became an office boy, but by keeping eyes & ears open I was able to take a position of responsibility & to pass the Institution Examination after a good deal of trouble to prove myself satisfactory to the Council. Of course I have always felt the difficulty of success for want of funds. The consequence is that one often feels disgusted with the world as it exists today & I sometimes think I must be of socialistic tendencies. In the desire to understand more of Socialism I thought I might be permitted to write you. You can doubtless tell me what is best to read or do to understand the true principles of Socialism.

I know you must be always very busy but I trust you will excuse me for encroaching on your time & thanking you in anticipation.

I am,

Yours very truly

Ben C. Apps

---

[1] Apps was a surveyor and land agent. His letter arrived in the wake of the immense amounts of London press notices and is given here as an example of the significance of the correspondence, as is the case with the previous letter in this collection.

728. To Mr Evans

Hofstra ALS

Spade House
Sandgate

[unknown date, but possibly late December 1907]

Dear Mr. Evans,

Will you run down here to lunch one day? Then I can explain to you what an entirely futile person I am to put anyone in the way of anything. I spin theories about conduct, & try to write novels & I have never done any practical social work in my life. There are trains to Shorncliffe (which is my best station) or Folkestone Central that will enable you to get here about 1:30. I shall be here nearly all January & I could meet any train.

Very sincerely yours

H.G. Wells

729. To 'Vernon Lee'

Colby, ALS

[Sandgate]

[sometime in 1907?]

My Dear Miss Paget,

Your letter just to hand. Here is a rather stolid note by way of reply. I did see your article in the Albany & for a time it made me quite featherheaded. You did somehow make it seem true mingling intoxicating praise with reality as Americans put liquors into innocent grape fruits. Your inscription of your book will give me another whirling time. I am really almost proud – no, I mean properly proud – of having got you.

Where are you fighting Pragmatists? I am a Pragmatist. I am going to send you, if you will forgive me (it is not too late to write & countermand) a typed M.S. on my metaphysical beliefs.[1] It is on thin paper (you will have to put an opaque white sheet of paper behind each page, but it is compact).

I do not know about your [*illegible word*] I have been very sorry to hear of your painful times & your illness. I wish I understood better.

I will tell Shaw

Yours ever,

H.G. Wells

We long to come to Florence but I am extravagant, times are hard & I shall have to stick here & grind resolutely until the autumn before I can afford a holiday.

---

[1] Probably an early version of his Credo, see letter 732. Paget's book may have been *Gospels of Anarchy* which appeared at the end of 1907.

730. To Sidney Low

Illinois, Typed Transcription

National Liberal Club
Whitehall Place

[Autumn 1907]

My dear Low.

Here I've just got a prelude to a new book on Socialism done, beauty of the Embankment by night, desolating shock of figures on seats, moral, when you, with <u>your</u> eyes for these vivid effects, hit on the same thing (yesterday's Morning Post). Well, I shall stick to what I've done, but I perceive it may be necessary to divide the world between us.[1]

Yours ever,

H.G.

[1] Wells's *New Worlds For Old* was about to be serialized, and also to appear as a book. Low was in process of writing a series entitled, 'The Discovery of England', which was appearing in the *Morning Post*. The two writers were working the same territory.

731. To Harold Monro[1]

Boston, ALS

Sandgate Oct. 28. 07

My Dear Monro,

I can't spare time to go anywhere before Christmas, so clearly I can't come to your Samurai Conference.[2] Here is a draft of a credo.

Yours ever,
H. G. Wells

[1] See letter 695.

[2] After the publication of *A Modern Utopia* in 1905, Samurai Societies sprang up in England. Wells's credo occurs in an earlier draft form in holograph, as well as a typescript: we print the typescript below.

732. To several addressees

Illinois, AL

Jenny. I want ten copies of this. Send with missing letter.

CREDO[1]

1. I believe that I possess a mind of limited capacity and an essential if sometimes only slight inaccuracy and that I am thereby debarred from any final knowledge, any knowledge of permanent and ultimate things.

2. I see the Universe in a state of flux, all Being as I conceive it is becoming.

3. In order to steady and determine my life, which otherwise remains aimless

and unsatisfactory, I declare that this ultimately incomprehensible Universe about me is systematic and not chaotic and that I and my will and the determinations I make, and likewise all other things are important to that scheme. I cannot prove this. I make this declaration as an Act of Faith.

4. I do not call this systematic quality in the Universe God, but I do not dispute its being called God. And I am often disposed to talk of it as God's Will or God's Purpose. I believe that this "God's Purpose" as many people would call it, works in and through me, and the more earnestly I think and seek out what is right in my mind and heart, the nearer am I at one with it, the better everything is. But I am unable to say or prove why this should be so.

5. I am disposed to believe and I do believe that my Ego is as it were derived from my species and detached from it to the end that I may gather experience and add to the increasing thought and acquisitions of the species. I believe that a species moves forward unconsciously to a consciousness of itself and to a collective being, and that love is an emotional realization of this collective being (however partial) and that right action is what forwards it. I am a Socialist because to me Socialism is a practical material aspect of this awakening through will of the conscious collective being of humanity.

6. My ideal of living is to live as fully as possible, to know and express as much as possible, to leave permanent results of my individual self behind me when my life ends. For me my master gift and passion is imaginative construction and especially in relation to the making for humanity of an ideal world-state. To that I seek to subordinate all my other gifts, powers and passions. But what other people should plan and seek for themselves I cannot say.

---

[1] Although it was not a formal letter, this credo in various forms was circulated among his friends for comment in 1907–8. This version is the last of several.

733. To the Editor, *North Devon Herald*[1]

PLS

Spade House
Sandgate, Kent

October 29, 1907

In your issue of the 28th inst. you publish in your correspondence columns a statement that "Mr. H. G. Wells declares 'that family life is incompatible with Socialism' and proclaims that the natural goal of Socialism is 'free love'"[2] This is absolute untruth. I shall be obliged by your prompt retraction and apology. In addition, I shall be glad if you will ask "E.W.B" for the source of his statement, if any, as I am particularly anxious to get to the root of the constantly recurring libels.[3]

Yours, etc.,
H.G. Wells

[1] This letter and the next are printed out of chronological order, because they indicate how these matters hung on in the small country weeklies, long after they were dead elsewhere.
[2] On 24 October 1907, p. 3, a long letter from E.W.B. of Barnstaple to the *North Devon Herald* was published under the title, 'Socialism'. Wells responded with this letter, published 7 November 1907, p. 5, "Novelist and Socialism."
[3] E.W.B. responded that the source of the statement was the Bottomley pamphlet, as Wells certainly knew. He also cited the reviews of *In The Days of the Comet* which had appeared in *The Times* on 15 September 1906. E.W.B. said that if Wells had been misquoted, he would apologize. E.W.B. wrote a rather lame response which appeared on 21 November. In this same issue G.Y. also responded to E.W.B. and quoted the *New Age* letter from Wells in its entirety. He suggested that E.W.B. had more apologies to make.

734. To the Editor, *North Devon Herald*[1]

PLS

Spade House
Sandgate [*c.* 11 November 1907]

I can only repeat that E.W.B.'s statement about my opinions is grossly untrue. I have dealt with Mr. Bottomley and the pamphlet to which he refers elsewhere. It seems to me quite extraordinarily unintelligent, even by the standards of Anti-Socialist writing, that E.W.B. cannot go to my books for his evidence, instead of relying upon Mr. Bottomley's scurrilous publication. The "Times" review quotation published at the height of the Book War, was adequately answered, and the other passage has only to be read in its context, which the ingenious Mr. Bottomley omitted, to appear in an entirely different light. Why does not E.W.B. get and read "Socialism and the Family" for himself and try to undersand what I am driving at, instead of repeating these second-hand libels?

Very sincerely yours,
H.G. Wells

[1] This is Wells's second letter. It appeared on p. 2, 21 November 1907 under the title 'H. G. Wells and Socialism'. This entire controversy over Socialism in 1907 and 1908 deserves more detailed analytical treatment than is possible here, as many newspapers carried long columns, of which the Wells controversy was only part.

735. To Edmund Gosse

Leeds, ALS

The Reform Club
London

November 18. 07

My dear Gosse,

I really find it hard to acknowledge your book. One has written so many letters of acknowledgement & praised this or that until one feels there is nothing left at all in the world but long sticks of stereo[1] for these occasions. And this thing isn't a book that can be fitted by any of the common phrases. It lives, it breathes, it is warm & kind like a friend. One turns it round & looks at it here & there & looks again & recounts little fragments to others who have read it & tells anecdotes about it. I've long since ceased to make class lists of books. Either they were unique or riveting or they don't matter. But now I have got it, this is a book I could as ill spare as any book. And I perceive I may begin to know you. If I complain at all it is that you have told [the story] for leisure & that you have not told enough of the devolutions of your family at this end. One could go on with a good appetite to the rest of your autobiography. In the end your father is left strong & clear, but you, as you cease to be a boy, wriggle[?] out of the book. I can see excellent reasons why this should be so but still I would rather it were not so.

I thank you for this book & for giving me a copy from your own hand.[2]

Yours ever
H. G. Wells

[1] Matter printed directly from a stereo-metal plate. Today we use the word 'boilerplate' to indicate such printing.

[2] This is Gosse's classic autobiography, *Father and Son*, originally published in 1907.

736. To the Editor, *Nature*

PLS

[Spade House] [mid-December 1907]

May I have a line to correct Sir William Thiselton-Dyer's impression (p. 126) that the tragic story of The Pure White Mother and the Coal Black Babe was accepted by me "as accurate and in perfect good faith". I suppose I ought to have underlined the gentle sneer at a feeling transcending the natural blackness of a negro. At any rate, I told the anecdote simply to illustrate the nonsense people will talk under the influence of race mania, and I hope it will not be added too hastily to the accumulation of evidence on the Mendellian side.[1]

H.G. Wells

---

[1] The anecdote appeared in Wells's discussion of his first visit to the United States, *The Future in America* (1906). The book, in fact, is exemplary on the issues of race, especially for its time. Wells sought out and interviewed Booker T. Washington and other black leaders, describing their experiences and their views in his book. There is less racism in the writings of Wells than virtually anyone in public life at that time. The letter appeared originally in *Nature*, 19 December 1907, p. 149.

Gregor Johann Mendel (1822–84) was the founder of genetics. His work on the principles of heredity based on experiments with peas remained unrecognized until 1900.

737. To Upton Sinclair[1]

Indiana, ACCS

Spade House
Sandgate Nov. 28. 07

Dear Sinclair

The teams will have a triumphal procession through England. But we've got too much work to do to join you except in the spirit. Our warmest good wishes for the experiment.

Yours ever
H.G. Wells

[1] This is the first known letter between the two Socialist writers. Sinclair (1878–1968) had just published his most famous book, *The Jungle* (New York, 1906), an exposé of the packing trade. He was apparently planning a trip to England, but whether it materialized or not is unknown.

738. To an unknown member of the Whitefriars Club[1]

Hofstra, ALS

[Sandgate] 13 – 12 – 07.

My Dear Sir,

I shall be very pleased to dine with the Whitefriars Club on the date you name & I shall be greatly obliged to you if you will tell me whether you expect any speech & how it comes in.

Yours very faithfully
H.G. Wells

[1] Wells's subscription receipt from the Whitefriars club for annual dues for 1908, 1 guinea, is in the editor's collection.

739. To Julia Dawson[1]

PLS

Sandgate [*c.* December 25, 1907]

The Woman's cause and the Socialist Cause are one and the same causes.
H. G. Wells

[1] Dawson conducted a weekly women's page in *The Clarion*. Wells sent her New Year's Greetings, which appeared in the magazine on 27 December 1907, p. 7. Others were printed as well.

740. To Cosmo Rowe[1]

Illinois, AL

Spade House
Sandgate

Boxing Day [1907]

Dear old Rowe,

I'm grieved to hear you have been cut about & I do hope it goes well with your head. But what the Devil do you mean coming to Folkestone & not coming to Spade House? I'll punch your head if you do that again.

[*letter ends here*]

[1] The name is virtually illegible, but the text sounds as though it is a letter to Cosmo Rowe.

741. To Mr Clark[1]

Hofstra, ALS

[Spade House
Sandgate]

Dec. 28. 07.

My dear Clark.

I am delighted by your letter and the news of your success. It was a fortunate day for me that brought you to my door & gave me the good fortune of helping you. I hope we may call each other friends for many years. Go on & prosper & believe me

Always yours very sincerely
H.G. Wells

Mrs. Wells & the children are very jolly & Mrs. Wells sends her very friendly greetings.

[1] Otherwise unknown

742. To Fred Wells

Illinois, AL

Spade House
Sandgate

Jan 14. 08

Dear old Fred,

I was very shocked to get Lewis's letter on Saturday night & to hear of poor old you sick & sinking in hospital on Christmas Eve. I was just in time to get off that reply telegram (please thank Lewis warmly for his reply) & I held the letter over a day or so to get news of you before sending on to Dad. He was dreadfully disturbed, Frank says, & greatly relieved by the telegram. I hope when this reaches you you will be well on the way to vigour again. I enclose old Frank's letter, just to show you that you're still cared for in the old home.

[*two thirds of page three and four have been cut away*]

here while she has done the furniture of some people in Folkestone.

N.B. Enclo. See postage is right

743. To Edward Pease

LSE, ALS
(read at Bromley, photocopy)

Spade House
Sandgate

[*c.* Feb. 1908]

Dear Pease,

Can you say in F. News that Fabians are reminded that <u>New Worlds For Old</u> will be published by Messrs. Constable on March 2nd & that it appears to be <u>the</u> text book for middle class propaganda. Following the soundest Fabian traditions proofs of this book have been read & numerous suggestions made by Sidney Webb, Bernard Shaw & several other members of the society.

Yours ever,
H.G. Wells

744. To Winston Churchill[1]

Bromley (photocopy), ALS

[London?] [1908]

Dear Mr. Churchill,

Here is the real Socialist case. I do hope you'll find time to look through it. It isn't quite your monster, much less is it Smith's monster.

Yours ever,
H.G. Wells[2]

---

[1] This letter and the next were presentation letters enclosed in books written by Wells and presented to Churchill. They were photocopied for the Bromley archive while in Sir Winston Churchill's library. Their precise location today is unknown. There were other exchanges but often the Wellsian side of the correspondence has been lost. Churchill once asked Wells for 'more jam with the suet' in his political commentary. These letters and others are described in my 'Winston Churchill and H. G. Wells: Edwardians in the Twentieth Century', in *Cahiers Victoriens et Edouardiens*, no. 30, Octobre 1989, pp. 93–116.

[2] This letter was attached to a copy of *New Worlds For Old*. 'Smith's monster' probably refers to F. E. Smith (1872–1930), a close associate of Churchill's, later to become Attorney General and Earl of Birkenhead.

745. To Winston Churchill[1]

Bromley (photocopy), ALS

The Reform Club
Pall Mall, S.W. [1908]

My dear Churchill,

Here in a sort of intellectual hari-kari is my inmost self. I place it at your feet.

Very sincerely yours,
H.G. Wells

---

[1] This letter is attached to a copy of Wells's *First and Last Things*.

746. Amber Reeves to H. G. Wells[1]

Illinois, ALS

Clough Hall
Newnham College
Cambridge [1908]

Dear Mr. H.G.,

Thank you very much for your letters and Mrs. Wells for her love. Getting letters from you is a tremendous joy, and makes me work hard for days.

Of course you must answer the lady. She would be ever so disappointed if you didn't. But please speak the truth and do not indulge what Professor Marshall calls your lobster-salad imagination. (He is a horrid old man and a liar.) I think her name is Hevens. Ruth Frederika Hevens. Still it would be delightful to get them to start a Utopians out there. I expect their rules would be different and instructive.[2]

I am working quite hard at Moral Science and very hard at Fabians. We have affiliated at length to both the Fabians and the S.L.P. but the whole University rang with the struggle. The men are frightfully pleased with themselves because they brought in a Socialist motion at the Union and were only defeated by 100-70. I am in evil odour with the authorities for the moment because I said revolutionary things at a public meeting – The one you were to have spoken at. I was too frightened to know what I did say, with two chaperones glaring at me, but the men are delighted. By the way Mr Keeling says if you don't come next term, you will be a skunk. If you don't come I shall be so unhappy that I shall fail in my tripos.[3] If you could see how I love getting letters from you, you would write again some day.

Yours ever,
Amber Reeves

---

[1] This letter, written by Amber Reeves while she was still a student, is included along with three others written at different times because it indicates the quality of the relationship for the Socialist woman who bore him a daughter and who remained a significant part of his life until the end.

[2] This may possibly refer to an effort to begin a Utopian society in New Zealand where Reeves came from. Her father had been Governor General.

[3] Ben Keeling was a well-known young Socialist and a very good friend of Wells. He was killed in France in 1916. Wells wrote an introduction to a collection of his letters brought together by his fiancée, Emily Townsend, *Keeling Letters and Recollections* (London, 1918).

747. To Violet Paget

Colby, ALS

Spade House
Sandgate [early Spring 1908]

Dear Vernon Lee,

In order not to write volumes I am writing a short note in a train. Because really there is nothing for it but a long talk & on the whole I am inclined to prepare notes for that so as to miss as little as possible. I rejoice over the marginalia to the Faith[1] M.S., which indeed is just the sort of collaboration I had the impudence to hope from you. I want to talk about that & two books of yours I have read – one of which your publisher says you have sent me. As for the New Worlds For Old, I doubt if much will arise between us out of that. So please make it two or three nights this time at Sandgate. Would you like to meet – have you met William James? He may be at Rye about mid July.

Yours very gratefully
H.G. Wells

---

[1] Probably the manuscript that became his major philosophical statement, *First and Last Things*, which he circulated widely among his friends prior to publication. It could also have been his *Credo*.

748. To Violet Paget

Colby, ALS

Spade House
Sandgate [early Spring 1908]

Dear Miss Paget,

P.S. By the bye, are you likely to have a short story or anything of that jewelled nature to publish about September or October next? There is a prospect of a magazine in which we are to print what the dull editor will not suffer. There are to be poems by Hardy, something by Anatole France, criticism by James, & a big novel I can't "serialize". In fact it is a revolt against present apprehensions. The proposal is to share profits among the contributors according to the length of contributions.*

Yours ever,
H.G. Wells

* But as we want a constellation at first we do not appeal for long contributions.

749. To Ford Madox Hueffer

Cornell, Typed Transcription

[Spade House,
Sandgate, Kent] [date unknown, early in 1908]

Dear Hueffer,

Put Lady Sassoon down and please return me the letters I sent you. And put down Mrs. J.H. Green, 38 Grosvenor Road. Will you write Lady Elcho and McTaggart, giving especial care to the spelling of Evan Charteris' name, as it is the Wemyss's surname. I can't read your P.S. beginning "tell Mrs. Wells ——" Oh! don't forget to ask Arnold Bennett for a Five-Towns story.

Yours ever,
H.G.

750. To Harold Monro[1]

Boston, ALS

Spade House
Sandgate Feb 8, 08

My Dear Monro,

Very many thanks for "Judas" a fine vision very well done. It has pleased me very much & set me thinking. Your irritated scheming practical man is wonderfully constructed & felt. By humanizing him you have done something for me in the way of humanizing Christ. Shelton tells simple.

If you have any views or ideas I'd be glad to have them.

Yours very sincerely
H.G. Wells

---

[1] Wells had sent Monro a copy of his Credo when it was circulated. See letters 695 and 731. Monro at one time proposed organizing a New Republic Society, or a Samurai Society. Wells addressed one such Proto-Samurai Society in 1906 at the LSE, with Beatrice Webb in the chair. But, as with Plato's Guardians, with whom there is a strong affinity, the Samurai never grew beyond the discussion stage.

751. To the Editor, *Labour Leader*[1]

Illinois, ALS

Spade House
Sandgate [early February 1908]

Dear Sir,

It is quite true that I live in my own house with servants (four to be exact & a gardener) on fair & pleasant terms. I have a second class season ticket to London (not first as stated but Shaw & Coit I understand go first) & a tennis lawn, a garden study, a rock garden & other luxuries. I haven't ever given 10/6 for a driver but I don't see why I should not do so if I chose. I take holidays abroad. But my chief luxury is Socialism. This has cost me in time & energy, in damaged sales for my books, a loss in the last four years of at least £2000 and that is only the beginning of the damage it will do to the solid world of success I have within my grasp. It is quite worth it.

I travel second class because I am not crowded in a second class carriage & can read books & write letters & arrive at my destination better fit for work than if I travelled third. I would travel first if I could afford it. I live in comfort & as pleasantly as possible because so I think & work without stress. All the thinking for Socialism has been done by men of such independence & leisure. I insure my life heavily & invest what I can so as not to be worried & tempted for the sake of my wife and children. I mix with all sorts of people, peers & plutocrats & both cheeseparers[?] & dressmakers & work girls & clerks & shop assistants & so on & they are all worth knowing. I want to go about freely, watch & taste the way of living of all sorts of people. I want everybody to have at least as much ease, leisure & freedom as I have myself & that is why I am a Socialist. With a sensibly reorganized social & economic system I believe that that is quite practicable & so I am doing my best to bring that about. But I see no sense at all in making myself & my wife uncomfortable & inefficient, keeping myself off from associating with any but the working class & risking the lives & education of my children by going to live in some infernal slum or other at a period of a week or so. I don't believe in anyone having to do that. Why should I set an example? What possible good would that do?

I think militant Socialists have to drop this queer unrealistic idea that everyone who becomes a Socialist has to abandon house, leisure & comfort. When social organization will provide young women with a way of living more wholesome & interesting than domestic science (at present the alternative is factory employment) and sees every wife with cheap electricity & domestic conveniences that will displant not only the need of hired help, I am quite ready to alter my way of living but not before. I don't believe that Socialists desire any such sacrifices & I am constantly preaching to middle class & professional that it is untrue that Socialism demands any such fanatical sacrifice as your correspondent suggests. Socialism is a clean sound principle for destroying poverty & dependence. I mean to go on working for it. – & in the meantime having just as good a time & just as many pleasant things as I can.

H. G. Wells

---

[1] A whispering campaign arose concerning how some Socialists lived with the implication that, as a Socialist, a person was supposed to share his wealth. Wells was asked to comment on this and he responded with a letter to the editor of *The Labour Leader*, which published the letter 14 February 1908, under the heading, 'Ought Socialists to Live Poor: How I Live'. We print here the original which differs slightly from the published version. Relatively few of Wells's original letters to the press occur in this form.

752. To Sidney Webb

Illinois, Typed Extract

[London?] 9/3/08

[Dear Mr. Webb,]

[...] I happen to be something of a teacher & I want to get out of that piece of apparatus [the Basis of the Fabian Society] very much. Why can't you and

Shaw let me throw it out now.... You won't even let me enlist & train forces for you to handle. You two men are the most intolerable egotists, narrow, suspicious, obstructive, I have ever met.

753. To the Editor, *New Age*[1]

PLS

[Spade House
Kent] [April 1908]

The challenge business is, I think, overdone. May I say in reply to Mr. Max Hirsch's proposal that I should put in writing about that pamphet of his that if he will send a copy (I've not kept one) and his present address to me, I will read through his thing, blue pencil the worst bits, writing "M" misrepresentation, and "A" for Abuse and return it to him. Then if he and the editor agree, he can argue about the justice of my assertions in the New Age. But I wonder if it will arouse anyone very much so.

H.G. Wells

---

[1] Wells often found himself challenged by those who thought he should deal with them singly. Max Hirsch, an Australian, had written a pamphlet to which Wells had made a passing reference. When Hirsch responded to that letter, which was published on 8 August 1908, p. 299, Wells refused to file a formal answer. The editor of the *New Age* summarized Wells's objections in a condensed form, noting that Hirsch had a history of such challenges.

754. To the Editor, *New Age*[1]

PLS

[Spade House
Sandgate, Kent] [*c.* 25 March 1908]

Belloc has framed an admirable question and put the third possibility before us very clearly, the possibility of "dividing up" as an alternative to Socialism. By the three possibilities, I mean (1) the unchecked development of our present plutocratic system, (2) Socialism, and (3) the deliberate artificial checking of the concentration of property. This third possibility is the implicit ideal behind much contempary legislation and many contemporary proposals, behind graduated Income-tax proposals, graduated taxation of large holdings of land and the like. It seems to me the American ideal, so far as there remains an American ideal. Belloc does a great service in putting it in clear, well-chosen phrases, because it is very extensively confused with Socialism.

He asks: *Given a social system in which the modern means of production are widely distributed among the citizens, why should it not endure?*

Well, all these questions are questions of judgment and not proof. I think it would not endure because of the unconceivable mental and moral strain it would put upon the citizen as politician. You see Belloc's question would be quite readily answered in the affirmative did he omit the word *modern*. A social system of small holdings and small traders and owners working their property is as permanent a social system as we can imagine. It is the Chinese type of social system. But if we are to have the large enterprise and machine, the organized production, and the small owner, then that small owner must be a shareholder. He may be completely independent or partially employed for wages, but the property he will "legally control" he will only work indirectly through his elected board of directors. So that this American ideal of Belloc's resolves itself into the economic conrol of that social system through a great multitude of boards of directors responsible only to the shareholders for dividends, and into the least gratifying form of "owning" for the individual citizen. I do not see what can possibly prevent the development of a director class and the virtual rule of the country through them, and I do not see how such a community can protect itself effectually from the misconduct of directors. Production will certainly be run for dividends, with all the consequent evils, and the law will always be fighting at a disadvantage against the natural tendency of all large businesses to negotiate rather than to compete. In the end, I believe the aggregatory forces will beat any set of laws against aggregation you could contrive. It seems to me that Belloc's proposal as an alternative to Socialism is simply the suggestion of the least efficient as against the most efficient way of managing wholesale production, and all to meet an alleged passion in the individual to "own".

While the disadvantages and instabilities of Belloc's little-owners-of-big-concerns ideal are at a maximum, the compensating sense of ownership that recommends it to him, is only by an infinitesimal difference greater than the sense of ownership a citizen in a Socialist state would have as a shareholder in that State. So that were his project possible I do not see, even on his own principles, that it could be very desirable.

I think that answers the question raised, and I hope Mr. Dexter will appreciate the severity of my manner in this reply.

H. G. Wells

---

[1] Although Wells did not take up the challenge from Hirsch, he was usually happy to debate with Hilaire Belloc. In fact their debates lasted for well over twenty years. This piece appeared in the issue of 28 March 1908, p. 429, as 'An Answer'. A minor theme in the discussion of Socialism in 1906–8 concerned the somewhat related doctrines of Social Credit and Distributionism. Belloc, and later G. K. Chesterton, were in favour of the latter doctrine. It was based, roughly, on the idea that in some regular way, all goods should be shared and distributed among all who adhered to the social contract implied.

755. An open letter to an elector in N.W. Manchester[1]

PLS

Sandgate April 21, 1908

My Dear Sir, -

You are at present considering how you may vote at the imminent election in your constituency. I take it that, in common with the great mass of active-minded people in this country, you have been deeply moved and interested by the Socialist movement, which has been urged upon your attention by every sort of speaker from dukes to dustmen, and also by Mr. J. St. Loe Strachey in a series of letters in "The Spectator" of exceptional distinction. You may not have been made a Socialist, but you will have come to realise how much is just in the Socialist case, how much is fine and possible in its proposals.

You desire the development of a constructive State which shall exist for all men and be served by all men, the establishment of a wider security and comfort and of a definite minimum of welfare below which no one should be allowed to fall. You wish to see men living less and less for the mean end of private gain, and the accumulation of wealth and more and more for the nobler purposes of public service and honour. It is quite possible that, misled by the wide application of the Socialist name, you may think that these ends will be best forwarded by voting for the professedly Socialist candidate, Mr. Irving.

I want very earnestly to point out to that this is not so. I want to point out to you that Mr. Irving is not a representative Socialist candidate; he has little or no prospect of return, and the diversion of your vote, which would, I assume, go otherwise to Mr. Winston Churcill, will simply favour the return of an exceptionally undesirable person, Mr. Joynson-Hicks.

You may think that in spite of that it may be well to vote for Mr. Irving simply because he calls himself a Socialist, for the sake of the demonstration in favour of all constructive ideals. That would be all very well if Mr. Irving was, indeed, a good representative of modern Socialism. Were he a properly accredited candidate, chosen beforehand from out the constituency, and supported by the centre organization of the Independent Labour Party and the Labour vote, I should have nothing to say against him. But he is not that.

"The Labour Leader", the official organ of the Independent Labour Party in Great Britain, in its issue of April 17th very distinctly says he is not. The local Socialist organizations did not invite or desire his candidature. He has, I regret to say, decided to come in from outside as a delegate of the so-called Social Democratic Party. Mr. Irving has done sturdy work for Socialism in the past, but at this election, he is representative not of Socialism as a whole and of the great organizing projects it has developed in the last quarter-century, but of that extreme, old-fashioned, and implacable type of Socialist theory, limited, doctrinaire, and cantankerous, which has done so much to retard the development of a sound and statesmanlike propaganda in Great Britain.

Not everyone who calls himself a Socialist is necessarily a representative of our movement; and it is becoming more and more desirable to distinguish clearly between the two wings of Socialism, or, to put it more justly, between the main body of British Socialism and the Social Democratic wing, between that broadly constructive and essentially British Socialism, on the one hand, of which the Independent Labour Party is at present the political expression, standing to-day for all that is noblest and most hopeful in the awakening consciousness of our democracy, and on the other the extreme and relatively small left wing, harsh, impracticable, insubordinate, a mere disloyal minority, altogether alien to that compromising yet persistently creative disposition, that practicality and charity and sanity which are the peculiar politicial virtue, both of the British people and of that real and vital Socialist movement which more and more embodies its ideals.

For nothing is more remarkable than the political sanity of the main Socialist movement at the present time, its general and increasing enfranchisement from narrow and and intolerant attitudes. We realise fully that the organized State of the future must be made out of such elements of order and progress as exist to-day. We aim at no sudden revelations, no dramatic replacement of class by class. We work steadily to increase the proportion of labour representation in Parliament, and diminish the power of narrow, anti-social and demoralising propertied interests, but we recognize and welcome the co-operation of all men of good intent. The political system of tomorrow must develop, we are fully persuaded, out of the traditions of the governing class of to-day. And though Mr. Churchill is not a Socialist, though he stands as a member of a party that is strongly tainted by the memories of Victorian individualism, though he refuses the letter of our teaching, we recognise in his active and still rapidly developing and broadening mind, in his fair and statesmanlike utterances, and, in particular, in his recent assertion of the need of a national minimum, a spirit entirely in accordance with the spirit of our movement, and one with which it is both our duty and intention to go just as far as we can.

A man, because he is a believer in the vitalising influence of modern Socialism, is not necessarily bound to vote for a candidate because he labels himself Socialist. Indeed, by doing so he may be inflicting a real injury at this moment upon Socialist development. But, every voter with an breadth of outlook in N.W. Manchester, whether he be a Socialist or not, is bound to do his utmost to secure the rejection of Mr. Joynson-Hicks.

I have no hesitation in saying that Mr. Joynson-Hicks represents absolutely the worst element in British political life at the present time, that he stands for debased politics, for the Americanization, in the worst sense, of our public life. He is far more of the type of a party unit in the House of Representatives than an English member of Parliament. He is an entirely undistinguished man, and involved, I notice, in all these ridiculour reversals of opinion and self-contradictions natural to a man of his personal indeterminateness. In contrast with Mr. Churchill's brilliant career and vivid personality, he is an obscure and ineffectual nobody. I know nothing, and want to know nothing of his social standing or of his private quality, and I do not suppose I should ever have heard of his name before this time if it were not that I keep myself informed by means of Press cuttings of the progress of Socialist discussion. But among the multitude of speakers who were busy last year in bespattering the great constructive proposals of modern Socialism with insult and misrepresentation his name was conspicuous through his witless use of the clipped and forged quotations which formed the ammunition of the great anti-Socialist campaign, and through his vile abuse of Socialist leaders.

For example, he called Mr. Keir Hardie a "leprous traitor". He was industrious with the foolish lie that Socialism is atheism. He declared, knowing it as he must have done to be childishly untrue, that "the very essence of Socialism was that all the Ten Commandments should be swept away". He invented wonderful unknown Socialist books which he would not "dare read to an audience of English men and English women". Nothing, indeed, seemed too foul or too foolish for Mr. Joynson-Hicks to spout at as great and honourable a popular movement as England has ever seen.

I think it is most necessary that North-West Manchester should not forget Mr. Joynson-Hicks's method of controversy at the present juncture. This question of fair and decent public discussion is one of supreme importance, far more important than any other single issue before you – land, liquor, tariff, or what not. If the English are to lose our habit of freely and generously expressing and criticising ideas, if one party or movement is to set out to blacken and vilify another public movement, if senseless misstatements of an adversary's opinions are to endorse such methods and send the user to Parliament, then it seems to me our national outlook is a gloomy one.

I think this question of elementary decency in public discussion transcends party lines. Whatever side we back, the fight must be a fair one. I would be the first to admit as a reasonable Socialist that there is a strong case to be made and powerful arguments to be advanced against Socialism. They do not convince me, but I acknowledge their validity. I can understand and respect the attitude of such an antagonist as Mr. Mallock, for example. But this anti-Socialist propaganda, of which Mr. Joynson-Hicks is a typical representative, has not made out a case. It has failed quite amazingly to make out a case. It is scarcely too much to say it has not attempted to make out a case. Throughout it has treated the ordinary voter as a fool, who must be humbugged, and not a man who must be reasoned with. It has been from first to last a campaign of lies and controversial tricks and base imputations, an outrage upon and an insult to the intelligence of our common people, and to the splendid constructive dreams they are developing. It has been a campaign to drag in scandal and personalities, and in every way to embitter and degrade political life, to foul the names of antagonists, and exacerbate class feeling.

The question every Conservative gentleman, every Unionist, every constructive-minded Tariff Reformer in North-West Manchester has to ask himself in the next three days is whether this sort of thing is to be the New Politics. Are men who cannot be trusted to make a quotation to be presently trusted to draft a tariff? And if the new age of politics is not to sink below the old, if the typically English traditions of national compromise, of fairness, moderation and mutual honourableness, of patient collective development in which every class participates, are to be maintained, then I do not see how they or anyone can support Mr. Joynson-Hicks. And the effective way not to support Mr. Joynson-Hicks on this present occasion is to vote for Mr. Winston Churchill.[2]

Yours, etc.
H.G. Wells

[1] This open letter appeared in the *Daily Mail*, 21 April 1908. Some parts of it have been reprinted in my 'Winston Churchill and H. G. Wells' in *Cahiers Victoriens et Edouardiens* No. 30 (Montpellier, 1989).

[2] Churchill had held the seat in 1906, but his recent appointment as President of the Board of Trade, by the Prime Minister, Asquith, required him to seek re-election under the rules of that time. The Tories were keen to unseat Churchill, because he had 'crossed the floor' and had led the fight in 1906 against them. In the event, Joynson-Hicks won the seat with a poll of 5,417. Churchill received 4,988 and Irving 276. The margin of 429 votes was a Tory swing of 6.4 per cent from the previous general election. It was a hard-fought campaign, but Churchill's victory in 1906 had been an anomaly, as the seat was at best marginal for the Liberals having been held by the Tories since the mid-nineteenth century. Wells's letter was a nine days' wonder, but he could have hardly done less for his friend, Churchill, especially in opposition to the man who had smeared Wells in 1906 in the 'free love' controversy. Wells and Joynson-Hicks, curiously enough both native sons of Bromley, later became good acquaintances, served on the Air Board together and even visited each others homes. It was a bit much, of course, for Wells to indicate that he did not know Joynson-Hicks, as they had exchanged several letters concerning his charges against Wells; see letters 702, 704 and 707. Joynson-Hicks's responses are at Illinois.

756 To H. J. F. Miles

Hofstra, APCS

Sandgate [postmarked May 22 08 13]

Dear Sir,

I regret very much that I do not know sufficient facts to justify my supporting this memorial to Mr. Asquith.[1]

Very sincerely yours
H.G. Wells

---

[1] Apparently Wells had been asked to contribute to a petition of some sort to Asquith.

757. To Fred Wells

Illinois, ALS

Spade House
Sandgate [*c.* 1908][1]

My dear Freddy,

I'm glad to hear you are better. I should have written to you before but I'm tied up in knots with a damned novel that won't come right.[2] We are looking forward to your coming over to see us. I want to keep at my novel for a week or so & early in June, William James & his wife have promised to come for a night or so to us. He's an American professor lecturing at Oxford & he hasn't been able to fix a date yet, but as soon as he does I will let you know & then perhaps you won't mind fitting in. I thought you would like to cycle out here, perhaps with Frank. You ought to get in some exercise.

Yours ever,
The Busswhacker

Love to the Parent. I am very sorry to hear of his foot. Something must be done with that this summer.

---

[1] Another hand has marked this letter as June 1908, but that must be incorrect.
[2] Very probably *Ann Veronica*, but it might be the beginning of *Mr. Polly*.

758. To Methuen

Illinois, TLS

[Spade House
Sandgate] [May 1908]

My dear Methuen,

In that case your accounts are not in order as they show you to have sold off copies at remainder prices. If that is not remaindering, what is? I am asking Mrs Wells to send the account in question and the agreement to my solicitor to clear up this point.[1]

Yours ever,
H. G. W.

[1] Whatever the problem this letter apparently solved it as no further correspondence exists.

759. To William James

Illinois, ALS

[Sandgate?] [*c.* May 1908]

My dear James,

We are full of pleasant expectations & will do our best using will & prayer to assure fine weather. We shall regret Mrs James but delight in Miss James. There is staying with us a Miss Reeves who is just your daughter's age. She has recently attained a transient notoriety by getting a first in Part II of the Moral Science Tripos at Cambridge & is so accomplished that she can speak Hegelian. Her father is the New Zealand High Commissioner & initiated the advanced legislation that makes that country so interesting politically. Mrs. J.P. Reeves, the mother of this historian & a pleasant talker, & Mary Austin the playwright will be in London. Otherwise, the heavens are clear.[1]

Yours ever,
H.G. Wells

[1] Hurried writing, age and indistinct xeroxes combine to make parts of this letter virtually illegible.

760. To Frank Harris

Texas, ALS

Spade House
Sandgate [1908][1]

My dear Harris.

I don't think I shall be able to join in the chorus of praise of the Bomb. I had hoped to do so in the English Review but Hueffer seems to value that vehicle of commendations his own and anyhow there are difficulties. I wish rather you hadn't asked me & I wish you hadn't made that generous allusion to the pay being all right. Damn your pay anyhow. I quite see the necessity we are under of speaking publicly & frequently about good work, but there's also the necessity of getting good work done. I've got my own things in hand & if I did break out into what would look like officious patronage of my betters, I don't think I should start with the Bomb. Have you read Bennett's Old Wives' Tale? It's a bigger thing. The Bomb puzzles me and if I did write about it I should have to pound air into it a good deal. It has an art of being based on documents. It's tremendously real in places & then passes into a sort of blandness. As a statement for the case for anarchism, it's neither from the inside or the outside. I think if I did write about it, I shouldn't so much praise as analyse.

Yours was a very impressive speech at the Ross dinner though I think you overdid your mighty scorn of "Your Grace and my lords."

Yours ever,
H.G. Wells

[1] *The Bomb* and *The Old Wives' Tale* appeared in 1908, so this letter must be from that time. The Ross dinner was a testimonial given by two hundred of Robert Ross's friends in recognition of his contributions to literature and especially as literary executor for Oscar Wilde.

761. To Violet Hunt

Cornell, APC

[London?] [postmarked 15 July 08]

E's at home. So's she. Come dahn to tea.

The secretary[1]

[1] A humorous invitation to tea from Wells and Catherine to Violet Hunt.

762. To Graham Wallas

LSE, AL

[Spade House
Sandgate] [1908]

[Dear Wallas,]

Your connections are admirably helpful. I accept with particular pleasure your points about the Basis. It's just on the points on this matter I'm apt to go wrong. I'll put it straight.

I'm looking forward to your proofs though I doubt if I'll be able to do you any equivalent service.[1]

[1] In this letter and the next, Wells is discussing Wallas's book, *Human Nature in Politics*, which came out in late 1908.

763. To Graham Wallas

LSE, ALS

Spade House
Sandgate [*c.* 1908][1]

My dear Wallas,

I was just finishing up a novel – all writers are egotists – & so I did not write a line & put off writing day to day, about your book. I think it is in many ways a fine & richly suggestive book & likely to become cardinal in the campaign of discussing democracy that lies before us. It is full of admirably chosen instances & a sort of irony that is very characteristic of you. I am trying myself to plan out a novel that shall give scope to the discussions of many of the points you raise & Amber Reeves who will be more or less with you next session at the school of Economics is proposing a thesis upon Incentive that may or may not be a brilliant contribution to the growing body of criticism.[2]

Yours ever,

H.G. Wells p.t.o.

Our united love to Mrs. Wallas & May.

---

[1] It is difficult to determine when this letter was written. Although Wells and Wallas had been close, and Wells had commented on the earlier manuscripts of *Human Nature in Politics*, this is the last extant letter for a decade. There is some evidence that Audrey Wallas found the Amber Reeves affair distasteful and relations between the two men were probably limited as a result.

[2] If I am right in my dating, the proposed novel would be *The New Machiavelli*.

764. To E.R. Pease[1]

LSE, TLS

Spade House

Sandgate, Kent

September 16th, 1908

My dear Pease,

I shall be obliged if you will tell my colleagues on the Executive and the Society generally that I am resigning my position upon the Executive now and that I propose to become a subscriber instead of a member at the end of the present year. I have had this course of action under consideration for some time and it is only after much hesitation that I have decided to take it. It will, I think, save much misunderstanding if you will print this letter, in which I am stating as compactly and simply as I can, my reasons for withdrawing from an active participation in Fabian affairs.

Essentially the position is this: I find myself disagreeing with the Basis which forms the Confession of Faith of the Society and discontented with the general form of our activities. So long as I could consider the Basis a document that might presently be altered and the policy of the Society as a policy that would develop and change, I have remained a member. I have had it in my mind that I might presently take part in a vigorous campaign for a revised basis and a revised Propaganda. But when I calculate the forces against such a campaign, the inevitable opposition and irritation that must ensue and the probable net results of what would certainly be an irksome and distressful conflict, I am forced to conclude that the effort is, for me at least, not worth making. Moreover I want very much to concentrate myself now upon the writing of novels for some years, and so I have taken the alternative course and sent in my resignation.

My chief objection to the Basis is its disregard of that claim of every child upon the State which is primary and fundamental to my conception of Socialism. A scheme which proposes to leave mother and child economically dependent upon the father is to me not Socialism at all but a miserable perversion of Socialism. It forbids the practical freedom of women and leaves the essential evils of the Individualist system untouched. I see the hopelessness of any attempt to force this recognition upon the Fabian Society at the present time, and I do not care to remain permanently identified with formulae that misstate my views by this terrible omission.

In addition I think the repudiation of compensation in the Basis is opposed to all those ideas of orderly social development inherent in modern Socialism. And I realize more and more the need for insistence upon the immense educational and administrative reconstructions that are necessary to save Socialism from futility. I have lost hope in the Fabian Society contributing effectually to the education of the movement in this direction, & to borrow a convenient Americanism I have no use for a Fabian Society that is not developing and spreading ideas.

Let me add that I think the period of opportunity for a propaganda to the British middle classes on Fabian lines is at an end. That opportunity came and found us divided in theory and undecided in action. The petty growth that is going on is a mere mockery of the things we might have done. It is however no good lamenting our might-have-beens and it is to other media and other methods that we must now look for the spread and elaboration of those collectivist ideas which all of us have at heart.

Very sincerely yours,
H.G. Wells

---

[1] This letter is Wells's formal resignation from the Fabian Society. It appeared in the *Fabian News* for September 1908. I am, however, following a carbon typescript sent to the Society, but which has some minor emendations in Wells's hand, and a photocopy of the original which is in the Fabian papers at the LSE. I read this photocopy at Bromley. What is interesting is that Catherine Wells continued to be a member, sit on the executive board, and participate in meetings for another two years after this time. Her name appears fairly frequently in the reports of meetings in *Fabian News*.

765. To Bernard Shaw

British Museum, ALS
50552 ff. 21-2

Sandgate [early October 1908]

I think you do me an injustice. I don't mean in your general estimate of my character – but in the Bland troubles.

However, you take your line. It's possible you don't know the whole situation.

Well, I had some handsome ambitions the last twelve month & they've come to nothing – nothing measured by what I wanted – and your friendship & the Webb's among other assets, have gone for my gross of green spectacles.[1] Because it was all nonsense to keep up sham amiabilities. I've said and written things that change relationships and the old attitudes are over for ever. On the whole I don't retract the things I've said & done – bad & good together it's one. I'm damnably sorry we're all made so.

And damn the Blands! All through it's been that infernal household of lies that has tainted this affair & put me off my game. You don't for one moment begin to understand. You've judged me in that matter & they're you are!

Yours ever,
H.G. Wells

[1] The reference to a gross of green spectacles comes from Oliver Goldsmith's (1728–74) novel *The Vicar of Wakefield* (1766) where needed money is exchanged for these worthless items. They play a part as well in L. Frank Baum's populist novel, *The Wizard of Oz*.

766. To Ford Madox Hueffer[1]

Cornell, ALS

Spade House
Sandgate. 28. Sept. 1908

Dear Hueffer,

I enclose two letters, one from Lady Elcho, and one from Lady Desborough. Please read and return. I do not fail to pursue these ladies with subscription forms. Tell me shall I write to Lady Tennant? If that succeeds you will of course have to print just what she sends. Tell me also what you think of the Evan Charteris proposal. He is, by the bye, a great friend of Gosse, whom you are, I submit, rather an ass not to propitiate. It is funny that both Mallock and I should have gone for that same diary. Has Anatole France pulled through? I judge by the Chronicle paragraph. I rather promised him to their people.

Yours ever,

H.G.

Please return enclosed letters.

---

[1] This letter and a few more which follow deal with the creation of *The English Review*. The quarterly was edited by Hueffer. Wells advanced some funds for the magazine and solicited submissions and subscriptions among his friends. His novel, *Tono Bungay* was serialised in the journal, and in fact the book's publication was delayed because of problems in getting the magazine underway.

767. To Violet Paget

Colby, ALS

Grand Hotel
Adelboden, [Switzerland] [Autumn 1908]

Dear Vernon Lee,

The English Review is a frightful failure financially & I doubt if any of us poor dears will get any money. Hueffer has some idea of involving me in the liabilities of an honourable – from – the literary point of view but otherwise questionable enterprise, by declaring I said I was a proprietor in a letter to you. I hope not. Anyhow, I wasn't. Please tell me what I said (to Sandgate). The arrangement was that Duffield was to print and publish & do everything except advertise, to get his out of pocket expenses & ten per cent thereon + one fifth of what is left out of the receipts. The remaining 4/5 were to go to Hueffer who would retain 2/5 for his advertising, editing, etc. & divide the remaining 2/5 between the contributors pro rata – this quite independent of what he chose to pay for advertisement.

Yours ever,

H.G. Wells

768. To Violet Paget

Colby, ALS

Spade House
Sandgate

17th Oct 1908

Urgent
Secret
Terrible

Dear Vernon Lee

Is there anyone in Florence called "Isabel[1]Sherrill Dodge". Is it a he or a she & what is its name when it writes please? It wants advice about a son of six.

Yours ever,
H.G. Wells

You are doing that story for The English Review, eh?

[1] When I read this while preparing my biography of Wells, I thought the name was Mabel Sherrill Dodge, whom I took to be the famous New York and Arizona left wing hostess. I am not sure who it is now.

769. To T. L. Humberstone

Illinois, ANS

Spade House
Sandgate

[postmarked Oc 24 08]

Dear Humberstone

I'm too pressed just now to take a hand in that shindy.

Yours very truly,
H. G. Wells

770. To Mrs Tooley[1]

Illinois, Typed Transcription

Spade House
Sandgate, Kent [October-November 1908]

Dear Mrs. Tooley,

No more straw!

The M.S. is from 'The War in the Air' just published by Bell.

I believe that somewhere I have a photograph of my father that is rather good but I can't put my hand on it. If I get it I'll send it you.

I do all my work in M.S. Then it is typed, then I correct it & recorrect it.

I have 2 sons, no other children. No "early struggles" of any sort. My life has been easy & uneventful. My father was a tradesman of Bromley who was also a professional cricketer. I was apprenticed to a draper when I was 13, I did not like it, I tried a chemist & a draper again & then after a year at Midhurst Grammar School went to the Royal Coll of Science for three years until I was 20. Then for a time I was an assistant master in a private school, a science lecturer, a journalist & a dramatic critic. First book the Time Machine (date in Who's Who).

No books of mine are autobiographical though of course I use all my experiences.

Health sound but the fact that a football accident when I was 21 led to a serious but by no means wonderful illness when I was 35 has given rise to a legend of permanent ill health. Really very sound, go for long walks of 20 miles or so (favourite exercise) play tennis ardently but badly & so on. Cheerful disposition but when I was little boy had a severe cut over the eye. This has left a scar which is much more visible in a photograph than in reality. Hence many photographs, especially when badly reproduced give a distressful face (worse case enclosed, from Burk's As Others See Us. He came & stayed in my home & then published this.) Hence a theory of a saddened life. Early struggles, saddened life, permanent Bad health, jaundiced outlook. All nonsense, Madam.

Yours very sincerely,
H.G. Wells

---

[1] Mrs Tooley was apparently a journalist, or perhaps a local historian.

771. To Maurice Baring

Illinois, ALS

Spade House
Sandgate

Nov. 6, [1908]
[*in another hand*]

My Dear Baring,

There are two of you the same as me. There is a fine expressive man who writes books & there is an individual in the flesh who is either shy or drunk. Russian Essays is an admirable book, it makes me catch at one's adjectives before they get out of hand. Sympathetic & vast & a sort of depth of underlying & the sense of beauty alive & active, – I would value it if it came from a stranger and I should want to know you if I didn't.

Are you coming to the Ross doings? I hope so. It has been a great thing in the way of friendship that little man did, in putting Wilde's reputation out of the curious book catalogues into decent reception again.[1]

Yours ever,
H.G.

---

[1] Wells is referring to Baring's *Russian Essays* (London, 1908). Robert Ross was Wilde's literary executor, and friend. He was responsible for placement of the Epstein monument on Wilde's grave in Pere Lachaise. Wells was prominent in this cause. The 'Ross doings' was a banquet given by the friends of Wilde and Ross to honour Ross and his work. Wells gave the main toast at the banquet. Ross and Wells remained close throughout Ross's life. There was a second Ross dinner, which was more public, in December 1914. There has been some confusion over the two events.

772. To Fisher Unwin

Illinois, ALS

Spade House
Sandgate

[November 1908]

Typed Copy Sent

My dear Fisher Unwin,

Yes, I'm afraid I did modify the terms by suggesting an anticipation of the payment I proposed. Perhaps that wasn't fair game. Still I understand you to meet me by suggesting three payments of £500. After all that's a difference of twenty or thirty pounds interest more or less. I'm quite willing to meet you in that matter by making the payments, £480, £490 & £500 (total £1470).

—

The translation rights of this or any book are quite out of the discussion. Don't let's say any more about that.

—

I can help you thus far about the serial that I will deliver copy as far as finished – two copies you can have – on signature of the agreement. I think I shall be able to send you the whole thing before December, but I like to hold a m.s. for a week or so to re-read.

—

Nothing can be settled about the subsequent books at present unless you are disposed to buy it as a pig in a poke for £2225 on an identical agreement. You see the serial rights are the book. It's not possible to separate book rights & serial rights because as you know the publishers who own magazines always want them together. I found in the case of Kipps that a previous agreement for the book rights with Macmillan gave me practically no market for the serial at all except the Pall Mall Magazine. I don't think any sane mean would plonk down £2225 for the book at the present time, but if it turns out to be a good serial it will be costing all that. (I got £500 for Kipps & nothing in America because of the hampering book agreements).

Look here! will this additional clause satisfy your craving for some lien on the next book. If so, add it to the agreement & let's settle the thing.

(And the author further agrees with the Publisher to sell him either the next book or the next book but one completed after the completion of Ann Veronica, the said book being a novel & not shorter than 70,000 words in length, if he, the Publisher, chooses to buy it, upon an agreement similar to this agreement except in so far that the purchase price will be £2225, and that the dates of publication will differ. And the Author shall determine which of his books he shall offer to the Publisher under the conditions of the clause and the publisher shall in no wise be bound to the said book. The Author shall submit to the publisher the M.S. of the said book or a completed portion not less than 50,000 words in length at any time he thinks fit after the date of this present agreement & the publisher shall decide within two calendar months of the receipt of the M.S. whether or not he will avail himself of the option herewith conceded him.)

Now this is all I can do to meet you. Take it or leave it.

Yours ever,

H. G. Wells

I shall dine at the Reform on Wednesday, but I shan't be there after nine.

773. To P. Cazenove[1]

Illinois, ALS

Spade House
Sandgate

Nov. 10. 08

My dear Cazenove.

I don't think that Hutchinson can safely reckon on a sale of 10,000 for any books of mine. I think I can make a book that will be quite safe to do that but that introduces ultra-authentical elements. The last fantastic novel In The Days of the Comet did 5,300 at 6/- and 2560 Colonial which was a descent from Kipps which went over at 6/-. What the War in the Air will do, I don't know. In The Days of the Comet was as you know complicated by a disagreeable "free-love" shindy & was advertised by the Times at some scalping prices within a week of publication. The earlier books I find I cannot calculate. They are mixed up with existing and suchlike editions. The War of the Worlds only did about 6,000 at 6/-, and The Food of the Gods about the same or less, I believe, but I fancy the accounts are with Pinker.

As for the lease arrangement – I don't like it. My last lease was to Fisher Unwin & just at the end he made a sale of 2,000 copies outright to Heinemann who goes on selling the book to this day. I want £3000 clear (n.b. after deducting agent's fees) and for that I'm prepared to sell all rights (except translation & dramatic rights) and to mark out a season during which no other book shall be published. I strongly advise you not to be too specific at the present time with H. except to make the irreducible price quite clear. Then let me have a talk to him.

After all, there's no hurry.

Yours ever
H. G. Wells

---

[1] Cazenove was a sometime agent for Wells's work and an author, editor and general literary figure. Wells was never quite happy with his agents; he was soon to use A.P. Watt almost exclusively, but even there he often worked alone.

774. To P. Cazenove[1]

Indiana, AL

[London] [date stamped 16 Dec 1908]

Dear Cazenove,

No paper but this – I'm writing in the train. Obviously the suffragette book wasn't your business. It could have been if F.U. hadn't crumpled up. You see, I take my poor old failure of Tono Bungay as a standard (& Kipps also) & I've got this new blessed book off my hands for half as much money again & half the work these others have given me. F.U. bought it without seeing it & I've had none of the publishers & editors criticisms or anything of that sort. Frankly Casenove I want money to work upon. If I can get it through agents I will & if I can't I shall get it my own way. You've been first rate for popular serial work but you have been not at all effective for long serious fiction & for the First & Last Things stuff. Constables would, I feel certain, have haggled over the novel if they had seen it. &

[*remainder of letter missing*]

[1]This letter is tipped into a copy of Wells's novel, *Kipps*, in the Lilly Library.

775. To the Editor, *New Age*[1]

PLS

[Spade House
Sandgate] [mid December 1908]

Life is not only short but urgent, so that one must write of things in a kind of shorthand, but I think that will convey my point to Belloc any how.

H.G. Wells

[1] Wells's squib was carried at the end of a long article by Hilaire Belloc analyzing Wells's work and philosophy, *The New Age*, 17 December 1908.

776. To Ford Madox Hueffer

Cornell, Typed Transcription

Spade House
Sandgate [late in 1908]

My dear Hueffer,

I hope you understand clearly that I do not consider that things are yet arranged for the use of "Tono Bungay" as a serial. We have not defined terms, and nothing is secured to prevent the publication of the magazine amounting to an anticipatory publication of the book. I hope this will make quite plain that as things stand, you are <u>not</u> free to serialize "Tono Bungay."

Yours ever,
H.G. Wells

777. To Fred Wells

Illinois, ALS

Spade House
Sandgate [early in 1909]

Dear old Freddy,

Here's luck to The Shop! I hope you'll do better than Ruth who I am afraid is going to make a mess of things. – mainly because she thinks gross receipts are profits.[1] But to tell the truth I'm inclined to bet on your pulling through. You play most games carefully & well & keeping shop is just another game of that sort.

The children were delighted with the insects which have gone into a museum.

Best good wishes from
The Busswhacker

[1] Probably a reference to his cousin Ruth Neal, daughter of another of his mother's sisters. Wells sent money to her from time to time. Fred Wells had just opened a draper's shop, with some other sideline goods for sale, in South Africa. The shop was a success, apparently: there are several photographs of it.

778. To Ford Madox Hueffer

Cornell, Typed Transcription

Spade House Jan. 28. 1909
[*in another hand*]

Dear Hueffer,

All's well that ends well, and I don't distrust anyone, but it's just simple plain foolishness that I don't let in Macmillans in any sort of way. I agree Duckworth is admirable, but it's only just now that I learn that it is Duckworth. If you knew the quantity of messes we've had this year about American copyrights, overlapping and so on, through assuming that so and so or so and so would "see that everything necessary" was done, you'd quite understand my absolute determination to take no more avoidable risks.

Yours ever,
H.G. Wells

What dates do you propose? I think Macmillan would probably like to publish in March or April.

Forgive my hard ways.

779. To Ford Madox Hueffer

Cornell, APCS

Spade House
Sandgate [postmarked 5. Feb. 09]

Mr Hueffer must be perfectly aware that I had no authority to offer Miss Paget any terms for her story. I told her the terms upon which contributions were to be made as far as I understood them.

H.G. Wells

780. To Beatrice Webb

Illinois, ALS

Spade House
Sandgate

Feb. 22. 09

Dear Mrs. Webb,

Very many thanks for the Poor Law volumes.[1] I've been reading in them with interest & I shall value them for many reasons. But, what a mass of stuff it all is! I had hoped for a fuller & more illuminating introduction. I suppose you two got a good deal pressed for time – at any rate I shall value[?] this broad & scientific handling that made Industrial Democracy your high water mark of achievement. You don't by any means make the quality of your differences from the Majority Report plain, and your case in the slightest degree convincing. Perhaps I have been led to expect too much, but at any rate, I am left wondering just what it is you think you are up to. All literature & all science is digestion & I've been wondering at times lately whether your later views as to dietary couldn't with advantage be applied to intellectual things. You two people are doing so much detailed work that it seems ungracious to chastize you but I believe you will do more permanent & effectual things if there were more thought & less report & societing[?]. In my student days I saw so much industrious piling up of ill assorted facts that this dusty glimmer does not impress me. What does impress me is illumination.

We've just got back from Adelboden & I find among a list of other things that the Fabian Society with a sort of wicked obstinacy is going to reprint that old essay about Adam coming with a case for & taking the first bite of land & so on & so on – child of thirteen economics – with a definite quotation from G.B.S. (Shaw!) to say that that is all that is specific about Socialism. It strikes me as being as aimless & silly a proceeding as it is possible to imagine.[2]

Good Wishes to Webb,
Yours ever
H.G. Wells

---

[1] In November 1905 a Royal Commission was named to study the English Poor Law and the Relief of Distress. The Law, which dated to medieval times, no longer met the circumstances of modern industrial life. Some reform had occurred in the 1840s, but the law was still insufficient. Twenty persons sat on the Commission and Beatrice Webb became a major factor, producing a Minority Report in two volumes titled, *The Break-Up of the Poor Law: Being Part One of the Minority Report of the Poor Law Commission* (London: Longmans Green, 1909) and *The*

Public Organization of the Labour Market: Being Part Two of the Minority Report of the Poor Law Commission (London: Longmans-Green, 1909). Beatrice Webb in her letter of 24 February 1909 told Wells, 'What an interesting letter – quite the most interesting you have ever written me – I enshrine it with due honour in my diary! Lots of people will agree with you in all you say – and you say it so well.'

[2] Although this is certainly strong criticism of the Minority Report of The Poor Law Commission, which was thought, in many ways, to be the high point of the Webbs's analytical thinking, Wells never wavered in his *public* support for this work. As a writer, and on the more active side in the Fabian Society, his exasperation with their turgid prose comes through clearly, however. Much of his problem with the Fabian Society came in the area of presentation – which Wells sought to do succinctly and clearly in words which any reader could follow.

781. To Beatrice Webb[1]

LSE, ALS

Spade House
Sandgate [late February 1909]

Perhaps my letter was ungenerous but the provocation to hurt your good piece of work as you treated mine & to be just wilfully unsympathetic was too great. You & Sidney have the knack of destroying people & I think you have to consider me among the destroyed. I've tried to do something towards educating the big popular socialist movement & I've even had a generous moment for Webb. He's been the ready ally of Bland or anyone to minimize my influence. And now he's gone out into the ridiculous frontiers of forcing your Minority Report upon the Fabian Society, after a season spent in extracting that stale Basis, paragraph by paragraph & with the society just publishing a tract to show that it has learned nothing & forgotten nothing since the beginning attack which expressly repudiates the essential principles of your report. I give up trying to cooperate with the two of you. I don't see what you are up to in relation to me.

But really your report is as you know a very great piece of work & quite after my own heart.

Very sincerely yours,
H.G.Wells

---

[1] Beatrice Webb wrote back on 28 February urging Wells not to shun the Webbs, and to apologize to him for a remark she had made about *Tono Bungay* which did not represent her true feelings. Relationships were cool, however, and grew even cooler when *The New Machiavelli* appeared in another two years. The serial, even more stringent on the Webb-Bailey personae, began in May, 1910.

782. To Henry Newbolt

Hofstra, ALS

Spade House
Sandgate,   17. iii. 09.

Dear Newbolt,

The book is good all through and curiously [cunningly?] expressive of an attitude of mind. I'm bound to be quoting it soon. But the Tournament – the Tournament is Golly! – writing and telling – just wonderful. All that first Book ranks on the level of couldn't possibly be better. [1]

Yours ever,
H.G.

[1] Newbolt had sent Wells his recently published *The New June* (London: Smith Elder, 1909). This letter also appears in Margaret Newbolt, *Sir Henry Newbolt*, p. 134.

783. To Ford Madox Hueffer

Cornell, Typed Transcription

Spade House   Mar. 29. 09.

Dear Mr. Hueffer.

I shall be obliged if you will either return to me or tell me that you have in safe keeping a MS of Sir Sydney Olivier's that I sent you last winter. I shall also be glad if you will send me a statement of accounts showing the contributors position with regard to the English Review. Who are the present proprietors? You will remember that it was agreed that the concern should be wound up at the fourth number, and as I am acting for Miss Paget as well as myself in this matter I am obliged to ask you for definite statements.

Very sincerely yours,
H.G. Wells

784. To Ford Madox Hueffer

Cornell, Typed Transcription

Spade House

29 March or earlier
[*in one hand*]
Feb. 1909
[*in another hand*]

My dear Hueffer.

Will you please tell me (1) whether you propose to issue a fourth number of the English Review, and (2) if you do, what you propose to do with regard to the payment of Vernon Lee (who wishes me to act for him) and myself?

Very sincerely yours,
H.G. Wells

785. To Ford Madox Hueffer

Cornell, Typed Transcription

Spade House
Sandgate

Apl 2. 09.

Dear Mr. Hueffer.

Your letter says nothing about Sir Sydney Olivier's MS. What has become of it? I am very anxious to have that particular item set straight.

With regard to the payment of Miss Paget and myself, I will confess that we have never based any extravagant hopes on your enterprise. I would like to see Miss Paget paid something, and if you could make a proposal to put her upon the footing of an ordinary contributor, I should have no objection (subject to Sir Sydney Olivier's MS being secured) to waive any golden anticipations I may have formed of the sale of the goodwill of the Review. You will then have your mind and conscience cleared of these three contributors altogether and you will be relieved from such quaint, but I should think irksome, necessities as you impose upon yourself at present, of pretending not to be yourself when speaking through the telephone to me, and of corresponding in strange and oblique manners. All these antics have been totally superfluous from the outset. I never expected anything from your review, and I was quite willing to help it as I have done.

Yours ever,
H.G. Wells

786. To the Editor, *Christian Commonwealth*[1]

PLS

[Spade House
Sandgate] [*c.* 5 May 1909]

Dear Sir, -

You have honoured me by asking me for an article upon the present position of the I. L. P., and were I not bound to get on with a book that cannot conveniently be interrupted, I would certainly do it for you. As it is, I cannot refrain from stating my position in this matter. It seems to me that it is the duty of everyone connected with the Socialist party, big or little, to think this situation out thoroughly, make a definite decision and state it for what it is worth.

For my own part, I have no hesitation in saying that my confidence is wholly with Keir Hardie, Snowden, and Ramsay Macdonald. There are no men fit to replace them in the party. They and their associates stand for all that is sane and practicable and hopeful in Socialist politics. I don't believe in Grayson. I think he has all the levity of youth added to an instability that will last his lifetime. He may do all sorts of things in the world, but politically he will never be anything but a nuisance to his own side. I wouldn't lend him a horse. If I found myself commanding a beseiged fort short of food, water, and ammunition, and hard pressed, and Grayson was in the fort, I should put him outside.

Blatchford has never been one of my idols. He strikes me as touchily vain and excitable, a shy obscure man overpraised for his valiant roaring, who would rather roar like a lion than do anything else in the world. He would insist upon roaring during a night attack. "Let me roar! Let the old lion roar once! They will want to hear me roar!"

Hyndman and Quelch, too, I don't believe in. I have watched all these men pretty closely during the last few years, and I do believe there is a strong ingredient of spite, the proverbial spite of the impotent, in the wrecking tactics they have pursued.

Shaw, again, is in matters political as matters educational, a perverse eccentric, a wit with an outstanding genius for contrast and surprise, a gross sentimentalist in cynic's motley, adorable as a friend and hopelessly tiresome as an associate.

The "Clarion" the other day deplored "personalities" in this discussion, but it is all a question of personalities. These men I have named are the various types of the trouble in Socialist politics, Grayson the generous, impatient, unstable, as the type of the ruling *genus* of the family, and for other genera, Blatchford the limitlessly vain, Hyndman the difficult-tempered, inflexible doctrinaire, Quelch the embittered, Shaw the fastidious stylist with no outstanding of solid purpose yet is veiled however thinly by trite or inadequate expressions. You could classify all the recalcitrant Socialists under these leading species. Haden Guest, for example, is a Shawistical Grayson, and Taylor of the "New Age", a Hyndmanitic Grayson possibly with Pankhurstian affinities.

I think I speak for almost all commonplace, sensible men when I declare that the alternative in Socialist politics to loyalty to the old I. L. P. group is simply no Socialist politics at all. To build on these others would be like building on a hill of soapsuds and sodawater.

Very truly yours,
H. G. Wells

[1] In the wake of the problems in the Fabian Society, and the effects of the Anti-Socialist campaign, many Socialists in the United Kingdom had begun to seek a firm direction. This Christian Socialist newspaper asked Wells to comment on his views. They printed his letter in their issue of 12 May 1909 under the heading, 'The Position of the I.L.P'.

787. To H. A. Jones

Illinois, Typed Transcription

Spade House
Sandgate [24 May 1909]

My dear Jones,

It's just occurred to me that you might like to think of buying my house. Don't be alarmed! But I want very much to leave this place and live in London soon by reason of a web of almost impalpable reasons that affect people of our temperament, and the house is therefore in danger of going very cheap. You like to work down here very much I know and the house gives you practically all you get at Folkestone Hotel – a roof or so for week ends, a garden, a sense of proprietorship and the probability of letting or lending it when you don't want it yourself. It has cost me in all about £2800 or £2900 and I have been asking £3200 and I should be willing to leave about a third of the price on mortgage for seven or eight years at least at 4 or 4½ %. Also it is to let furnished for the summer if you want to try it.

There is no harm in letting you know this anyhow.

Yours ever,
H.G. Wells

788. To Elizabeth Robins[1]

Texas, ALS

[London] [26 May 1909]

Dear Miss Robins,

Certainly I'll come to lunch on June 2d. And your note & the sight of your handwriting has come just when it was most needed & welcome. I didn't know where you were or I think I should have been writing to you to tell you I want very urgently to talk to you. I do! Don't be alarmed! But I want advice, and advice of just the sort that you can give me, very badly. An hours talk with you may, I think do numerous things for me. We but have after all met very little, but there is, I feel, a sort of understanding between us people of the imaginative life. I'm free certainly this week except Friday when I must be in London and engaged between twelve & five. Please help me.

Yours ever,
H.G. Wells

[1] Elizabeth Robins (1862–1952) was to emerge later as a radical feminist, beginning her work as a significant suffragette. She wrote the play *Votes for Women* (1907). She was a founder of *Time and Tide* and wrote an important early radical feminist novel, *Ancilla's Share* which Wells reviewed in the *Westminster Gazette*, 30 August 1924. She knew Amber Reeves well, and acted as a go-between and confidante for Wells and the Reeves family during Amber's pregnancy and marriage.

789. To Elizabeth Robins

Texas, ALS

[Spade House
Sandgate] [1? June 1909]

Dear Elizabeth Robins,

Very many thanks. I see plainly that whatever else may happen, I must be with Amber soon & have her in quiet & comfort away from these stresses. But I am exceedingly anxious not to do things precipitously & that is why I want her in lodgings somewhere for a few weeks, peacefully & companionably housed before the big smash of taking her occurs. I want to have just the right place found & ready. I sold the house on Friday (this quite between ourselves) & I am taking a place in Hampstead, I think, & moving the family there. Naturally, that eats up time & brains. I want time & elbow room if I am to pull this affair off & it is practically impossible for me to get Amber into that longed-for cottage under a month from now. That is why I am so keen to get her into apartments & with the fever for action in her brain a little allayed. I don't want you to be in any way a party to any subsequent proceedings but I should be most grateful if you could let her stay in a pacific cottage round near Hatfield until my train of supplies & outfitting are ready to come into action. If I take her now the whole affair will smash & if she stays in London she will smash. I want to negociate a pause. I've got several people's lives entangled about me, I'm doing all I can to get things triumphantly out of the mess, & Amber's state of tension is forcing my hand, spoiling my game & precipitating a catastrophe. If I could only feel she was right for a month, I might get the whole business in train – oh! brilliantly.

But are <u>you</u> ill? I don't like the feel of letters in pencil & who is that nurse for? – you or Mrs Simmonds? I shall kick myself if I think I've come badgering you with my complications just on the verge of breakdown. Well, anyhow, my warmest thanks & good wishes to you.

Yours ever,
H.G.

790. To Elizabeth Robins

Texas, ACCS

17, Church Row
Hampstead [3 ?June 1909]

Dear Elizabeth Robins,

I think the great search is over. There will be no divorce but Amber will live at Blythe & hold her own alone refusing to live with her husband. There never has been as a matter of fact any grounds for a divorce & there won't be but I shall see her & help her. She won't want for money. I think that is the solution that will most commend itself to you. If at any time you find yourself with Mrs. Reeves, I don't mind at all your letting her know I asked your advice once & that you know about things. She sadly wants heartening over her daughter. We'll all be glad to see you – us here, or Amber at Blythe (especially).

Yours ever,
H.G.Wellls

791. To Elizabeth Robins

Texas, ALS

[London] [14 June 1909]

Dear Miss Robins,

I'm still glowing with you & all sorts of impressions round & about you & it's a humble thing to have to confess that your note to Mrs. Snowden[?] didn't get posted until this morning. I couldn't get any hand on that address before. I have very great doubts if it will get to her or him until long after your lunch because almost certainly both of them will be away campaigning for Whitsuntide & I know they'll leave letters to accumulate in their servantless flat. I wish I could put my hands on them certainly for you. I'd like to bring them to please you. I saw Amber on Friday & she is coming down to you on the 4th, though her mother doesn't think it proper for her to go about without her husband. I think it will be possible for her to get away from him & go into farm house lodging almost at once. Then I propose to find a cottage, clean it & paint it & furnish it without an owner for it, & have it lent to her. She'll be quite content to live in it with a servant girl – though she'd prefer to put out that nervous little head of hers & pull me in after it & shut the door.[1]

Yours ever,

H.G.Wells

---

[1] Amber Reeves was pregnant with Wells's child. In order to protect the Victorian sensibilities of her mother, she had married a suitor, Rivers Blanco-White, in an apparent platonic marriage. Catherine and Wells did not split up, although they did sell Spade House and move to Hampstead. Amber was moved to a cottage in Blythe, where she took the baby after it was born. Catherine Wells, Beatrice Webb, and other acquaintances came to visit her and the new child, as did her husband and Wells. Not everyone was as sanguine about the relationship, and it was in the middle 1930s before Wells and Blanco-White agreed to meet socially, although Wells continued to see Amber on a more or less regular basis. The child was named Anna Jane.

792. To Elizabeth Robins

Texas, ALS

[London] [19 June 1909]

Dear Miss Robins,

No! You're getting away from the realities of the case more & more. And so old proper persons crop up & you aren't helpful. When you treat my Comet book as advocating "free love" & you talk about me in my "character of experimentalist" you just drag in irritating matters. I don't think you can help me any more except by absolute silence about this to everyone. Amber & I must work out our situation without help. We wanted both that she should be away from her husband & with some social backing. We haven't managed the latter & she's alone away in Hertfordshire. As for being "quit" of her! Have you ever in all your life known what it was to have a community of flesh & blood & pain & understanding with another human being? You can't get quit.

Yours ever,

H.G. Wells

793. To unknown addressees

Illinois, TCCD[1]

[Spade House,
Sandgate, Kent]

June, 1907
[*in another hand*]

Why I Joined the National Committee

I have joined the National Committee very much as a drop of water, when it encounters a pailful, lines up with the rest. The Minority report, boldly planned and magnificently done, expresses just that deliberately Constructive Socialism which I have always advocated. And I am glad of this opportunity to underline and accentuate my adhesion because it is possible that the recent antagonism of Webb and myself in Fabian affairs may give rise to misapprehension in the matter. I had sought to replace the sterile and uninspiring Basis of the Fabian Society by a statement of broadly constructive aims, and for reasons that I still fail to grasp, I did not get the support of either Shaw or Webb in that enterprise. Well, that is over now, and I have left the Fabian Society. All the more gladly do I adopt the Minority Report as my banner.

H.G. Wells

[1] I have seen this in a draft on correspondence cards, and it was published in *Christian Commonwealth* 30 June 1909. It was addressed to anyone, especially in the Fabian Society, who may have had questions about supporting the Minority Report of the Poor Law Reform Commission. This letter was also published in the first edition, but not the second, of a pamphlet, *The Charter of the Poor* (London, 1909). The newspaper and the pamphlet were made up mainly of such testimonials. The pamphlet marked the founding of a supporting National Committee to Aid Poor Law Reform.

794. To Elizabeth Robins

Texas, ALS

Spade House
Sandgate [13 July 1909]

Dear Elizabeth Robins

I wrote you a cross rude letter & I bow beneath your feet. (But you were wrong about me) I'm putting Amber into Blythe.

Forgive me for everthing,
Yours ever,
H.G. Wells

P.T.O.
I've just been to Blythe & it's admirable.[1]

[1] This letter is in response to an apology from Robins to Wells, of 12 July which appears in draft form on the obverse of this letter.

795. To Elizabeth Robins

Texas, ALS

17, Church Row
Hampstead [7? August 1909]

Come and see us if you are in London.
[*with an arrow drawn to the address*]

Dear Miss Robins,

You ought to know how things are settling down. Amber is in Blythe. There will not be a divorce – a quite satisfactory treaty has been made about that. I shall be about at Blythe a good deal and Blanco-White will come down for weekends. Everybody is going to be ostentatiously friendly with everybody & honi-soit-qui-mal-y-pense.[1] Amber seems likely to be very happy in Blythe. At present she has two puppies & my two little boys to satisfy her abounding maternity – while we move to Hampstead. It is well to pretend to Mrs. Reeves that I don't exist if you meet her.

Yours ever,
H.G. Wells

[1] The motto of the Order of the Garter – shamed be he who thinks evil of it.

796. To George Meek

Illinois, ALS

After Friday

15 [*crossed out*] Church Row
Hampstead [August 1909]

My Dear Meek,

I am moving from here[1] – having sold the house & the men are rolling up carpets & so forth. I am sending your M.S. back. My wife read it & she says that it has the same touching quality, the same fine sense of detail & the same faults as your autobiography. She says it is a bad length – she herself is a story writer you know – and that you make the mistake of writing about things you don't know – the Jewish financier, e.g. Sorry I can't give it more attention but life is being damnably urgent & troublesome with me just now.

Yours ever,
H.G. Wells

[1] Spade House

797. To the Editor, *British Weekly*[1]

Illinois, ADLS

17, Church Row
Hampstead [*c.* August 1909]

Dear Sir,

It is quite characteristic of The British Weekly to decide that a novel ought to be a hundred thousand words in length & assume that a writer who runs to greater lengths than that 'spins out' his story, but I do not see why you should expect me to discuss anything so silly. No doubt that representative organ of British criticism will go on to tell the world the right size of a picture. Why not let it?

Yours very sincerely,
H.G. Wells

[1] This letter may have been sent to the *British Weekly*, but if so, it was apparently not published. At the top of the letter, encircled, are the words in Wells's hand , 'Add Too long novels' and in another circle, '1gms' . This may indicate that another letter went out, or it may indicate that no letter was sent.

798. To Elizabeth Robins

Texas, ACCS

[London] [July or August, 1909]

Dear Elizabeth Robbins [*struck out*] Robins,
Please forgive that, it was my wife's surname.

You've got rather away from our situation & I don't think you quite understand how we look at these things. The child wasn't an accident. But anyhow Amber is away in apartments now & we're going on working out our affair without dragging in anyone else. I trust you implicitly not to discuss this knowledge with anyone & particularly not with Mrs. Reeves, who is not only foolish but treacherous & may precipitate some horrible misadventure if you gave her any inkling of what is or may be fact. And anyhow it is very good

& kind of you to give me all the warnings against my baser self. I am afraid I have to judge right & wrong by my own standards.

Yours very gratefully,
H.G.Wells

799. To Lord Esher[1]

Illinois, Typed Transcription

[London] August 23rd, 1909

[Dear Lord Esher]

I don't think I know anything at all of military matters but since warfare is evidently to be waged in the future very largely with novel and untried appliances, I suppose an active and well trained imagination is sometimes able to provide suggestions – my training has I think served to keep my imagination if anything rather too much alive. Of course I shall be only too delighted and flattered to meet you in London when you return.

Yours very sincerely,
H.G. Wells

[1] Viscount Esher was a confidant of the Royal Family and at this time involved in what the Prince of Wales described as the 'imperative duty of maintaining an Army capable of successfully resisting any attack'.

800. To Bernard Shaw

Illinois, ALS

[Spade House
Sandgate] 24th August 1909

My Dear Shaw

Occasionally you don't simply rise to a difficult situation, but soar above it & I withdraw anything you would like withdrawn from our correspondence of the last two years or so. There is no use in giving details about this affair. The world being full of asses and cowards it will be very disagreeable[?] for Blanco-White and his wife if these stories get any decent backing, that is all. Matters are very much as you surmise. We should all be very happy & proud of ourselves if we hadn't the feeling of being harried and barked at by dogs. Amber has got a little cottage in Blythe, Dean Road Woldingham[?]. B.W. works in London, & goes down in his leisure time. I like him & am unblushingly fond of her & I go down there quite often. The Reeves don't know how often & the heavens will fall if Reeves does. My children are staying there now while Jane goes to London. It will be nice & amusing if you ran down to Blythe one day Amber is going to have a child early in the New Year & she can't go about & see people.

Yours ever,
(in a gust of violent friendliness)
H.G.

801. Amber Reeves Blanco-White to Catherine Wells[1]

Illinois, ALS

Blythe [24–5 August 1909]

Dearest Jane,

Many thanks for your sons. They have been perfectly delightful and I'm awfully sorry they are going. They've been very well here, I think, and even Esther remarked to me that "They are tidy little boys, they tickle me to death." Vedder & Grundy will have to go into black bows.

Fraulein will doubtless explain to you that some of the linen you sent is at the wash. Towels, it is, I think – I did go over the list and see them packed but have forgotten. I'll send them on as soon as they come back.

I tried to wring from the boys some admission that perhaps they would like to come again, but they only say that they can't see ahead to the time when they will have explored the heath with sufficient thoroughness. I hope that day will come though.

You'll come yourself as soon as you really get over the house, won't you?

Did you know that one rub of Wood Milne shoeshine keeps boots bright for days? I see from a bill head on my desk that it does. Thought you might find the hint useful.

Dear Jane what ought one to per week prepare ahead for feeding four people? Rivers and H.G. and visitors and the day counting as one. Things are awfully dear here locally, and if you get them from London you have to pay 2/- each time from the station. You might say about though because I want to fix a proper allowance for things.

Best love
from
Amber

---

[1] Certainly one of the more unusual and one of the most 'civilised' letters in this collection. Amber, entertaining Wells's and Catherine's children, thanking her for linen, and sending messages back by the boy's governess, while Catherine went to London. Vedder and Grundy were probably her two dogs.

802. To George Meek

Illinois, ALS

17, Church Row
Hampstead [1909?]

My dear Meek,

I've written Constable.[1] I'm very busy.[2]

Yours ever,
H.G. Wells

---

[1] Constable published the book *George Meek: Bathchairman by Himself* (Constable: London, 1910).

[2] There is a whole sheaf of letters to Meek, but almost none of them are dated, so placement of the letters in this collection is tentative.

803. To George Meek

Illinois, ALS

17, Church Row
Hampstead [September? 1909
possibly 1910]

Dear Meek,

No. I stick to my promise to pay that last instalment.[1] If I might offer advice, it is that you should now do some very simple, intimate, unaffected short stories (not too lurid or tragic) about the kind of people you know intimately, & try the English Review with them (mention my name.)

Yours ever,

H.G. Wells

Austin Harrison Esq',
English Review
c/o Chapman & Hall
11 Henretta Street
W.C.

Let me know of your passage through London – we might arrange a lunch here for the three of you & a few admirers.

[1] Wells had set up a cycle of payments to Meek, when he agreed to help with the book; see letter 818.

804. To Mary Barrie[1]

ALS

17, Church Row
Hampstead

[early 1910][2]

My dear Mrs. Barrie,

How are things going with you? I'm concerned by vague rumours that everything isn't well between Barrie & you. Can't someone do something? I don't like to think of you as getting poor and embittered & that's the turn the stories give things. My best respects to Cannan, too.

I've had rather a bad time. Amber & I are being forced never to see or write to each other. I suppose it is the same thing in the long run – except that I rather hanker after bolting – but it hurts horribly & leaves one the prey to all sorts of moods. Anyway we've brought a very jolly little daughter into the world.

Good wishes to you

Yours ever,

H. G. Wells

[1] Mary Barrie was the separated wife of the playwright, James Barrie. She was about to marry Gilbert Cannan, after seven years of separation. Wells was fond of both of them. These remarkably understanding letters appear in a biography of Barrie, Janet Dunbar, *J.M. Barrie: The Man Behind the Image* (London: Collins, 1970), pp. 178, 181. One of them also carried a small drawing of a heart with the names Gilbert and Mary inside it. At the top of the heart are the words, 'This is a picture of my heart', and the sketch is signed, 'Uncle H.G'. A facsimile of the drawing also appears in Andrew Birkin, *J.M. Barrie and the Lost Boys* (New York: Clarkson Potter, 1979), p. 176. According to Birkin, Wells, Henry James, A. E. W. Mason, Maurice Hewlett, Arthur Pinero, William Archer, Beerbohm Tree, and others, wrote a circular letter to the London press that 'as a mark of respect and gratitude to a writer of genius' they abstain from heavy coverage of the divorce case,which was heard beginning 13 October 1910, since he is 'a man for whom the inevitable pain of these proceedings would be greatly increased by publicity'. In the event coverage was slight. I have not located this joint letter. The marriage with Cannan was not very successful as he spent many years in mental institutions.

[2] My original dating of the letters to Mary Barrie as 1909 was incorrect. They must have been written in early 1910, as the baby was born on December 31/January 1.

805. To Mary Barrie

ALS

17, Church Row
Hampstead [early 1910]

Dear Mrs Barrie,

Sillies you are! Go & live together & get Babies as soon as you can like two sensible people. One could think there was magic in marriage. Fancy you & your friends conspiring to glorify the Damned old Fetish. Also – and this is impertinence – I wouldn't marry if I were you unless you know you are going to have Babys. No earthly reason why you should for if so be you soon should disagree, it gives you both amazing powers of making Hell for one another. So take an old Sinner's advice & *tell* them you are married when the time comes, & don't marry unless there is a child to legitimate. I'll always say I know you are & declare I was a witness at the registry office if you want confirmation. This by the way, but affairs go on – tumultuously & with complications – but quite well on the whole. Too long a story to tell. Of course I don't leave Jane. Why should I? But as Shaw says, incorrect rumours are the best concealment in the world. Thanks for your valiant denials. Poor recluse! You have our warmest sympathy.

H. G. W.

806. To George Meek

Illinois, ALS

Blythe
Woldingham
Sussex [August-September 1909][1]

My dear Meek,

Good wishes for the M.S. I wish I could help you further.
Yours ever,
H.G. Wells

[1] Dating derived from the heading. The cottage where Amber was living before the baby was born was located at Blythe.

807. To George Meek

Illinois, ALS

~~Westminster Chambers~~
~~13, Victoria Street~~
~~London, S.W.~~ [August-September 1909?]

[*This address is crossed out, and the legend, in Wells's hand, 'Reply to Spade House, Sandgate', appears. This address is that of The High Commissioner, New Zealand, Amber Reeves's father.*]

Dear Meek,

I've got the story & shall read it as soon as a confounded paper on American Social Conditions is done.[1] But it certainly isn't too long. Rather the other way round.

Yours ever
H.G. Wells

Did you get that opening section of novel or wasn't it sent you?

[1] This paper is somewhat elusive, at least in its magazine form. Wells lists it as being published in a non-existing journal. It may have been a piece for a multi-authored history of the world, which came out in 1908–9. A version of it appeared in *An Englishman Looks at the World* (1914), which was published in America under the title, *Social Forces in England and America.* I have seen a corrected proof of this work, set up as a pamphlet to be published by Fifield. I do not think that it was ever published. The text is about sixty pages in type.

808. To George Meek

Illinois, ACCS

Spade House
Sandgate [September, 1909]

My dear Meek,

I'm just now through with your story. I will write about it later but I want to tell you there is a gap between the Billington[?] School & the American farm. Have you missed sending some of the M.S. or what has happened?

Yours ever,
H.G. Wells

809. To George Meek

Illinois, ALS

17, Church Row
Hampstead [1909]

My dear Meek,

I am glad you are trying to do something for yourself & I will remember your pitch if I have any friends going to Brighton. I have no old clothes to spare at present but I will bear your needs in mind.

Yours sincerely,
H.G. Wells

810. To George Meek

Illinois, ACCS

17 Church Row
Hampstead [late 1909?]

Dear Meek,

Will you study enclosed & carefully fill up the form & write the letter indicated & then return the whole galleys to me. Ars longa, vita brevis.

Best Wishes,
H.G. Wells

811. To George Meek

Illinois, ACCS

17, Church Row
Hampstead [1909-1910?]

Dear Meek,

You'll get £5 tomorrow.

Yours ever,
H.G. Wells

812. To Beatrice Webb

Illinois, ALS

17, Church Row
Hampstead [September ? 1909]

Dear Mrs. Webb,

I wrote to Webb some days ago about a story you are telling (under pledge of secrecy) about me. It isn't a true story, Webb is lying about the source of it, & it does the ugliest injustice to Mr. Blanco-White. Webb has not answered my letter. So far as I can judge the tale engendered[?] in its present form in Well Hall & you extracted it from that very unfortunate[?] young man you employ, Colegate. I think it would have been more in accordance with your pose as an A, if you had given me a chance of refusing or correcting this scandal before you began putting it about among my friends & his.

I didn't, of course, when I came on that Committee of yours for the Break Up of the Poor Law conditions understand that there were to be these collateral activities. You know best how far my name will be worth anything after you have finished this campaign against me, but anyhow I put my imagination in your hands to use as you think fit for the cause.

I asked Webb to tell me, at any rate, who he was telling about this. Practically you are leaving Amber & myself no alternative but a public smash to clear up this intolerable sneaking nastiness about us. We've made pretty big sacrifices to mind that & it's bound to hurt Blanco-White, the Reeves's & my wife very dreadfully. But when people of your sort act as channels for the machinations[?] of the Bland-Colegate type, there's nothing else possible but the open.

Yours very sincerely,
H.G. Wells

813. To Maurice Baring

Illinois, ALS

17, Church Row
Hampstead

[10 September 1909]

My dear Baring,

The book of short stories pleased me very much indeed, though I swear for the space of a second that you didn't devote the Calypso story to me, with its two ornithologists & everything. I liked the flute player, & the fluting Changling as well as any & the man who gave good advice & the resort story & the parody of Belloc ran these close. I wait now for your complete [*illegible word*] writer. Note my telephone number[1] & my address – one minute from the tube. Don't listen to evil stories about me for even if the facts are right the values are always manly & believe me and

Yours
H.G.

[1] Wells's telephone number at that time, Hampstead 3489 was printed on his stationery.

814. To George Meek

Illinois, ALS

Spade House
Sandgate [September 1909]

My dear Meek,

I have now read your M.S. through (I found the missing part on my return here) and I find it extremely interesting. But I am in great doubt what can be done with it. I do not know of any publisher who would be likely to print it as it stands. To me it is good living stuff. There have been moments when I have been tempted to set to work to write it up & make a long novel out of it. I think it wants some sort of careful revision anyhow. I'll think over it. I really believe something can be done with it but for the life of me I don't yet see my way.

My wife will look into the matter of that suit & I hope find something not too thin to send you in a few days time.

Very sincerely yours
H.G. Wells

815. To Mr Oyler

Hofstra, ALS

17, Church Row
Hampstead Sept 12 09

Dear Mr Oyler,

Your article is very interesting & well written indeed. I haven't the remotest idea of how you ought to place yourself in life. These interludes are among the trying & unstable places of existence. You'll find your job coming along to your hands soon enough I expect.

Very Sincerely yours
H.G. Wells

816. To Violet Paget

Colby, ALS

17, Church Row
Hampstead

[September 1909][1]

Dear "Sister in Utopia,"

This world is very resonant & transparent & I perceive you have been listening to scandal about me & avoiding me, instead of coming to me to find out just what the moral values were, as I think you ought to have done. I'm very sorry for I had wanted to talk to you – very sorry indeed. And it wasn't kind to my wife who likes & admires you beyond measure. Well, I forgive you because I know the complications of life & if at any time you would like to know me again, I'm altogether at your service. I've done nothing I'm ashamed of. I had meant to write to you a long letter against your symbols of the laurel bough – it must have been very long if I had written all I meant to do.

Good bye for a time.
Very Sincerely yours
H.G. Wells

[1] This is the first in a series of at least four letters written by Wells to 'Vernon Lee' which discuss Amber Reeves and her pregnancy. Wells apparently delayed writing to her as he knew she would be more censorious, or he thought so, in any case.

817. To Violet Paget

Colby, ALS

17, Church Row
Hampstead

Tuesday [September 1909]

Dear "Vernon Lee,"

Your letter is just what I might have expected – warmest thanks for it. I can't talk about things now. It's vital to us all that we should be left alone to straighten out our affairs in our own way – & thought of & dealt with generously. So – until we can talk next year let us leave this. Will you, if you can, silence talks & hasty judges & believe me always.

Very much yours
H.G. Wells

818. To George Meek

Illinois, ALS

Spade House
Sandgate Sept 18th, 1909

VERY PRIVATE

My dear Meek,

I have been thinking over the story & what may be done with it. At present it is 35000 words long (about) & the ordinary novel is 70000 words, so that as it is it could hardly be published except let us say as a shilling pamphlet & as that form does not pay to advertise & push it would probably yield you nothing or next to nothing. Also I doubt if my publisher would take it up in its present form as a literary speculation at all. I don't think many people will see in it without help the quality of gentleness & fine feeling which claims me. It has many superficial faults, crude expressions, want of knowledge of various sorts & so on, that might blind many readers to its merits.

Also I have a very strong artistic impulse to use your stuff for a purpose of my own. I want to rewrite it in a different setting. I was recently at a big house near Windsor for the Ascot week end. It was rather a splendid party; there was an ex-Prime Minister, an ex-Viceroy, a prior foreign minister, a duchess & so on & everything was very glittering & magnificent. Well, I want to begin by describing the party at dinner & then how my thoughts went back to your m.s. which I had been reading upstairs in my room before dinner. Then I shall describe you as you came to me at Sandgate & go on with your story. I shall show that you are just exactly as fine as these people & discuss the marvel of your sort of life & their sort of life being in the same world. I think I can see a tremendous piece of writing in this, a tremendous criticism not only of their beliefs but yours & the whole system. The week end will be described, the

Sunday morning, the tennis in the afternoon & a gossip on the lawn, the men seriously will walk across the picture, & then I shall plunge back into your story. Finally I shall begin to talk to these people about your M.S. & the whole social problem.[1]

That's my scheme. But when it comes to fixing up arrangements, I am perplexed. For me such a book means a year of writing & as I spread my work out & later on open & put it down again, I may not get the thing done until 1910. Also, I've got to live in a certain scale; if the book sells it will sell largely on my prestige; & I can't think of anything like going halves on what will be got out of it. I can't afford to give so large or anything like so large a portion of my earnings to you because in the same time it is equally open to me to put in all the time at a piece of work wholly my own. But here is a proposal which you must think over & which is really very much fairer than it will strike you at first – all things considered. Suppose I buy your story for £30 paid in the following way; £5 by Oct. 1st & £5 on Dec 22nd (for Christmas) Then I may want you to write up altogether 20,000 words more, supplying particulars & I may want to come along & talk to you as I get into the job. Well, I will pay you £5 for each 10,000 words written if they are written before May 1st & August 1st respectively & if they are not because I haven't asked for them, I'll pay the fivers on these dates. Finally the last £10 when the book is published or on June 1st 1910 whichever comes first. Then I will get what I can out of the book. I may get anything between £250 & £1000 or even more. I will pay you one tenth of my nett except (i.e. after deducting against fees & so forth) after deducting the advance of £30. In this way you will certainly get £30 towards your personal expenses while you write other things & you may get a decent sum in addition, you will learn a lot about writing & you will get a considerable publicity. The book will appear as a collaboration by H.G. Wells & George Meek (I can't have any damned 'pen names') & we will call that bath chairman our hero, William Deedes or Henry Drew or some such south of England name.[2]

Will you think this over carefully & let me know. If you agree will you recapitulate my terms & then we shall have a virtual agreement.

Very sincerely yours,
H.G. Wells

---

[1] This idea is retained as a paragraph in Wells's introduction to the published book. This letter may have been written during Royal Ascot from the country house of the Desboroughs. See letter 848.

[2] A document in the Meek files dated Sept 16/08 lays out the terms of the agreement, essentially as it appears in this letter, but either the date of that document or this letter is in error. Both are in either Wells's or Catherine's hand.

819. To Violet Paget

Colby College, ACCS

17, Church Row
Hampstead [3 or 4 October 1909]

Dear Miss Paget

Will you come to lunch or supper on Sunday or Monday just as it pleases you. We'll talk like nice human beings as occasion determines & we shall both be very glad indeed to see you.

Yours ever
H.G. Wells

820. To George Meek

Illinois, ACCS

17, Church Row
Hampstead [1909?]

Dear Meek,

Aren't you a bit exacting with Maurice Baring? He is not very wealthy, he has all sorts of claims on him. Belloc is frightfully hard up. Have you written your uncle about that bond. It would be cheaper to pay the C.P.R.[1] to cable in that matter than to keep on indefinitely troubled. M.B. & I will stand the expense of that.

Yours ever,
H.G. Wells

The book is out. I will send on such cuttings as reach me.

---

[1] Canadian Pacific Railroad. Meek's uncle lived in Vancouver, British Columbia, Canada, and had recently visited him, the story of which fills in the latter part of Meek's book. Meek was on the verge of possibly migrating, or at least travelling in North America, and he was hoping for a loan of money and a gift of clothes from Baring, and Belloc, both of whom had met him, and thought his book important.

821. To George Meek

Illinois, ACCS

Spade House
Sandgate [Autumn 1909]

My dear Meek,

Don't count on anything yet – not even on publication. I am giving the whole thing careful thought but it is a difficult business.

Very sincerely yours
H.G. Wells

822. To Violet Paget

Colby, ALS

17, Church Row
Hampstead [end November 1909]

My Dear Miss Paget.

Many thanks for your letter, though I think I've got to write about the things I know & feel, even if it scatters my "public" to the four quarters of heaven. The facts of the scandal are perfectly plain & simple but they can't be published broadcast in their simplicity. I was & am in love with a girl half my age, we have a quite peculiar and intense mental intimacy, which is the finest & best thing we have had or can have in our lives again – & we have loved one another physically & she is going to bear me a child. We have made the most careful & elaborate plans to save this from scandalizing our friends & the public & all that was wrecked by the violence of her father. She attempted very assiduously[?] to cover the situation by marrying a man who is devoted to her & who promised to leave her alone for so long as she pleased & promised us free intercourse – on an understanding of course that we rigidly respected that we shall cease to be in common parlance lovers. Certain people just wouldn't permit this to happen – people who ruin mostly our character & quality. We are fighting to keep in touch with each other which is a matter of quite vital importance to both of us &

we mean to keep in touch. From this buds & branches, complications, situations, misstatements, lyings. The present clamour for our divorce & that we should marry or have an absolute separation. There you are! You won't for a moment tolerate it I know – nobody seems going to tolerate it.- I won't leave my wife whose life is built up on mine or my sons who have a need of me. I won't give up my thinking & meeting with my lover. I mean somehow to see my friend & my child & I mean to protect her to the best of my power from the urgent people who want to force her to make her marriage a "real one."

And that's all.

Yours ever,
H.G. Wells [1]

---

[1] Her letter in response to this letter was dated 22 December. This, and some others to Wells may also be found in Peter Gunn, *Vernon Lee: Violet Paget, 1865–1935* (London: OUP, 1984).

823. To the Editor, *Spectator*[1]

PLS

17 Church Row
Hampstead

[*c.* 1 December 1909]

Sir, – My attention has been called to your strenuous review of my last book, "Ann Veronica." under the heading, "A Poisonous Book." I have considered that review very carefully, and after a first phase of natural resentment, I am disposed to acquit the writer of anything but an entirely honest and intolerant difference of opinion. I would like with your permission to offer a few remarks upon that difference, because I think very wide issues are involved in your suggestion that my book should be burnt, so the speak, by the common hangman and myself trampled underfoot.

My book was written primarily to express the resentment and distress which many women feel nowadays at their unavoidable practical dependence upon some individual man not of their deliberate choice, and in full sympathy with the natural but perhaps anarchistic and anti-social idea that it is intolerable to have sexual relations with a man with whom she is not in love, and natural and desirable and admirable for her to want them, and still more so to want children by a man of her own selection. Now these may be very shocking ideas indeed, but it is not the first time they have erupted into literature, and I submit that a case can be made out for tolerating their discussion. The case lies in the fact that the opposite arrangment by which a woman is subdued, first to her father, and to a husband of his choice, is not in our present phase of civilisation working satisfactorily. I do not, of course, expect you to attach any great value to the distress, inconvenience, and even misery that this inflicts upon many women, over-educated to a painful degree of delicacy of perception; but I know your keen and vigorous patriotism, and it seems to me that you overlook the fact that in practice the arrangement you manifestly approve is not giving the Modern State enough children, or fine enough childen for its needs. Your ideals have had the fullest play in the United States of America among the once prolific population of English and Dutch descent. There, if anywhere, the Christian ideal of marriage and woman's purity, as you conceive it, has prevailed exclusively. So late as 1906 the Gorki incident in New York called attention to the continuing vigour of these conceptions. And yet that colonial strain has dwindled to a mere fraction of the population of the United States, and still dwindles. In France, again, the man-ruled family has become insufficiently prolific for the public need. People of your persuasion have denounced "race suicide" with a quite remarkable eloquence, but it has produced no appreciable effect on the decline. Now I explain this decline, rightly or wrongly, by the fact that the man in a man-ruled family, which is competing for existence with other families, has not only no great national passion for offsping, but has also under our present conditions every practical inducement to limit their number, that there is an enormous pressure as well as an enormous temptation, for the wife to shirk what you, I think, would join with me in regarding as her chief public duty; and so I believe that the development of civilisation demands a review of the constitution of the family and of our conventions of the relations of man and women, which will give the natural instincts of women freer play. I have come to this belief after years of thought and hesitation, and I mean to give it expression. The Family *does not work* as it used to do, and we do not know why, and we have to look into it. With the best will in the world to damage my book, your reviewer could not find anything at all to call pornographic in it, and so I enter my plea for an arrest of judgment and liberty of discussion in this vitally important field.

I am, Sir, etc.,

H. G. Wells

---

[1] Wells was ever vigilant for 'unfair' reviews of his work. After the anti-Socialist campaign, and the attacks on *In The Days of the Comet*, he became more vigilant. When *Ann Veronica*, the story of a young woman liberated by her assertiveness, was published, the book was hailed by those sympathetic to feminism and Socialism. It was thoroughly disliked by more conventional papers. Such a paper was the *Spectator*. Wells responded to the review with this letter, headed

'An Open Question', 4 December 1909, p. 945. The editor responded with an even longer letter, summarising the debate and saying that he believed that Wells deserved a hearing, but declined being drawn into a general discussion of Wells's views, in the novel or elsewhere.

824. To. H. A. Jones

Illinois/Texas, Typed Transcription[1]

The Reform Club
[London] [late 1909]

My dear Jones

I haven't written plays for a number of reasons, but one of the chief of these was the persuasion that my work might in end be made abortive by the incalculable whim of the Censor. His recent obstinate campaign against Shaw does I think justify my discretion.

Yours sincerely,
H. G. Wells

[1] This letter has another letter at the bottom from Wells to Mrs Thorne, Jones's daughter, giving her permission to use this letter in a memoir of her father. It appears in volume 4.

825. To Thomas Seccombe[1]

Korn, ACCS

17, Church Row
Hampstead [*c.* end 1909?]

Dear Seccombe,

"Milly" is to be matched for us. See enclosed. Let's all three lunch at some restaurant (me host) on Wednesday. You write Meek & say which & I'll keep the day open.

Yours ever,
H.G.

[1] Seccombe (f. before 1914) was an author, mainly of children's books, who was interested in the theatre, and was close to George Gissing. He also worked on the *Dictionary of National Biography* (*DNB*) and wrote the appreciation of Wells which appeared in the *Bookman* double issue of August 1914 devoted to Wells and his work.

826. To Mr Lee[1]

Illinois, ALS

17, Church Row
Hampstead [1909-10]

My dear Lee.

Warmest thanks – for the pamphlet which I shall read with the greatest interest, & which I see by my first cursory study is full of print.

Yours ever
H. G. Wells

[1] Lee is unknown.

827. To 'Vernon Lee'

Colby, ALS

17, Church Row
Hampstead New Years Eve
[31 December 1909]

Dear Friend,

I have a little daughter born this morning. You wrote me the kindest letter & I clutch very eagerly at the friendship that you say is still mine.[1] I don't think that there is any faultless apology for Amber & me. We've been merry & half passionate, – there's no excuse except that we loved very greatly & were both inordinately greedy of life. Anyhow now we've got to stand a great deal – of which the worst is separation – & we're doing it chiefly for love of my wife & my boys.

Best wishes for you for the New Year
H. G. Wells

[1] In her letter of 22 December 1909, Paget had remarked, 'what grieves me is not that those who have eaten the cake or drunk the wine should pay the price of it, but that part of that price should be paid by others who have not had their share. ... My experience as a woman and as a friend of women persuades me that a girl, however much she may have read and thought and talked, however willing she may think herself to assume certain responsibilities, cannot know what she is about as a married or older woman would, and that the unwritten code is right when it considers that an experienced man owes her protection from himself – from herself ... but one thing you and I do, I feel sure, agree upon, namely that although those who are not tempted cannot judge of the difficulty of resisting, those on the other hand, who *are* tempted, cannot judge of the need which the community has of demanding that temptation should be resisted". She signed the letter, 'Your *Sister in Utopia*' and affectionate friend'.

828. To Edmund Gosse

Leeds, ACCS

[London] [1909-1910]

My dear Gosse

I'm afraid I didn't quite do our friend[1] justice the other day. There has been a very great strain on account of his wife's ill health, which has at last become very grave. It seems she has tuberculous kidney. They've really been forced to break up homes once or twice. I think I was harsh about his general position, the hardships of strained virtue. He probably is damned hard up, it's largely no fault of his own, & Fifth Queen, & Privy Seal & The Fifth Queen Crowned are three remarkably good novels.

Very sincerely yours
H. G. Wells

p.t.o.

I write this off in a hurry. I was very pleased to have your book & when I have read it I shall express my gratitude more fully.

[1] Ford Madox Ford (Hueffer) (1873–1939) was a novelist and editor. His editing, especially of the *English Review* and the *Transatlantic Review*, was significant in creating the ideas behind modernist writing.

829. To Edmund Gosse

Leeds, ACCS

17, Church Row
Hampstead [1909-1910]

My dear Gosse,

On reflection I hand this on to you.[1] I can't take on this job. I spend four or five hundred a year on various poor relations & it's as much as my income justifies. But, you know, I know, various "sources" which might perhaps find a relief in the Gissing direction. I can't quite see what he's doing with his brother's M.S.S. They weren't left to him.

Yours very sincerely
H. G. Wells

[1] This letter and the next refer to an effort by Algernon Gissing, George Gissing's brother, to obtain funds as he was in straitened circumstances.

830. To Edward Clodd

Leeds, ALS

17 Church Row
Hampstead [1909-1910]

Dear Clodd,

I don't care after the hideous fuss made by the Gissing family about my obituary notice to incur fresh hostility by being mixed up in any further Gissingism. And it's doubtful after all the Library Committee bother & so on at Manchester, if my name wouldn't be rather a deterrent to the subscription-list people than otherwise.[1] Also Arthur[?] hasn't written me. But it's a good idea. You support it & make them at any rate get the name of the highest living authority on Gissing, – Thomas Seccombe.

Yours ever
H. G. Wells

[1] Wells is referring to the contretemps created when a library committee at Manchester banned circulation of his novel, *Ann Veronica*.

831. To an unknown addressee

Illinois, ALS

17, Church Row
Hampstead [1909-1910]

My dear Sir,

Very many thanks for your letter. I would be very amused & grateful to learn the subtleties of Pope Joan from you. But -. Have you ever written a novel? I am now in the distresses of concluding a new one & a thing of morals & usefulness.[1] May I telephone one day in the next month instead of making a definite appointment?

Very sincerely yours,
H. G. Wells

[1] The novel is the *New Machiavelli*. Pope Joan was a parlour game of the period. Wells was fond of such games, especially charades and little theatre productions.

832. To Harry Leon Wilson[1]

Bancroft, ALS

17, Church Row
Hampstead [1909-1910]

My dear Wilson,

At last I've really read The Seeker & a very fine novel it is. Mostly I read no novels. I don't read much at all, & then comes a period of adventurous opening of books. The Seeker is a novel after my own heart, just the story of travel & happenings amusing views & beliefs, that I most like to write myself. And to an English reader it's tremendously illuminating. Extraordinary vermin an American Episcopalian bishop must be, a thing against nature, like a Yorkshire Buddhist or a Swiss Mahometan. What else have you done that you'd like me to read?

Yours ever,
H. G. Wells

[1] This letter is misdated, in another hand, as 1904 but it may have been written in early 1913. From the heading of the stationery the two other letters to Wilson, 933 and 934, are probably both from 1913 as well. Harry Leon Wilson (1867–1929) was a satirical writer whose subjects were mainly about California idiosyncracies. His best known works were *Ruggles of Red Gap* (1915) and *Merton of the Movies* (1922).

833. To Elizabeth Healey

Illinois, ACCS

The Reform Club
London [early January 1910]

Dear Miss Healey,

I'm going to write you a long letter soon, but I've awful dread. All the rumours are true & false in various measure. Mrs. Blanco-White has got a pretty little daughter anyhow. I'm afraid I've behaved rather scandalous but no how mean in the past year. Believe everything scandalous & nothing mean about me & you'll be fairly right.

Yours ever,
H. G. Wells

834. To Thomas Seccombe

Korn, ACCS

17, Church Row
Hampstead [1910?]

Damn it! Seccombe! I've already corrected the proofs once & you send me on <u>your</u> amendments on an uncorrected proof. Please incorporate my first corrections. Consider what I've accepted & rejected on this & then on a nice fresh proof insert your final product. But I must <u>name</u> [*illegible word*] once or I won't sign the introduction.

Yours ever,
H.G.

835. To Thomas Seccombe

Korn, ALS

17, Church Row
Hampstead [c. 1910]

My dear Seccombe,

Here is a proof of Meek's introduction. If you will let me have a proof of his stuff, when you read the proof of this, I will enlarge the praise of him by a thousand words or so.

Yours ever,
H.G.

836. To Ford Madox Hueffer

Cornell, Typed Transcription

17, Church Row
Hampstead [early 1910?]

Dear Hueffer,

I can assure you I never for a moment suspected your motives in that matter, or for a moment bore resentment on account of it. And don't too readily believe base and ugly versions of this story that is going about. There is a lot of very foolish and groundless virtuous indignation at large – always.

Yours ever,
H.G. Wells

837. 'Vernon Lee' to H. G. Wells[1]

Illinois, AL

Florence January 19, 1910

Dear Mr. Wells, Dear Friend,

I don't know exactly what it is I want to write, except what I wrote last represented only one half of me and represented it in a cut & dry, crude, pedantic, self-righteous form. I do think all that. But I think and feel also that you are one of the greatest and dearest of living persons, and that your books, even your worst, are far above the best thought and work of those who fall foul of them.

And, dear Mr. Wells, since I speak of falling foul (and in the literal sense 'foul') of your books, I want to say again and after oh such sickening discussions of Ann Veronica that you must not 'give' all of those who are faithful to you the misery of the discussions which will ensue if at this moment you wish more than can be connected with your personality or interpreted in the light of your own case.

P.S. If you have a book dealing with love, etc. ready, hold it back till it can be read for what it is. People will forget if you don't remind them. I am not counselling cowardice. If I thought people could behold your reasons and arguments, I should say 'write it all out boldly and take your case directly'. But anything you write now will be merely skimmed as a test for dirty Puritan comment.

Some think A.V. was stealing another woman's man & Capes was just like Ramage!! There's a run on the book for its 'psychological interest'.

[*The letter simply ends here, and probably it is what she sent to Wells at the time.*]

[1] The storm over Wells's writings – not the quality but the frankness of the material discussed – was not confined to the press. Colleagues and friends also wrote of their own feelings, most of which consisted of advising him to do what he must, but perhaps try to soften and delay his attack on contemporary morality.

838. To 'Vernon Lee'

Colby, ALS

Reform Club
Pall Mall, S.W. [postmarked Jan. 28 1910]

Dear Vernon Lee,

Your letter has really moved me. But a writer must follow his instincts & I fear very much you won't like my book after next, because it will be open to most of the objections you urge against it. To think of possible misconstructions & your influence is to give one's soul into the hands of the vagrancy of tyrants. The next book anyhow has no "love" in it, except the love of pleasant hours – this I hope will console you & in the one to which I refer love is a great disturbing force. It is Love & Mr. Lewisham on again in a bigger scale, but the man is now a statesman. It may be you won't altogether regret it, in spite of the 'love' in it. I never sought my influence, such as it is, never cultivated it & set no value upon it for myself or others. I can't I feel even study my defenders. That will be to turn literature into a sort of pamphleteering.

Forgive me for the pig-headed thing I am, & believe always,

Your very affectionately
(& gratefully)
H.G. Wells

839. To George Meek

Illinois, ACCS

Spade House
Sandgate [? January 1910]

My dear Meek,

I had a very busy time this Christmas & my wife misunderstood the agreement between us. I'm very sorry indeed about that delay & I do hope it won't put you out too much. I've not touched the book yet, I've been at work on another. I've had it all typed though and I will get at it later & either collaboration as I said or try & get it published as it is. If I do the latter I will make a bargain for you & we will treat what I shall have paid as a loan (without interest).

Yours ever,
H.G. Wells

840. To George Meek

Illinois, ALS

Spade House
Sandgate [January-February 1910]

My dear Meek,

I have been thinking over your story. In many ways it is very fine indeed & I think it will be a better thing standing alone than as a book of collaboration. But if I were you I would not use assumed names but tell everything & make it a human document of the sincerest sort. I want you to write in more stuff & more detail (of your life after 21) so as to make it upwards of twice the present length and then I propose to write an introduction with a description of you. I think it would be well to keep the photographs you send me & the others you have on hand as they might be very useful for illustrations.

You will see by the typed copy I sent you what I think you ought to do in the way of amending the style but the matter you insist I leave to you. Remember how ignorant most people are of the details of your sort of life. Most men of your experience are quite inexpressive. There's no end of C.O.S.[1] facts but living facts & how it feels are what I want people to get from you. So go ahead & perhaps we may be able to get the book out in 1910.

Yours ever

H.G. Wells

I mean to come on to you one of the these days on my bicycle.

---

[1] C.O.S. may stand for Charity Organisation Society.

841. To R. D. Blumenfeld[1]

Illinois, ALS

17, Church Row
Hampstead

[early 1910]

Dear R.D.B.

I merely praised your last review & said it was good business. I will write you an article just to show I'm not monopolized but not just now. I've purged my mind & I'm going back to my work.

Yours ever,

H.G.

---

[1] Blumenfeld was an essayist and editor. He and Wells were, from 1912 until 1930, to be tenants of the Countess of Warwick. His *R.D.B.'S Diary 1887–1914* (London: Heinemann, 1930) has some entries which concern Wells. His autobiography *All in One Lifetime* (London: Benn, 1931) prints more of the diary up to the end of 1919, as well as offering other materials on Wells and his time. Blumenfeld edited the *Daily Express* from 1904 to 1932.

842. To Elizabeth Robins

Texas, ALS

17, Church Row
Hampstead

Jan 9th, 10

Dear Miss Robins,

I don't understand your note. I have been asked to read a passage from one of my books at a suffrage meeting & I've agreed to do so. I thought I understood my own attitude, but perhaps you know it better. Anyhow I wish you'd explain.

Yours ever,
H. G. Wells

843. To Elizabeth Robins

Texas, ALS

[London]

[*c.* mid January 1910]

Dear Elizabeth Robins,

I do think I've a right to know my own opinions. I do believe, I have believed, in women's suffrage – I don't believe in the Pethick-Lawrence–Pankhurst movement. There's absolutely nothing in Ann Veronica against the suffrage & only a gentle kindly criticism of the suffragette side of it. Still if your committee chooses to refuse what it has first asked for, I'm quite ready to be nice to it in the matter, & let it off.

I'm glad you've been thinking of me a little. I felt you'd vanished from my world. Amber's got a jolly little daughter. Reeves is talking right and left on the character of the Pathetic Noble Tender Father injured by a blackguard, & probably making things so hopelessly disagreeable for Amber that she'll probably make me take her away as soon as she can get about again – in theory she is perfectly able to do at any time.

Good wishes for the New Year,
Yours ever,
H.G. Wells

844. To Edmund Gosse

Leeds, ALS

17, Church Row
Hampstead

Feb. 8. 10

My dear Gosse,

I was frightfully sorry to have missed you yesterday. I had no idea you were coming to lunch – I thought there was merely a chance of your calling sometime during the day. My liver happened to be enlarged something frightful & so I went for a long walk with it & Rothenstein (in the same revolting condition) – to Totteridge & all sorts of places. The viscus is now in order again, but I deplore the price.

Yours ever,
H. G. Wells

(Come again & say you are coming please)

845. To Robert Ross

Illinois, Typed Transcription

17, Church Row
Hampstead

[*c.* 1910-11]

Dear Bobby,

Holland came last night and was delightful.[1] He says you're in the dumps and ill. That distresses me very much. Don't. Can I be of any use. Your friends love you Bobby.

Yours ever,
H.G.

[1] Vyvyan Holland, Oscar Wilde's son

846. To Ford Madox Ford

Cornell, Typed Transcription

17, Church Row
Hampstead [*c.* early 1910]

Dear Hueffer,

I have made no claim upon the English Review on account of "Tono Bungay." I told Harrison the terms upon which you had the serial rights. I presume if there is a dividend I am entitled to a share, but I have taken no steps to secure one. What is happening?

Very sincerely yours,
H.G. Wells

847. To George Meek

Illinois, ALS

Court Lodge
Stansted
Wrotham, Kent
Reply 17 Church Road, Hampstead May. 10. 10

Dear Meek,

Here's your letter – a very nice human document.

Everyone likes the book who's read it. I've hopes of tapping a new source of help for you.

Very sincerely yours,
H.G.Wells

848. To George Meek

Illinois, ACCS

17 Church Row
Hampstead [Spring 1910]

Have I got your address right?

Dear Meek,

I've just rec'd enclosed cheque. Will you write to Llewellyn Roberts, the Sec'y of the Fund 40 Denison House 296 Vauxhall Bridge Rd., S.W. & say something graceful to the Committee & let me know how you stand. I thought subject to your approval you'd better have £5 at a time until you start for America & keep as much in reserve as you can until then, so as to go comfortable. Probably I shall bring my boys to see Windsor Castle next week in which case I'll have a shot at you. Windsor is part of my youth. I was junior apprentice at Rodgers & Denyers, the drapers, when I was 13 until a furious battle with the junior porter (& other incidents) ended my career.

Yours sincerely,
H.G. Wells

I couldn't get over to you from the Desboroughs – Chesterton came over on Sunday afternoon.

849. To George Meek

Illinois, ACCS

17 Church Row
Hampstead [1910]

Dear Meek,

Send me your particulars please, what's owing, how you stand for tickets & a berth to Vancouver & all thats necessary to get things in a fortnight.

Yours ever,
H.G. Wells

850. To George Meek

Illinois, ACCS

17 Church Row
Hampstead [1910]

Dear Meek,

Glad you've got the tickets & I hope everything will fix up all right. I was at Maurice Baring's last night & he said he'd greatly like to see you again before you go. His address is 6 North Street Westminster. You'd better write & ask him when you can see him. "The Honble" in front of his name on the envelope as he happens to be the son of some peer or other, but otherwise you treat him as you treat anybody. He knows no end about Russia & his pantomime is highly commended.

Good wishes

Yours ever,
H.G. Wells

851. To E. A.[1]

Hofstra, ALS

17 Church Row
Hampstead [?1910][2]

Dear E.A.

I am working & writing like God. But I shall try & come see you next week, D.V. I shall ring you up & try to catch you.

Yours ever,
H.G.

[1] Exactly who this letter is addressed to is problematic. Wells did know a woman, Mrs. E. Arias, as E.A, and she appears in some places as 'Ettie Rout' but that name was probably a later nickname. She published a memoir in 1922 with three letter excerpts from Wells to her therein. It is just possible that the letter is to (Enoch) Arnold Bennett, although Wells does not normally use this style in writing to him.

[2] Although the date is unknown, they knew each other by 1910 for they had each attended a party given by Marie Belloc-Lowndes at that time.

852. To Ella Hepworth Dixon[1]

Illinois, ACCS

17, Church Row
Hampstead [*c.* May 1910]

Dear Miss Dixon,

On Thursday we shall be in Blackburn[2] with the infants. Gip has had an operation for appendicitis & we are living more or less in a Surrey farmhouse for a few weeks. He was operated upon Friday three weeks ago – last Friday he was pursuing me on the crest of Blackdown full tilt screaming, "Scalp him!"

Not bad for modern surgery.

Very sincerely yours,
H.G. Wells

---

[1] Ella Hepworth Dixon was a poet, actress, and writer. She spent much of the summer of 1911 with the Wells family in Normandy while Easton Glebe was being renovated. Many people thought she was the original of the central character in Max Beerbohm's novel, *Zuleika Dobson*, and Wells frequently addressed her in that way.

[2] The Wells family may have been staying at Blackburn Cottage at the foot of Blackdown. This location is near Liss where his family lived and Haslemere where his friend Harold Monro was located. This location was determined through a fine piece of detective work by Patrick Parrinder who studied the Ordnance Survey maps of 1900. See letters 863 and 875.

853. To John Galsworthy

PLS

[Spade House
Sandgate, Kent] [early May? 1910]

My dear Galsworthy,

I was sorry not to get to you the other day. I'd been thinking a lot about Justice, and these other plays that are following seem likely to overlay the things one has thought. It seems to me that Justice, so far as the question of art goes, just establishes and vindicates you.[1] (I didn't see Strife.) I've always opposed myself to your very austere method hitherto. I've not liked a sort of cold hardness in much of your work, but since it leads you at last to the quite tremendous force of the play — well, I give in.

What keeps my mind busy about Justice is the riddle of the evil of all this cruelty of order. I've set on the bench at Folkestone and last year I went over Wormwood Scrubbs[2] — I remember too blundering years ago upon the condemned cells at Exeter one bright sunny afternoon — and I've felt all your play so finely and essentially conveys. But it isn't a system that is wrong. Another system will give kindred cruelties. If people abolish solitary confinement, for instance, some new horror will creep into the substituted treatment. We've got to back into the sources of law and control.[3]

Do you get Press cuttings? I was struck by a little thing in Punch about your house being burgled. I've cut it out and stuck it into my copy of Justice, because that incredibly base denseness of spirit seems to me to lie very near the heart of the problem.

Yrs. ever,
H.G.

---

[1] Galsworthy's play opened on 21 February 1910 to rave reviews and much discussion in the press, and made a contribution to the reform of the prison system. This letter, whose date is uncertain, appears in H. V. Marrot, *The Life and Letters of John Galsworthy* (New York: Scribner, 1930), pp. 259–60. Galsworthy's response is also printed there.

[2] Wormwood Scrubs is a massive prison in London, famous for its forbidding exterior. Galsworthy spent a day at Hampstead with Wells on 3 April 1910 along with William Rothenstein, and he sat for a portrait in the afternoon. Galsworthy described the conversation with Wells while they were on a walk as 'mainly the business of the imaginative man in relation to the state of the country. We agree that it's not our business to dogmatize as to define solutions' (pp. 280–1 of Marrot's book, quoting from the diary which Galsworthy had just begun to keep).

[3] Wells and Catherine served as Justices of the Peace in the county of Kent. This account suggests that it was not a perfunctory position listening to dreary cases of trespass.

854. To Leon Bourgeois[1]

Boston, ALS

17, Church Row
Hampstead

Friday [*c.* May 1910]

My dear Bourgeois,

I don't know Davray's[2] private address now & relations are rather strained at present as I have (after years of patience) terminated our standing agreement for translations & set out to look for a new translator.

Yours ever,
H.G. Wells

[1] I am not sure whether or not this is the same person who later served in a number of cabinets in the Third Republic of France.

[2] Henri Davray had been Wells's most faithful translator into French. He did use others from time to time, but he also went back to Davray. However, Davray's last translations may have been *The War in the Air* (1910) and *Ann Veronica* (1912). What the problem was between the two men is not known. Certainly Davray thought Wells a great man and in 1931 published a book with an essay on translating Wells, *Pages Choisies* (Paris: Albin Michel, 1931), pp. 7–18, followed by selections from Wells's work which made up the main body of the text. André Gide thought the selection of Davray especially felicitous. Davray's last words in his essay were, 'Il est une des plus prodigieuses intelligences de notre époque, et peut-être de tous les temps.' (He is one of the most prodigiously intelligent persons of our time, and perhaps all time.)

855. To the Editor, *Daily Mail*[1]

PLS

17, Church Row
Hampstead [*c.* 12 June 1910]

Sir, – I do not wish to detract from the sterling worth, the rich emotion for goodness and breadth and activity as such, the vague splendour of amiable sentiments, that pervades the Roosevelt crescendo, but it does happen to be what is called in Washington a "lie" to say that I advocate the abolition of the family. I quite recognize that to convey such meanings as Mr. Roosevelt affects, a certain rough unsentimental treatment of fact is necessary, but as I have been frequently very explicit upon this issue; I submit he has gone too far. I *do*, on the other hand, advocate the endowment of Motherhood because of that lamentable fall in the birth-rate that Mr. Roosevelt deplores and as a corrective to that practical abolition of the family which individualist competition has brought about.

H.G. Wells

[1] Wells's letter was headed, 'Mr. Wells and Family Life' when it was published 13 June 1910. Teddy Roosevelt's comments had occurred during a triumphant tour of Europe after he had left the presidency. The exact same letter was printed in the Fort Worth (Texas) *Star-Telegram*, 1 July 1910; there it was entitled 'Family Life'. Wells had visited Roosevelt in the White House on his tour of America in 1906.

856. To the Editor, *Daily Mail*[1]

PLS

17 Church-row
Hampstead

[15 June 1910]

Sir, – I am glad to see Mr. Cooper Rawson's letter in your issue of June 15, because it gives me an opportunity of denying with quite Rooseveltian emphasis this stupid misrepresentation of my views based on two or three clipped and misunderstood quotations from my writings. May I say then that I believe, have always believed, and have always made perfectly clear to any honest and intelligent reader of my books that I regard the association of father, mother and children in one group – and if that isn't the family, what is? – as the NORMAL, MOST NECESSARY, AND MOST DESIRABLE HUMAN GROUPING.

There it is for what it is worth – I should be grateful if you would put it into as Rooseveltian type as you can – though I have no doubt that these miserable hired liars that the Anti-Socialists disgrace themselves by sending about the country will keep on year after year in speech and handbill using these passages to trick the careless hearer and reader into the belief that I have taught the exact opposite.

What do these quotations he cites even in their clipped condition amount to?

In the first place I declare I want the State family and not the independent, privately owned family. Now is there such a thing outside the dreams of "free-love" as an altogether private family? Hasn't every family to be state-recognized now? Hasn't every child and every woman rights sustained by the State as against the head of the family now? Does Mr. Cooper Rawson really want to make the family a private and secret and anti-social thing? Or what queer, uncalled-for nastiness does he contrive to import, all out of his head, into my words?

And for the life of me I cannot conceive how a mind of ordinary capacity and common honesty can see in the second quotation any attack on the Family. I say the Socialist does not regard the institution of marriage as a permanent thing. Well, is it a permanent thing? Is anyone who can read so ignorant and dense as not to know that the institution has been profoundly changed in the last hundred years by the establishment of a divorce court, by the Married Women and Property Act, by separation orders, and that even now a Royal Commission is sitting and discussing whether it should be changed further. It is an institution that varies in every civilised country in the world and in every state of the American Union, and if Mr. Cooper Rawson thinks that is permanence, I can only ask Mr. Cooper Rawson to take lessons in the elements of English speech. The pamphlet "Socialism and the Family" from which these extracts are taken, would, I should have thought made both these points clear to a cow. And upon these two poor instances he bases his attack, and a thousand readers as slap-dash as he will carry away the impression that I have been contradicting myself and I am insidiously and mysteriously the enemy of all they hold dear in family life.

Oh! I do wish people would think what words and sentences mean! Everywhere this foolish, bawling, incompetent controversy, this dust and muddle of slovenly apprehension and angry, thick-headed, misdirected, virtuous indignation chokes our public discussion, [it] stifles our national thought. The thick head behind the "thick stick", stupidly rampant, unashamed, aggressive, persecuting, assails our national outlook. Every attempt to clarify thought and establish workable generalisations goes down under a rush of stampeding strenuosity. [2]

And this is an age and in the presence of needs that call for thought as subtle as electricity, and as firm and flexible as tempered steel.

H. G. Wells

---

[1] The day after Wells's first response to the charges of Teddy Roosevelt, he was answered by Cooper Rawson (16 June 1910) citing Wells's words in the November 1906 *Fortnightly Review*. Wells responded, under the heading 'Mr. H. G. Wells and Marriage', in the issue of 16 June 1910.

[2] This paragraph is a masterful example of invective. Wells plays tunes on all of Theodore Roosevelt's ideas, ranging from his oft-quoted African proverb, 'Speak softly and carry a big stick', to his advocacy of '*The Strenuous Life*', the title of a book of his writings.

857. To Henry James

Illinois, ALS

17, Church Row
Hampstead

Aug. 31, 1910

My dear James,

I've heard of your brother's death with a sense of enormous personal loss. As you know I've seen very little of him but he's been something big and reassuring in my background for many years & what I saw of him at Rye & Sandgate gave me a very living affection for him. I can imagine something of what his death means to you. I'm filled with impotent concern for you. That all this great edifice of ripened understandings and charities and lucidities should be swept out of the world leaves me baffled and helplessly distressed.

Yours very sincerely
H.G. Wells

858. To Frederick Macmillan

Illinois, TCC

[London] [*c.* 26 September 1910]

OBVIOUSLY PRIVATE

[My dear Macmillan]

Are the Baileys [in The New Machiavelli] a libellous picture of the Webbs?

That is quite right. I made a pretty recognizable picture of them in the second book & it now occurs to me that I wasn't free to use them as characters in the subsequent style in that account. But the difficulty is quite easily met. I'm looking at the story & it is perfectly easy to make a false bottom so to speak to the Bailey's by introducing another couple to do the unpleasant work of book five. Of course all the rest of the Bailey stuff is extending flattery to the Webbs; and there you are!

[Is this your difficulty? & if so, let's go on.][1]

[1] The copies of these letters I used (see note to letter 698) are slightly smudged and a few words are conjectural in the last sentence. There are descriptive changes in the characters from the serial to that published as the novel. The serial appeared from May to October in the *English Review*. The novel was brought out by John Lane in London in 1911 as Wells and Macmillan were unable to agree on the contents of the work, see letter 861.

859. To W. Heinemann[1]

Illinois, ALS[2]

17, Church Row
Hampstead

Sept. 30 [1910]

Dear Heineman

I won't discuss alteration until I see you. I've every confidence in you etc.

About agreement as I hope it will be model for subsequent ones I want it clear to prevent discussions later. I'll stick to it if you will, except the fiction advance must be a £1000.

(A.) British colonial rights – not continental
& omitting Canada.

(B.) 25% British

(C.) 4½ Colonial

(D.) 7 years term from the date of the publication by you after last book by me. i.e., so long as you go on publishing books by me, the 7 year term continues to be put on in date. The 7 year term applies to all books of mine published by you.

E. You to have option of refusing each subsequent novel (except see below) on above terms until refuse one.

F. In event of your bankruptcy or dissolution of partnership all rights to revert to me & you to assign no rights without my consent

G. Within 2½ years after publication you may issue cheap edition at less than 1/1 (13d.) at 1d. royalty & £150 advance – if not I am free to arrange same

H. All unspecified rights retained by author.

Suggest Macmillan has Marjorie[3] – for Autumn 1911. & H. begin with 1912 novel.

H. G. Wells

---

[1] When Macmillan began to shy away from *The New Machiavelli*, Wells began negotiations with Heinemann. This letter relates to that discussion. Heinemann did not publish the book, and Wells's next three novels of human relationships, *Marriage* (1912), *The Passionate Friends*

(1913) and *The Wife of Sir Isaac Harman* (1914) were all published by Macmillan, the last books by Wells to be published by them.

[2] Although signed by Wells, virtually the entire letter is in Catherine Wells's handwriting.

[3] *Marjorie* was the name originally given to *Marriage*.

860. To William Heinemann

Illinois, ACS

17, Church Row
Hampstead

Oct. 1 1910.

Dear Heineman

The extension of our agreement to cover future books was suggested by me simply to reconcile you to the 1911 trouble. I want also to modify it by specifying not simply novels but "novels of over 100,000 words". What I want is a series of line of battle ships – so to speak & if I choose to do – Mr. Polly it will have to be left out.[1]

How far are you going to back me up if this other 1911 book leads to a row with Macmillan? Suppose he says if he can't have the next book he won't pay or guarantee anything. I suppose ... solicitor & see how I stand for breach of agreement. Will you make cheques on a/c New M. £750 – £500 now & I take my chance of getting what I can out of Macmillan & make it an ordinary cheque on a/c.

H. G. W.

[1] *The History of Mr Polly* was published later in this year by Thomas Nelson.

861. To Frederick Macmillan

Illinois, TCC

[London] October 2, 1910

[Dear Macmillan]

[I cannot accept your proposed changes on The New Machiavelli.] Our poor rejected "Ann Veronica" is selling very fast both here and in New York. Well, The New Machiavelli is a book of altogether better calibre than A.V. It's the political companion to Tono Bungay & I want to have a guaranteed royalty of more than 10,000.

I don't altogether agree at this prospect of giddy elevation but I want to see myself going up – & being properly aided up – the scale to twenty to thirty thousand in the country. Kipps, Tono Bungay, and The New Machiavelli are steps in my growth.

[Sincerely yours,
H.G. Wells]

862. To Morris Colles[1]

Boston, ALS

17, Church Row
Hampstead Oct 30, 10

My Dear Colles,

Thanks for your letter which clears this transaction happy for everybody but not I hope our regular acquaintance. I've a children's birthday party to work off next week & then I contemplate a dash somewhere for a holiday. When I'm fit company for a human being I hope we may meet again..

Yours sincerely,
H. G. Wells

[1] William Morris Colles (d. 1926), Managing Director of the Author's Syndidate, acted as an agent for Wells, usually dealing with US serial rights.

863. To Elizabeth Robins

Texas, ALS

17, Church Row
Hampstead

Nov. 21, 1910

Dear Miss Robins,

I thought you'd deserted me altogether. I was very glad to get your letter but very sorry indeed at the news it held. I do hope your eyes will get all possible benefit from Arisbrand[?], & that I'll hear of you at work again in a very short time.

I've been in Blackdown working at a book that excites me very much & my life is very full. I've got more friends than I ever had before, fewer acquaintances & lots of absurd enemies, & it is all to the good. J.A. Spender (as a sample) is never going to speak to me again. I am to be cut & insulted & ruined & pulverized, whereas you know I belong to a race that lives to 85 & doesn't age before seventy. I can live for twenty years now without earning two hundred a year, I've only just begun to do my best work & I'm cheerfully pugnacious. But I wish I could see Amber at times. After this year we shall write – & so far as I'm concerned & I'm pretty sure as far as she is concerned, nothing has altered or can alter between us.

I'm sorry I missed the Harper's talk. I hope some day for another.

Yours ever,
H.G. Wells

I hope you see Amber sometimes. Her book ought to be done by now & it ought to get a little show before she does better.

864. To an unknown addressee

Texas, ALS

17, Church Row
Hampstead [1910–11]

RIGHT O
Typed short stories
BUT
Ask this young man to write a
covering letter beginning with a
mention of your name
or else
they go into a SHOOT
which returns them
with
The Utmost Violence Unread

H.G.

865. To Thomas Seccombe

Illinois, ALS

17, Church Row
Hampstead [1910-11]

Dear Seccombe

There's an old school friend of Jane's, Dorothy Richardson has her eye on you. She wants to submit a scheme for a book – Quakerism to Constable, & I think myself she'd be likely to do very well indeed. She's got a real philosophical twist (which is rare in petticoats) & she's been soaking in Quakerism for the last four years. Will you give her an ear. I never do this sort of thing simply because I'm asked to, but I really believe in Miss Richardson.

Yours ever,
H. G. Wells

866. To Edmund Gosse

Leeds, ALS

17, Church Row
Hampstead [end 1910]

My dear Gosse,

Your letter fills me with terror, dismay and perplexity. I adore you & James but I am bitterly, incurably, destructively against Literary Academies[1] & further I have taken OATHS to have no dealings (save only bloodshed, rapine & the like) with this Academic Committee as such. This I did with Bennett & another.

Yours ever,
H.G. Wells

Sir Wm Robertson Nicoll arranging who shall exist in English literature with Mr Edmund Gosse

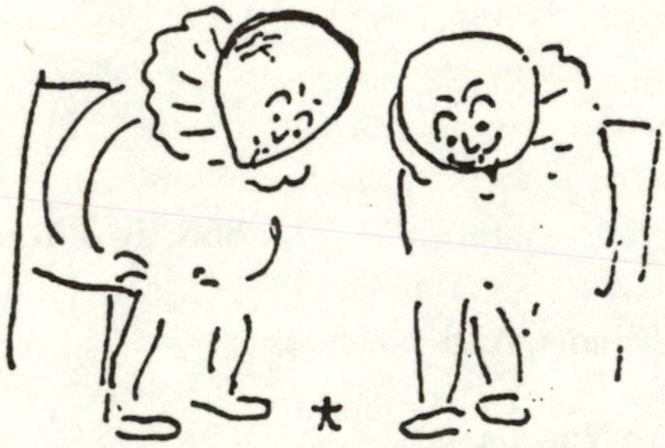

Mr Pember of the British Academy takes his place among the Immortals (modestly but firmly)[2]

[1] Wells attacked the idea, in an ironic way, of an Academy of Letters in Britain in an article in the *Eye-Witness*, 26 September 1911, 'The Academic Committee', pp. 464–5.
[2] These two 'picshuas' also appeared in an article in *The Strand*, vol. 41, 1911, 'Author and Artist Too', p. 4; see also letter 871.

867. To D. Appleton & Co.[1]

Bromley, ALS

Hotel Schweizerhof
Wengen, Switzerland

Tuesday, Jan 17. 1911
[receipt date stamped 29 Jan 1911]

My dear Sir,

(Please note the change of my permanent address to 17 Church Row, Hampstead, N.W.)

I shall be very glad to discuss the future with Mr. Sears [2] when he is in London. I shall be here until the end of the month & then I shall probably be in Berlin for a fortnight. After that I shall be in London & on the telephone again.

I may however say that my relations with Mr. Duffield are very friendly & that I am disposed to give him a preference for my future work. He took up Tono Bungay & made a success of it after I had had the humiliation of offering it to a number of New York firms & failing to then secure the terms I asked for it – something like a quarter of what Mr. Duffield had secured for me. Moreover I do not think your firm has done all there is to be done with the Sea Lady. That is a very good book with many enthusiastic friends & I am told that the way to secure a copy in America is to advertise for one secondhand. It lies dormant in your hands and I think an effective understanding with me lies in the direction of a successful renewal of that great characteristic piece of my work.

Very sincerely yours,
H.G.Wells

---

[1] Wells was by this time a good financial prospect, and he frequently received letters of inquiry from various publishers, in this case an American firm.
[2] Sears was an editor with Appleton in New York.

868. To Robert Ross

Illinois, Typed Transcription

Grand Hotel
Wengen, Switzerland [January-February 1911]

My dear Bobbie,

I'm starting home from here tomorrow and not going on to Berlin. I'm ill and we're all ill. Jane went home last Sunday week. She had one day ski-ing and then got ill suddenly – a sort of complication that will involve an operation and she's been in bed at Church Row ever since. I stayed on here with the children and Fraulein and we've all had influenza and are now with vile coughs and restive temperatures. Church Row will be a hospital when we get back on Friday; it's like God that dear little Hans the squirrel should suddenly die. Life under these circumstances comes down to personal and physical feelings and the New Machiavelli publication which ought to have been a gorgeous spree is just wasted on us. We'll have to get out of Church Row, I think, to a larger, airier warmer house with a garden for the children and more space. – so tell your friends that's how it stands. I feel we're a cranky lot and got to be taken care of. Lord! how influenza takes the Pride and Adventure out of a man! Have you found a house we might like, – a warm house where you can feel well when you're ill. That's what I want now.

Yours ever,

H.G.

O. Reginald's[1] written me a nice letter – will you please give him my love and tell him how things are.

---

[1] Reginald ('Reggie') Turner, who lived in Florence. His letters to Wells survive but almost none of Wells to him, see Stanley Weintraub, *Reggie* which is the standard life.

869. To T. L. Humberstone

Illinois, ANS

17, Church Row
Hampstead

[postmarked Feb 20 11]

O — I say. isn't there a bill for the R. C. S. dinner? I had champagne & Apollinaris[1] & things. ? ? ? ?

H. G. Wells

[1] Probably the mineral water of that name.

870. To an unknown addressee[1]

AL

[London]

[*c.* early March 1911]

I do not see that I have any grounds for complaint if the Birmingham ratepayers choose to have their fiction filtered through the mind of Mr. Burman and to allow him to reject anything that he finds difficult or uncongenial. If Mr. Burman, under the stimulus of the interviewer, adds a trifle of insult to my exclusion and claims to suggest that I make my books "suggestive" in order to cover my "literary deficiencies" it is really not my affair. As 'Bagshot' suggests in the Westminster Gazette, the best way to attack an author you do not like is to abuse his style: Mr. Burman acts under sound advice and goes only a little further in imputing base motives. These are the recognized methods of British criticism, and I must confess my interest in Mr. Burman remains slight and impersonal.

[1] In 1911 Wells's novel, *The New Machiavelli* was banned by the Free Libraries Committee of the Birmingham City Council. A cutting from a newspaper which reported this action was sent to Wells and this is his reply. It appeared in a story which was an account of an interview with a Mr. J. H. Burman who was chair of the Book Sub-Committee. The letter was quoted in detail in *The Times*, 29 March 1911. The story concluded by saying that Wolverhampton Free Libraries Committee allowed *The New Machiavelli* to be circulated, but they banned *Ann Veronica*. Their comment on *The New Machiavelli* was 'that there is much of unquestioned literary merit in it and it can in no way be harmful if used with discretion'. The article was entitled, ' Fiction and Morals: Mr. H. G. Wells's Novels'.

871. To Henry James[1]

Illinois, ALS

17, Church Row
Hampstead [25 April 1911]

My dear James.

I've been putting off answering your letter[2] because I wanted to answer it properly & here at last comes the meagre apology for a response to the most illuminating of comments. So far as it is loving chastisement I think I wholly agree & kiss the rod. You put your sense of the turbid confusion, the strain & violence of my book so beautifully that almost they seem merits. But oh! some day when I am settled-er, if ever, I will do better. I agree about the 'first person'. The only artistic 'first person' is the onlooker speculative 'first person', & God helping me, this shall be the last of my gushing Hari-Karis. But the guts & guts & guts & guts I've poured out all over the blessed libraries & J. A. Spender & everybody! I am against all sorts of people festooned with the apparently unlimited stuff....[3]

No! – This shall be the end of it.

I wish you were over here. I rarely go to the Reform without a strange wild hope of seeing you. In June I am going with all my household to a house in France & I shall return to London in October. Thenabouts perhaps you'll be out.

Very sincerely yours,
H. G. Wells

---

[1] Although this letter appears in Leon Edel and Gordon Ray, eds, *Henry James and H.G. Wells* (Urbana and London, 1958), it is important enough also to be included in this collection. James was in the United States at the time of writing. Wells, however, was about to deliver his strongest attack on Jamesian ideas on writing in his lecture (early May, 1911) 'The Contemporary Novel', which was in circulation in both the English and French press by June of 1911.

[2] A letter dated 3 March 1911 in which James acknowledged reception and reading of *The New Machiavelli*. James's letter to Wells provides both praise, but also a good deal of negative comment, including the phrase, 'your capacity for chewing up the thickness off the world in such enormous mouthfulls, while you fairly slobber, so to speak, with the multitudinous taste....' This latter comment is quite similar to the squeezed and dirty orange metaphor of James in his 1914 pieces, 'The Younger Generation', in *The Times Literary Supplement*, 19 March and 2 April 1914. Feelings were very intense on these matters, as when Walter Emanuel wrote a piece on illustrating one's personal letters, 'Author and Artist, Too', which appeared in *The Strand*, vol. 41 (February, 1911), p. 4. Two of Wells caricatures in this piece were provided with comments about the state of English Literature. We show them as illustrations beneath letter 866.

[3] Spender was editor of the *Westminster Gazette* and was in the van of this sort of criticism. He was lampooned, along with others, in Wells's pastiche of James, *Boon* (London, 1915).

872. To the Editor, *The Times*[1]

PLS

Maison de Canal[2]
Pont de L'Arche
France

[mid June 1911]

Sir, – I have read with great interest your leading article of June 14, and the admirable criticism of your Dramatic Critic upon which it is based and I find myself in very complete agreement with it. It is certainly true that, whatever our institutions and ideas, the normal state of the great mass of adult humanity will remain as it is at present – a state of monogamic marriage. That is the specific human grouping, as manifestly a part of the human lot as the possession of shoulder-blades or the absence of wings. But it has to be recognized that there may be very great variatons in the conditions which may be imposed upon those who enter into this natural and necessary grouping, and there seems to me to be altogether too strong an implication in your article that the many dramatists and authors who are attempting in the face of much hostile misrepresentation, a fair and open discussion of sexual life are necessarily attacking marriage as such and necessarily advocating some inconceivable promiscuity called Free Love as the happy consequence of its "abolition". The scurrilous Pharisee raises his head again in the world of criticism, and it is not perhaps superfluous to point out that all discussion of marriage in novel and play is not necessarily destructive and anarchistic. There are signs of an imminent "mobbing" of contemporary literature which it is still perhaps not too late to avert.

In the first place, a large proportion of current writing upon these topics directs itself against that pre-nuptial ignorance which is so productive of subsequent misery in married life. A large proportion not only of our young women, but, in perhaps a coarser form, of our young men, come to this cardinal step blankly, or what is perhaps even worse, grossly unprepared for its trials and difficulties. Many, no doubt, thanks to the ineptitude of human charity, muddle through to a sort of lamed happiness at last, but all the problems arising out of this evil secrecy and indirectness of initiation are not only fair material for treatment in novel and play, but need urgently to be dealt with in novel and play, because it is only so that they are likely to reach the minds of the persons most concerned. Their discussion has nothing whatever to do with any anarchistic depravity.

And next there is a criticism of the conditions of the married state which is not simply desirable, but necessary nowadays, and which lies entirely apart from any attempt to inaugurate an age of licence. Many of us think that the bond as it is tied at present permits of many nearly intolerable cruelties and tyrannies, that it puts great numbers of women into a position of shameful subservience, that in cases, exceptional indeed but by no means inconsiderable, it works evil not only for the partners, but for the children and the race. A criticism of the conditions of a contract is not a proposal to destroy that contract; it may be the most helpful step in its reestablishment. To point out that the institution of marriage is a clumsy thing is not necessarily to propose its abolition.

Very sincerely yours,
H.G. Wells

[1] This letter appeared in *The Times* on 24 June under the title, 'The Discussion of Marriage'.
[2] The Wellses were living at this French address while their new home, Little Easton Rectory, was being renovated.

873. To George Meek

Illinois, ALS

17, Church Row
Hampstead [late Spring 1911]

My dear Meek,

You can write a ripping article or book now.[1] "How I went to Canada." telling simply & faithfully the story. – Your uncle, your hopes & dreams, & then the absurd series of muddles that has happened since. Keep up your heart & give my best regards to Mrs. Meek & tell her to keep up hers. In Buxton & Belloc you have influential friends. I'm just going down to my boys at Haselmere, but I shall be in London after next Saturday. The misfortunes of the man are the material of the artist.

Yours ever,
H.G. Wells

[1] What happened to Meek in Canada we do not know. He apparently attempted a book based on Wells's suggestions, see letter 878, but without success.

874. To J. W. Robertson-Scott

Illinois, APCS

17, Church Row,
Hampstead [postmarked 18 March 1911]

1. I think the concentration of rooms round the open fireplace & and the casual ventilation of fireplace, window & door is a source of discomfort that only habit makes us tolerate. I want to live all over my rooms & I've never been able to do so in any house I have occupied.

2. The general substitution of horizontal for vertical arrangements everywhere seems an immense improvement to me. My ideal house is a two story house with no underground parts. In middle class homes the development of the narrow passage "hall" into an interesting central apartment pleases me extremely.

H. G. Wells [1]

---

[1] The Wells family was about to move to Little Easton Rectory, but before they did so the building had to be renovated.

875. To Lillah McCarthy[1]

Texas, ACCS

17, Church Row
Hampstead [April? 1911]

My dear Lillah,

I'm bowed down with complications. I've found a farm right up on Blackdown & I can have it for us from now to the 6th of May. I want to go there. Also I deeply want to come to you. May I – I bow down at your feet & beat my head – may I put you off two weeks? The farm is let after May 6th & I do so want to get us all down there. See?

Tell Barker[2] nothing on earth will shake my (if anything) growing conviction that the Madras House is splendid work. I seem to be one of the many who will readily talk it back. I saw Prunella & liked it tremendously.

Yours ever,
H.G.

[1] Lillah McCarthy was a premiere actress of this time and a good friend of Wells.
[2] Barker is Granville Barker, her husband, a play writer and theatre manager. They had originally met through Shaw and the Fabian Society.

876. To Violet Paget

Colby, ALS

17 Church Row
Hampstead [late Spring 1911]

Dear Miss Paget,

I've just found your letter here. I'm here for a day or so to look at some county weekend things – & I'll take it back to Jane to answer more fully. But I hasten to tell you that the night boat reaches Dieppe about three & the corresponding train drops you at Rouen at something after four. There you can either bargain with a cabman (20 francs will do it) and drive the twelve miles to Pont de l'Arche or wait for a train at five something to Pont de l'Arche.[1]

Yours ever,
H.G. Wells

[1] The Wells family stayed in Normandy while their new home at Easton Glebe was being renovated. They entertained Ella Hepworth Dixon, Ray Lankester, and others, as well as Violet Paget at this *pied à terre*.

877. To F. A.H. Eyle

Boston, ALS

17, Church Road
Hampstead [early 1911]

My Dear Sir

I shall be pleased to talk about the production of Kipps,[1] about March 1st.

Very sincerely yrs
H. G. Wells

[1] A stage adaptation of the novel was presented at the Vaudeville theatre in London during the season of 1912.

878. To George Meek

Illinois, ALS

Maison du Canal
Pont-de-l'Arche (Eure) [Summer 1911]

My dear Meek,

I don't agree with your coming back before you've got stuff to sell, but you're as old as I am & as able to guide your own affairs as I am to guide mine. So I wish you good luck.

Yours very sincerely,
H.G. Wells

879. To Lillah McCarthy

Texas, APCS

Pont d'l'Arche
Eure, France [postmarked Juillet 19, 1911]

This sort of thing & a row & so on in. A rather jolly river on which we have a boat.[1]

Better come,
H.G.

[1] The house was in fact on a canal, but there was a boat and the family and guests often picnicked on a nearby island.

880. To Frank C. Wells

Illinois, APCS

Eure, France [postmarked Juillet 30[?] 1911]

Just to remind you of your August walks & stay here. I want to organize a walk from Havre here, so get if you can a knapsack for your night things & we'll send all the rest of your luggage by train from Havre.

881. To Maurice Baring

Illinois, ANS

Maison du Canal
Pont-de-l'Arche (Eure) [*c.* August 1911]

Dear Baring,

We [*encircled*] (Oh! – C.W.) found your pin!
Thank you endlessly for my beautiful boxes.[?]
They will (one does another up) last me all my happy life.

Yours ever,
H.G.

882. E. Ray Lankester to H.G. Wells[1]

Illinois, ALS

[London] September 13, 1911

My dear Wells,

[*Lankester told Wells that he had a strong sexual attraction for women, and that he had determined that there were really two kinds of women, one, 'naughty but fascinating', the other, 'angelic creatures', or 'angeloids'. This second group, he felt, should only be approached with the intention of marriage and with the assent of the family. While he was strongly involved with the first group, he placed the second 'on a pedestal and should as soon thought of temporary amusement or a passionate outburst with one of them as robbing a bank'. He thought Wells had been exceptional and that Wells's point of view.*]

... seemed to be determined by the fact that you had not appreciated the merits of professional ladies before you were led off by a quasi-angelic female into conduct which should be reserved for the alcoves of a professional and you have maintained your taste for what I may call the aberrant angelic female who the professionals would say takes the bread out of honest women's mouths.

[*He considered that Wells had been fortunate to marry Catherine.*]

I have never reached that phase of happiness – now at my age, I know how great is the good fortune of those who have a devoted wife ready to bear and do everything for the sake of the man and her children. If I were in such a case and in natural need of the relief and nervous rest given by 'naughtiness' – I would seek it from the best type of professional lady at my leisure and keep it a dead secret. That is, I imagine, what hundreds of men do.

[*Wells and Lankester apparently continued this conversation, now mainly dealing with group and communal marriages, which, of course, was close to Wells's own ménage. In one further letter to Wells, dated 1 February 1912, Lankester returned to his lesson for Wells.*]

The difficulty in adopting practical polygamy and unlimited selection in the male, is, I think, that we have not for some centuries played that game but another – and consequently the women are not trained to meet the difficulties of the new game, nor are other men duly advised and ready for it. Even as it is – I have constantly observed that girls of fine qualities and great beauty – are snatched up and as it were infatuated by this or that young man of no merit but reckless audacity – simply because the chance was that the reckless youth appeared on the scene and proposed marriage – not because there was selection based upon adequate experience either on the man's or the girl's part.[2]

---

[1] E. Ray Lankester, Director of the Natural History Museum, and a bachelor, was a close friend of Wells. Their correspondence spanned nearly thirty years, but Wells's letters to Lankester do not appear to have survived. After visiting Wells at Pont de L'Arche, Lankester wrote to him at length continuing their discussion and summarizing on sexuality.

[2] Although Wells might have resented this frank comment he did not take offence.

883. To D. Appleton & Co.

Bromley, ALS

17, Church Row
Hampstead [*c.* September 1911]

My Dear Sir,

I am very greatly obliged to you for a copy of The Grain of Dust which I have read with the utmost interest & think is a very powerful and illuminating story.

Very sincerely yours
H.G. Wells

884. To Robert Ross

Illinois, APC Transcription

Emmerich, Austria 7.9.11.

Two people you know are having a very good time on the Rhine. They are anonymous but here are their portraits. To secure impartiality we have drawn each other.

[*Card is written in alternate handwritings with sketches of Wells and Catherine, who had sent the card to Ross.*]

885. To Fred Wells

Illinois, ALS

17 Church Row
Hampstead, N.W.
~~Maison du Canal, Pont-de-l'Arche (Eure)~~ [early Autumn 1911]
Enclo.

Dear Fred,

Here's a cousin & I know you specialize in cousins. How are you? We've spent the last four months in France & had a very amusing time. I bicycled part of the way home & should have done it all, with the two boys, but for rain & punctures. They are getting on, & both are going in for the College of Preceptors exam at Christmas. They don't go to school but have a tutor & governess at home & if they don't get on in the world, it won't be for want of education. They both speak French & German very well.[1]

We like the house & are keeping it on but we find we want fresh air outside London so I have taken The Rectory, Little Easton, Essex & we are furnishing it, in order to be abler to go to & fro between the houses as we feel disposed. It is a pretty little place standing quite alone in the middle of a big park of Lady Warwick's (who is on very friendly terms) so that the boys will be able to live wild about the park while we are down there.[2] Things go very well with us. My last book has sold nearly 23,000 [3] which is nearly double any predecessor & my income keeps well ahead of expenditures. How are you getting on? In a little time now, next April, I hope to be transmitting the balance of that insurance transaction to you.

Frank keeps jolly. He & old Carolyn[?] came & spent a week in France. We had two boats on the Seine & rowed as if we were back at Surly Hall.

Love from us all,

H.G.

---

[1] The College of Preceptors examination, and their education generally are treated quite comprehensively by M. M. Mayer, *H.G. Wells and His Family* (Edinburgh: International Publishing Co., 1955). Mayer was the governess mentioned in the letter.

[2] In the event, the Wells's did not retain the Church Row house for very long. Easton became home, with a flat in London for those times when some or all of the family came up to town.

[3] This was *The New Machiavelli*.

886. To Ella Hepworth Dixon

Illinois, ALS

17, Church Row
Hampstead

[*c.* September-October 1911]

May I come to the Wild Geese as you asked me. Please when is it? Then all about the play.

H.G.

887. To Amy Burgess[1]

Bromley, ALS

Rosemeath
Liss, Hants. Oct. 15 1911

My dear Amy Burgess,

You will I know be sorry to hear my Father is dead. He died suddenly & quite particularly of heart failure on Friday morning. I know you write to him & I know he valued your friendship very greatly. Very many thanks for your letters. My brother Frank joins with me in warmest regards.

Yours very sincerely
H.G. Wells

[1] Wells's second cousin

888. To Ella Hepworth Dixon

Illinois, ACCS

17, Church Row
Hampstead [October-November 1911]

Dear, dear Ella,

Send along the play. The book is done. Kipps is done. All my beautiful mind is waiting, waiting, waiting for you.

Yours ever,
HeGee

889. To Ella Hepworth Dixon

Illinois, ACCS

17, Church Row
Hampstead
[October-November 1911]

Dear Ella,

Get on writing that play. The Little Theatre waits for you – so do I. When I have your copy in hand, I will do all sorts of things to it but I must have something to work on.

Yours ever,
H.G.

890. To Maurice Baring

Illinois, APCS

Hotel Victoria
Wence [Bern]
[postmarked 6. 11. 11.]

Thanks from all of us, [J] G. & Frank.

Dear Maurice,

I'm doubtful if this will reach you so I'm compact. I agree about Beethoven & I echo also your longing for London. I'm here with all my family down with influennza.

H.G.

Back next week.

891. To Edmund Gosse

Leeds, ACCS

17, Church Row
Hampstead [early December 1911]

My dear Gosse,

A Danish newspaper wants me to do a reverence to Brandes on his 70th birthday. You know my colossal ignorances. Where can I most simply & surely acquire the knowledge needed for an apt & elegant remark? I don't like not to do the thing if I can.

Yours sincerely,
H.G. Wells [1]

---

[1] I have not seen Wells's piece. Georg Brandes was a Danish poet and author and a friend of Gosse, who translated his work into English.

892. To Edmund Gosse

Leeds, ALS

17, Church Row
Hampstead [16 December 1911]

My dear Gosse,

Very many thanks indeed for your prompt help. I shall get the book & display its knowledge as my own.

All good wishes to you & Mrs. Gosse, to help you through Christmas time. We go to our quiet Rectory in Essex to have a real English Christmas.

Yours ever
H. G. Wells

893. To Edmund Gosse

Leeds, ALS

17, Church Row
Hampstead [mid-December 1911]

My dear Gosse,

I've read Two Visits to Denmark & got all I need from that & the Encyclopedia to write up my compliment to Brandes. But that done, I'm reading Two Visits for my pleasure & with extreme delight. You do the Fog household wonderfully. One must go to Father and Son to find anything to touch some of that writing.[1] It's so delicate, so sweet spirited & good tempered & at the same time rich & full bodied. When someday I get to work on the monograph upon The Natural History of British Reputations, which is to immortalize me, I shall devote a chapter to you. You're known & you're admired & so on, but you really don't get a tithe of your right. I think I have threatened you already with an article on Father & Son. This renews my determination. I will. It will make you feel like a young hoarding with the bill stickers at work on it. It is odd you should dedicate your book to Low, who next to you, is the most undervalued writer of our time. A book like Two Visits ought to come out like a Royal Visit or Opening a Public Palace or New Years Day or anything else public & memorable, whereas I did not know it was published this season until you told me.

Best Wishes for a New Year,
Yours ever,
H.G. Wells

[1] Wells is referring to Gosse's autobiography *Father and Son* published anonymously in 1907, a book still read as an important autobiographical statement and comment on father-son relationships.

894. To Edmund Gosse

Leeds, ALS

[London] [1911?]

Dear Gosse,

I will come if I can but I can assure you she is, if kindly treated, docile & amiable – & perfectly well behaved. If at all troublesome, which I do not for a moment expect, offer her an ice. I like dancing very much & want to come but she says I wave my legs too much.[1] She says my dancing is all very well for large unconfined spaces but unsuitable for polite society. She has got a room in the hotel.

I will try to come but she says dances excite me to violence. She would not mind my coming if Mrs. Gosse was giving a Maffick[2] – but this she says is a dance. She is sure you would not like the way I go on.

Rot! I say, and, unless she locks them up, come I will.

Yours ever,

H.G.

She says I "hurl" my legs. You can't want a man who hurls his legs.

---

[1] The last sentence is on the back of a Spade House correspondence card. Who the 'she' with the strong opinions is is not known. It might be Catherine Wells, although this is more jocular than Wells ever is when he writes about her.

[2] The slang word which meant celebration and came from the wild outbursts of joy after Mafeking was relieved in 1900 during the Second Boer War having endured 217 days of siege.

895. To Violet Paget

Colby, ALS

17, Church Row
Hampstead [1911]

My dear Vernon Lee,

I knew you wouldn't like The New Machiavelli, or for a time after you've read it, me. I didn't repent or apologize for the book, which I'm proud of, but my affections run on different lines I think from yours, & it makes no difference to my very warm regard for you, that you should not see it as I would like you to see it. Don't come to us while there is a strained feeling on your part toward us, there's none on ours to you. I think a day will come when you will forgive me The New Machiavelli, & and anyhow dear Vernon Lee,

I am yours very warmly & admiringly & affectionately,

H.G. Wells.

896. To Ella Hepworth Dixon[1]

Boston, ALS

Church Row
Hampstead [1911?]

Brightest and dearest,

We shall be at Easton on the 27th. I am passionately excited over my book after next, but if I can get an idea for that playlet I will. At present it just does nothing in my mind.

Your adoring Sultan
H.G.

[1] This also appears in Ella Hepworth Dixon's memoir, *As I Knew Them* (London: Hutchinson, 1930), p. 208.

897. To an unknown addressee

Korn, ALS

17 Church Row
Hampstead [1911]

My dear Sir,

I regret the delay in answering your letter but I have been travelling about, it was left behind, and I have only just received it. The inconsistencies you find in my work will all very largely disappear if you will realise firstly that The New Machiavelli is a work of fiction & that Remington is an attempt to express the ideas of Tory Democracy in an intellectualized coherent form. Remington is not H.G.Wells but just simply himself & secondly the The Modern Utopia is Utopian & experimental. Even in The Modern Utopia however, you will find a very careful indication of the importance of the "Poëtic" class of mind, a very fully developed sense of my distrust of the official. This also appeared in a very early work, When the Sleeper Wakes, & you will find it very fully dealt with in my interesting essay in a forthcoming work of essays,

The Great State, which Messrs Harper Bros will publish in England and America next month. I wish you could read this latter book before completing your revision of your book as it will be a very complete restatement of the British progressive position.

Yours very sincerely,
H.G.Wells

898. To Richard Le Gallienne[1]

Texas, ALS

[London] [1911?]

My dear LeGallienne,

How difficult you are to get at! I'll come along on Friday.

Yours ever,
H.G.

[1] Richard Le Gallienne (1866–1947) was a poet and essayist; he later lived in New York City. His first success was *Quest for the Golden Girl* in 1896. Wells reviewed the book fairly well in *Saturday Review* 6 March 1897, pp. 249–50 under the heading, 'The Lost Quest'.

899. To Richard Le Gallienne

Texas, ALS

[London] [probably Summer 1911]

My dear Le Gallienne,

What have I to do with times & seasons? Will you come on any of the following days – Monday, Tuesday, Wed. Thursday, Friday, Saty, or Sunday – all of which suit me equally well. If you ride in early before the sun is up very far & will have an early cold lunch, tea on the canal which is lush & beautiful in this weather & a more serious meal about 7.

Thanks very much for [*illegible title*] which I shall value exceedingly – opinion after greater deliberation.

I've just come upon your letter having been away on a cycling tour until last night.

Yours ever,
H.G.

900. To an unknown addressee

Hofstra, ALS

17, Church Row
Hampstead
Little Easton Rectory [*in Wells's writing*] [date unknown]

Dear Sir,

Many thanks for the jolly little book. My name is alright to sign for the purpose you name.

Very faithfully yours,
H.G. Wells

901. To Morley Roberts

Illinois, ACCS

17, Church Row
Hampstead [*c.* 1911-12]

My dear Roberts,

It was very natural for you to be angry & it's for me to apologize again for the absurdly irritating muddle my domestic made.[1]

Here are some G.G. letters – all I can put my hands on.[2] I'm off to Little Easton Rectory, Dunmow, Essex today & I shall be up again next week.

Yours ever,
H.G.

My wife tells me the letters are buried deep, she doesn't quite know where. But she is sure she can find them & you shall have them as soon as they are found.

[1] Roberts came to call on Wells who was hard at work at the time. A servant, who did not know Roberts, denied him admission. Roberts was furious, and this letter is Wells's apology. They were never really close again, although they saw each other from time to time.

[2] The remaining Gissing letters were probably with Frank Swinnerton, who was working on his biography. Eventually Roberts saw all that were available.

902. To Edwin Pugh[1]

Illinois, ALS

17 Church Row
N.W. [*c.* 1911-12]

Dear Pugh,

Following an excellent precept & the Fashion of the work I wrote to acknowledge your book briefly & I trust elegantly, before I had read it. I was disposed to think it might be good. I've read it now with an admiration that grew steadily until Ricky appeared & then anyhow I didn't decline. It has your best writing & some of it is quite wonderful. I guess (this is a trivial detail) that your man wasn't originally destined for the bar & a K.Cship. He writes "seems to me" & things like that in the earlier chapters. I hope the book will go. It deserves to anyhow. The Lord deals gently with me. My personal unpopularity is immense but amusing & people listen with blanched faces to the tale of my vices & go & buy my books. Really I lead a life of unspotted virtue mostly at a little old Rectory I have in Essex. My two little boys are a continuing joy & I am taking them off to Switzerland tomorrow. Bowkett[2] is stranded in Madeira & can't get home (God keep him there). His wife divorced him two years ago & has been near death with rheumatic fever. Conrad I've given up since he went on the Academic Committee & took a Civil List pension. I hope you detest Morley Roberts Gissing book.

Good wishes
H.G.

[1] Edwin Pugh (1874–1930) was an author. He had just finished *The Charles Dickens Originals* (London, 1911).

[2] Almost certainly one of the two Bowkett brothers who were fellow students in Bromley with Wells. They had drifted into relative want, and Maurice emerged in the 1930s as an object of Wells's philanthropy. There are a few letters from both Maurice and Sidney Bowkett to Wells, but none from Wells to them have survived apparently.

903. To Miss Van Dyke[1]

Bancroft, ALS

52, St. James's Court
Buckingham Gate, S.W. [date unknown]

Dear Miss Van Dyke,

I've read Wallace Irwin's book right through with much admiration & fellow feeling. "Wings" & the "Highest" I like best of all & then "Ideal Gentleman". I suppose in any classification of short stories, Irwin's work & my short stories must be lumped together in the same "school" so that my very warm approach is an instinct approval. I've been along that track. I shall look out for more of Wallace Irwin & I am greatly obliged to you for sending Pilgrims on a Hill to me.

Very sincerely yours,
H.G. Wells

[1] Miss Van Dyke may have been a publisher's representative. Irwin (1876–1959) was known for *Letters of A Japanese Schoolboy* (New York: Doubleday Page, 1909).

904. To Mr Norman[1]

Boston, ALS

17, Church Row
Hampstead [date unknown]

My dear Norman,

When you find a thing happens to you like your dismissal you can be pretty sure that the diplomacy of the Minority Report is busy. Now the New Age will follow the Crusader.

Very sincerely yours,
H.G. Wells

We both know Bobby Ross by the bye. Will you come and have lunch at the Reform one day?

[1] Norman is otherwise unknown.

905. To Edmund Gosse

Leeds, ALS

17, Church Row
Hampstead   Jan. 31, 1912

My dear Gosse,

I've been away or I would have answered your post card before this. I too think that this proposed bill of McKenna's is likely to be a serious & mischievous nuisance to decent artists, but I cannot imagine what to do.[1] It doesn't help for me after Ann Veronica rows & the like to write and complain about it. What is wanted is to get some liberal minded bishop or a respectable peer to speak out & organize a watching committee.

Yours ever,
H.G. Wells

[1] Wells and others kept a careful watch for new attempts at censorship; he signed many letters to the press opposing censorhip. The legislation proposed by Reginald McKenna was not enacted. For another statement of his views on theatrical censorship see his letter, which was also signed by John Galsworthy, John Masefield, Bernard Shaw and others, to *The Times*, 14 February 1912.

906. To Martin Secker

Illinois, Typed Transcription

Reply to
17 Church Row
[Hampstead]   [February 1912][1]

Dear Sir.

I learn that you have sold the American rights of my article upon George Gissing to the New York Times. My price for these American rights is £20. Of course you had no more right to sell them than you have to sell

Devonshire House & I shall be obliged if you will let me know what you propose to do to regularize this remarkable position.

Yours very sincerely
H. G. Wells

[1] The original transcriber dated this letter in 1913, but that cannot be correct. I have been unable to trace an American printing of this article.

907. To Martin Secker

Illinois, Typed Transcription

[17 Church Row
Hampstead] Feb 14 1912

My dear Sir,

I've not replied to your letter for some time as I wanted to think it over & not do anything further in a burst of anti-publisher indignation. I'm now quite cool & very ready to accept your explanations. Please let me have your cheque for the 15 dollars & we will let the matter drop.

Yours very sincerely
H. G. Wells

Martin Secker, Esq.
5 John St.
Adelphi

908. To the Editor, *The Times*[1]

PLS

17, Church Row
Hampstead [5? March 1912]

Sir, – In common with the rest of the world, I am deeply interested in the possibilities of a settlement of the present coal strike, and I shall be glad if you will permit me to point out two consideratons that seem to me to be quite fundamentally important in this problem. The first of these is the extreme suspicion of the men. They appear to be resolved not to return to work until they have a completely specific agreement that will leave nothing to subsequent discussion. I will not attempt to explain the origins of such suspicion, whether it be the work of insidious "agitators" or the vicious fruit of previous disappointments, or the reflection of our sordid political prepossessions in the popular mind; the fact remains that it is there to an extent quite unpredecented in British labour quarrels. The general deterioration of our political tone is manifesting itself in this struggle. The men behave no longer as though they believed our political leaders are in the last resort gentlemen, but as though they considered them in the worst sense of the words lawyers and "exploiters". I do not, I say, wish to discuss the sources of this persuasion, much less would I justify it. It is so, and for the present problem it cannot be altered. The Government is dealing with a mass of men hopelessly shy of promises or subsequent adjustments, and the only conceivable way of getting to a settlement with such men is absolute frankness and explicitness to the utmost detail.

And that brings me to the second essential fact to which I would call attention – the ignorance of our rulers. The men have submitted a detailed demand for a specific *minimum* wage in every district. They seem, to an unbiased observer like myself, to have prepared that demand with considerable care and moderation. We are told that what they ask is in several cases unreasonable. If that is so, why are our expensive Government officials and why are the owners unprepared with an alternate schedule that is reasonable and will permit of a working profit? This strike has been coming visibly for a long time. Why haven't the "experts" a detailed, lucid statement to make that could be put up against the men's specific claim? This struggle, I submit, is amazingly discreditable to the English governing class. It is a worse disillusionment than the South African war. Here are the men on the one hand, clear, informed, exact; here are the owners and the Government on the other, windy and vague, and standing on their dignity. In my small experience of business transactions I have always refused to deal with people who stood on their dignity when I wanted accounts and figures. The people we trust to govern us seem to have been taken by surprise after a full half-year's warning, to be inadequately informed and planless. They didn't know; they didn't even know they ought to know. I sit over my dwindling fire full of the apprehension of discomforts to come, and it is not against the miners that my resentment gathers. It is against the traditions and shame of party politics, against the organization of ignorance by the public schools, against the systematic exploitation of Parliament by lawyers that leaves us now with nothing but shifty politicians in a crisis that calls in vain for knowledge and statecraft.

The miners, and not only the miners but the workers generally, are restless and out of hand. The situation is stupendously dangerous, we must go back 130 years to find a solution as dangerous. If this strike goes on it will go on to social revolution and something indistinguishable from civil war. Let the ruling and owning classes stop a resistance that is at once planless and extraordinarily exasperating, give in at once to demands that are still clear and finite, stop this struggle now at any price, and then, with such haste as they can, set about learning their business a little more thoroughly than they know it at present time and recovering that confidence which has until recently been given them in such generous measure by the mass of British workers.

H.G. Wells[2]

---

[1] In late February 1912 850,000 miners went on strike, asking for a new wage scale of five shillings a day for men, and two shillings for boys. Negotiations failed and the men were forced back to work by Parliamentary action. The strike ended on 12 April. Wells wrote this letter in early March and it was published in *The Times* on 7 March 1912. Since then it has appeared in a collection of letters to the Editor of *The Times*, *The First Cuckoo*, and it was reprinted in the paper on 7 March 1982.

[2] Wells's concerns over these labour problems were offered in an originally six (finally eight) part statement in the *Daily Mail*, running from 13, 14, 15, 16, 17, 20 May, 5, 7 June 1912, under the title 'The Labour Unrest'. The articles were also published in a separate pamphlet under the same title. Dozens of other writers across the country also wrote in to participate in what became a great national debate over the issues of labour and capital. In addition to his standard calls for reform in technical education, and housing, Wells also called for popular representation and a social contract.

909. To the Editor, *The Freewoman*[1]

PLS

[London] [1? March 1912]

THE FREEWOMAN is too bright and intelligent a paper to indulge in wilful misrepresentation of a position she doesn't approve of, but she is rather wickedly wrong about what she calls, begging the question to begin with, The State Endowment of Mothers. It's the State Endowment of Motherhood she's thinking of, which is a very different thing. It's not human beings we want to buy and enslave, it's a social service, a collective need, we want to sustain.

Here are the answers to her questions, from one who has staked his poor reputation for intelligence on the State Endowment of Motherhood.

1. Does State endowment of mothers mean an adequate subsistence grant to mothers – say, £100 a year or so? or is it a dole to mothers – perhaps 5s a week?

1. It means an adequate subsistence for the child and for the mother so far as the child needs her. "How much" depends upon the standard of life prevailing in the community and upon the resources available.

2. Endowing the mother, does the State propose to make her subsistence grant sufficient for the child also, and, if not, on whom does the cost of maintenance of the child fall?

2. See answer to 1.

3. For what period before birth is the grant to be in operation – nine months, six months, three months, or one?

3. A matter of common sense and convenience. Six months perhaps.

4. If the child lives, how long is the grant to continue – one year, three years, or seven years, or what?

4. The payments will be made to the mother as first and principal guardian of the child so long as it needs a guardian.

5. If the child dies, is the mother to continue to be endowed, or, being deprived of her child , is she to lose her endowment as well?

5. The payments only concern the child, and cease with its life.

6. If the period during which endowment is fixed extends through a number of years, will not women be able to earn their livelihood by continuously giving birth to a small number of children?

6. I presume that the payments will be a pretty complete maintenance for both mother and child before birth and until the child no longer engrosses the whole of a woman's attention. Afterwards I presume it will fall in amount so as to prevent a woman living parasitically on a solitary child. But there is no reason why a woman disposed to specialise as a mother should not do so through many years.

7. After spending the best years of their lives in bearing children, are women to be thrown aside when their bearing period is over? If not, will not a State pension be necessary at the close of the period?

7. This is only a special aspect of old age pensions, and is not relevant to the present discussion. It applies equally well to sterile women who have spent the best years in teaching or editing.

8. If this is so, does not this amount to a permanent State maintenance of all adult fertile females?

8. That depends upon (a) the adult fertile females and (b) the ability of the State to discourage excesses of philoprogenitiveness by diminishing allowances.

9. If to the number of most females maintained by the State there be added on the number of children they bear (perhaps also State endowed; certainly not self-supporting), can such a State avoid bankruptcy?

9. This is the general question of Socialism and the available resources of a civilised community. The community *now* supports (through extravagant and wasteful individual media) *all* non-productive females and *all* the children in it.

10. Of whom, for financial purposes, is this State which is to provide such maintenance composed other than money-earning men and a few sterile women"

10. Productive people always have and always will produce everything that is spent in the community.

11. On whom is the motherhood tax to be levied?

11. Why suppose there is to be a tax ad hoc?

12. Is it to be a poll-tax on adult men and women, including bachelors and spinsters?

12. Nonsense! *Think!* I'm surprised at you.

13. Is it worth while taxing mothers in order to refund them their money?

13. My *dear* lady! If you go on like this—!

14. Will the protected position of mothers lead to a rush into motherhood?

14. No greater rush need be feared than exists now. It would be quite easy to check an increase of the population by diminishing allowances, and to stop a fall by increasing them.

15. If so, is this increase in the population wanted?

15. Answered.

16. Is there to be any limit to the number of a woman's family?

16. No compulsory limit is necessary – a financial discouragement of excess works very effectively nowadays. (Cp. ex-President Roosevelt on "Race Suicide".)

17. If so, on what grounds is limitation to be made?

17. Welfare of the children and society generally.

17a. Will endowment increase with size of family?

17a. Abundantly answered already.

18. Are all women to be eligible for motherhood?

18. I imagine it would be possible to define "unfitness" and of course the State will not endow the motherhood of unfit women so far as unfitness can be defined.

19. If not, what is to be the standard of eligibility?

19. There we fall back on the wisdom of the medical profession.

20. Who is to set the standard?

20. The collective intelligence working through the organs of Government.

21. Will the standard be a physical or mental one, or both?

21. Both.

22. Will the State require to exercise restricting rights over the selection of fathers?

22. So far as "unfitness" can be satisfactorily defined.

23. If so, by what standard will fathers be judged?

23. Same answer as 20-21. Sauce – goose – gander.

24. Will the State-endowed mother have full control over her allowance, or

24. She is guardian and trustee for the child, and I suppose she will be removable in case of culpable negligence or manifest incapacity.

25. Will the father be able to exercise rights over it?

25. I think not, but there are many who are with me thus far who depart from me. I think a father ought to have a right of action to dispossess an incompetent, vicious, or extravagant mother and set her aside, but the role of the

normal father should be, I think, one of friendly advice, and not of legally sustained intervention.

26. To whom does the child of the State-endowed mother belong?

26. To itself, with the mother normally acting as its guardian.

27. If it belongs to the State, will not the State have to provide for its maintenance until capable of earning its own livliehood?

27. Even without the first hypothesis, yes.

28. Would marriage be necessary as a qualification for endowment?

28. "Marriage" may mean all sorts of different things, but I think that people ought not to incur the liability to parentage without forethought and public formalities. But then I have very liberal views about divorce and marriage; so liberal that I will leave 29, 30, and 31 unanswered. After all, these are quite secondary questions, not affecting the principle of endowment, but only its application.

[29. If so, and the mother should complain of the poor quality of her child from the particular stock, would the State allow her to choose a father outside the marriage bond?

30. If so, why enforce marriage?

31. If it should be maintained that the mother should choose rightly at the outset, and it not be counter-maintained that in these things you never can tell?]

Your constant reader,
H.G. Wells

---

[1] The most important feminist journal of its time, *The Freewoman*, offered a platform to women such as Josephine Baker and Rebecca West. They did not oppose contributions from men, and, in the case of someone like Wells, they welcomed his contributions. He had put the case for a pension for mothers – an endowment of motherhood he called it – as early as 1904. The first letter is an important part of the debate over Endowments for Women. The editors of the paper and Wells exchanged public views and this led to a full-blown debate. The first letter, written at about the same time as the previous letter to *The Times* published on 7 March 1912, gives Wells's responses to queries put by the editors of the journal. The queries were reprinted as part of the letter and they are printed in italic type here. A second letter, also printed on p. 1 of the journal, 21 March 1912 under the title, "Woman Endowed", provided a forum for his ideas in the debate over this controversial proposal. After his letter the editors responded to his queries in a nearly full-page article. They certainly respected his views and welcomed his support, but he was not enough of a feminist. In fact, one would say that he was more of a realist.

910. To Upton Sinclair

Indiana, ALS

17, Church Row,
Hampstead [Spring 1912]

My dear Sinclair,

I can't back that book.[1] I've been considering it & when I can find time I shall write you a letter discussing the whole question. Just now I'm too involved with a book of my own. The story is full of fine stuff but I can't find that birth chapter permissible.

Yours ever,
H.G. Wells

[1] Sinclair was about to move into self-publishing as he felt he had been badly treated by his publishers. This may refer to a request for some backing from Wells.

911. To the Editor, *The Freewoman*

PLS

[London] [mid-March 1912]

Madam, – Your comments upon my complete answers to your questions about the Endowment of Motherhood leave little for me to say further in the way of controversy. You admit that children will be State-maintained in a large measure up to the age of eighteen or twenty-one, and the State Endowment of Motherhood is really nothing more than that *plus* the assertion that the legitimate guardian of a child is its mother. It's odd you won't take that concluding step. What remains of your case – if anything can be said to remain – it is not so much a survival as a relapse – rests apparently upon an extraordinary assumption that women are, or can be made, equivalent economically to men, and that over and above that normal citizenship they are capable of bearing and rearing their own children. That is, I think, a quite impossible assumption. Sex is a graver handicap to a woman than a man – economically. Womanhood is not someting superadded to the normal citizen; it is something taking up time, nervous energy, room in the body and room in the mind. It is something carved out of the normal citizen. Apart from child-bearing, it means a periodic disablement for a large number of women, and the only possible way in which women generally can be put upon a footing of equal and honourable competition and fellowship with men is to correct this natural economic handicap by a collective endowment. Sex in a man is a handicap only through women, not in itself. It does not incapacitate him; it may rule his being, but it does not invade it; for him it is not a physical let and encumbrance, but only a desire and a possible obsession. It is for men quite as much as for women that the endowment of motherhood is needed. I can see no other way of escape from our present state of affairs in which women, hampered, needy, and economically inferior, live under a constant provocation to loot the superior earnings of men by exciting and playing upon their passions.

I should be glad, dear madam, if the endowment of motherhood is not the way of escape, to learn what is your way. Do you really suppose a state of affairs is possible in which most women as well as most men will be "productive", and while the women keep both themselves and their children, the men will keep only themselves? I may have missed something in your able leading articles, but that is what you seem to be driving at. You owe it to your readers to develop your Utopia of Freewomen a little more fully than you have done. I want, madam, to know how you propose to keep *us* and the women with a weakness for "dependence" upon us, in order, in your magnificent commonweal of Freewomen, each sure of a job and a minimum wage of thirty shillings, and each containing herself and at least ninety-nine per cent of one child thereon. There is, you know, the Philoprogenitive Male, sometimes a person of considerable earning power. How will your Thirty Shillings a Week Mother feel when her not very expensively turned out child comes in comparison with the three or four rather elaborately cared for darlings of the lady in alliance with the Philoprogenitive Male? I want to know more about that minimum wage of thirty shillings. Is it for everyone in the State, or only for the women, and if the latter, then aren't you after all getting round to something more extreme than my Endowment of Motherhood, an Endowment of Feminity? I respect your courage and your spirit, dear madam, but at times I find you very far from being clear or consistent.

Very sincerely yours,
H.G. Wells

912. To Gertrude Kingston[1]

Illinois, ALS

17 Church Row
Hampstead [early 1912]

Dear Miss Kingston,

The business affairs of "Kipps" lie between Bright & Bezier & it will simply complicate things if I interfere.[2] There is however another affair which I would like to talk over with you later when time is riper. I have sketched out a little play very suitable for the Little Theatre in collaboration with Miss Ella Hepworth Dixon. It is a one act thing that might play for perhaps an hour & really original & amusing. I will write you about it later.

Yours sincerely,
H.G. Wells

---

[1] Kingston was an actress, producer, suffragette, and friend of both Wells and Shaw.

[2] A stage production of *Kipps*, adapted by Rudolf Bezier, was given at the Vaudeville Theatre in 1912. O. S. Lawrence, Christine Silver and Helen Haye played the leads. The Dixon play, tentatively entitled, *Dicky Touchwood*, never went beyond the toy theatre trials in France during August 1911.

913. To an unknown correspondent

Boston, ALS

17, Church Road
Hampstead [receipt stamp 11/2/1912]

My dear Sir,

You are quite at liberty to quote any three passages (not consecutive) of less than a thousand words in length from the N. Machiavelli & I feel very greatly complimented by your choice. I've cruel duties through May this year & I'm going to a house I've taken in France in June to escape the coronation.[1] I shall not be back in England until October but then I hope we may have the pleasure of meeting.

Very sincerely yours,
H. G. Wells

[1] The coronation of King George V took place on the morning of Thursday, 22 June 1911, so from the date of the receipt stamp this letter was either long delayed before posting or in the post.

914. To the Editor, *The Eye-Witness*

PLS

17, Church Row
Hampstead — June 11, 1912

Sir, – Mr. Street writes in your columns:

> It is a mistake to suppose (as Mr. Wells supposes) that the average workman from the light of his reading and ideals looks on them (the rich) and the luxuries with contempt.

Mr. Wells supposes nothing of the sort and there is nothing he has ever said or written to justify this careless invention of Mr. Street's. It is a casual lie.

H.G. Wells [1]

[1] Street responded, in the issue of 18 July 1912, that he had taken the Wells quotation from part III of *The Labour Unrest* and, although he was exaggerating somewhat, he was praising and applauding Wells's work, certainly not attacking him. He urged Wells to calm down and show self-restraint, as did Arthur Quiller-Couch, who said that Wells and Street were both too good to be involved in this sort of exchange. Wells then responded with letter 921.

915. To the Editor, *The Nation*[1]

PLS

[London] — [*c.* early June 1912]

Sir:

In what professes I suppose to be a review of The Great State, you give your readers a fanciful intellectual biography of myself. Regarded as a way of evading a serious discussion of ideas there is no doubt much to be said for this form of attack. But your reviewer appears to be one of those people who can neither read or remember, and his amiable interpretations of my character are marred by the entire untruthfulness of his statements. He gives a series of sketches of my phases; his whole intention being manifestly to insinuate that once I was a typical member of the Fabian Society, that I quarrelled with that obscure & now I believe extinct body, & that my entire intellectual life has been determined by my relations to it.

He gives a fancy sketch of my "Anticipations" (written in 1900 before I had any relations at all with the Fabian Society & which he declares I wrote "when the Fabian spell was working") in which he pretends that the book is a Utopian work – he hasn't even grasped the meaning of the title — & attributes to me the conception that "rapid transport & Eugenics were to be the pillars of the State". As a matter of fact there is a chapter in Mankind in the Making (1903) devoted to a careful destructive criticism of Eugenic proposals, a chapter I would endorse without a word of alteration today.

Then, entangling himself with a "A Modern Utopia", he goes on to ascribe to me that ridiculous opposition of "character" & "intellect" which was originally invented I believe by public schoolmasters to excuse their bad teaching, & caught up by the wire-pulling class in their attack on competitive examinations. I cannot imagine how anyone with an average knowledge of the meaning of words can assume that my distinction between poiëtic & kinetic types is such an apposition.

"A Modern Utopia" (1905) was written after certain leading members of the Fabian Society attracted by my "Anticipations" had invaded me with requests to come into the Fabian Society & stimulate it. I thought the Society was badly in need of stimulation, & I went into it, & from the beginning to the end of my connexion with it I was in conflict with that awful priggishness and that vanity of disingenuousness which have done so much to make social constructive proposals seem dangerous & ridiculous in this country. From first to last I was at issue with Fabianism. Yet now according to your reviewer comes my last, my "anti-Fabian" phase. I have just, he declares, flared out into opposition of the "Servile State", that bureaucratic tyranny which once, he implies, I supported.[2] Your reviewer has never I suppose heard of "The Sleeper Awakes" (1899) which is an anticipation and a vehement attack on just that specialization & regimentation of labour which we writers in "The Great State" are attacking, thirteen years later, today. "The Food of the Gods" (1904) says in symbols nearly everything that the "Great State" puts now in reasoned terms.

I apologize Sir for this invasion of your space, but there comes a limit to one's patience under this method of criticism by invented biography & careless misstatement. Given a certain slovenliness of attention & anyone may be excused of inconsistency. A writer with the intellectual fluidities of your reviewer could find a mass of incoherence in the first four books of Euclid. He would think that what Euclid said about right angles he said about any angles, forget several of his definitions & suspect the influence of the "spell" of Todhunter. And he would point out how the excitable unstable mind of Euclid was obsessed by the idea of circles in his later books, and suppose that this was due to the accidental acquisition of a pair of compasses. I submit that this sort of thing is unworthy of the high traditions of the Nation.

Yours etc.,
H.G. Wells

[1] This letter was in response to a review of Wells and others, *The Great State* (London: Harper,1912) which appeared on 12 June 1912. However this copy is dated, in another hand, June 22, 1912. It was given the heading, 'Pot Shots at Criticism'.

[2] *The Servile State* was a very recently published attack on statism, written by Hilaire Belloc. This was a time when many thinkers were attempting to analyze and predict which sort of government would work best in the twentieth century.

916. To R. D. Blumenfeld[1]

Illinois, ANS

17, Church Row
Hampstead [undated, *c.* July 1912]

War game isn't available on Sunday but come over with a golf club[2]. We shall have Kauf(f]?)man(n?)] (F's & N's to taste) & his wife. One of the new rising American novelists He wrote the House of Bondage.[3]

[1] This may have been a hand delivered note.

[2] This note illustrates weekend life with the Wells family: a houseful of guests, and the Blumenfelds invited to join in. Unfortunately, the 'war game' is off for some reason. Wells invented games for his guests, and the war game refers to the famous organised game described in his *Little Wars* (1913); it is normally associated with Easton or Spade House. The Wells family were about to remove to Easton. The Blumenfelds were also to remove to the Essex countryside, and such weekends were famous, especially the last weekend of peace, in late July 1914.

[3] The writer and newspaper editor, Reginald Wright Kauffmann (1877–1950) had written this novel in 1910. At the time he was a Socialist, but moved steadily to the right, and ended his career editing very right wing newspapers in the United States.

917. To R. D. Blumenfeld

Illinois, ALS

Little Easton Rectory,
Dunmow [1912–15]

Dear R.D.B.

Here is the article, which you need not use if you do not like it. I have only done it to please you, & if it doesn't suit you don't use it.
And God bless you.

H.G.

[*A note at the bottom of the page in Catherine's Wells's hand says:*]

'If it is set up please send a proof, as the writing is very difficult to decipher, & please return the M.S. with the proof for comparison.'

918. To R. D. Blumenfeld

Illinois, ALS

Little Easton Rectory,
Dunmow [1912–15]

You see Uncle the difficulty is that the knee is not a dislocation but a sprain & Bartlett doesn't do sprains.

Your affectionate nephew,

H.G.

Come over with Daisy on Saturday evening. J. M. Barrie will be here & he will like R.D.Bs' when he gets over the first shock.

919. To Bertrand Russell[1]

Texas, ALS

Little Easton Rectory
Dunmow
[date unknown][2]

Dear Lord Russell,

I'm not quite sure if I shall be in England at the end of September. I may go to Denmark but if I am I shall be very sure indeed to come along to visit Huntingdown[?] once more.

Yours ever,
H.G. Wells

[1] Lord Russell (1865–1931) married Elizabeth von Arnim in 1916. Von Arnim was a good friend and for a short time, lover of Wells. There is one letter to her in volume 4.
[2] Although this could be anytime from 1911 to 1929, in fact, the address Little Easton Rectory certainly dates the letter before 1915. The late Summer of 1912 is likely.

920. To Ella Hepworth Dixon

Illinois, ANS

Easton Glebe
Dunmow
[date unknown][1]

Dearest Zuleika,

I'm so sorry we couldn't get to your tea. Coal shutes & week enders who want to have a LONG weekend, did us in. But I want to see both you & the Countess Lutzow. Couldn't we have a lunch somewhere next week? Say about the 12th. I will ask Jane to fix it up with you.

Yours ever,
H.G.

[1] Again the date could be any time from 1912 to 1928, but it is almost certainly after the Summer of 1915 as the name of their house was changed after an extensive renovation.

921. To the Editor, *The Eye-Witness*[1]

PLS

[17 Church Row,
Hampstead] July 25, 1912

Sir, – I was abusive; – I am an irascible small man, very distressed at the evils I can see, and feel and cannot remedy, and doing what I can to clear up things misunderstood. I desire an exquisite adherence to veracity and a sedulous understanding.

H.G. Wells

[1] See Letter 914. His original letter may have been longer. It was printed in a cramped corner of the newspaper and appears in this somewhat jumbled form.

922. To Upton Sinclair

Indiana, APCS

[Holland] [postmarked 27/7/12]

I don't know what is to be done. The best things is to get your friends to write to the best of the literary people & if warned them [*illegible words*].

As ever

H G.W.

923. To Upton Sinclair[1]

Indiana, APCS

[Address unknown] [1912]

Reply please to Hampstead
Dear Sinclair,

I'm packing up after a spell of hard work in these places. I hope to be back next week. I'll write or will you call on Mrs. W.

HGW

[1] Sinclair was living at the time in Hampstead.

924. To Upton Sinclair

Indiana, ALS

Little Easton Rectory
Dunmow [1912–15]

My dear Sinclair

I'm about – Though writing on my own paper & posting from home. My heartiest response to your friendly letter.

Yours ever
H. G. Wells

925. To Upton Sinclair

Indiana, ALS

Little Easton Rectory
Dunmow [1912–15]

My dear Sinclair

I think your new Bible will be tremendously interesting & send it my blessing. No publisher has any right to ask you anything for quotations. I retain always my "serial" rights which cause such occasions. But I think the book can have no better introduction than your modest foreword. Let it speak for itself.

Yours ever,
H G. Wells

926. To Perular Maxwell

Boston, ACCS

Little Easton Rectory
Dunmow [postmarked July 16 12]

Dear Mr. Perular Maxwell,

Very well. You shall have that letter for £3 provided that you do not tell how much you paid for it & provided you say you paid for it. This special message business which usually involves the expensive redirection of lengthy telegrams is being overdone & henceforth & always the price is going to be £20 irrespective of length, for answering any American papers.

Very sincerely yours,
H.G. Wells [1]

[1] The message and where it appeared have not been traced, unless it is the letter which appeared in facsimile in *The Bookman*, November 1912, p. 237. This letter is filled with Wells's drawings and appears to be directions for either the compositor or a sub-editor concerning *The New Machiavelli*.

927. To Mr Rideing

Boston, ALS

Little Easton Rectory
Dunmow [Summer 1912?]

Dear Mr. Rideing

I can't read your letter very well. What exactly are you offering for the article? Resort to a typist and let me know. I think I could do you something quite jolly about toys & games – either the game things or camping about in gardens. — In the piece of 2000 to 3000 words, but I had rather write it after Christmas as my time is very much engaged.[1]

Yours sincerely,
H.G. Wells

[1] This letter relates to Wells's two books for children, *Floor Games* (London: Palmer, 1911) and *Little Wars* (London: Palmer, 1913). Wells first mentions the games he had invented in *The New-Machiavelli* (London: John Lane, 1911). The text of *Little Wars* appeared in the *The Windsor Magazine* in two parts, December 1912 and January 1913. Whether there is another article is problematic.

928. To Mr Rideing

Boston, ALS

Little Easton Rectory
Dunmow [Summer 1912]

Will you modify your terms to 300 dollars for an article between 2000 & 3000 words in length?

Dear Mr. Rideing

I can't do that article now but if you will write to me in January att the Hotel du Parc, Vellar sur Ollen, Switzerland (where I shall be from Jan 15th onward) you will catch me in a state of leisure.

Very sincerely yours,
H. G. Wells

929. To Edmund Gosse

Leeds, ALS

17, Church Row
Hampstead [*c.* Summer 1912]

My dear Gosse,

Thanks for your Times letter. Can you help this with your signature. Mrs. Garnett is nearly blind, very ill, & with a husband, amiable in most ways, but no good for comfort.

Yours ever,
H.G. Wells [1]

[1] This letter may be some sort of appeal for Constance Garnett, the extraordinary translator of Russian fiction.

930. To the Editor, *The Freewoman*[1]

PLS

[London] [*c.* 1 September 1912]

Madam, – Keenly aware as I am of your great gifts and unprecedented intuitions, I think you carry your confidence in them too far when you set out to summarize for your large and appreciative circle of readers a book you quite manifestly have never seen. The "Great State" is not, as you intimate, a volume by me, but by a number of writers, and no one who had read my contribution would suppose that I advocated anything that could conceivably be called "Guild-Socialism". Neither is the Great State the Servile State which I foreshadowed in "When the Sleeper Wakes", and which Mr. Belloc subsequently christened. Foreseeing the possibility of slovenly readers, I supplemented the very exact distinctions in my "Great State" article with a diagram, which you have, of course, not seen, but which was intended to bring home to the meanest intelligence the essential difference between the ideal of the Great State, on the one hand, and the ideal of that Bureaucratic State (Servile State of Mr. Belloc) which I have always hated and opposed, and satirised and jeered at, on the other. That difference lies in *the entire absence of any specific labour class in the Great State*. You have heard somewhere of my adhesion to the idea of a universal labour conscription, a labour service for a year or so, as a necessary substitute for the subjugation of a labour class, and your rapid, mobile mind has leapt to the phrase "unregimented labour" and an entire inversion of my proposal.

Perhaps because of my greater modesty, I do read you with attention and amusement, and now that I am writing to you, madam, permit me to add to my correction of your brilliant misstatements my assurance that I do not believe you have any constructive ideas at all in your head, that you do not know what you want in economic and social organisation, that the wild cry for freedom which makes me so sympathetic with your paper, and which echoes through every column of it, is unsupported by the ghost of the shadow of an idea how to secure freedom. What is the good of writing that "economic arrangements will have to be adjusted to the Soul of man", if you are not prepared with anything remotely resembling a suggestion of how the adjustment is to be effected. My collaborators and I in the "Great State" do offer, among other matters, suggestions to that very end. Your paper, which was so promising as a breakaway from the monomania of the Vote, becomes more and more an irrational and inattentive clamouring of the same kind – mixed up amazingly with Mr. Kitson on currency. . . . [*They cut his letter here*]

I pray you, madam, to collect yourself, and I remain, as always, your sympathetic reader.

H.G. Wells

---

[1] In this letter, published on 5 September 1912, p. 312, Wells is defending his recently edited, *The Great State* against claims that he and his co-authors had proposed a scheme which could lead to a bureaucratic central government.

931. To Edmund Gosse

Leeds, ALS

Little Easton Rectory
Dunmow October 2 1912

My dear Gosse,

Large sections of me are altogether with you. The next book is just finished & is as hard as nails but the next after shall show the fruits of your admonitions.[1]

Yours ever,
H.G. Wells

[*At the foot of this letter Gosse wrote, 'In reply to a letter of mine expostulating with him for the increasing hardness and rhetorical quality of his inventions. E.G.'*]

---

[1] Gosse may have been commenting on *Marriage*. Wells's next two novels were *The Passionate Friends* (1913, in serial by March, 1913) and *The World Set Free*. Wells may also have been thinking of *The Wife of Sir Isaac Harman* which appears to have been planned as part of a group of novels dealing with marital relations. The series was interrupted by *The World Set Free*, see the two letters to A. T. Simmons early in 1913, 941 and 944.

932. To Morley Roberts

Illinois, ALS

Little Easton Rectory
Dunmow *c.* 5 Nov. 1912
[in another hand]

Dear Roberts,

I'm disappointed in the book. So far as my knowledge of facts goes it's blazingly inaccurate. I could have set you right upon a dozen points if you had shown me the proofs. Your estimate of Gabrielle is ridiculous. She was a tiresome weak sentimental genteel middle-class Frenchwoman who wrote her letters on thin paper & cursed them & she worried G's last moments of life out of him. I wish I could have praised the book. I can't. You may have thought about it for years but it isn't planned, it isn't written, it's shied on to paper.

Yours ever,

H.G. Wells

[*Below, in Roberts's hand:*] – I never meant him to see Maitland [the name Gissing was given in the novel] [*illegible word*] has bitter page. No real review, only chaff![1]

---

[1] Wells was much less savage in his review, probably because he still felt some responsibility for Gissing's estate. He liked Swinnerton's book much better. Wells's review article entitled, 'The Truth About Gissing', appeared in *Rhythm* (Literary Supplement), December, 1912, pp. i-iv.

933. To an unknown correspondent

Hofstra, ALS

17, Church Row
Hampstead [*c.* late 1912]

Dear Sir,

Thank you very much for the Cambridge Magazine.[1] If art was not so long & life so busy very gladly would I not fill pages & talk to the Heretics.

Yours ever,

H.G. Wells

---

[1] Wells is probably referring to one of the first long critical articles about his work, written by Sir Hume Hordon, Bart., 'The Popularity of H.G. Wells and Arnold Bennett', *Oxford and Cambridge Review*, no. 25 (November, 1912), pp. 80–86.

934. To Mr Sears[1]

Bromley, ALS

17, Church Row
Hampstead [probably 1912]

Dear Mr. Sears,

The Great State is in the press & will appear in April – Harpers on both sides.

I'm very much fixed up ahead now for my books. I don't think I shall have anything to negociate until 1915.

Yours ever,

H.G. Wells

[*The letter has the word FILE in Well's hand at the bottom of the page*.]

---

[1] See letter 867 for Wells's first contact with Sears.

935. To J. W. Robertson-Scott

Hofstra, APCS

Hotel du Parc
Villars sur Ollen [postmarked 17-1-13]

Very many thanks for your thought of us but we are here for a month now.

Yours

H.G. Wells

936. To Mr Maxwell[1]

Boston, ALS

Little Easton Rectory
Dunmow
Essex [*all in Wells's hand*] [*c.* early 1913]

My dear Mr. Maxwell,

I'll call it The Human Adventure.[2] It's got a wider scope than The Task Before Mankind. It's a bit of what spiteful people call "fine writing" about Man & the Universe. I trust you'll prefer it to a kind of Daily Mail article in interest. It shall be 1500 exactly.

Yours ever,

H.G.

---

[1] Perhaps the same Maxwell as letter 926.

[2] The Human Adventure appeared in *Hearst's Magazine* in November, 1912, pp. 110–13. It was republished initially in *An Englishman Looks at the World* and more recently in Patrick Parrinder, ed., *The Discovery of the Future* (London: Wells Society, 1989). Other writers have given the *Daily Mail* as a source for this piece, but I have been unable to locate it there.

937. To Harry Leon Wilson

Bancroft, ACCS

17, Church Row
Hampstead

Mar. 8, 1913.
[*in another hand*]

I'd love to have that book dedicated to me.[1] Your letter is the sole joy of my declining years. And don't read Marriage in serial form. It's cut atrociously (between ourselves). The book will be entire.

Yours ever,
H.G. Wells

[1] Which book was dedicated to Wells is not known.

938. To Harry Leon Wilson

Bancroft, ALS

17, Church Row
Hampstead

1913?
[*in another hand*]

Dear Wilson,

I'm proud beyond measure of my god-son. When can you come and we must dine & drink immortality to him. You're the fourth author to so honour me, Archer, Vernon Lee, Joseph Conrad & now you. I feel like a mortal who is still trying to run about mortal while the gods have half made him into a constellation. But indeed B.B. is extraordinarily well done. Go on. And presently take your courage in both hands, abandon all thought of pleasing your publisher & bookseller, & give us a long, leisurely, full American novel. It's up to you to do that.

Yours ever,
H.G. Wells

939. To Violet Paget

Colby, ALS

Little Easton Rectory
Dunmow

Brissago, on my way home
[Spring ?1913]

My dear Miss Paget,

Your maid – it was no [*illegible word*] – it was a maid – was inflexible. I said, "Uno venuto dos Inglesi terra solominute vedere la Signorina Paget. Questa e il solo joerno possible mobile." — no go! [1]

That night I had to dine with some men; the moment I parted, I rushed in order to save you vain telephoning. But, listen! – a secret. There is to be a little flat 52 St. James's Court, S.W. St. J's Ct. is a private address with a telephone exchange. You ring it up & ask for 52. I only tell few people this much. But Little Easton is to be my 'official' address.

Yours ever,
H.G. Wells

[1] Wells's Italian, written in his tiny script, is extremely difficult to read. But he is apparently describing his efforts to see Vernon Lee in her Florence home. This letter, without a date, must have been written in the spring of 1913.

940. To Elizabeth Healey

Illinois, ALS

52, St. James Court
Buckingham Gate, S.W.

[*c.* May 1913]

Dear Mrs. Bruce,[1]

I'm just back from a month in France & Italy, a comparatively hard month & I am up to my ears in work. But I will remember there is a haven of tea & talk at Tothill Street close at hand & I will try & look in more often.

Yours ever,
H.G.

[1] Healey had recently married a professor of mathematics at Cardiff University named Herbert Bruce (1877–1935).

941. To A. T. Simmons[1]

Illinois, ALS

Chalet Soleil
Randoyne sur Sierre
Switzerland [early Summer 1913]

Beloved Tommy (with love to R.A.G.)

I've been away from England for some time while Jane has been moving 17 Church Row partly to Little Easton & partly to 54 St.James's Court & I've suddenly broken out into one of the good old scientific romances again. And I suddenly want to know quite the latest about atomic theory and sources of energy. I've read and mastered Soddy's very good little book[2] and I want more. My idea is taken from Soddy. Men are supposed to find out how to set up some atomic degeneration in the heavy elements just as they found out long ago how to set up burning in coal. Hence, limitless energy. Now will you do me the kindness to write under the enclosed just whatever books will give me tips for this. I shall be coming back to London June 8th so don't put more than 2 or 3 books down, or if more have the others particularly the heavy ones sent to St. James's Court & believe me,

Yours ever,
H.G.

And at the beginning so at the end, love to R.A.G.

[1] This letter and letter 944 were printed in part in the Sydney, Australia, *Morning Herald*, 23 February 1946 in an article written by 'Tommy' Simmons's widow, Winifred. Why they were published in Sydney rather than anywhere else is puzzling. The address from which they were sent was the Swiss home of Elizabeth Von Arnim, with whom Wells was having a brief but passionate love affair. Part of *The World Set Free* was written at her chalet.
[2] Frederick Soddy (1877–1956) was a leading authority on radioactivity and the 'very good little book' was almost certainly his *Interpretation of Radium.*

942. To an unknown addressee

Korn, ALS

Little Easton Rectory
Dunmow [Summer ?1913]

Dear Madam,

Very many thanks for your interesting letter & my congratulations to your sons, who have a mother, so boy spirited. You will be interested to know that the late Mr. George Wyndham fought over our research of Middleborough both with Colonel Sykes last year & was keenly interested in Little Wars. I like your home paper work & games! – Meanwhile I never thought of hairpins.[1]

Yours very sincerely,
H.G. Wells

[1] This letter is to someone who read and liked Wells's games, and had made a suggestion which he valued. It is another piece of evidence to his openness and kindness to those who wrote to him. *Little Wars* occasionally replayed battles from the past, although it was a more *ad libitum* game usually.

943. To S. L. Bensusan[1]

Korn, ALS

Easton Glebe
Dunmow [1913?]

Dear Bensusan,

I feel just as though you had written the book of Job. I don't know why, & as if this lovely book you have given me came from that author. My warmest thanks & it will be among my most treasured possessions.

Yours sincerely,
H.G.

[1] Another friend and co-tenant of the Countess of Warwick. Bensusan was a writer and editor.

A literary weekend at Easton, 1913. Back row, R. D. Blumenfeld, Catherine Wells. Front row, Mrs Marian Bensusan, Mrs Hugh Cramber-Byng, H.G.W., Frank Wells, Lady Warwick, Lady Mercy Greville (her daughter), G. P. (Gip) Wells, Hugh Cranmer-Byng, S. L. Bensusan. (Getty Images)

944. To A. T. Simmons and R. A. Gregory

Illinois, ALS

Chalet Soleil
Montana sur Sierre
Switzerland [early Summer 1913]

My dear Tommy & Gregory,

It's like you two to hunt me up all these papers & put my feet into the way they ought to have gone four or five years ago. I think of doing a story about what would happen to the world if atomic degeneration could be set up in one or two of the heavy commoner metals, artificially induced radioactively in fact – and as I haven't done anything of this sort for some time, I'm quite amused. I shall be back in England now in a week or so. I've been away and chiefly here working very hard, while Jane has been moving our London establishment partly to Little Easton & partly to 52, St. James's Court. Everything is going very pleasantly & well with me just now, as I hope it finds you. I shall telephone you when I get to London and we must meet to celebrate my return to science.[1]

Yours ever,
H.G.

St. James's Court has a private branch exchange. You ring up the court and then ask for 52.

---

[1] When *The World Set Free* appeared. Wells wrote on the dedication page, 'To Frederick Soddy's "Interpretation of Radium". This story, which owes long passages to the eleventh chapter of that book, acknowledges and inscribes itself.' Soddy, who was also the author of *A Study of the Radio Active Elements* (1912–4), worked with the Curies and was awarded the Nobel Prize in Physics in 1921. He and Wells later met and shared several political platforms in later years. The original letters are at Illinois.

945. To Morris Colles

Boston, ALS

Little Easton Rectory
Dunmow

29 Aug 13
[date stamped by recipient]

My Dear Colles,

I got your note written partly in ink and partly in heart's blood. I've not counted much on the serialization of Lady Harman & I quite understand your difficulties.[1] But I look to you to squeeze me something out of it — It seems to me much better suited to monthly than weekly use & usable in large chunks.

Yours ever,
H. G. Wells

[1] *The Wife of Sir Isaac Harman* was not serialized.

946. To the Editor, *The New Witness*

PLS

Little Easton Rectory
Dunmow

[*c.* 7 September 1913]

Sir, – Your correspondent, "An Irishman", with his fun Liberals and his fun Conservatives, fails altogether to enforce the peculiar merit of Proportional Representation, which is that it makes the return of a well-known, politically-trusted man <u>who is neither Liberal nor Conservative</u> as inevitable as is his rejection under the present system. Moreover, it kills the undistinguished party nominee. Proportional Representation[1] as the Proportional Representation Society advocates it, could never have admitted a Herbert Samuel to the House of Commons.[2]

Yours very sincerely,
H.G. Wells

[1] Wells was a life-long adherent to the principles of Proportional Representation for elections to

Parliament. He is here answering 'An Irishman' who proposed a better party selection in the issues of 28 August and 4 September 1913 in *The New Witness*. 'An Irishman' thanked him for his analysis in the issue of 18 September. Wells's comment appears on 11 September 1913, p.595.

[2] Herbert Samuel (later Viscount Samuel) was at this time Postmaster-General in Asquith's Liberal government.

947. To C. H. Grinding[1]

Korn, APCS

Easton Glebe — 24 Sept 13

I'm up to my neck in work & I can't promise to read these books. Vorlet's book on the Countryside sounds very interesting.

H. G. Wells

---

[1] Grinding is not known.

948. To the Editor, *Daily Mail*[1]

PLS

Little Easton Rectory
Dunmow — [15? October 1913]

Sir, – Your contributor, Mrs. Lilian Hensman, scolds me with admirable vigour, but upon insufficient evidence, for supporting 'eugenics'.

I admire her free, fine feminine style of discussing matters so greatly that I regret the necessity I am under in declaring that not only do I not support eugenicists and the Eugenics Society, but that I have written an entirely destructive criticism of their proposals.

What sent Mrs. Lilian Hensman girding at me was, I perceive, not one of my books, of which she is no doubt spiritually ignorant, but the absurd proceedings of a gentleman named Bolce, who has recently taken my name (and my portrait) in vain in the columns of a contemporary [newspaper]. Mr. Bolce came to my house a year or so ago to take photographs of me for a magazine, and secured, among others, one of himself and myself in conversation. He has since become the father of a child who has been named – I think unfortunately – Eugenetta. He declares that his wife was with him when he visited me – I did not know she was his wife, I imagined she was an assistant operator – and that my conversation was calculated to improve the prospects of the incipient Eugenetta. (I doubt if he will think so now.) He has further declared in print, and the thing will no doubt go around the Press of the world, that I take a profound interest in Eugenetta and what he is pleased to consider the eugenic experiment of her birth and upbringing. This is what has aroused the swift eloquence of Mrs. Lilian Hensman, and it is absolutely untrue. I had never heard of Eugenetta until she blazed into publicity a week or so ago; it is my sincerest wish that I may never hear of her again; and I do not believe that any of these antics of her parents before her birth will have the slightest effect in mitigating her heredity. (Will American papers please copy?) I am altogether an unbeliever in the inheritance of acquired characteristics.

I must apologize for this intrusion upon your space, but surely my work gives plentiful scope for Mrs. Lilian Hensman's invective without a complete inversion of the opinions I hold.

H. G. Wells

---

[1] During the ten or fifteen years after the rediscovery of the Mendelian experiments on heredity at the beginning of the twentieth century, there was an enormous increase into research on plant and animal breeding and also a great deal of non-scientific speculation. Wells, as a scientist, was interested in these matters and he wrote a dozen articles or reviews on the subject of eugenics, the attempt to improve the stock by programmes of selective breeding. Wells considered experimentation with humans unethical, and called for very careful scrutiny of all such experiments and their purported results. He became involved in a notorious case in October, 1913, when an English couple by the name of Bolce claimed that they had produced an eugenically pure baby girl, who was given the name Eugenetta. The child, six months old, was reported by the parents to be receiving strict care on eugenic principles 'seriously, in faith and reverence, and with scientific care'. They had begun to exhibit the child on a stage circuit and 'in order to preserve the child's sense of humour' had called on Jerome K. Jerome, Harry Lauder, George Robey, Wilkie Bard and H. G. Wells. Upon hearing of this, a woman named Lilian Hensman wrote a letter to the *Daily Mail* chastising Wells for his part in it. He wrote back in self-defence. Later a stock breeder in England, Hardine Cox, wrote congratulating Wells on his position. The Hensman letter appeared on 16 October 1916. Wells's letter was printed on 18 October under the title 'Nonsense about Eugenic Babies' and Cox's letter appeared on 21 October.

949. To Fenner Brockway

PLS

[London] October 23, 1913

Dear Mr. Brockway,[1]

I perceive you are exhorting me. You are doing so because someone has told you I have "rejected Socialism". As I have not rejected Socialism your exhortation is not so well aimed as it would have been if you had had a clearer apprehension of my position. In several books, "Anticipations", to begin with, "The Modern Utopia", and "New Worlds For Old", and various tracts, such as "This Misery of Boots", none of which you seem to have heard of, I have stated my faith as clearly as any Socialist has ever done, and I have never repudiatated those books.

I wrote them to be used for Socialist propaganda; it is not my fault that they are not so used; if the leaders the Socialists have chosen find other books and tracts serve their purposes better, I do not see that it follows that I am no longer a Socialist. It is true I do not belong to any Socialist organisation, but that is because I am not clever in organisation and they hamper rather than help me.

I left the Social Democratic Party because it was hopelessly doctrinaire, and I left the Fabian Society, as a study of the Fabian News will show, because I could not induce that body to alter its Basis and confess to the citizenship of women and the endowment of motherhood. From first to last in my relationship with the Fabian Society – I was bitterly antagonistic to the furtive methods of the Webbs. I loathe their game. I believe their cunning and contagious vanity has held back the cause of Socialism in England for a quarter of a century. But the Webbs are not Socialism any more than the vanity of the Pankhurst family is the emancipation of women.

There is a sentence in your letter which I will notice because I think it puts into print what has been going on underground for a long time about me. It is your suggestion that "something in my own life" has led to some abandonment of Socialism. There has been no abandonment of Socialism and there is nothing in my own life which I would not bring to the light with a good heart if I were not hampered, as any honest man is hampered, by the discretions that the tactics and concealments of the people connected with me demand. So hampered, I am the prey in Socialist circles of vague and apparently incurable scandals, distorted stories, and stories partially or wholly untrue. While you Socialists prefer scandal to Socialism I am helpless to do any more for your movement.

But I do wish that when next you go over these delicious exercises in imaginative testimony, of which I am the unworthy nucleus, you will try and get hold at least of the dates and order of my quarrel with Fabianism. You will then realise that the campaign of scandal against me *followed* a series of bitter attacks upon Webb Socialism. In no other world but the Anglo-Saxon world would it be possible to neutralise the work of an earnest writer by industriously declaring that he practiced what he professed (for that is the range of the more substantial of these stories that have come to my ears about myself) and by maintaining in the teeth of common sense and manifest fact that he was the "original" of every unorthodox character he had ever put into a novel.

Well, anyhow, it does not make me any the less a Socialist because I prefer the quiet of a country rectory to the atmosphere of feverish curiosities, wrong-headed accusations, and imbecile political ambitions that I breathed in Socialist circles. There are, I hope, a good many years ahead of me, and before I die I believe I shall altogether live down the remarkable legend that my attacks upon a dwarfish perversion of Socialism that I detest, upon the profound corruption of Liberalism, and upon the meanness of Parliamentary Socialism and Labour politics are dictated by some obscure private feud arising out of mysteries in my private life.

There, Mr. Brockway, is my still opener answer to your well-meant but ill-advised open letter.

Yours sincerely,
H. G. Wells.

---

[1] This is an open letter, to Fenner Brockway, in response to an Open Letter to Wells from Brockway in *The Labour Leader*. A second Brockway response appeared immediately after the letter from Wells. Brockway (1888–1988) was a militant pacifist and was imprisoned during the First World War for his views. He served in Parliament from 1929–31 and from 1950–64. He edited the *Labour Leader* for many years in the First World War period.

950. To D. Appleton and Co.[1]

Bromley, ALS

Easton Glebe
Dunmow 15 Nov. 1913
[*in pencil*]

Dear Sir,

By this time I think the fate of The Atom Frees the World is settled. It is a new 'romance of science' story but in a different bigger & maturer style.

Yours sincerely,
H.G. Wells

[1] This title given here was Wells's preferred title (he offered a half dozen to his publishers) for *The World Set Free*. Wells occasionally had problems with titles and this book had more than a dozen prospective versions. *Star-Begotten*, published in the mid-1930s, had close to fifty alternatives before it was actually decided upon.

951. To D. Appleton and Co.

Bromley, ACCS

52, St. James's Court
Buckingham Gate, S.W. 18 Nov. '13
[*in pencil in another hand*]

Dear Sir,

Sir Isaac Harman's wife[1] was arranged for (September next) long ago. And my price for that sort of story is getting very high. The Atom was your chance.

Yours very sincerely,
H.G. Wells

[1] Wells's novel *The Wife of Sir Isaac Harman* was published in September 1914 (London, Macmillan).

952. To Curtis Brown

Illinois, AN

[London] 25? November 1913[1]

Private and in The Utmost Confidence. I stick to my Colles in spite of these luscious suggestions. But I hope he will make sure of something The book must be out in September 1914.

[1] Note written in the bottom margin: on a letter of November 24, 1913 from Curtis Brown, an author's agent. Brown took Wells to task for selling his material at too low a price and opened by offering to discuss a proposal to sell books in cheaper bindings for a shilling. But he went on to say, 'Also, unless you sold the American serial rights of "The Wife of Sir Isaac Harman" for over $7,500, I wish you'd give our people first shot at the next serial for America. If you got over $7,500 for the American serial rights alone, then I'm "licked," for that was the best brick I could make with what straw I had. If you didn't — well, the chance is probably gone now, for I found something else that served the purpose; but I would be glad to have you know that this was the price my editor finally said he would pay for the story.'

953. To Mrs G. K. Chesterton

Illinois, ALS

Spade House
Sandgate [undated – *c.* 1913]

Dear Mrs. Chesterton,

God forbid that I should seem a pig [*small drawing of a pig*] and indeed I am not and of all the joys in life nothing would delight me more than a controversy with G.K.C., whom indeed I adore. [*a drawing of a small Wells adoring a large Chesterton*].

But – I have been recklessly promising all and everyone who asks me to lecture or debate; 'If I ever do so again it will be for you', and if once I break that vow I took last year.-

Also we are really quite in agreement.[1] It's a mere difference in fundamental theory which doesn't really matter a rap – except for after dinner purposes.

Yours ever,
H.G. Wells

[1] Wells and Chesterton remained friends throughout their lives, although they argued about theology continually. In fact Wells is said to have remarked that the only two writers of his lifetime with whom he had never quarrelled were Chesterton and Bennett. One might add Swinnerton to that today.

954. To M.S.

Hofstra, ALS

On board R.M.S. "Adriatic". [date unknown][1]

Dear M.S.,

This is awful copy but if you get it very carefully typed & read & scrutinized before the damned Compositor gets hold of it you will find it goes all right I think. It would be well to send me a proof if time permits.

Warm & Good Wishes

H.G.

[1] The shelf cards for this item at Hofstra list it as to 'Dear Sir', and give it a date of 8 April 1903. The copy I am using is addressed to 'Dear M.S'. and has no discernible date. In addition, the printed date on the stationery is ________ 191[?] which suggests sometime prior to the first World War. If we did not have these facts, I would suggest that the letter is to Margaret Sanger, and that it discusses the manuscript introduction to Sanger's book, *The Pivot of Civilisation* (London: Cape, 1922) for which Wells provided an introduction, but that is regrettably probably not true. However, if he were using out-of-date stationery, it could have been written to Sanger. All of Wells letters to Sanger, as far as I can tell, are located in the Sanger papers at Smith College, so this letter is a mystery.

955. To Lady Randolph

Hofstra, ACCS

52, St. James's Court
Buckingham Gate, S.W.1 [date unknown]

Dear Lady Randolph,

I shall most earnestly try to get to the happenings on the 13th. In these difficult times with Peach exploding right & left of us, we can never be sure, but to the best of my knowledge & belief The Virtuous Republican will be there.

& is
yours ever
H.G. Wells

956. To Frederick Macmillan et al[1]

McMaster, ALS

[London] [late 1913]

My dear [Sir],

I have been in some doubt about the title of the new book, which I proposed originally to call The Atom Liberates the World. This title I now want to restore & retain for all purposes except in the serialization in the Century Magazine. Under the importuning of the Century Co., I agreed to alter it to The Human Adventure & as I dislike very strongly to have work published under different titles in E. & A. I was so ill-advised as to propose to make the alteration in all cases. But, 'The Human Adventure' is battered & trite. It suggests the Great Adventure & all sorts of adventures & I return very gladly to the former title.[2]

Yours ever,
H.G. Wells

---

[1] This letter was sent to Sir Frederick Macmillan in London, Sir F. W. Lane at the Macmillan Co. in New York, the Editor of *The Strand* and Mr Harrison at 17 Tavistock St.

[2] It was too late however, so the book was published under the title *The World Set Free*. The *Century Magazine* used the alternate title for part of their serialisation. Wells had already used 'The Human Adventure' as the title of a shorter piece in 1912.

957 . To Gertrude Kingston[1]

Illinois, Photostat, Transcription

National Liberal Club

Nov. 19, 1913

Confidential
OK

Great Catherine
Little Mother
Darling,

I enjoyed you greatly — & please God, I will come again & see you some more. But why oh why! do you precede it with one hour of dull pretentious sham realistic sentimental flummery? Take that silly play off, my dear, take it off at once, & save Great Catherine from the fate of Androcles which was damned like a cat with a brick of a curtain raiser round its neck.

Your admiring subject
H.G. Wells

[1] Wells is referring to a double-bill of short plays put together for Kingston by Shaw. *Great Catherine*, with a curtain-raiser *Between Sunset and Dawn* by Hermon Ould, opened at the Vaudeville Theatre on 18 December 1913. The play was withdrawn after thirty performances. It concerned the life of Catherine the Great of Russia and Kington received strong positive reviews herself.

958. To Richard Curle[1]

Curle, APC

17, Church Row
Hampstead

[*c.* 1913]

Sir,

You are drunk with Conrad. You have got a style before you have got a story & God help you. "The Inquest" is the best of that book load.

[1] It is unfortunate that the correspondence of most people to Joseph Conrad was destroyed. In the case of Wells, only two letters survive, and neither of them of great consequence. Two letters which relate to their friendship are undated postcards from Wells to Richard Curle, an important Conrad collector and student. They appear in the 1995 catalogue devoted to Richard Curle items, issued by Stone Trough Books, Yorkshire.

959. To Richard Curle

APC

17, Church Row
Hampstead [*a short time later*]

Dear Sir,

If I thought the book "damned rot" or you a fool I shouldn't have sent the card I did. There are easier ways for an overworked journalist. But the stuff's stiff with literary pretensions.

960. To Robert Ross

Illinois, Transcription

Easton Rectory
Dunmow [November 1913]

Dear Bobby,

I think that this January I shall take a little journey to Berlin, Warsaw and Moscow. Will you tell me all the wise things I ought to do and all the thick clothes I ought to wear, and please note on the 26th we have Anthony Hope and his Mrs., and Mr and Mrs. Townsend and the Haynes to dinner and on the 28th. Oliviers and Clutton Brock and Mohammed Ali, a voluble Indian and afterwards other Indians will come and on either day your good little self would be a joy if it came in and talked after 9.30.[1]

Yours ever,
H.G.

[1] Anthony Hope, novelist, author of *The Prisoner of Zenda;* the Haynes are E. S. P. Haynes, a friend from the Fabian days and Wells's solicitor and his wife. Arthur Clutton Brock was an author and literary critic. The Oliviers were Wells's good friends Sydney Olivier, recently Governor General of the British West Indies, and his wife.

961. To Lillah McCarthy

Texas, APCS

[Spain] [*c.* 1913]

Dear Lillah,

Jane's been home a week – ill. Gip has the influenza. I've had it, Frankie had it. Sounds lucky you didn't come. The remarkable thing is that in spite of these capers, it's been a good holiday. Back in time to see you in the flesh.

H.G.

962. To Frank Harris

Texas, ALS

Little Easton Rectory
Dunmow [*c.* 1913]

My dear Harris,

I've read Unpathed Waters with great admiration but all the same I 'd love to have a copy from you.

Yours ever,
H.G.

963. To Catherine Wells

Illinois, APCS

[France] 1913
[*in another hand*][1]

P.S.
I haven't Ollendorf's address so will you please write them at once to say that I saw B.K. on my way through Paris & that he agrees to the cancellation of the contract & will offer no opposition to their publication of my book. Tell him I am writing to him & that I hope to have the understanding between us duly documented by his reply. Little B.K. was rather pitiful but quite incompetent.

H.G.

---

[1] This post card may have been sent while in France in early 1913, or on his way to Russia in January, 1914. My best guess is 1913. It is the second of two, and the first one is apparently missing. B.K. was a publisher in Paris.

964. To A. G. Gardiner[1]

Gardiner, ALS

Little Easton Rectory
Dunmow [*c.* end 1913]

Dear Gardiner,

You remember talks & walks & things that I'd supposed clean forgotten. I'm very pleased to be written about by you but I confess I don't recognize the portrait; a simple, sluggish rather melancholy & timid man is what I am & God knows it anyhow.

'Tis cracker; & it isn't me.

Come & see us soon,

H.G.

---

[1] Gardiner was the editor of the *Daily News*.

965. To A. G. Gardiner

Gardiner, ALS

Little Easton Rectory
Dunmow [end 1913-beginning 1914]

Dear Gardiner,

No, my affect[ion] is for the editor of the Daily News. I'd love to do an article to please you & I'd not haggle about price, but just now I'm really so overworked I can't promise to turn out anything more. I don't think there is any immediate future for the Feminist movement until the Pankhurst's are out of the way.

Yours,
H.G. Wells

966. To A. G. Gardiner

Gardiner, ALS

Little Easton Rectory
Dunmow [end 1913-early 1914]

Dear Gardiner,

Right O.

I'll do you another in about a week's time.[1]

But don't alter my title next time. I'll try to make it more declamatory.

Yours ever,
H.G. Wells

[1] He did write a piece comparing England and Russia, from which he had just returned from a short visit, *Daily News*, 21 February 1914, 'Russia and England: A Study in Contrasts'. Another version appeared in *Harper's Magazine* April, 1914, pp. 6–7, 'Russia and England'.

967. To Mr Sharp[1]

Yale, ALS

Spade House
Sandgate
[*c*. 1914?][2]

Dear Sharp,

See here.

Yours ever,
H.G. Wells

[1] This letter might be addressed to Clifford Sharp, but what occurred to bring the letter about is unknown.

[2] Date assigned at Yale, but this seems unlikely given the Spade House letterhead.

968. To Fred J. Wells

Illinois, ALS

Little Easton Rectory
Dunmow
Jan 16, 14

Dear little Freddy,

Do you keep your head out of water through all the rioting & troubles? I am very keenly interested in the last rows because I want to introduce a scene in my next book of the shooting etc in J'burg. Will you send me any good accounts of the trouble. I'd be so grateful if you would. [1]

I' m just off to Russia for a month. I shall go to St. Petersburg & Moscow & be back about the 14th of February. Jane stays at home.The boys have just been in for the College of Preceptors exam again. Gip, second class, & Frank, third class. Gip has got very high marks for French & German & both have passed but the exact positions will not be known until later.

Affectionate Brother
The Busswhacker

[1] This is the scene of the riot, and the death of Benham in *The Research Magnificent* (London: Macmillan, 1915).

969. To Catherine Wells

Illinois, ALS

Little Easton Rectory
Dunmow
[*but obviously on the train*
from Berlin to St Petersburg] [24 January 1914]

Dear Mummy,

Russia is <u>most</u> amoosing.[1] Exactly like the stage Russia, – guard in huge furry cap and top boots. No first class place free so I have to travel second with a first class ticket. Nobody shocked. In Berlin they could have fainted at the thought. High carriages & everybody running about with tea.

This compartment holds four, is papered with an ordinary wall paper, has a door & is bigger than my bedroom at Sandgate used to be. Everything is shabby. Outside are unfenced wilderness with deep snow, stunted firs & silver birch & (rarely) stunted hovels. Nobody speaks French or German, & the man who called up my passport called me Vowles. I shall post this in St. Petersburg, where I hope for letters.

Love,
Bins.

---

[1] Wells was travelling on his first trip to Russia. The letter was apparently written on the train and it is a rather uneven script, see his articles in *Daily News* and *Harper's Magazine*, foonote to letter 966.

970. To Elizabeth Healey

Illinois, APCS

Russia [January 1914]

The book awaits me in England. Good wishes to you for Italy. Let me known when you go & I'll ask Vernon Lee to give you tea & show you her garden.

H.G.

971. To Robert Ross

Illinois, APC, Transcription

[Russia] [4 February 1914]

I have been to Tretyakov [?] today to see your ikons. Bobby! you are a superstitious infidel.

972. To Rebecca West[1]

Yale, AL, Extracts

[Russia] [late January 1914]

[Dear Rebecca,]

[...] I go through this horde of sensual beasts [Berlin] like a Tennysonian knight. I exercise no self control, but I just can't think of any delyts like Panther's[2] delyts.

[...] St. Petersburg is more like Rebecca than any capital I have seen, alive and dark and untidy (but trying to be better) and mysteriously beautiful.

[...] Get Wales ready.[3] I think of that happy thing cuddled up in your soft flesh and your dear warm blood. I'm so glad we've made it.

[...] You are Mrs. West, I am Mr. West. Write and arrange that you are to stay at Llandudno until your baby is born. Mr. West is in the cinematograph business, and he has to write things. He wants a quiet room to work in and he has to have a separate bedroom. (Though he proposes to spend much time in your delicious bed). You also write. Make this clear and get everything comfortably arranged. That house has to be our home. We have to settle down and work there and love there and live there, and you have to see that it is all right. You have go to take care of me and have me fed and peaceful and comfortable. You are going to be my wife. We will have great mysteries in each other's arms, we shall walk together and eat together and talk together. You are the woman and you are to be the maker and ruler in all this life. (Our income is about £400 or £450 a year.) Panther, I love you as I have never loved anyone. I love you like a first love. I give myself to you. I am glad beyond any gladness that we are to have a child. I kiss your feet. I kiss your shoulders, and the soft side of your body. I want to come into the home you are to make for me. I shall hurry home for it. Get it ready. Make it our success. I will go down with you there after the 20th. Come up to London for some days and get clothes and things to be the young wife of a decent intelligent man.[4]

---

[1] These extracts are from four letters written by Wells to Rebecca West while he was on his trip to Russia. Rebecca had recently learned that she was pregnant. The letters concern such matters as where she is to have the child, and as an underlying motif, whether Wells will leave Catherine and come to live with Rebecca. The extracts are given for their general interest, but the letters of West and Wells are used with great effect in Gordon Ray, *H.G. Wells and Rebecca West*, (Yale: New Haven; London: Macmillan, 1974).

[2] Her *nom d'amour* in this relationship. His was Jaguar. Anthony West, their child, was given Panther as a middle name.

[3] The couple had thought of Rebecca's removal to Llandudno in Wales while she was awaiting the arrival of the child. In the event, Wales was not suitable, but an apartment was found on Victoria Avenue, now Street, in Hunstanton on the Norfolk coast.

[4] They maintained their home in a house called Brig-y-don for six months from late February. Wells usually spent the middle of the week there, commuting from Bishop's Stortford by rail. Anthony was born on 4 August, the weekend the First World War began. They soon abandoned the Hunstanton house and Rebecca moved with Anthony to Braughing in Hertfordshire, only a dozen miles from Little Easton. Wells cycled to visit her at first, although he soon purchased his first car, which was given the name 'Gladys'. Little Easton was in the process of a complete renovation, and for some months Wells spent most of his time in London and at Braughing. He was less and less at Dunmow, and this led to friction, and his letter 985 to Catherine. Eventually it became obvious that Wells was not going to divorce Catherine and marry Rebecca. He maintained the second family in Alderton, and other locations in and around London. Gordon Ray attributes much of the change of plans to the demands of the war on Wells, but, in addition to this, his ties to Catherine were too strong to change. She, for her part, acted as a sympathetic older aunt or something similar, much as she had in the case of Amber and her baby.

973. To Morris Colles[1]

Hofstra, ALS

Little Easton Rectory
Dunmow

[date stamped by
recipient 25 Feb 14]

My dear Colles,

What is the need for all this cabling? I understood the £800 was a firm offer. If it is so, then surely all the business of securing copyright, sending duplicate copies and so on, is not my affair.

I don't care to burden myself with such correspondence as that of the P. M. M. (i.e. Vincent) just now. Especially as Vincent asks the price.

Yours ever,
H.G. Wells

---

[1] Colles was still handling some of Wells's literary business in North America.

974. To Morris Colles

Hofstra, ALS

52, St James's Court
Buckingham Gate, S.W.

[date stamped by
recipient 2 Mar 14]

Dear Colles,

You really must get something out Lady Harman. You are up against time & that gives you an excuse for concessions. So sound the depth of the Graphic (as well as Ingram). I should have thought there is considerable scope for characterization in illustrating the story.[1]

Yours ever
H.G. Wells

---

[1] These two letters concern the illustration and publication of *The Wife of Sir Isaac Harman*.

975. To an unknown addressee

Boston, ALS

52, St. James's Court
Buckingham Gate, S.W. [a date stamp receipt 7 April 1914]

Dear Sirs,

Your dictionary stands upon a little special table in my study & I use it constantly. I find it in every way the best for me. I particularly like its being in one volume & its marginal indices which facilitate reference enormously. [*another word is crossed out and replaced by this one*] I have not yet caught it out in errors or deficiency. The copy you formerly sent me now does duty in my boys' school room. For them, though not for me, that older edition is preferable because of the relegation of some words to the foot of the page & because of the clumped collection of illustrations at the end. That is probably handy when the forgotten name of some animal or leather good or music instrument or such like things has to be recalled. I hope you will continue to sell that edition also, it is the best dictionary ever issued for schoolroom use.

Yours very sincerely
H.G. Wells [1]

---

[1] It was very unlike Wells to endorse a product, as he seems to here. One has to assume that he really liked the dictionary, which was almost certainly *Webster's New International Dictionary*, 2nd edition.

976. To Mr Reed

ACC, Extract

52 St. James's Court
S.W. 1 [date unknown]

[*In 1982, the firm of Francis Edwards Ltd., offered, in their catalogue no. 1041, a signed correspondence card from Wells to a Mr Reed. Wells said he was too busy*] [...] to work on a committee...But I shall be an interested associate... [*Wells also said that he would sign*] [...] your invitation to that personal committee...

977. To Rebecca West

Yale, AL[1]

[London] April 14, 1914

Dear little Mate,

Fing I like talking to
Fing I like to sit about with not talking
Person that it's pleasant to be against.
Dear, dusky, dear-eyed Panther
Warm kind Companion
The world bores me to death
(Or rather my world does)
It bores me and irritates me
When I am away from you.
I like the feel of you.
Like the noises you make
I love your faults
I love your voice
I love your truth
I love your affectations
I love you.

---

[1] This letter also appears in Gordon N. Ray, *H. G. Wells and Rebecca West* (Yale: Yale University Press; London: Macmillan, 1974).

978. To Maurice Baring[1]

Illinois, ALS

Little Easton Rectory
Dunmow [*c*. June 1914]

My dear Maurice,

Here you are off again! I wanted to see you very much, but I have been much engaged & out of town with various many productions. I thought you were still in England & ready to hand, then before I can get with you, you are back in Russia again. I am very near exhaustion[?] & shall rejoice in a book by Russians steadily[?]. Lycandopoulos is here this weekend, Williams & his wife next. [*illegible word*] by a strong opinion in a passionate argument with Zangwill & another Hebrew on the growth of the Pale. I've just had a delightful [?] from the Ridley's

Come back and talk presently,
Yours ever,
H.G.

---

[1] This letter, although only partially legible, does indicate how widely some of the questions of the first World War period were discussed. Unfortunately, these discussions were nearly always outside official circles.

979. To Philip Guedalla[1]

Illinois, Transcription

[Easton Glebe] [probably 1914]

Dear Mr. Guedalla,

You kept in the train I gather. But what happened to you or the train afterwards? Bliss does not know. Poor Bliss is very much out of things at present. He was severely injured while offering his services as a special constable the other day. He is in bed & he won't speak to me because he says I have tried to steal his reputation as an author.[2]

Yours very sincerely,
H.G. Wells

---

[1] Among the closest friends of the Wells family after they settled in Dunmow was the author and biographer, Philip Guedalla (1889–1944). The whereabouts of the Guedalla papers is unknown, but in 1977 M. A. L. Bloch, working on Guedalla, made several partial transcripts of correspondence to Guedalla from the Wellses. Although most of them are from Catherine, those from Wells himself deserve a place in this work. These are partial transcriptions done by another, however.

[2] This is a jokey letter, referring to Wells's pseudonym, Reginald Bliss, in his parody of Henry James, *Boon*, (London: Fisher Unwin, 1915). This may make the date of the letter 1915 rather than 1914.

980. To Philip Guedalla

Illinois, Transcription

[Easton Glebe] [undated, *c.* 1914]

My Dear Guedalla,

Would you care to run down here for a weekend? If so we'd be very pleased if you'd come. Next weekend there'll be two of Sir Sidney Olivier's daughters & a Mrs. de Boer so there will be much scope for a young man of grace & charm. We shall try to organize a game of hockey for Sunday afternoon.

Yours ever,
H.G. Wells

981. To Mr Gilmer[1]

Boston, ACCS

Little Easton Rectory
Dunmow

[date stamped by recipient,
13 July 14]

Dear Mr. Gilmer,

I shall post you tomorrow the first sixty-seventy thousand of the Research Magnificent fit to print. I did not know it would be possible to do this. If you can save the Empire longer[?], do. But Note. This amount of copy must last six months.

H. G. Wells

[1] Although this letter sounds as though it dealt with serial publication of *The Research Magnificent*, none is known. It may have been cancelled in the wake of the war, which soon overran many aspects of everyday life. The next letter deals with this same matter, as well as others concerning the novel.

982. To Mr Bigelow

Boston, ALS

Little Easton Rectory
Dunmow [early Summer 1914]

Dear Mr. Bigelow,

I'm sending you under a separate cover all that is finished of the Research Magnificent. One chapter, a large many coloured blossom, remains to be done. It exists now in a horribly incomplete M.S. that's not even typed. I confide this M.S. to you. It is peculiarly mine this book & I trust you to show it to nobody who is not in the deal with you & to take great care to return it to me safely. The typed M.S. is an early stage of the manufacture & much has been done upon it since.

You carry H.G. Wells & all his fortunes practically. The book publication will be Sept or Oct 1915 & I much prefer that the serial appearance did not end until the book was ripe to appear.[1]

Yours ever,
H. G. Wells

[1] *The Research Magnificent* was not serialized.

983. To Robert Ross

Illinois, Transcription

Reply H.West
c/o Mrs. Crum
Brig-y-don
Hunstanton[1] [July-August 1914]

Dear Bobby,

If life presses too hard and you want a complete change for a day or two, come down and see the Wests at Hunstanton, (c/o Mrs. Crum, Victoria Avenue). They have a spare bedroom and are kind gossiping creatures, Mrs.

West is Brown and now dreadfully big with young, she has a dear ugliness that grows upon the affection. Mr. West adores her. They go down on to the beach where they have a hut and he bathes and then one sits about in a dry bathing suit gossiping. That is all.

H.G.W.

---

[1] The Wells-West home while she awaited the birth of Anthony. Wells was able to visit her most weeks, by leaving Easton at noon on Sunday, taking the train to King's Lynn, and on to Hunstanton, returning to London on Monday night or Tuesday morning. Anthony was born on 4 August 1914. This is the time when charges of slander against Alfred Douglas, brought by Ross in the trial at which Wells testified, were about to come to court. Both Wells and Edmund Gosse testified to the high ethical standards of Ross. Wells's testimony was published in some detail in the *Daily Express*, 27 November 1914.

984. To the Editor, *The Times*[1]

PLS

Little Easton Rectory
Dunmow [6? August 1914]

Sir, – There is now no thought in the mind of any reasonable Englishman but to bring this war to a speedy and successful conclusion. Every man with any military training will be already in touch with his proper centre for utilization, and with that sort of man I, who am altogether untrained, have no concern. But I wish to point out that there is in the country a great mass of useful untrained material available and that it may be very readily called upon at the present time by the establishmnent of local committees. I suggest the formation at once of corps of local volunteers for use in local services, keeping order, transport, guerilla work in case of a raid, and forth. I have in mind particularly the boy of 15, the man of 47, the mass of the untrained, the Boy Scouts and ex-Boy Scouts who have not gone on to any military training. There is no reason why all the surplus material should not be enrolled now. With it would be a considerable quantity of bicycles, small cars, and other material. This last line need not be drilled; it should not be expected to use either bayonet or spade; but upon the east and south coast at any rate it should have bandoliers, rifles, and Brownings (for close fighting) available, and by way of uniform it should have a badge. Perhaps it would not be a very effective fighting force, but it would permit of the release of a considerable number of men now keeping order, controlling transport, or doing the like work. Nobody wants to be a non-combatant in a war of this sort.

Very sincerely yours,
H.G. Wells

---

[1] This letter, which appeared on 8 August, was preceded on the page by a similar call from Arthur Conan Doyle.

985. To Catherine Wells

Illinois, ALS

[London] [August 1914]

Dear little Mother,

Please send this, correct anything in error, make obscure words plain & send it to the Daily News. Or, if you think proper, have it typed.[1]

* I shall come to Bishop Stortford by the usual afternoon train on Thursday. *

About your letter. I have thought over the business of rebuilding the house. I think [:]

My abundant absences just at present is due to my need here, not to any hostility to my home.[2]

My irritability at home is due to the unsettled feeling due to plumbing. I do not think you understand what a torment it is to an impatient man to feel the phantom future home failing to realize itself. I hate things unfinished & out of place. I want things settled. I want a home to live in & have people in to. – people one can talk with. At present home is a noisy unsympathetic, uninteresting muddle. I want to get at it. I want to see it changing. I feel like Removals. When we get it all cleared up perhaps it will be possible to get human beings interested in things that matter about us again. Anyhow we must try. What'ever else is done, it is impossible for the Rectory to go on as it is going now, so that I cannot bring a visitor down or get to feel that my work is anything but an income-getting toil. It must be changed in that respect.

And also when I have been at the Rectory for a few days, I get into a state of irritability because of sexual exasperation. Later on I shall be able to get pacified in London. – for that business I still fail to see any perfect solution, I confess. But the present situation is particularly calculated to make a peaceful sojourn at L. Easton impossible. Later in every respect I think it will be better. The brute fact is that I am not & never have been – if there is such a thing – a passionate lover. I am affectionate & tremendously interested in things & bodily vigorous and I want a healthy woman handy to steady my nerves & leave my mind free for real things. I love you very warmly, you are in so many things, love of my love & flesh of my flesh & [illegible word] making. I must keep you. I like your company & I doubt about never spending that holiday together again & so on. But the other thing is a physical necessity. That's the real hitch.

Let us get on with this home & make it roomy. I think I can see a state of things ahead, when I shall live between London & Little Easton, work hard, get my hands in some organ of expression, group myself with some vigorous people.

Bins[3]

---

[1] The piece being discussed is his letter to the *Daily News*, 989 below.

[2] Perhaps true, but Rebecca West had just delivered his child, Anthony West, on 4 August, 1914, and these demands were strong. In any case Catherine would have had some anxiety no matter how strong their bond, as this child, unlike Anna Jane Blanco-White, did not have a convenient surrogate father.

[3] This is obviously an important letter, which allows an insight into this extraordinary marriage. The sexual anxieties are remarkably clear, although it is worth pointing out that Wells sent letters on such occasions at least as a preliminary to, if not a substitute for, face-to-face conversation This reading is slightly different from the one given in my biography of Wells, but I feel that this is the more accurate after eleven more years of looking at this and other letters. However the letter, which is one of the most important in the entire collection, in many ways is also one of the most difficult to decipher. The handwriting, as always when Wells was distraught, is tiny. The spacing is unusual, and, as a result, some of the word readings are therefore problematical. The letter is undated, and my reason for placing the letter in 1914 are the frank sexual references. Rebecca West had given birth to Anthony West early on 4 August 1914. The renovation of their home was also an irritant. Another matter which may have caused stress for Wells is that his letter coincided with his testimony, along with Edmund Gosse and Vyvyan Holland, to the upstanding character of Robbie Ross. Ross had brought a writ of slander against Lord Alfred Douglas, the son of the Marquess of Queensbury, and the other person who was prominent in the trial of Oscar Wilde. The Ross case was dropped with a writ of *nolle prosequi* by the Crown. However, most observers thought that Ross had been vindicated by the proceedings. Wells was prepared to help Ross at any time, but taking the witness box may have been a somewhat daunting matter. Wells never referred to this event in his correspondence to my knowledge; see below for correspondence dealing with a testimonial dinner for Ross.

986. To the Editor, *The Times*

PLS

Dunmow [16 August 1914]

Sir. – You permitted me to make a suggestion some days ago that the services of untrained men and men rather too young or too old for sustained active service in the field could be made very useful at this time in the form of local service corps. This very obvious idea has, of course, occurred to very many other people, and in a great number of localities committees have already sprung up to carry it out. The uses of such local bodies, so soon as they are embodied and recognized, may include the organization of a messenger service in conjunction with the local Boy Scouts, the provision of sentries, work in connexion with emergency measures for the protection of the people's food supply, transport, hospital and suchlike services, and, in the now highly improbable event of a raid, the waylaying and capture of scouts, sniping of advancing enemies, and hedge and ditch guerilla work generally.

For all these purposes these local forces must be under military discipline and they must have a uniform that will secure them recognition and authority and protect them from butchery in the event of capture. I suggest that this uniform should be at once decided upon and that it should be provided by the men themselves and be of the simplest kind. It might be a cloth or tweed suit of any description, preferably brownish or grey, on which has been sewn a collar and cuffs of red cloth or flannel and a red stripe on the trousers or breeches. The hat might be the common soft felt hat, with a red band attached to it. To this might be added a belt and cross bands of unbleached linen or calico. Such an improvised uniform could be made in an hour in any village in England, and directly it was officially adopted it could be protected from imitation by the ordinary laws forbidding abuses of the King's uniform. It would leave the whole countryside free to convert itself immediately into a bed of stinging nettles against raiders so soon as rifles and ammunition came to hand. In many places they are at hand.[1]

Yours sincerely,
H G Wells

[1] Wells anticipates in this letter the mobilisation of civilian defence which played such an important part in the Second World War. His letters caused a heated debate over whether ordinary folk should be allowed to possess weapons, even in the emergency. This letter appeared in *The Times* on 17 August, 1914 under the heading, 'A Uniform for Irregulars'.

987. To Robert Ross

Illinois, Transcription

52, St. James's Court
S.W [postmarked Aug. 18th, 1914]

Dear Bobby,

I am remaking my will. If I die before, Jane manages everything, if she dies first I shall make another will in the ordinary course of things, but I am providing also for the chance that we may get killed (practically) together. That is a very remote chance indeed but I want to cover it. In that case will you be my literary executor?

Yours ever,
H.G.

988. To the Editor, *The Times*[1]

PLS

52, St. James's Court
Buckingham Gate, S.W. [19 August 1914]

Sir, – I would like to thank Sir Foster Cunliffe for his consideration of my two brief and quite unexpert suggestions. He does a little exaggerate my intention when he supposes that I intended my calico and flannel uniforms and my enrolment of boys under serviceable age and men past the prime as a method of "developing our reserves of men". That is not my business. I was thinking of the residuum of men. When all the "efficients" have been swept up into the organized fighting machine (about which I am as competent to write as I am to pilot an aeroplane) there are those who remain over and who may still be useful in less exhausting ways. Many of them would be non-combatant ways. What chance there was of a raid some weeks ago, it has now, I suppose, vanished; but I suggested nevertheless the possibility of arms and of participation in fighting – "guerilla" was an ill-chosen word for it – because I suppose I am primarily a psychologist, and I believe that it would make a profound difference in the spirit in which the voluntary service was done and in the feeling of the countryside, if at the back of it all was the idea of service to the death. And I suppose even the presence of scattered men in the hedges and ditches all over the countryside, with rifles and as much uniform as the law requires, even if they were men who could neither march very much nor sustain any of the heavier fatigues of warfare, would be an extraordinary check upon hostile scouting and preferable to the spectacle of the same men standing at their doors and gazing helplessly at the passing enemy. But the whole thing, as I conceive it, is something marginal.

I would not in a moment interfere with the working and development of the official war machine. I would, therefore, suggest that too exclusive an insistence upon the "machine" may lead to the refusal and discouragement of much exterior enthusiasm without any corresponding advantage to the machine.

Yours, etc.,
H.G. Wells

[1] This letter appeared on 20 August under the heading, 'The Untrained and Unfit'.

989. To the Editor, *Daily News*[1]

PLS

St. James's Court, S.W. August 20 [1914]

Sir, – Lord Eversley's letter seems to me to express with the greatest clearness and ability just that attitude of mind which is most likely to render Liberalism feeble and futile in the present crisis. He objects apparently to such low people as Mr. Shaw and myself, "a popular writer of plays", and a nobody, from expressing any views at all about the outcome of this war. In the next column to his communication S. L. H. with that tremendous elaboration which has made him the terror of the parish magazine throughout the country, sneers at some unfortunate gentlemen at Congleton who has speculated about coming things. In a recent leading article, too, you have spoken of any remapping of Eastern Europe as "premature". The idea of the "Daily News" seems, indeed, to be that we Liberals should leave these questions of settlement to our "betters", that we should drift along with blank minds, closed eyes and open mouths, ready for any Peace that may be presently thrust upon us. It is no longer to be "Peace at any Price"; it is to be "Any Peace at any Price". I found myself, with amazement, for the first time in my life, invoking the name of Gladstone. He at any rate had no delusions about the dangerous artificiality of the Austrian empire, no panic fear of Russia, and no foolish idea that the East of Europe was no business of ours.

Surely it is still in Liberalism to resolve that the settlement of this vast upheaval is to be a people's settlement, understood by the people and willed by the people. Lord Eversley in his account of my proffered views does me no sort of justice. He sees me as a presumptuous person rushing in with ideas where great statesmen fear to tread. He omits to note that I said and repeated that I was an ignorant person, that I felt the intricacy of the difficulties of the settlement, but the only possible alternative to such a full discussion of the outlook now as these redrawings of the map of Europe will promote secret diplomatic settlement that will leave the world worse off than it was before the war. It is a choice between backstairs arrangements or the creation of a common Liberal purpose by such common, blatant people as Shaw and myself (and Mr. Lowe of Congleton). Incidentally, I may note that I did not say Alsace is "to be given to Switzerland".

I would implore Liberals not to let this sort of blank-mindedness, this pseudo-sage, intellectual laziness, this easy dread of "prematurity" carry them into a merely passive and obstructive position. Things are on the move now, as for a century they may never be again. A sane settlement of Europe may wipe out a hundred festering wrongs, reduce the reasons for armaments to a minimum, open a new and cleaner page in the history of mankind. Surely there is more life in Liberalism than that it should play the part of a drag, and no other part, in these tremendous happenings.[2]

H. G. Wells

---

[1] This letter appeared in the *Daily News and Leader* on 21 August 1914 under the heading, 'The Object of the War'.

[2] From the very first weekend of the war, Wells saw it as an opportunity to rid the world of dictatorships, redraw the boundaries of Europe and hasten the coming of world peace. He feared the diplomacy of the foreign offices, and in his comments on secret diplomacy predicted what actually happened. He also saw the war as a possible agent to electoral change, a move to Republicanism and to Popular Representation. He devoted an immense amount of effort to these goals throughout the war, and this letter is part of that campaign. He produced a short book from eleven of his earliest articles entitled *The War That Will End War* (London: Frank and Cecil Palmer, 1914).

990. To the Editor, *The Times*[1]

PLS

[London] [23 August 1914]

Sir, – May I protest in the strongest terms against Mr. Foster Cunliffe's proposal that because the Germans might burn villages and shoot promiscuously if they were afflicted by untrained irregulars, therefore we untrained men should not take whatever steps were possible to us to delay and inconvenience a raiding invader? This seems to me to set a premium upon brutality on the part of the invader and cowardice on the part of the invaded.

Very sincerely yours,
H.G. Wells

---

[1] This piece is a follow-up to others; it appeared on 24 August 1914. One problem which emerged was the class issue of whether or not guns should be available to these irregular troops if they were formed.

991. To Edward Carpenter[1]

PL

[London] [29 August 1914]

In offering you our congratulations on the completion of your seventieth year, we would express to you (and, we speak, we are sure, the thoughts of a very large number of other readers and friends) the feelings of admiration and gratitude with which we regard your life work.

Your books, with no aid but that of their own originality and power, have found their way among all classes of people in our own and many other lands, and they have everywhere brought with them a message of fellowship and gladness. At a time when society is confused and overburdened by its own restlessness and artificiality, your writings have called us back to the vital facts of Nature, to the need of simplicity and calmness; of just dealing between man and man; of free and equal citizenship; of love, beauty, and humanity in our daily life.

We thank you for the genius with which you have interpreted great spiritual truths; for the deep conviction underlying all your teaching that wisdom must be sought not only in the study of external nature, but also in a fuller knowledge of the human heart; for your insistence upon the truth that there can be no real wealth or happiness for the individual apart from his fellows; for your fidelity and countless services to the cause of the poor and friendless; for the light you have thrown on so many social problems; and for the equal courage, delicacy, and directness with which you have discussed various questions of sex, the study of which is essential to a right understanding of human nature.

We have spoken of your many readers and friends, but in your case, to a degree seldom attained by writers, your readers are your friends, for your works have that rare quality which reveals the "man behind the book", and that personal attraction which results only from the the widest sympathy and fellow-feeling. For this , most of all, we thank you – the spirit of comradeship which has endeared your name to all who know you, and to many who to yourself are unknown.

---

[1] Carpenter was an important Socialist thinker and writer, loved by his colleagues on the left. He was seventy years old on 29 August 1914, and more than fifty eminent people including Wells subscribed to an address to him to which he responded. It all appeared in *The Labour Leader*, 3 September 1914, under the heading 'Is There No Progress?', p. 2. One would be hard pressed to find a significant name of the time who did not sign, including Wells.

992. To the Editor, *Labour Leader*[1]

PLS

[London] [30? August 1914]

Sir, – Our country is fighting for existence. No one who remains sane can suppose we have any other alternative before us now except victory, or destruction. I would like to know, therefore, what good Mr. Keir Hardie and Mr.Ramsay MacDonald imagine they are doing at the present time by trying to misrepresent the negotiations that preceded the war and suggesting that in some way we are cheats in defending the neutrality of Belgium. What do they want to happen now? Are we to sue for peace? Will Mr. Keir Hardie and Mr. MacDonald answer that question? And, if not, what are we to do? The small section of the working class that still reads the LABOUR LEADER is, no doubt, waiting for guidance. What lead are Messrs. Hardie and MacDonald going to give it?

And have these ex-leaders of Labour nothing in all the world to offer in this tremendous crisis and opportunity except a whining criticism of the acts of Sir Edward Grey?

The great argument against our fighting to destroy, if we can, the huge war machine of Germany that has hung over our national life like a nightmare appears to be that Russia will profit. Russia is represented as a Bogey of the most terrible sort. I gave the fullest and clearest reasons against this Russian superstition in the issue of the Nation immediately preceding your last issue of the LABOUR LEADER. To that issue "Vernon Lee" has contributed an article entitled, "A Reply to H.G. Wells", in which she raises the same great Russian scarecrow and entirely ignores my Nation article. I cannot go on writing one article over and over again, and so I must refer your readers to that Nation article for my countervailing view. It is at your disposal to print or quote at any length you like. It knocks the bottom out of all this nonsense which represents Russia as a kind of worst devil and the Kaiser-Krupp Prussian system as the clean, white fabric of a delightful yet disciplined civilisation, which not only aspires but deserves to dominate the world. Why, even the Poles hate Germany more than they do Russia.

If "Vernon Lee" wrote her "reply" to me before she saw the Nation article, I shall be obliged to her if she will consider the latter as my answer to her, and I shall be interested to see how she proposes to meet the case I make therein.

Very sincerely yours

H.G. Wells

---

[1] An issue on which the left was divided when the First World War began, concerned Russian participation in the war. Some on the left felt that Russia was a totalitarian nation, and should be avoided. Others, like Wells, thought the war might prove to be a liberating force in Russia. Wells's friend, 'Vernon Lee', was on the other side from Wells and her stance was also attached to her pacifist beliefs. This letter responds to hers and others under the heading, 'The Russian Menace; H.G. Wells says it is a Bogey: Is it?' The editor of the *Labour Leader* responded, just below Wells's letter, with an article of his own on similar subjects. All of this appeared in the issue of 3 September 1914, p.5.

993. To the Editor, *Labour Leader*[1]

PLS

[London?] [*c.* 15 September 1914]

Sir, – When I read Miss Paget's previous contribution to your pages it did not occur to me that she was "laughing" at me. I thought she was just over-excited when she called my articles "manifestoes" and accused me, quite out of her imagination, of using the "Sword of God Tag" and so forth. I accept with regret the correction that she is in a state of merriment. This unseemly mirth is blinding her to even the precise words of the article she is "answering". It may be great fun to say that I asked Americans to "refuse to furnish Germany with food on their neutral ships" when as a matter of fact I suggested to Americans that it was undesirable to countenance the purchase of German liners by America in time of war and their use in victualling the German Army, but such humour is not controversy. Nor is it controversy to accuse me of ignoring Mr. Snowden's pamphlet upon the "Kruppism" of this country when I have quoted it and used it in my articles, when I have made it as plain as daylight that that evil is constantly in my mind.

But my case is that the intensive cultivation of militarism by Germany, the military machine which we are all (except for Miss Paget, the I.L.P., and Mr. Jim Larkin's people) doing our best to smash, has been the strength of the trade throughout the world. Miss Paget in her careless queston-begging way writes that "Krupp armament and scare mongering" business has had its "*exact* counterparts throughout the world", when the vitally important fact is that they have not been exact counterparts, but unavoidable and inferior reflections. And abuse of French "rottenness" – I do not see it – in comparison with the moral exaltation of Gemany comes ungraciously in the columns of a paper that I had supposed democratic and Republican. The French, like the Americans, wash their financial dirty linen in public. It is characteristic of republics, and, on the whole, it is better than never washing your dirty linen at all. No doubt Miss Paget thinks the Kaiser is a simple, poor man.

Now in the comparison of Russia and Germany, which is the gist of this argument, I am forced to declare my conviction that Miss Paget knows nothing whatever of Russia. She will not learn. It is not my own poor little observations in Germany and Russia that I would set against her opinions, opinions evidently made in Germany, but the views of our friend Maurice Baring, of Doctor Harold Williams, of Mr. Hagberg Wright, of Mr. Nabokoff, the editor of the occasionally suppressed Reich, and one of the most brilliant Liberal statesmen in Russia, of Sienkowicz, the Polish patriot novelist, of Prince Kropotkin's daughter, of Mr. Zangwill, who has been imploring people to let Russian Jews know their own business in this affair. All these people, in spite of pogroms, strifes, and exile, believe in the Liberal possibilities of Russia. None of them believe in the Liberal possibilities of an unchastened Prussian militarism. All of them beg and pray Miss Paget and Mr. Keir Hardie and the German Jews of America to abandon them to Russia. Against these opinions of Russian and Pole and Jew that I have quoted I cannot, for all my respect for Miss Paget, bring myself to attach very much counter-vailing weight to what the editor of the Berliner Tageblatt told Miss Paget eighteen months ago about the beautiful democratic developments that were going to happen presently to the Kingdom of Prussia. As between the Liberalism of the private talk of the editor of the Berliner Tageblatt and Prussian militarism, it is evident that Prussian militarism got its blow in first.

I do not know whether I need say very much about the "strong and uncompromising reply" of Mr. Keir Hardie. I am glad to see that he has at last, a month late, picked up the idea that there is more in this business than a chance to get back at that irritating person Sir Edward Grey. In a compact passage he summarises most of what I have been saying in the Liberal press during the past few weeks, and tells me that is what the I.L.P. is going to "do". I doubt if the I.L.P. will. Other people will try to do it, while the I.L.P. yaps at their heels. He calls me a war-monger. Why does he not think of the meaning of words? Evidently he has read nothing that I have written about the crisis at all except my few allusions to himself. If he has, then he is either drunk or mad to say that I am "shouting with the multitude". I am working with all my being for Socialism and the peace of the world. My complaint against him is that he is doing nothing for Socialism or disarmament in this crisis because of an ignorant terror of Russia. As for his "whining" – confound it! he whines. He writes – his English is bad, but one can see what he means – "But after all Mr. Wells has a reputation not only in newspaper articles, but in his books, of taking a mean advantage of those whom he does not like." I owe that reputation to the spiteful lying chatter of the shabbiest scum of Socialism. But what a bit of dirt to aim at me! The "mean advantage" of which he complains in this case is that I described his activities and the activities of Mr. Ramsay MacDonald in perfectly plain language.

Yours very sincerely,

H.G. Wells

---

[1] When the First World War broke out the issue of support for the war also divided old friends, sometimes with bitter-sweet results. Such was the case again with 'Vernon Lee' (Violet Paget) and Wells. She felt that only a pacifist view was legitimate while Wells thought the war might allow world government to develop. They exchanged letters in the press, and eventually drew apart. It was not until the mid-1920s that the two old friends were able to overcome their wartime anger. This piece is a letter from Wells to Paget, which happened to be published on 17 September 1914 in answer to her earlier writing. On the same page the editor chose to publish another 'Vernon Lee' article, 'Facing Realities', which did not mention Wells but did offer her views on his ideas. In this period articles, letters and comments flowed freely and spilled from one paper to another. This piece was also read in draft form at Illinois where Wells gave it the title, *VERNON LEE'S PERSUASIONS (and a Note on Mr. Keir Hardie)*. At the top of the draft is a statement, 'Recopy middle sheet. Transfer corrections on the others, duplicate and post to the *Labour Leader*. The letter sent must have my signature.'

994. To the Editor, *Labour Leader*[1]

PL

[London] [*c.* 20 September 1914]

Mr. Wells draws attention to the fact that Mr. Israel Zangwill has appealed to the Jews of America and other neutral countries not to let the shadow of Russia alienate their sympathy from the causes of the Allies. Of that we are aware, but Mr. Zangwill's support of Britain only makes the more notable his contempt which he has expressed for Mr. Wells's views on Russia.[2]

[1] Quoted in a news story, not in the letters column. This is one part of a controversy about remarks made by several writers and editors of *Labour Leader* and *The Times*. It is in response, along with a separate letter from C. Hagbert Wright, to a leading article about Wells's and Wright's views, published on 17 September 1914. Wells's letter appeared on 24 September. Hagbert Wright, who is so closely involved with Wells in these matters, was librarian of the London Library.

[2] The issue of the possibility of Palestine becoming a Jewish homeland always underlies these discussions and others.

995. To Mr Clancey[1]

Illinois, ALS

London Library
St. James's Square
London S.W. [mid September 1914]

Dear Clancey.

Make six copies of this.[2] Send one (accompanied by the last sheet of this [with] the signatures) to the Labour Leader & keep the others against any further need.

Yours ever,
H. G. Wells

[1] Probably an employee of the London Library.

[2] This letter is accompanied by a six page draft of a letter in Wells's hand, and a seventh page in another hand with the signatures of C. Hagberg Wright and Wells. It was published in its entirety in the *Daily Chronicle* of 22 September 1914, under the lead 'Our Ally Russia: Some

Misconceptions and a Protest', signed by the two men. It also appeared in an edited version in *The Times* 22 September 1914. This latter printing was accompanied by a short letter from Wells, saying that the enclosed letter was sent to the *Labour Leader* for publication in their leader pages. Wells went on to say that it had not been printed therein. This fact had not however prevented the editor of the *Labour Leader* from quoting one sentence from it and then devoting a column 'to the vehement abuse of its two writers. Will local papers in Labour constituencies please note these I. L. P. methods?

Very sincerely yours,
H. G. Wells'

The Times gave the story the original proposed heading, 'The Penny Dreadful Idea of Russia: A Protest'. The *Chronicle* story provided a copy of the letter to *The Times* dated 21 September 1914 for their readers. The next letter, 996, is produced from the holograph. The copies in the newspapers do not differ very much from this heavily worked draft. Copies of the accompanying letter to *The Times* were also sent to the *Daily Citizen*, *Daily Express*, *Daily News*, *Daily Herald*, *Justice* and *Daily Telegraph* with the words, 'Will local papers in Labour constituencies please note these I.L.P. methods'.

996. To the Editor, *Labour Leader*

Illinois, ALS

[The London Library] [mid September 1914]

The Penny Dreadful Idea of Russia : A Protest

Sir.

We notice with extreme regret that two of the more prominent members of the Socialist wing of the Labour Party, Mr. Kier Hardie & Mr. Ramsay MacDonald, are devoting their very great energies & abilities to a campaign against the present war on account of some fancied diabolical quality of our ally Russia. This is a time of supreme importance to labour. Extraordinary dislocations are occurring in our economic system, hundreds of thousands of men are being taken into employment by the state & the lives & welfare of millions are being profoundly altered for ever. Naturally we look to these gentlemen to join with the other representatives of labour & help such as ourselves who cannot pretend to a profound knowledge of labour conditions, to do our utmost to secure better & fairer conditions of life in the new state of affairs that is being brought about by this revolutionary war. Unhappily they do nothing of the sort, & it has even been left to the President of the Anti-Socialist League to support a minimum wage for our soldiers of a pound a week. Meanwhile Mr. Keir Hardie & Mr. Ramsay MacDonald are displaying the most minute & wonderful & distorted knowledge of diplomatic details, that soar far above the simple practical affairs of White Papers, ambassadors and treaties, in the earnest attempt to show that the burning of a few towns & villages in Belgium & the crushing of France, has nothing to do with the business of this more fortunate country. Both Mr. Keir Hardie & Mr. MacDonald have travelled widely, but neither of them appear to have ever visited Russia or to have any ideas about Russia that have not been devised from popular fiction & melodrama. On this basis they are in a position to assure us that all Russia's declared intentions towards Finn & Pole & Jew are lies & that distrust of Russia is of far more importance to working men than their own concerns. This is an opinion not shared by the scores of thousands of Jews such as that hero Osnas whose capture of a standard has met with such prompt and general recognition in Petrograd, nor is it shared by that great patriotic novelist, Sienkowwicz[1] who stands as the very symbol of Polish nationality. We who can claim to some slight knowledge of Russian conditions, declare our convictions that Russia has long wavered between the Prussian connexion & the traditions of the Holy Alliance on the one hand & her present association with liberal forces on the other. We do not deny her efforts in the past to realize the ideals of Russian intolerance. But this war has made her definitely liberal by linking her almost indissolubly with the western liberal powers. Unless we repulse her. That liberalism is our hope, it is a reasonable hope; to deny it now, to condemn the whole future of a people because of some violence in the past is the insanity of distrust. Already we learn that the reassembling of the Duma which would have occurred in the ordinary course of things next year is to take place earlier & the free promises of the Tzar to Jews & Poles & Finns are to be embodied in legislation. Men of every party & every tradition in Russia, except the extreme reactionaries, hail this war with passionate enthusiasm. But what are such facts as these to the preformed intuitions of Mr. Keir Hardie & Mr. Ramsay MacDonald? On the other hand they deplore our conflict with the cultivated & amiable Prussian Empire. Its huge fleet, it's inexhaustible store of submarine mines, its carefully concealed preparation of hundreds of bomb-dropping aeroplanes, & Zeppelins, its great system of strategic railways upon the Belgian & Polish frontiers, its secret manufacture of vast siege guns, its incessant increases of stupendous army, its leap, prepared & armed, into this war, they regard as evidence of an excessive anxiety to keep the peace. Had we but let Germany reduce Russia to the present position of Austria in a Three-Emperor League, "finish" Belgium & France the peace of the world, the security of Britain, the welfare of our millions of workers would have been assured for

ever. We might then have given up building more war ships confident in the Kaiser's secured good will, but for the wickedness of Sir Edward Grey.
We protest against this insult to the intelligence & self respect of our fellow Britons which Mr. Hardie & Mr. MacDonald are offering, & we protest still more strongly against the stupid, ignorant, mischievous misrepresentation of a great, kindly, friendly people upon which their case is based.

C. Hagberg Wright
H. G. Wells

---

[1] Henryk Sienkiewicz (1846–1916) was a Polish novelist of considerable repute. He wrote a major trilogy of Polish literature beginning with *Fire and Sword* (1884), but is probably best known for his *Quo Vadis* of 1896. He received the Nobel Prize for Literature in 1905. Nothing more is known of the exploit of the captured standard which must have occurred in the earliest days of the conflict.

997. To the Editor, *Daily Citizen*

Illinois, ALS

Little Easton Rectory
Dunmow [mid September 1914][1]

Sir

The enclosed letter was sent to the "Labour Leader" for publication in this weeks' issue. It has not been published therein. That fact has not however restrained the editor of the Labour Leader from quoting one sentence & then devoting a column to the venomous abuse of its two authors.

Very sincerely yours
H. G. Wells

---

[1] Although the original specified that copies should go to the *Daily Express*, *Daily News*, *Daily Chronicle*, *Daily Herald*, *Justice*, *The Times* and *Daily Telegraph*, I have only searched for it in *The Times* and *Daily Chronicle*.

998. To the Editor, *Labour Leader*[1]

Illinois, ADLS

Little Easton Rectory
Dunmow [after 25 September 1914]

Sir.

As you see fit to "answer" a letter from Mr. Wright & myself which (except for one misleading extract) you do not care to print, & as you "answer" it chiefly by abuse & personal insult, I do not see that I need to go on discussing you, with your readers in your columns. They can judge between us. But as you deny my statement that Mr. Zangwill asks you to leave the Russian Jews to judge for themselves about the war & as you attempt to support it by quoting Mr. Zangwill's comparative disapproval of a number of non-Jewish writers about Russia, perhaps you will hearten yourself to put in some obscure corner the pronouncement of Mr. Zangwill enclosed, which you have hitherto found it convenient to overlook.

Yours very sincerely,
H. G. Wells

[1] This letter was not published. It appears in draft holograph in the Wells papers at Illinois.

999. To the Editor, *The Nation*[1]

PLS

52, St. James's Court
Buckingham Gate, S.W. October 1, 1914

Sir, – No! I will write no more in THE NATION for a time. I admit the completest failure. I leave the field and return to my "fiction". What I have had to say in THE NATION about the war is "balderdash" if Mr. Ramsay MacDonald and the rest of the advanced opinion choose to have it so. What people will not understand can never be realized, and it is as clear as daylight, from the responses I got to the few things I have said, that either I have talked wisdom to deaf ears or nonsense and, anyhow, quite impracticable things. Mr. John

Bailey crowns my conviction. I haven't the heart to argue with him; he is so entirely like everybody. He has, it seems, never heard before of that idea of public service for anyone which was first broached by another insane dreamer, an American lunatic named William James, in his "Moral Equivalent for War".

It is, says Mr. John Bailey, a "fantastically absurd proposal", and, confound it! he's right; it is in a world of Mr. John Baileys. And what does it matter if I did not suggest any sort of State control for newspapers? Mr. Bailey jumps to the conclusion that I did, and I suppose it is the normal process of the human mind to suppose that when one suggests that newspapers are bribeable, and that a *financial control* by the State, similar to the control exercised over banks and insurance companies, would prevent the systematic bribery of the press by a hostile power – that means a State editor. But I would as soon play croquet with Alice in Wonderland as go on with these ridiculous attempts to reason with Liberals about Liberalism. The honours are entirely with Mr. John Bailey. *His* world -

Yours, etc., H.G. Wells

---

[1] When the First World War began, it posed an immense problem for Socialists. Should they elect not to participate in the war, or should their natonalism determine their approach to the conflict. Ultimately many Socialists saw the war as among the latter struggles of capitalism, but national pride dominated in virtually all cases in England, France and Germany. Wells supported the war from the beginning, and his views were bolstered by his phrase, 'The war to end war'. Not everyone was in full support, however, and this letter to *The Nation* (UK), published 3 October 1918, under the heading 'Mr. Wells's Pacifist State', provides information on the debate in the left in the late Summer and early Autumn of 1914. Wells's ideas that the war could lead to world government of some sort did not convince many people on the Liberal left. Many Socialists and pacifists thought that although such an organization might result from the war, they did not wish to participate in the war itself.

1000. To the Editor, *The Nation*[1]

PLS

London October 2, 1914

Sir: I will not trouble your readers with a lengthy reply to the remarkable "message" apropos of myself which Miss Paget ("Vernon Lee") has written you. For the most part she answers herself, or what she has to say has been quite adequately counteracted by other articles and letters in your columns. But most of your readers will not have read the article by me in relation to what she writes, and as manifestly she has misread it in her excitement, you will, I know, permit me to correct her upon certain specific points.

She declares I want America to "starve" the German people. There was no such suggestion in my article. So far as the internal Austrian and German food supply is concerned, Germany can, with a little economy go on feeding herself without importation for an indefinite time. But feeding her armies at the front is a different matter. As my article poined out – a thing "Vernon Lee" has overlooked or ignored – the Rhine is a natural supply canal for these armies and the peculiar position of Holland renders it much more convenient to supply them from America via Rotterdam, if America does see fit to play in such a game, than from the threatened granaries of Pommerania and Silesia. In the long struggle which is now reaching its climax, the question of supply is a dominating factor, and so I have no quarrel with the editor who threw up my phrase of Victualing Our Enemies into large type. That is exactly what I meant, our enemies, the German army, and exactly what "Vernon Lee" failed to grasp in her haste.

As for the "thousands of British men and women" who share my former friend's "shame and disgust" at my proposals, I ask you not to believe in their existence. Probably not a score of them have misread me, as "Vernon Lee" has done. I am instead puzzled and distressed by these onslaughts of hers upon me, by her scarcely sane abuse of Republican France, by her quotation, with approval, of mere abuse of Professor Harmack's description of Russia as a "Byzantine and Mongol semi-barbarism". She even accuses me of flattering America, in spite of the fact that I sent her my little book upon "The Future in America" when it appeared. She will end, I know, by calling me "pro-British", the last sin of which a true-born Englishman is capable. Whatever other losses or gains this war brings about, it has, I fear, lost "Vernon Lee". But we shall do our best to reconquer her for the sake of many precious things she gave us before she was won from us by Berlin.

H.G. Wells

---

[1] The last in the series of letters exchanged in the press by Wells and "Vernon Lee" and others over his desire to bring Germany to book once the war began. This appeared in *The Nation* (New York), 22 October 1914, p. 495, under the heading, 'Mr Wells and "Vernon Lee"'.

1001. To the Editor, *The Times*[1]

PLS

[London] [*c.* 25 October 1914]

Sir, – At the outset of the war I made a suggestion in your columns for the enrolment of all that surplus of manhood and patriotic feeling which remains after every man available for systematic military operations has been taken. My idea was that comparatively undrilled boys and older men, not sound enough for campaigning, armed with rifles, able to shoot straight with them, and using local means of transport, bicycles, cars, and so forth would be a quite effective check upon an enemy's scouting, a danger to his supplies, and even a force capable of holding up a raiding advance, more particularly if that advance was poor in horses and artillery, as an overseas raid was likely to be. I suggested too, that the mere enrolment and arming of the population would have a powerful educational effect in steadying and unifying the spirit of our people. My suggestion was received with what seemed even a forced amusement by the "experts". I was told that I knew nothing about warfare, and the Germans would not permit us to do anything of the sort. The Germans, it seems, are the authorities in these matters, a point I overlooked. They would refuse to recognize men with only improvised uniforms, they would shoot their prisoners – not that I proposed that my irregulars should become prisoners – and burn the adjacent villages. This seemed to be an entirely adequate reply from the point of view of the expert mind, and I gathered that the proper role for such an able-bodied citizen as myself was to keep indoors while the invader was about and supply him as haughtily as possible with light refreshments and anything else he chose to requisition. I am also reminded that if only men like myself had obeyed their expert advice and worked in the past for national service and the general submission of everything to expert military directions, these troubles would not have arisen. There would be no surplus of manhood and everything would have gone a smoothly and as well for England as – the Press Censorship.

For a time I was silenced. Under war conditions it is always a difficult question to determine how far it is better to obey poor, or even bad, directions or to criticize them in the hope of getting better. But the course of the war since that correspondence and the revival of the idea of a raid by your Military Correspondent provoke me to return to the discussion. Frankly, I do not believe in that raid, and I think we play the German game in letting our minds dwell upon it. I am supposed to be a person of feverish imagination, but even by lashing my imagination to its ruddiest I cannot, in these days of wireless telegraphy, see a properly-equipped German force, nor even so trivial a handful as 20,000 of them, getting itself with guns, motors, ammunition, and provisions upon British soil. I cannot even see a mere landing of infantrymen. I believe in that raid even less than I do in the suggested raid of navigables that has darkened London. I admit the risk of a few aeroplane bombs in London, but I do not see why people should be subjected to danger, darkness, and inconvenience on account of that one-in-a-million risk. Still, as the trained mind does insist upon treating all unenlisted civilians as panic-stricken imbeciles and upon frightening old ladies and influential people with these remote possibilities, and as it is likely that these alarms may lead to the retention of troops in England when their point of maximum effectiveness is manifestly in France, it becomes necessary to insist upon the ability of our civilian population, if only the authorities will permit the small amount of organization and preparation needed, to deal quite successfully with any raid that in an extremity of German "boldness" may be attempted.[2]

And, in the first place, let the expert have no illusions as to what we ordinary people are going to do if we find German soldiers in England one morning. We are going to fight. If we cannot fight with rifles, we shall fight with shot guns, and if we cannot fight according to Rules of War apparently made by Germans for the restraint of British military experts, we will fight according to our inner light. Many men, and not a few women,will turn out to shoot Germans. There will be no preventing them after the Belgian stories. If the experts attempt any pedantic interference, we will shoot the experts. I know that in this matter I speak for so sufficient a number of people that it will be quite useless and hopelessly dangerous and foolish for any expert-instructed minority to remain "tame". They will get shot, and their houses will be burnt according to the established German rules and methods on our account, so they may just as well turn out in the first place, and get some shooting as a consolation in advance for their inevitable troubles. And if the raiders, cut off by the sea from their supports, ill-equipped as they will certainly be, and against odds, are so badly advised as to try terror-striking reprisals on the Belgian pattern, we irregulars will, of course, massacre every German straggler we can put a gun to. Naturally. Such a procedure may be sanguinary, but it is just the common sense of the situation. We shall hang the officers and shoot the men. A German raid to England will in fact not be fought – it will be lynched. War is war and reprisals and striking terror are games that two can play at. This is the latent temper of the British countryside, and the sooner the authorities take it in hand and regularize it the better will be the outlook in the remote event of the hypothetical raid getting home to us. Levity is a national characteristic, but submissiveness is not. Under sufficient provocation, the English are capable of very dangerous bad temper, and the expert is dreaming who thinks of a German expedition moving through an apathetic Essex, for example, resisted by only the official forces trained and in training.

And, whatever one may think of the possibility of raids, I venture to suggest that the time has come when the present exclusive specialization of our combatant energy upon the production of regulation armies should cease. The gathering of these will go on anyhow; there are unlimited men ready for intelligent direction. Now that the shortage of supplies and accommodation has been remedied the enlistment sluices need only be opened again. The rank and file of the country is its strength; there is no need, and there never has been any need, for Press hysterics about recruiting. But there is wanted a far more vigorous stimulation of the manufacture of material – if only exports and rich people will turn their minds to that. It is the trading and manufacturing class that needs goading at the present time. It is very satisfactory to send troops to France, but in France there are still great numbers of able-bodied trained Frenchmen not fully equipped. It is our national duty and privilege to be the storehouse and arsenal of the Allies. Our factories for clothing and material of all sorts should be working day and night. There is the point to which enthusiasm should be turned. It is just as heroic and just as useful to the country to kill yourself making belts and boots as it is to die in a trench. But our organization for the enrolment and utilization of people not for the firing line, is still amazingly unsatisfactory. The one convenient alternative to enlistment as a combatant at present is hospital work. But it is really far more urgent to direct enthusiasm and energy now – to the production of war material. If this war does not end, as all the civilised world hopes it will end, in the complete victory of the Allies, our failure will not be through any shortage of men, but through a shortage of gear and organizing ability. It will not be through a default of the people, but through the slackness of the governing class.

Now so far as the enrolment of us goes, of the surplus people who are willing to be armed and to be used for quasi-military work at home, but who are not of an age or not of a physique or who are already in shop or office serving some quite useful purpose at home, we want certain very simple things from the authorities. We want the military status that is conveyed by a specific enrolment and some sort of uniform. We want accessible arms. They need not be modern service weapons; the rifles of ten years ago are quite good enough for the possible need we shall have for them. And we want to be sure that in the possible event of an invasion the Government will have the decision to give every man in the country a military status by at once resorting to the *levee en masse*. Given a recognized local organization and some advice – it would not take a week of General Baden-Powell's time, for example, to produce a special training book for us – we could set to work upon our own local drill, rifle practice, and exercises, in such hours and ways as best suited our locality. We could also organize the local transport, list local supplies and arrange for their removal or destruction if threatened.

Finally, we could set to work to convert a number of ordinary cars into fighting cars by reconstructing them and armouring them and exercising crews. And having developed a discipline and self-respect as a fighting force, we should be available not only for fighting work at home, in the extremely improbable event of a raid, but also for all kinds of supplementary purposes, as a reserve of motor drivers, as a supply of physically-exercised and half-trained recruits in the events of an extended standard, and as a guarantee of national discipline under any unexpected stress. Above all, we should be relieving the real fighting forces of the country for the decisive area, which is, in France and Belgium now, and will, I hope, be in Westphalia before the spring.

At present we non-army people are doing only a fraction of what we would like to do for our country. We are not being used. We are made to feel out of it, and we watch the not always very able proceedings of the military authorities and the international mischief-making of the Censorship with a bitter resentment that is restrained only by the supreme gravity of the crisis. For my part I entertain three Belgians and make a young officer possible by supplementing his expenses and my wife knits things. A neighbour, an able-bodied man of 42 and an excellent shot, is occasionally permitted to carry a recruit to Chelmsford. If I try to use my pen on behalf of my country abroad, where I have a few friends and readers, what I write is exposed to the clumsy editing and delays of anonymous and apparently irresponsible officials. So practically I am doing nothing and a great number are doing very little more. The authorities are concentrated upon the creation of an army numerically vast, and for the rest they seem to think that the chief function of government is inhibition. Their available energy and ability is taxed to the utmost in maintaining the fighting line, and it is sheer greed for direction that has led to their systematic thwarting of civilian cooperation. Let me warn them of the boredom and irritation they are causing. This is a people's war, a war against militarism; it is not a war for the greater glory of British diplomatists, officials and people in uniforms. It is our war, not their war, and the very last thing we intend to result from it is a permanently increased importance for the military caste.

Yours very sincerely,
H.G. Wells

---

[1] This letter appeared in the paper, 31 October 1914, under the heading, 'Mr Wells on Invasion: The Civilian's Place in Home Warfare'. Wells's collection of essays, *The War That Will End War*, was published at the same time as this piece. That book, which includes articles not included here, needs to be read in this context.

[2] German zeppelins and long distance aircraft did bomb London several times, and there was fairly substantial loss of life. The underground played a role as an air raid shelter during these visits. In addition German naval vessels also shelled the port of Hartlepool in the northeast of England, with loss of life.

1002. To Victor Fisher

Boston, ALS

52, St. James's Court
Buckingham Gate, S.W. [October? 1914]

Dear Victor Fisher,

[I am very sorry indeed that I cannot come to your meeting on November 13.] War is a frightful and an evil state of affairs, worse almost than the Peace of Herbert Spencer, it is the dreadful punishment of Competition rather than Co-operation among nations, as poverty and social decay are the dreadful consequences of Competition rather than Co-operation among individuals. Until nations and men learn to forget themselves in the common good of mankind, poverty and war will be the substance of men's lives. We have to organise the peace and social justice of the world, we have to educate mankind to these ends, as thoroughly as the Germans have organised their state and trained their children for this war of pride and oppression upon mankind.

The Programme of Socialism is not complete unless it includes the Peace of the World, and that is to be secured, not by indolence and cowardice posing as a Mystical Pacificism, but by the strenuous resolve of all free peoples to beat down the armed threat in their midst.

The triumph of the German Emperor in this war means the end of Democracy for centuries. THE DEMOCRATIC SOCIALIST WHO IS NOT DOING HIS UTMOST TO-DAY TO OVERTHROW GERMAN IMPERIALISM IS EITHER A DELIBERATE TRAITOR OR A HOPELESS FOOL.

Yours sincerely,
H. G. WELLS[1]

---

[1] This letter was written to Victor Fisher after the rather vicious exchanges on the left of the Socialist movement in the *Labour Leader* and elsewhere in the month after the war began. It was printed in a one page handbill, with the title *Britain v. Germany: The Socialist Point of View. Letter from the famous Socialist writer*, by the National Socialist Defence Committee at The Utopia Press, London, and circulated in the street and at public meetings; see illustration on facing page. The portion of the letter that is in square brackets appears only in the original.

BRITAIN *v.* GERMANY

The Socialist Point of View.

Letter from the famous Socialist writer,

H. G. WELLS

DEAR VICTOR FISHER,

War is a frightful and an evil state of affairs, worse almost than the Peace of Herbert Spencer; it is the dreadful punishment of Competition instead of Co-operation among nations, as poverty and social decay are the dreadful consequences of Competition instead of Co-operation among individuals. Until nations and men learn to forget themselves in the common good of mankind, poverty and war will be the substance of men's lives. We have to organise the peace and social justice of the world, we have to educate mankind to these ends, as thoroughly as the Germans have organised their state and trained their children for this war of pride and aggression upon mankind.

The Programme of Socialism is not complete unless it includes the Peace of the World, and that is to be secured, not by indolence and cowardice posing as a Mystical Pacifism, but by the strenuous resolve of all free peoples to beat down the armed threat in their midst.

The triumph of the German Emperor in this war means the end of Democracy for centuries. THE DEMOCRATIC SOCIALIST WHO IS NOT DOING HIS UTMOST TO-DAY TO OVERTHROW GERMAN IMPERIALISM IS EITHER A DELIBERATE TRAITOR OR A HOPELESS FOOL.

Yours sincerely,

(Signed) **H. G. WELLS.**

Issued by the

NATIONAL SOCIALIST DEFENCE COMMITTEE,

Hon Sec., VICTOR FISHER, 22 Buckingham Street; Adelphi, London. W.C.

THE UTOPIA PRESS (T.U. and 48 hours), 44, Worship Street, London, E.C.

1003. To an unknown addressee[1]

McMaster, ALS

[London] [late 1914?]

Dear Sir,

Your Mrs. Martin's Man is most amazing good. I couldn't resist the impulse to tell you so. It's real & alive & feeling all through. You'll have to work to publish it in the midst of the war confusion, but even that won't drown so fine a thing as yours.

Yours very sincerely,
H.G. Wellls

I shall put it into old James's thoughts about the fact of publishing, but there's something wrong about his judgment. He puts Lawrence up against Walpole which is nonsense.

---

[1] Nothing is known about his correspondent, or his work. The letter is important, though, for it demonstrates how Wells could find time to read manuscripts, even with the war and his domestic situation topmost in his mind.

1004. To Israel Zangwill[1]

PLS

Little Easton Rectory
Dunmow November 4, 1914

To Mr. Zangwill
(Per Favour of the "Daily Chronicle")

Dear Mr. Zangwill,

And now, what is to prevent the Jews having Palestine and restoring a real Judaea?

Yours very sincerely,
H.G. Wells[2]

[1] Zangwill, a novelist and tireless advocate of a Jewish homeland in Palestine, was a good friend of Wells. This exchange between him and Wells took place in the press. Both men had other unnamed addressees in mind when they published these letters.

[2] Zangwill responded with a letter, dated 9 November 1914, saying he dared not speculate. The solutions of the problems must be gradual; the rights of others cannot be forgotten, 'but it is in the air'.

1005. To the Editor, *The Times*[1]

PLS

52, St. James's Court
Buckingham Gate, S.W. [*c.* 1 December 1914]

Sir, – May I, as one of those who threatened to shoot anyhow, reassure my neighbours, Lord Warwick and Mr. Arnold Bennett? Now that there is a serious and recognized organization of home defence on foot, the very sound and bitter justification we unqualified men had in uttering these threats disappears. I do not regret having uttered them, but I regret that they should have been in any degree necessary to overcome the indolence or professional satisfaction of the authorities. So now let every man join something recognized and get his gun. I very gladly admit that my threat has completely served its purpose, and I withdraw it and disavow it, and fold it up and put it away. Let us get on now with the work of perfecting our home defence. Let us get trenches dug at every possible position to meet a raid, and let us know where we are to go and what we are to do when the raiders come. It is as clear as daylight now that to end the war it will be necessary to hit Germany hard next year in Germany with every available soldier. It is quite possible that the moment for the knockout blow will come before the naval situation has changed essentially. By that time the million volunteers of Lord Desborough and Sir Arthur Conan Doyle should be fit to put an entirely satisfactory defensive fight with any score of thousand Germans that could rush the narrow seas. Every organized man of 50 in England means another British soldier in Germany for the final grapple.

And now that I am writing to you, Sir, may I ask also through your column whether it is not time to take measures to staunch the intolerable torrent of bosh in the Press about the slackness of recruiting? We are getting all the men we want, and we are steadily bringing up our lagging equipment to the demands of this generous supply of men. The country swarms with khaki, and by next spring it is manifest that, quite apart from the maintenance of our forces at present at the front, we shall have a magnificent and fully equipped additional host of a million and a half at our disposal for the concluding campaign. Yet a certain section of the Press maintains an imbecile torrent of lamentation, of abuse of "slackers", of ludicrous suggestions for meeting this entirely imaginary lack of men. The effect of all this cackle upon our national prestige in neutral countries must be enormous. And it will go far to persuade our Allies that our people are shirking their legitimate share in the burden of the war. That and the shameful campaign against harmless Anglicized Germans are two very disgraceful and mischievous stains upon our public conduct in this war. They have robbed us of much of the dignity of our cause. They have done the country more harm than the loss of a half dozen battleships.

Yours sincerely,
H.G. Wells

---

[1] Wells's proposals to arm a 'home guard militia' brought down a class protest of considerable strength. The fear of revolution was never far from the minds of the ruling class. Wells's response to this feeling was printed 5 December 1914, under the heading 'Promiscuous Shooting'.

1006. To Fred Wells

Illinois, ALS

52, St. James's Court
Buckingham Gate, S.W. Dec. 6th 1914

My dear Fred,

I'm afraid you'll be astonished at getting a letter from me, because nobody, not even the kindest person would call me a good regular correspondent, & it is far too long since either of us has written to you. But that is all the more reason why I should hurry up & write now! I hope the war isn't disturbing your prosperity. Here of course it has made things seem very strange, all our friends who are of permitted age are in Khaki, & the streets swarm with soldiers & men on encampment in the parks, all London is nearly dark at night save for big search lights in the sky. And of course we think of hardly anything at all except the war & what bears on it. It's a tremendous struggle. But as for ourselves, you want to hear the news. We are all extremely well, and it is not long since Frank was at Little Easton, looking very well too. Gip & Frank have left home for the first term at school. They are at Oundle School. Northamptonshire. It is a public school of about 350 boys, with very fine new buildings & splendid laboratories for science work & very large workshops and engineering buildings with a lot of machinery of every kind. It is a school with a particularly strong modern engineering side as well as the usual classics side. They seem quite happy, & seem to be doing well. Gip belongs to the school corps & has a khaki uniform & drills with a gun – I cannot help feeling very selfishly glad that both boys are too young for the army.[1]

We have left the Rectory at Little Easton for about four months, in the hands of builders, because we have got a long lease of it now. We wanted to improve the house before we settle down for our middle age! So H.G. & I are up here which is the little London flat we keep going nowadays, & for the Xmas holidays I've taken a little furnished house at L. Easton for the boys & us to spend that time in. H.G. has just finished a long book, a very fine novel, in which he has introduced the Johannesburg riots, written up from those newspapers you sent him which he was much glad of.[2] It will not be published until next autumn. I hope you got your copy of <u>Sir Isaac Harman</u> safely & liked it.

I must really have some photographs of the boys taken, just for <u>you</u>. There have been no photographs since they were only children, & you will want to know what they look like by this time. My mother is fairly well, living in London. Now write & tell us how you are youself.

With love from us both,

Affectionately

Amy[3]

---

[1] Wells and Catherine searched for a long time for a suitable school for the boys, who were allowed a say in the matter as well. Their final choice was heavily influenced by the headmaster, F. W. Sanderson, who had advanced ideas on education, see Anonymous, *Sanderson of Oundle* (1923) which was largely written by Wells, and Wells's biography, *The Story of a Great Schoolmaster* (London: Chatto & Windus 1924) and William George Walker, *A History of the Oundle Schools* (London: for the Grocer's Company, 1956), especially chapters 17 and 18.

[2] *The Research Magnificent*

[3] This is such a useful letter about family affairs that it seemed appropriate to include it. It is worth noticing that she signs herself by her real name, not Jane, even within the family.

1007. To Russian Men of Letters[1]

PLS

[London] [mid December 1914]

To Our Colleagues in Russia:

At this moment when your countrymen and ours are alike facing death for the deliverance of Europe, we English men of letters take the opportunity of uttering to you feelings which have been in our hearts for many years. You yourselves, perhaps, hardly realise what an inspiration Englishmen of the last two generations have found in your literature.

Many a writer among us can still call back from 10, or 20 or 30 years ago the feeling of delight and almost of bewilderment, with which he read his first Russian novel. Perhaps it was "Virgin Soil" or "Fathers and Sons", perhaps "War and Peace" or "Anna Karenina", perhaps "Crime and Punishment", or "The Idiot"; perhaps again, it was the work of some author still living. But many of us then felt, as our poet Keats felt on first reading Homer.

Like some watcher of the skies
When a new planet swims into his ken.

It was a strange world that opened before us, a world full of foreign names which we could neither pronounce or remember, of foreign customs and articles of daily life which we could not understand. Yet beneath all this strangeness there was a deep sense of discovering a new home, of meeting our unknown kindred, of finding expressed great burdens of thought which had lain half-spoken and unrealised at the depths of our own minds. The books were very different, one from another – sometimes they were mutually hostile – yet we found in all some quality which made them one and made us at one with them. We will not attempt to analyse that quality. It was, perhaps, in part that deep Russian tenderness which never derides but only pities and respects the unfortunate; in part that simple Russian sincerity which never fears to see the truth and to express it; but most of all it was that ever-present sense of spiritual values behind the material, and utterly transcending the material, which enables Russian literature to move so naturally in a world of the spirit, where there are no barriers between the ages and the nations, and all mankind is one.

And they call you "barbarians"! The fact should make us ask again what we mean by the words "culture" and "civilisation". Critics used once to call our Shakespeare a barbarian, and might equally well give the same name to

Aeschylus or Isaiah. All poets and prophets are in this sense barbarians, that they will not measure life by the standards of external "culture".

And it is at a time like this, when the material civilisation of Europe seems to have betrayed us and shown the lie at its heart, that we realise that the poets and prophets are right, and that we must, like them and like your great writers, once more see life with the simplicity of the barbarian or the child if we are to regain our peace and freedom and build up a better civilisation on the ruins of this that is crumbling. That task, we trust, will someday lie before us. When at last our victorious fleets and armies meet together and the allied nations of east and west set themselves to restore the well-being of many millions of ruined homes, France and Great Britain will assuredly bring their large contributions of goodwill and wisdom; but your country will have something to contribute which is all its own.

It is not only because of your valour in war and your acheivements in arts, science and letters that we rejoice to have you for allies and friends. It is for some quality in Russia itself, something both profound and human of which these achievements are the outcome and the expression. You, like us, entered upon this war to defend a weak and threatened nation which trusted you against the lawless aggression of a strong military power. You, like us, have continued it as a war of self-defence and self-emancipation. When the end comes and we can breathe again we will help one another to remember the spirit in which our allied nations took up arms, and thus work together in a changed Europe to protect the weak, to liberate the oppressed, and bring eventual healing to the wounds inflicted on suffering mankind both by ourselves and our enemies.

With assurances of our friendship and gratitude, we sign ourselves: -

William Archer, Maurice Baring, J. M. Barrie, Arnold Bennett, A. C. Bradley, Robert Bridges, Hall Caine, G.K. Chesterton, Arthur Conan Doyle, Nevill Forbes, John Galsworthy, Constance Garnett, Edward Garnett, A.P. Goudy, Thomas Hardy, Jane Harrison, Anthony Hope, Henry James, J. W Mackail, John Masefield, A.E.W. Mason, Aylmer Maude, Alice Meynall, Gilbert Murray, Henry Newbolt, Gilbert Parker, Ernest de Selincourt, May Sinclair, D. Mackenzie Wallace, Mary A. Ward, William Watson, H.G. Wells, Margaret L. Woods, C. Hagberg Wright.

---

[1] This joint letter appeared in the *Manchester Guardian*, 23 December 1914. It was accompanied by a moving leading article hailing the spirit of the letter, entitled 'The Bond of the Spirit'.

1008. To Robert Ross

Illinois, Transcription

52, St. James's Court, S.W. [December 1914]

My dear Bobbie,

The tumults of the war and the accidents of life come between us. I'm a homeless man save for this and a lodging in the country to which I retreat for work when London is insupportable. Little Easton is in the hands of builders and the house nearby we were to have occupied is in the grip of a licentious soldiery. But I am gradually adjusting myself to the new conditions and getting my mind onto a novel – about everything – of the usual pattern. When shall I see you again? I shall be up on Wednesday and lunching at the Reform.

Yours ever,
H.G.

1009. To friends of Robby Ross

Illinois, TLS

27 Connaught Square December, 1914

PRIVATE AND CONFIDENTIAL

We have good reason to think that many, besides the personal friends of ROBERT ROSS will welcome, at the present moment, an opportunity of testifying publicly to their admiration and regard for one who has been unfailingly at the disposal of any who claimed either his sympathy or his help. The calls that have thus been met with rare loyalty and courage will never be fully known, but in our time there has been no friendlier influence in the world of Art and Letters.

It is proposed that an address should be presented to Mr. Ross giving some expresson to this feeling and with it a portrait or other work of art; the choice of painter or of object being left to himself.

We desire to gather the names of those who would wish to join in one or both of those memorials, and venture to hope that we may count upon your support.

The terms of the address will be circulated later; the character of the gift will be determined in accordance with the response to this appeal and in consultation with Mr. Ross, by a committee formed from the subscribers.

Promises of support and subscriptions should be forwarded on the enclosed forms to the undersigned at the above address, cheques being made payable to the Hon. Secretaries, Robert Ross Fund and crossed "Barclay and Co., 19 Fleet Street".

When the list of signatories and of subscribers is complete we propose that their names should be published along with the address; until then we will ask you to regard the matter as confidential.

Overleaf will be found some names of those who have already interested themselves in the scheme and promised their support.[1]

Yours faithfully,

[D.S. MacColl

Robert C. Wirt] Hon. Secretaries

---

[1] Wells was among the eighty-nine signatories on the reverse side of this letter. He sent a cheque to the fund on 23 December 1914 for fifteen guineas. Here the world of letters was able to express its appreciation to Ross after the Douglas case was ended.

1010. To Mrs Fenner Brockway[1]

Churchill, ALS

52, St. James's Court
Buckingham Gate, S.W.

[date unknown,
probably late 1914]

Dear Mrs. Brockway,

Thank you for your kind letter. I doubt that Brockway has any reason to trouble his conscience about me. He didn't believe in me and he was right to do what he could to carry that disbelief to others. I'm a much tougher minded man than he is & as you know I differ fundamentally from him about the war. At the outset I said that this is the way to freedom, this is reality, the imperialists destroy themselves. In a hot controversy we had in the Labour Leader I stood up for Russia. The L.L. said Russia was barbaric. I prophesied the contrary. Was I right or L.L.? To-day Russia leads the world toward a republican world peace. Today I still say 'This is the war for freedom (& there is no freedom until a world peace is secure)'. Consequently I have set my face like flint against the C.O. attitude[2]. I do so still. It is to leave the war & the horror to the old regime. I wish I could persuade him to come out of this prison now & go to the front. Then he can stand with the old soldiers at the end & demand the freedom we have fought for. But what standing will men like Snowden & he have when it comes to reaping the harvest of this war? If all men had done as he has done the Kaiser would be Emperor of the world today; there would be no hiding place for free speech in all the world; there would be no talk of reconstruction possible. In defying German Imperialism, we destroy Russian, British & French & Italian imperialism. The price I reckon has scarcely been too high.

Very sincerely yours,
H.G. Wells

---

[1] After the rather rough handling of Wells by the *Labour Leader* after the First World War began, Fenner Brockway's wife apparently wrote to Wells in an apologetic manner.
[2] Refusal to serve in the armed forces on the grounds of conscience.

1011. To Mr Williams[1]

Illinois, ALS

Easton Glebe
Dunmow [1914?]

Dear Mr. Williams,

I have a very friendly letter from your sister in Sydney. We people here in England want to do all we can to make the country a second home to young Australians & so, I hope, you'll let me know when you are likely to be in London so that you can come & see me & have a gossip. But I'm a very busy man, going about hither & thither, so try & give me as long a notice as you can. Week-ends I'm usually at the address which heads this letter. Week middles I'm nearly always at 52, St. James's Court.
London
S.W. 1

Very sincerely yours,
H.G. Wells

---

[1] Mr Williams and his sister are unknown, unless they are cousins who had migrated to Australia.

1012. Dear Dr Collie[1]

Hofstra, ALS

Easton Glebe
Dunmow [date unknown]

Will this do? I'm down with flue[2] (dammit) and my brains won't compose anything else.

Yours ever
H.G. Wells

---

[1] Collie was the husband of Wilhemina Stitch, pen name of Ruth Collie, a writer of the time. She produced between twenty and thirty volumes of 'women's poetry' in the 1920s.
[2] Wells had a bad case of Spanish influenza in 1920, and perhaps this letter is as late as from that time. However he was fairly often the victim of upper respiratory infections during the winter months. He invariably spelled the word 'flue.'

1013. To Thomas Burke[1]

Indiana, ALS

Easton Glebe
Dunmow [date unknown]

Private

Dear Mr. Burke,

I acknowledged your book the other day. I hadn't read two pages. I just turned it over, saw 'Grant Richards trying for cheap advertisement' & put it with a number of the books that had come in. Yesterday I was in bed with a cold & my wife dug your book out. She thinks it rather horrible & I agree with Boots upon the quote of 'general circulation'. [2] But I think also that some of it is amazing beautiful and beautifully done. You remind me of Horace. He would have been much more at home in your Limehouse than at Dunmow. Your sense of the beauty in these lean little kids of the street is divine. I think I've been to Limehouse twice in my life but I know, as one does in really first class work, that you have given a beauty you have seen about another class, a beauty that will be there now visible to many who read you.

Very sincerely yours,
H.G. Wells

---

[1] Thomas Burke (1886–1945) was an author of many books about London life. Wells could have been reading *Nights in Town* (1915) or more probably *Limehouse Nights* (1916). He also wrote the *Streets of London* (1941).
[2] This probably refers to a description of the book by Boots (the chemist) lending library. Many establishments maintained lending libraries as the public library idea was still in its infancy.

1014. M. Lykiardopulos[1]

Boston, ALS

Easton Glebe,
Dunmow [early ?1915]

Dear Mr. Lykiardopulos,

I'll certainly speak to anyone who desires translation into Russian. I don't expect to be in London until Thursday or Friday of next week. Then I shall try to get you on General 3101 if you haven't started for Finland.

Yours
H.G.

---

[1] Lykiardopulos was the director of the Moscow Art Theatre, see letter 1278 in volume 3.

1015. To the Editor, *North Mail*[1]

PLS

London [end December 1914]

Sir, – At the time of Mr. Shaw's recent letter to you, I was ill in bed, and, I found, too feverish to write a temperate reply. I feel, however, that the issues he raises and the peculiar part he is playing in confusing the public mind, coupled with his direct appeal to my attention, call for some responses on my part, and now that I am returning to ordinary life again, I will, with your permission, deal with him, and add a word or two to what you have already allowed me to say on that muddleheadedness about Russia of which he is the noisiest example. It is impossible to ignore Mr. Shaw and there can be little doubt that he is doing a great deal of mischief at the present time.[2]

I do not mean mischief in neutral countries, but mischief at home.[3] A vast amount of nonsense has been written and said about the effect of our various writings upon neutral opinion, nonsense which had done much to excite Mr. Shaw to his present abnormal activities. I doubt if neutral countries are paying any attention to our voluminous "utterances". Why should they? All the writing in the world will not change the obvious rights and wrongs of this war. But there can be no doubt of the mischief and dissention the conspicuous repetition of this conventional muddlehead stuff about Russia is causing our home mentality.[4]

Mr. Shaw objects to my calling him muddleheaded. But I have always considered him muddleheaded. If I have not called him that in public before, it is simply because I thought the thing too obvious to need pointing out. We English are an indolent, indulgent people. We are apt to submit to a man's valuation of himself rather than face the boring task of pursuing him into the recesses of his unsoundness, and this weakness of ours is particularly evident in the case of such an indefatigible type as Mr. Shaw. We hump our backs. If we believe a man is systematically propagating some specific error we may take the trouble and combat him, but if we perceive he is flinging himself about in paroxysms of merely personal activity,we leave him alone, or if we notice him we notice him as we fling a hair-brush at a nocturnal cat, because the irritation has become intolerable.

And that is how things stand between Mr. Shaw and myself. I have been quite exceptionally and generously disposed to take him seriously and find out what he amounts to, and this is what I find he amounts to. He is an activity, a restless passion for attention. Behind that is a kind of jackdaw's hoard of other peoples notions, much from Samuel Butler, scraps of pseudo-philosophical phraseology such as that "Life Force" phrase he got from Doctor Guest, old Hammersmith economies, worn fragments of Herbert Spencer, some Neitzsche conveyed no doubt from the convenient handbook of Mr. Orage, shreds of theosophy, current suppositions, such as, for example, his idea that fear "poisons" meat, or that wool is a more natural and hygienic than cotton, sweepings of all sorts of "introduced" rubbish, but nothing anywhere of which one can say, "Here is the thought of a man." And it is just this incoherent emptiness, combined with an amazing knack of fluent inexactitude, which gives him his advantage in irresponsible attack, and which from his early repute as the Terror of the Fabian Society has spread his vague and unsubstantial fame about the globe far beyond the range to which even his confusedly entertaining intellectual farces would have taken it.

I will not ask your public to emulate my reading in the works of Mr Shaw; his letter in your issue of last Wednesday is quite sufficient to illustrate both his controversial methods and his intellectual quality. The first thing he does almost invariably in his controversies, if one may give his displays so dignified a name, is to create a distinctive serio-comic atmosphere, the "Shavian" atmosphere, by wild boasting about his mental clarity and facetious abuse of his antagonist. My mind, he declares, is "giving way", and so on. At this the well-trained Fabian spinster smiles almost maternally, and prepares for the next phrase of the "intellectual treat". This is a carefully untruthful statement of the antagonist's position. I say "carefully untruthful"; he does not err, he deliberately distorts.

In this instance, he declares that I think that Germany is holding out Finland as a bait to Sweden and so on. It is nothing to Mr Shaw that I did not suggest anything of the kind; the glib falsehood is necessary to his case, and he utters it with as light a conscience as if instead of offering rubbish as international politics he was introducing a panacea at a fair. And having thus prepared the ground, he proceeds to the main Shavian attack, a crack-brained explanation of why the antagonist maintains these alleged opinions, a demonstration of how ill-advised he is in doing so, and then what he really ought to do and think about the matter in hand. In regard to this Russian business, I am supposed to be in a state of bellicose enthusiasm; this is supposed to make eager to secure and fix the Russian alliance at any cost, and so I toady to the Czardom, write favourable lies about Russia, and generally behave like a scoundrel to forward these high aims. That, Mr Shaw assures his audience, is the simply psychology, not only of myself, but of all the literary men who have a good word to say for Russia at the present time. We know better, but we are telling these lies, "for the sake of presenting an unbroken front to the enemy".[5] And having satisfied himself and the loyal assenting Fabian spinster of the position of affairs, he goes on to show how fruitless such cunning is. "We have no need to propitiate the Czar; we are doing him a prodigious service in return for military aid which we all wish we could dispense with", and so on, and so on.

For some years I have been coming around to the idea that honesty is not a moral but an intellectual quality, and that real integrity is impossible to a confused mind. I think Mr Shaw's interpretation of the pro-Russian Englishman carries out the conviction. It is one of the commonest characteristics of the muddle-headed that they cannot understand that an opinion can be honestly held for its own sake. Mr Shaw, manifestly having no ideas whatever of his own, and being incapable of understanding authentic thought, does not know that it is possible to express an idea for its own sake and to be concerned about the truth; he thinks all utterances are calculated tactical statements; he thinks one expresses ideas for an end, in order to annoy somebody to do something; under every statement he looks for a motive; he is like those exasperating women who are always crying out, "Ah! I know why you said that." And as a consequence he flings out these intolerable insults to honourable writers without any sense of their gravity.

A postcard from some humble anonymous Shavian the other day put the thing with even greater directness by asking me: "What price your sticking up for Russian tyranny?" And I suppose the postcard writer would have been as incredulous as Mr Shaw that there was no end to serve and no price to be earned in the thing at all, and that the sole reason why I say that I am disposed to believe in the good intentions of the Czar, and that I believe firmly in the liberal future of Russia, is simply that I do so. The simpler a thing is the more difficult it is for the muddleheaded to understand, and you could have no finer display of the perfect muddlehead in action than Mr Shaw's treatment of those better informed people who reject the view he has adopted that Russia is Bogey, and Czar ought to be suddenly and violently replaced by God knows what. Some years ago I became interested in Russia. I took some pains to inform myself about Russia, and finally I went to the country. I formed the opinion that Russia and the Czardom were mischievously and almost systematically lied about in Britain and America, and long before this war broke out I was writing and saying as much.

I am, as Mr Shaw points out, a Republican but Republicanism begins at home, and I do not wish Russia "well rid of her Prussian Czar", because, firstly, they are not Prussian, but very distinctly national, and, secondly, I can imagine no possible substitute at the present time. I believe that the Russians are a very great people with a great future, and that they are in their general temperament, in their social disposition, and many of the insitutions more like the English and more capable of sympathetic cooperation with the English than any other people in the world. I think the melodramatic stuff that is talked and believed about Russia and the Czar is silly and dangerous rubbish, standing directly in the way to such a settlement of this war as will give the world a lasting peace, and so I say these things as plainly as I can. But Mr Shaw whose mind has never had a conviction, who has never grown up to a sense of varieties, is incapable of understanding this mental direction. He is naturally and honestly incapable of understanding intellectual honesty.

It is a trick of Mr Shaw's to "explain" the mental operations of the people he attacks. Commonly, he seems to make these fancy sketches for the mere satisfaction of representing people whom he is obliged to respect in a relation of intellectual and moral inferiority to himself. He describes with an artlessness which almost redeems his impertinence what goes on in Sir Edward Grey's head,[6] how Mr Asquith cries "Hurroo", and what ingenious cunning animated Professor Gilbert Murray and Mr. Archer and their associates in their letter to the Russian people.[7] Let me take a leaf out of his book and with a more decent motive and a steadier knowledge explain Mr Shaw. Mr Shaw is one of those perpetual children who live in a dream of make-believe, and the make-believe of Mr Shaw is that he is a person of incredible wisdom and subtly running the world. He is one of those beings to whom reality has never come. He is an elderly adolescent, still at play. To understand that is to have the clue to all Shavianism. The industrious curious who choose to examine the literature of the Fabian Society will find there the clearest evidence of his incurable belief that from its Clement's Inn cellar this little body has under his guidance influenced, frightened, guided, and hoodwinked the great political parties of Great Britain, and has been responsible for the whole of our social and political development of the last thirty years.

This delusion is the backbone of Mr Shaw's existence. It is his "Life Force". One cannot talk to him for twenty minutes without its coming to the surface. It takes the place with him of love or hate, or any passionate or impersonal end. And now under the intense excitements of the war it has become inflamed and amplified. In letters, articles, speeches, Mr Shaw – who has no kindred at this war, who has no children, who has no stake whatever to the future, to whom all life is still a boy's imaginative playground – makes believe that he is doing rare and wonderful things with international politics. He has invited us all to participate in his pastime. He gets in our way and thrusts himself upon our attention. Such fun! We are supposed to be playing with the nations as one plays with counters at a game; here is Scandinavian opinion being subtly permeated; here is America spinning round under the influence of artfully-designed elucidation; here, alas!, is somebody "wasting whitewash and boot polish" on the Czar. Some of us are busy producing "utterances designed to influence neutrals", and what we have to do is to "play steadily for sympathy with Western democracy and Western ideals".

All the world, indeed, is supposed to be hanging upon the magical wires we author-journalists are pulling. For some tactical purpose of infinite profundity Mr Shaw is being very stern and rude to Petrograd. He wants to play that that wicked, wicked raw head and bloody bones, the Czar, is reading over his letter of last Wednesday for the fourth time and shaking his Oriental crown. "I must be more careful. I must show them I am not as bad as Potsdam." 'Petrograd and Potsdam' is a dangerous alliteration.[8] If I do something to propitiate Mr Shaw's correspondent in Finland, perhaps Mr Shaw will not turn Britain and America against me.[9] And forthwith he does something Shaw-driven. Meanwhile, Sweden, a sea of upturned faces, says in unison, "But see how anti-Russian these Shaw-led British are. That is well for us." And so they write him numerous letters and do things also. But we others are not playing the game properly; we are encouraging the Czar. And so he dances on.

It is almost as if there were nothing happening in Flanders.[10] It is almost as if there were no pain in all the world. It is the inspiration of such delightful dreams that Mr Shaw now flings himself upon his typewriter and rattles out his broadsides. And nothing will stop him. All through the war we shall have this Shavian accompaniment; going on, like an idiot child screaming in a hospital, distorting, discrediting, confusing, and in the end, when it is all over, we shall have voluminnous pamphlets and prefaces explaining how modestly and dexterously he settled the Prussian hegemony and rearranged Europe. He is at present, when sane public discussion is of enormous importance, an almost unendurable nusiance. Gentleman who have carried make-believe only a few steps further write to me under imperial or divine signatures, from houses of rest in various parts of the country, explaining still more simply how Europe may be pacified, but for some reason nobody prints them. Mr Shaw gets printed. It is useless, I suppose, after all these years of impunity for him, to attempt to take Mr Shaw by the scruff of his intellectual neck, and tell him very loudly and distinctly, that he is mistaken, that the war is not a cesspool of idiot cunning, that most people are saying what they mean, and most people are acting directly toward the ends they desire. And that there is a very bloody and trying business called war afoot. He just has to – let go on making mischief, falsifying issues, lying about our national honour, lying about Russia, distracting and complicating the business before us – it is the fault of that critical indolence, that national intellectual apathy that has permeated his career – and we have to do now as well as we can with Mr Shaw in his glory, as if there was no Mr Shaw.

But having paid my long overdue tribute of a hair-brush to Mr Shaw, I would, before I conclude, like to repeat once more my protest at the dangerous ignorance of Russia, of which he is an example. He has simply, in his unthinking way, picked up and used ideas that are shared by great masses of ill-informed "advanced" people in Great Britain and America. Such ideas will tremendously encumber Western liberalism in its attempt to secure a permanent world peace at the end of this struggle. It is only by a world-wide network of treaties and the utmost international frankness and confidence that any extensive disarmament and any lasting peace can be made possible. If a large mass of Western people remain saturated with the idea that the mass of Russian people are savagely brutal, that the Russian government is a thing of insatiable ambition and incredible cunning and wickedness, and the daily life in Russia a profound misery occasionally enlivened by horrible cruelty, I see no hope for any such settlement. It is all very well for Mr Shaw to play at having such a devil country as his world of servile make-believe, but we who are not making believe, who can feel the stress of the trenches, who can imagine the hospitals and the sufferings, who have had to do with refugees from the war-tormented districts, and who are resolved to wring some good out of this great agony of manking, cannot afford to share in such foolery.

People have to clear their heads about Russia. There is a large and growing literature about Russia and books from Russia: Maurice Baring, Mackenzie Wallace, Stephen Graham, Garstin, a multitude of others, there is no excuse for any one who can read to share Mr Shaw's delusions. That critical indolence of ours who has left it to foolish sensational novels and ignorant melodrama to build up our conceptions of this great people, is fraught with disastrous consequences for the whole world. We want to bring the human realities of everyday Russia home to English minds; it is, I would venture to say, the next most important thing in our proper conduct of the war.

H.G.Wells

---

[1] When the First World War broke out, some on the left in Britain and the United States advocated a hands-off policy towards Russia. Wells demurred in a series of articles and letters in the *Labour Leader* most of which appear in this collection. The argument broke out again at the end of 1914, when Wells wrote an article for the *Daily Chronicle*, which was picked up and published in the *North Mail*, located in Newcastle-upon-Tyne. Shaw responded ironically to Wells with a sort of mock praise. Ford Madox Hueffer, still using that name, not Ford Madox Ford, replied to Shaw while supporting Wells. Wells then more or less ended the argument by writing a very long letter to the *Chronicle*, which was republished in the *North Mail*. The title varies: in London it was 'Muddleheadedness, Russia and Some Comment on Mr. Shaw'. In the North it was simply, 'Muddleheadness and Russia', but in their introductory squib, they remarked, 'The exposure of what is known as 'Shavianism' is ruthless in the extreme'.

[2] This literature is extensive. The opening salvoes were fired in the *Clarion* in July 1914, when Wells wrote a series of sharp articles on Shaw's arguments under the pseudonym 'Little Douglas'. These were followed by his letters to the *Chronicle* and other newspapers with C. Hagberg Wright, 'Our Ally Russia: Some Misconceptions and a Protest', 22 September 1914; 'Looking Ahead: The Future of the North of Europe', 18 December 1914; Shaw's response on 23 December 1914; Hueffer's defence of Wells, 24 December 1914; Wells's piece in *Harper's Weekly* 'The Liberal Fear of Russia', 19 September 1914; *Labour Leader* 'The Russian Menace: H. G. Wells Says It Is A Bogy', 3 September 1914; the debate that followed in that paper for a month to which Wells wrote, 'A Reply From H.G. Wells', 17 September 1914, and part of the Hagberg Wright letter with a strong leading article in opposition, 24 September 1914, as well as further discussion throughout October 1914 by many contributors; a Gilbert Murray letter to

the *Manchester Guardian*, 23 December 1914 written by Wells and Murray. Wells's letter to the *Times Educational Supplement*, 'Need of Russian Teaching in English Schools', 6 October 1914 are all useful in following this argument.

[3] The original Wells article also offered some comments on the relationship of Norway, Sweden and the Scandinavian peninsula with regard to Russia in the postwar world.

[4] There are six sub-headings in this article. Wells abominated sub-headings inserted by others; in this case, therefore, they have been omitted as he would not have tolerated them if he had had an opportunity of seeing them in advance.

[5] Here Wells is associating himself with such persons as Maurice Baring, Arthur Ransome, Bruce Lockhart, and Hugh Walpole.

[6] Grey was Foreign Secretary and best known today, perhaps, for the phrase, as the war began, 'The lights are going out all over Europe.'

[7] Murray was the distinguished Australian-born classical scholar whose translations of Greek drama were highly acclaimed. A friend of Wells, he was a life-long Liberal and worked diligently on the League of Nations between the wars. William Archer was a playwright. The letter, which Wells signed, was a welcome to the Russian peoples as allies when the war began; see letter 1007.

[8] Potsdam, close to Berlin, was the centre of the Kaiser's government, while Petrograd, also known as St Petersburg, was the seat of government of the Tsardom.

[9] Travel to Russia in those days usually involved a Baltic sea voyage and transport by rail from Helsinki to Petrograd. The railway station was the 'Finland station'. Finland was nominally free but in fact it was very closely monitored by Russia. Wells's allusion is to the fact that virtually every newspaper which had a northern Europe correspondent stationed that person in Finland. Helsinki was the centre of diplomatic talk, rumours, discussions and speculation.

[10] Belgium and Flanders were the scenes of the bloody trench fighting of this phase of the war. The battle names Ypres and Amiens were where men were dying in their thousands under horrible conditions.

1016. James Pinker to H. G. Wells

Illinois, ALS

[London] January 18, 1915

Dear Wells,

I have your letter. Of course, I should be very pleased to be your agent, but there would be no fun in the partial arrangement you suggest. I don't want to say anything against poor Cazenove, whom I liked, but as a matter of fact if you are content for your serials to be handled as they have been been for the last few years, any good tempered honest clerk can do it for you. I know all about the serial sales of the last few years, and although I do not suppose you mind the loss of money, the loss of prestige involved is serious, and work like yours ought not to be handled in that way.

Apart from this there is really a good piece of agenting to be done for you in America.

I believe there never was so fine a body of work frittered away in such a scandalous fashion. If your agent is responsible, he ought to have his tongue cut out, and if, as I suspect, it is your fault all I can say is you do not deserve to have written such books, and all you can say is "go to hell", and I suspect that is exactly what you will say. But never mind.

I am,

Yours very sincerely,

James B. Pinker

1017. To G. K. Chesterton

Illinois, Typed Transcription

[London] [sometime in 1915]

Dear old G.K.C.,

I'm so delighted to get a letter from you again. As soon as I can I will come to Beaconsfield and see you. I'm absurdly busy in bringing together the Rulers of the country and the scientific people of whom they are totally ignorant. Lloyd George has never heard of Ramsay – and so on, and the hash and muddle and quackery on our technical side is appalling. It all means boys' lives in Flanders and horrible waste and suffering. Well, anyhow if we've got only obscure and cramped and underpaid scientific men, we have a bunch of fine fat bishops and no end of tremendous lawyers. One of the best ideas for the Ypres position came from Robert Mond but the execution was too difficult for our officers to attempt. So we've got a row of wounded and mangled men that would reach from Beaconsfield to Great Marlow —just to show we don't take stock in these damned scientific people.

Yours ever,

H.G.

1018. James Pinker to H. G. Wells

Illinois, TLS

[London] January 26, 1915

Dear H.G.,

The proofs arrived this morning, and I need not say I am delighted to have them to read.

I wish we could have a talk, as I should not waste your time. You say there is nothing much doing at present, but as a matter of fact there is always something going for a big author, if the agent is handling him properly, as an institution and not as a writer of isolated books.

For instance, there is at the moment a chance of getting the Dent books. I remember we wanted years ago to do it and failed. About a couple of years ago, I could have done it, and by a curious coincidence there is what seems to me now a very good chance. This, I think, would leave only the Heinemann books outside, and as he binds them uniform with Macmillan's, that does not so much matter.

There is a great deal of this sort of work for an agent to do, and much of it produces no commission. For instance, when I went to America and arranged the uniform edition of Henry James's books, the labour and time involved were altogether out of proportion to the commission involved, but for men of your calibre the work has to be done if you are to be presented to the public in an adequate worthy manner.

Of course, you have made progress in America. Your work was bound to make effect, even if it were published in a cellar. I felt so strongly about it when I came back from America this time last year, that I wanted to approach you then, but I was afraid you would snub me.

You say I did not do brilliantly for you when I <u>was</u> handling your American business. I admit I made mistakes when I was acting for you, but the mistakes were due not to want of skill, or want of energy, but to a failure of courage in dealing with your personality. And in judging me, you must remember that it would have been very remarkable if I had stood up to you as I ought to have done. You would always at will dazzle me and make me forget that I was a better judge than you in all matters of business.

As a matter of fact, my dear H.G., there is only one point in which we are at variance. I should probably give you a much higher place than you would claim intellectually, but I should deny that you have the temper for business, for business ultimately is the problem of dealing with men.

Yours ever,

James B. Pinker[1]

---

[1] In the event Pinker did not act for Wells again.

1019. To Mr Rees

Larson, ALS

52, St. James Court [1]
Buckingham Gate, S.W. [early Spring ?1915]

Dear Mr. Rees,

I think that later I may do an article War Up to the Hilt. Have we ever discussed prices. I get 25 guineas for the ordinary articles I put into The Chronicle or News. For single special articles like this, I suppose I ought to set up a standard price. But I don't. I get £50 £75 and suchlike sums. What do you want to pay?

Very sincerely yrs.,
H.G. Wells

[1] Letter owned by Elmer Larson of Cleveland, Ohio; reprinted by permission

1020. To an unknown correspondent

Boston, ACCS

Easton Glebe
Dunmow [early 1915]

Dear Sir,

If you like my programme support it & me. I am bored by the dull hostility of the Labour Leader group. I had to object to the rot of the L.L. about Russia at the beginning of the war (since [*illegible word*] shown to be not part of the revolution), & I'm altogether opposed to the C.O. alternative. This is a war of liberation. Beat Germany — German imperialism, that is — & you begin a new age in human history. I would rather see both of my sons dead or mutilated in this war than have one of them a C.O. What is life for?

Yours ever,
H.G. Wells

1021. To the Editor, *Daily Chronicle*[1]

PLS

[London] February 3 [1915]

Sir, – If Mr. J. A. Hobson instead of "running his eye" down my article had read it, he might instead of knowing "what to expect" have found out what it was about. He misses everything of slightest importance of what I had to say and turns off his Four Points with the readiness of an overworked general practitioner confronted with a case he is too driven to diagnose. Then follows a line of abuse, "completely and consistently foolish", and we are to understand that the final wisdom of free trade had been spoken.

My article was based on the economic destruction of the French, Belgian and Polish industrial plant and the manifest fact that the German industrialism is militant. Mr. Hobson's running and habituated eye leaps these unfamiliar points. And even the four allegations which he imagines to be a reply to what he imagines I said, are really very, very silly propositions.

(1) Does it matter if "by damaging the industrialism and commerce of Germany we make the exaction of indemnities slow and difficult"? The longer Germany is oppressed by an indemnity, the slower will be the recovery of her military and naval estimates. You cannot both pay your indemnity and have it.

(2) "By compelling this country to continue producing, etc., ... will reduce to a considerable extent the productivity and income of our own nation." Well, what decent Englishman cares if that is so? I do not propose Protection that England may grow rich. I propose it that France, Belgium and Poland may recover. I do not want protection for British industries, I want it for the Allied industries. Will Mr. Hobson just stay his eye on that last sentence for a moment and try to think what it means?

(3) German "patriotism" will lie and scream about England anyhow. Why sacrifice Belgium to an argument?

(4) Having explained in (1) that an Allied Zollverein will lead to the impoverishment of Germany and prevent the payment of an indemnity, Mr. Hobson's really very birdlike mind is capable of asserting in (4) that the same cause will lead to a continuation of armament. On what conceivable financial basis? Indeed, I am astonished at Mr. Hobson.

H. G. Wells

[1] One area of debate as to the conduct of the war lay in the use of the tariff. Wells had strong opinions on this matter, and the following letter, printed 4 Febuary 1915 under the heading 'The

Tariff as An Instrument of War', is a clear statement of his views. His original article appeared on 1 February 1915, entitled "Looking Ahead: A Suggestion for Penalizing Germany's Commerce'. In it he proposed the formation of an Allied Zollverein, or customs union, after the war. He was attacked by J. H. Hobson on 2 February and others on 3 February which occasioned this letter. Wells returned to the subject on 13 February and later. His standards on wartime tariffs became an issue in the 1920s, both from his gadfly, H. A. Jones, but also a correspondent 'XYZ' in the *Westminster Gazette*; see volume 3 for this correspondence.

1022. To Ella Hepworth Dixon

Illinois, ANS

52, St. James's Court
Buckingham Gate, S.W. [date unknown]

Dearest Zuleika

The only characteristic thing so dear a lady as you can do is to burn that "gentleman's letter ! ! !" and forget about it. My dear, admit we all survive & don't we all admit him a foolish creature. Do, do end it. V.H. has her quite abnormal troubles.[1] They're desperately at bay under a brave appearance. I'm going to Barlem [tonight]. V. H. will certainly be there.

Your devoted
H. G.

[1] Probably V.H. is Violet Hunt. What the indiscreet letter may have contained is not known. Wells played a small role in maintaining Hunt's equilibrium.

1023. To the Editor, *Daily Chronicle*[1]

PLS

Little Easton Rectory
Dunmow [5? May 1915]

Sir, – Dr. Holland Rose, like so many of teeth-setting, say-nothing-but-abuse-your-fellow-countrymen "patriots", falls foul of my article in your issue of last Tuesday. He has not read it, but he does not like it, and in his stern, silent way he hastens to say so. He wants to keep it a secret from the world that we are bored by the war that Germany has thrust upon us. Never was there such an open secret. We are so bored that whatever cost we are resolved to carry it through to an end that will make its repetition impossible. I said that quite clearly in my article, but Dr. Holland Rose, in his sputtering haste to get in an obvious repartee and express his dislike of me, ignores that. Nor would a human being suspect that when he writes of my "lordly apportionment of German soil" he is referring to my very plain reminder that Alsace-Lorraine is primarily a question for France to settle and that Poland first concerns Russia.

I gather that Dr. Holland Rose poses as "a serious student of history". I thought serious students of history did at least acquire a certain care and accuracy in their reading, but when I find him declaring that I propose the annexation of the German north-west coast I wonder what has happened to the traditional Cambridge scholarship. I should imagine that only a completely untrained mind in a state of extravagant excitement could have so misread my words. For some reason, possibly humorous, Dr. Rose winds up this most regrettable outbreak by remarking "that this is not a time for controversy, still less for neurotic or splenetic outbreaks". Then why did he write his letter? Why did he not take the trouble to read slowly at least once the article he was setting out to revile, or at any rate the passages he was specifically attacking? And does he seriously propose to say nothing about what we are fighting for – "to encourage our brave boys at the front" – until – when? Until peace has been signed? I am dazzled by this learned and emotional gentleman.

H. G. Wells

---

[1] Wells's views continued to attract attention. He wrote a piece in the *Chronicle* called 'The Liberal Aim in the War: Why Should We Not discuss the Terms of Peace', on 4 May 1915. In it he suggested that a clear statement of war aims would help define the war better. Holland Rose replied to this article and Wells responded with this letter and the next. Rose (1855–1942) was the author of *Nationality as a Factor in Modern History* (London: Macmillan, 1916), and *The Origins of the War* (1915).

1024. To the Editor, *Daily Chronicle*[1]

PLS

[London] May 10, 1915

Sir, – If it pleases Dr. Holland Rose to declare that I said Britain was "weary" of the war when I said we were all bored by it and determined to end this Prussian business once for all, and that when I wrote "coast waters" I meant islands or coast or something else quite different, I can do no more than ask your readers not to believe him.

Nothing will ever shake my conviction that war and militrarism are regarded by the bulk of British people as intolerable bores, and that Prussianised Germany is being fought today not as a "rival for world empire", or anything of that silly sort, but as an outrageous world nuisance. It is absurd to trifle with the idea that this Prussian system of violent fools with their murder gas and their murder submarines should be left in possession of a yard of territory that is not strictly German, or with any access to the high seas. It is like questioning the wisdom of stopping rat-holes. Why Dr. Holland Rose should insist upon telling falsehoods about my suggestions puzzles me extravagantly. I never proposed the annexation of the "Frisian Islands", in that article. He has lost his sense of the meaning of words and of the elementary necessities of controversy.

H. G. Wells

[1] This letter, published 11 May 1915, continued the debate but it was somewhat overshadowed by the sinking of the *Lusitania* in this same week. Directly below Wells's letter is a six stanza poem, 'Lusitania' by Harold Begbie, with the opening lines, 'Who that can strike a blow/Now will refrain?/Who with the right to go/Now will remain?'

1025. To the Editor, *The Times*[1]

PLS

52, St. James's Court
Buckingham Gate, S.W. [*c.* 12 May 1915]

Sir, – It is with extreme distress that every reasonable British patriot must see the growth of a blood feud between the British and German peoples arising out of the atrocious war methods of the German government, and with, if possible, greater concern must he mark the large amount of stimulation this blood feud is receiving both in the Liberal and Conservative Press. Nothing can better serve the purpose of our enemies, nothing can inflict worse injuries upon humanity at large, than to hold each and every German accountable for the offences of the German Government and war control. Few of us wish to minimize the blackness of these crimes or to think that they will go unpunished, but to avenge them upon poor little barbers, upon prisoners of war, and unlucky naturalized Germans is, surely, not only the most contemptible, but the most foolish of retorts. I do not think I am a mawkish sentimentalist in this matter; I would assist very cheerfully indeed in the immersion of the Kaiser or any of his sons, or any one of the German higher command, in a pit of his own poison gas: I would be glad to have such a lynching on my conscience; I am all against fighting with the gloves on when the enemy fights foul; but these attacks upon insignificant and in ninety-nine cases out of a hundred quite innocent spirited individuals is an altogether different thing. [2] It plays the game of our real enemies, the Krupp-Kaiser group, the Prussian Court influences that have dominated and poisoned the whole Press and educational system of Germany, because it rallies about them in a common defensive the whole nation that we seek to liberate from their influence. Only too gladly will this system of wickedness escape the reckoning under the clouds and blind anger of a race war. All of us who have German and German-born friends know that they are amenable and reasonable human beings, neither better nor worse than the run of English people and as little malignant. It is to Germans finally that we must look for the reconstruction of Germany upon pacific and civilized lines; and it is abominable that a mere handful of scurrilous journalists, jealous brokers and butchers, and filching hooligans – many of them of serviceable age – should be allowed to falsify the issues of this war and discredit us in the eyes of the world.

Yours, etc.,

H.G. Wells

[1] Wells distinguished sharply between the German leadership, the alliance of Krupp with the Kaiser as he termed it, and the German people who he felt were not the real enemy. This piece appeared on 14 May 1915 under the heading, 'Playing the Enemy's Game'.

[2] A number of regrettable incidents had occurred involving people with German names and accents. A rough sort of street 'justice' had been applied. Most British people found it abhorrent.

1025. To the Editor, *The Times*[1]

PLS

[London] [*c.* 9 June 1915]

Dear Sir,

We have reconstructed our government & it is not for an innocent Englishman outside the world of politicians to summarize the advantages and disadvantages of the arrangement of the House of Commons. But there is a matter beyond the range of party politics which does still seem to need attention and which has been extraordinarily disregarded in all the discussions that led to the present Coalition and this is the very small part we are still giving the scientific mind and the small respect we are showing scientific method in the conduct of the war. I submit there is an urgent need to bring imaginative enterprise and our utmost resources of scientific knowledge to the assistance of the new-born energies of the Coalition; that this is not being done and that until it is done this war is likely to drag on and be infinitely more costly and infinitely less conclusive than it could and should be.

Modern war is essentially a struggle of gear and invention. It is not war under permanent conditions. In that respect it differs completely from pre-Napoleonic wars. Each side must be perpetually producing new devices, surprising and outwitting its opponent. Since this war began the German methods of fighting have changed again and again. They have produced novelty after novelty and each novelty has saved their men and unexpectedly destroyed ours. On our side we have produced hardly any novelty at all, except in the field of recruiting posters. It is high time that our rulers and our people come to recognize that the mere accumulation of great masses of men in khaki is a mere preliminary to the prosecution of the war. These masses make the body of an army, but neither its neck, head nor hands nor feet. In the field of aviation, for which the English and French temperaments are far better adapted than the German, there has been no energy of organization at all. There has been great individual gallantry and a magnificent use of the sparse material available, but no great development. We have produced an insufficient number of aviators and dribbled out an inadequate supply of machines. Insufficient and inadequate, that is to say, to such a war as this. We have taken no steps to produce larger and more fighting aeroplane capable of overtaking, fighting and destroying a Zeppelin, and we are as far as ever from making any systematic attacks in force through the air. Our utmost acheivements have been made by flights of a dozen or so machines. In the matter of artillery the want of intellectual and imaginative enterprise in our directors has prevented our keeping pace with the German improvements in trench construction; our shortage of high explosive has been notorious, and it has led us to the sacrifice of thousands of lives. Our Dardanelles exploit has been throughout unforeseeing and uninventive; we have produced no counterstroke to the enemy's submarine, and no efficient protection against his torpedoes. We still have to make an efficient use of poison gas and of armoured protection in advances against machine-guns in trench warfare. And so throughout almost the entire range of our belligerent activities, we are to this day being conservative, imitative, and amateurish when victory can fall only to the most vigorous employment of the best scientific knowlege of all conceivable needs and material. One instance of many will illustrate what I am driving at. Since this war began we have been piling up infantry recruits by the million and making strenuous efforts to equip them with rifles. In the meantime the actual experiences of the war have been fully verifying the speculations of imaginative theorists, and the Germans have been learning from their experiences. The idea that for defensive purposes one well-protected man with a small machine-gun is better than a row of rifleman is very obvious indeed, but we have disregarded it. The Germans are giving up the crowding of men for defensive (though the weakness of the national quality obliges them still to mass for attacks), and they are entrusting their very small and light machine-guns in many places to officers. They have, in fact, adopted for their 1915 model of trench defence the proper scientific thing. Against this we fire our shrapnel and hurl our infantry.

Now these inadequacies are not incurable failures. But they are likely to go on until we create some supplementary directive force, some council in which the creative factors in our national life, and particularly our scientific men and our younger scientific soldiers and sailors, have a fuller representation and stronger influence than they have in our present Government. It is not the work for which a great legal and political career fits a man. That training and experience, valuable as it is in the management of men and peoples, does indeed largely unfit men for this incessantly inventive work. A modern politician has no more special aptitude for making war than he has for diagnosing diseases or planning an electric railway system. It is a technical business. We want an acting sub-Government of scientific and technically competent men for this highly specialized task.

Such a sub-Government does in effect exist in Germany. It is more and more manifest that we are fighting no longer against that rhetorical system of ancient pretensions of which the Kaiser is the figure-head. In Flanders we are now up against the real strength of Germany; we are up against Westphalia and Frau Krupp's young men. Britain and France have to get their own brilliant young engineers and chemists to work against that splendid organization. Unless our politicians can add to the many debts we owe them, the crowning service of organizing science in war more thoroughly than they ever troubled to do it in peace, I do not see very great hope of a really glorious and satisfactory triumph for us in this monstrous struggle.

Very sincerely yours,

H.G. Wells

---

[1] By the Summer of 1915, with the war nearly a year old, it was clear to most observers that, even with a concentrated effort, the war was far from over. It was about this time that Wells began working on a method of sending information to the front lines by collapsible telephone and telegraph poles. He called this system 'telpherage', and it was widely discussed among military figures. He patented the invention, see Rose V. Tilly, 'The Search for Wells's Ropeways', *The Wellsian*, n.s. no. 9. This letter, under the heading, 'The Mobilisation of Invention' is a call for further inventive work to be done. It appeared on 11 June 1915.

1027. To the Editor, *The Times*[1]

PLS

[Easton Glebe
Dunmow] [*c.* 20 June 1915]

Sir, – The letter I ventured to send you some 10 or 12 days ago on the necessity of mobilizing our scientific and inventive forces has received so much attention that I am emboldened to send you some further remarks upon points that have arisen in my mind as an outcome of this discussion.

The present drift of things seems to be towards a committee or committees of distinguished men as a first step toward this mobilization, such, for example, is the suggestion of Principal Griffiths, and such is the proposal of Professor Armstrong. It is, however, possible to doubt whether a committee, even a small committee, would be the most suitable instrument to direct this particular business of rapidly taking up, examining, testing, and rejecting or developing new ideas. Committees are slow Parliamentary things, they do not so much divide as disperse responsibility, and what is needed here is promptitude and a single purpose. I believe that to bring about most rapidly and efficiently the application of our available sources of science and invention to the present war a more concentrated direction, possibly even a single person, supported by a proper organization, would be better. The direction itself must not be specialist. A direction possessing rather a high general intelligence than any great specialized knowledge is needed to correlate specialists. One wants a minor minister with something of the catholic understanding of Mr. Balfour and something of the push of Mr. Lloyd George. The task, when one comes to look into it, is not, I think, nearly so big or vague as it loomed at the first proposal. Quite a small organization might produce immense consequences in this matter. Let me by way of illustration sketch out what I may call a science and invention bureau as I would like to see it in operation.

Essentially I see it as a small department collateral rather than subordinate to the War Office and Admiralty. Neither of those actively fighting departments can at the same time fight and also conduct research and experiment; the mental states of the two procedures are antagonistic. No active administrative department can ever, I think, be expected to be continually innovating. The Admirality and the War Office in particular are both too occupied with the urgencies of the present struggle to entertain anything but completely worked-out ideas and fully demonstrated inventions. They cannot disperse their attention. Now the business of the bureau would be to stand between these great administrative departments and the flood of crude and imperfect suggestions that beats upon them so distractingly and unavailingly; it will examine, test and develop them, and present such as are found suitable in a finished form ready to find use in the fighting department. The bureau, I think, would do its work best if it were a responsible official bureau, because then it would have comparatively free access to official information; it would know more exactly what was being done and what needed to being done. Its directorate could be under military discipline as regards importing and discussing its secrets. That, however, is the ideal state of affairs. It would be quite possible for it to do a very considerable amount of useful and helpful work as a semi-official or even a merely sanctioned volunteer body, and that is the form in which I am making this present suggestion.

The organization of this board would consist first of an index (with a suitable system of cross references) of all the men and women with special scientific and technical knowledge and ability available, who could be called upon with advice, help and work upon the problems that would be its essential business. This index could be compiled very rapidly with the help and advice of the proprietors and editor of Nature and of the various leading technical journals, supplemented by the secretaries of our numerous scientfic and technical societies. If the people on this could be officially embodied as a scientific force, as a corps or services, so much the better. Secondly, the bureau would maintain a list of laboratories, institutions, and places free for experimental work. Under the educational department alone at the present time there must be very considerable resources for investigaton and experiment which are not being utilized for our national needs, and there are also numerous private laboratories. Thirdly, the bureau would need funds. These funds would be under the control of a small special committee which would sanction the directorates appropriations. This much would constitute the working body of the bureau; it's head and intelligence would be the director's office, or rather the directorial cranium, into which would come on the one hand a confused tumult of proposals and inventions from outside and from the War Office and the Admiralty an occasional inquiry or demand arising out of the experience and necessities of the war. Its business would be to convey the digested residuum of the former to the fighting departments, and, under suitable precautions, to see to the requisitions of the latter. The bureau, acting through the director's office would essentially be a clearing-house of ideas. It would weed out the absurd and impossible – probably 99 per cent of the matter sent it – it would sort and set aside for development the under-developed but intelligent suggestions; from its index it would develop a galaxy of capable and willing consultants to whom these suggestions, or questions arising out of these suggestions, would be submitted and promptly attended to, and it would in suitable cases provide funds, and immediately or mediately, direct trials and experiments. Except perhaps, in so far, as its waste-paper basket was concerned and the possible need for some convenient place for the receipt and rapid return of models and specimens – South Kensington could probably find a shed for that – the bureau need not be more than quite a small office; but I believe that its activities might be of incalcuable service in discovering, making available, and bringing into action methods by which this war might be hastened to a victorious end.

It would be interesting to see what promises of support for such an experiment as I have here indicated, are forthcoming – if it were decided to carry it out upon unofficial lines. What are needed are promises of subscriptions if the bureau materializes, promises of help from men of established scientific and technical positions, and offers of laboratory accommodations. What is still more essential is Government sanction and some access on the part of the directorate to confidential information. Given a satisfactory prospect of these four things, it will be possible to start at once in the long-delayed business of sorting out and developing inventive suggestions. The business of such a bureau might be made to-day; it might be at work within a week, it might be producing effects at the front within a month or six weeks of the present date.

Very truly yours,

H.G. Wells

---

[1] This appeared on 22 June 1915, under the headline, 'The Embodiment of Science. Mr. Wells's Plan. A Bureau for Inventors'. A spirited correspondence followed his suggestion.

1028. To an unknown addressee

Milwaukee, ALS

52, St. James's Court
S.W. [date unknown, *c.* July 1915]

Dear Sir,

No. – I think Lord Fisher <u>is</u> the man & very certainly the member you name isn't. Under Lord Fisher, who is a big figure & one <u>under whom all scientific men will willingly work</u>, there will be a bureau of energetic officials &

temporary volunteers & the department will not confine itself to naval requirements.

Very sincerely yours,
H.G. Wells

1029. To the Editor, *The Times*[1]

PLS

52, St. James's Court
Buckingham Gate, S.W. [*c.* 6 July 1915]

Sir, – Mr. G. H. Rayner writes to me complaining that you have stated that the correspondence upon the need for some organization of our inventive resources, which preceded the organization of Lord Fisher's new department, was "initiated" by myself. Mr. G.H. Rayner had written to you in the matter and you had printed his letter a week or so before the appearance of mine. The need for the thing had become so manifest that it is highly improbable that either Mr. Rayner's letter or my own had the slightest influence upon the developments that were afoot; but as Mr. G. H. Rayner seems to attach importance to this priority I shall be glad if you will acknowledge his claim to whatever initiative can be claimed in the matter.

Very truly yours,
H.G. Wells

[1] This letter appeared on 8 July 1915 under the headline 'Mobilization of Invention'.

1030. To Thomas Seccombe

Korn, ALS

Easton Glebe [Summer 1915]

Dear Seccombe,

Have you read Boon?

I'm sorry you're not a neighbour of the '<u>only woman writer who</u>

matters'.[1] I hope some day you'll call & see her. You needn't wait for my introductions.

Why not come and see the Glebe? Next week i.e. today fortnight, we are free for the weekend.

Yours ever,
H.G.

---

[1] Rebecca West

1031. To Fisher Unwin[1]

Illinois, ALS (Photostat)

Little Easton Rectory
Dunmow [1915?]

Mr. Reginald Bliss, whose little known manuscript treatise, "Whale in Captivity", attracted the attention of discerning critics some years ago has secured the now not uncommon privilege of a preface from Mr. H. G. Wells & his new book which bears the lengthy title of "The Mind of the Race, the Wild Asses of the Devil & the Last Trump", will be published by Mr. T. Fisher Unwin early in ____.

It is a discursive survey of contemporary intelligence illustrated with a number of curious pen and ink sketches by the author. It includes a description of the organization of a kind of literary Chautauqua conference of our literary world, a novel in the manner of Mr. Henry James, an informal & a celestial short story & many other matters of interest. Mr. Bliss is still a comparatively young man & has all the irreverance of youth. His father, under another name, is well known in the jam and pickle world & he himself is a graduate of Magdalen College Cambridge & a member of the A. F. C. He is unmarried but a structural defect in his shoulders has prevented his serving his country in the present crisis. He is a voracious reader of contemporary literature & he lives in a modest cottage near the village of High Easter in Essex, coming only very rarely to London & avoiding all avoidable social intercourse.

---

[1] This item is located in the Fisher Unwin files at Illinois in a photostat form. It appears to be a letter, probably not published, as a possible way of introducing 'Reginald Bliss', Wells's pseudonym in the first edition of his pastiche of Henry James's work, *Boon*.

Portraits of various celebrities. (Wild Asses)
By one who has never seen them. Features entirely deduced from public utterances.

Harold Begbie

St Loe Strachey

Mr Richard Le Gallienne

J. L. Garvin

Archbishop of Canterbury If he doesn't look like this then he ought to do so.

Editor of the Westminster Gazette

1032. To Henry James

Illinois, TCC

[London] July 8th, 1915

My dear James,

You write me so kind and frank a letter after my offences that I find it an immense embarrassment to reply to you. I have set before myself a gamin-esque ideal, I have a natural horror of dignity, finish and perfection, a horror a little enhanced by theory. You may take it that my sparring and punching at you is very much due to the feeling that you were "coming over" me, and that if I was not very careful, I should find myself giving way altogether to respect. There is of course a real and very fundamental difference in our innate and developed attitudes towards life and literature. To you literature like painting is an end, to me literature like architecture is a means, it has a use. Your view was, I felt, altogether too dominant in the world of criticism, and I assailed it in tones of harsh antagonism. And writing that stuff about you was the first escape I had from the obsession of this war. Boon is just a waste-paper basket. Some of it was written before I left my home in Sandgate, and it was while I was turning over some old papers that I came upon it, found it expressive and went on with it last December. I had rather be called a journalist than an artist, that is the essence of it, and there was no other antagonist possible than yourself. But since it was printed I have regretted a hundred times that I did not express our profound and incurable difference and contrast with a better grace. And believe me, my dear James, your very keenly appreciative reader, your warm if rebellious and resentful admirer, and for countless causes yours most gratefully and affectionately.

H.G. Wells[1]

---

[1] James suffered a serious stroke on 5 December 1915 while correcting the proofs on Rupert Brooke's *Letters From America.* On 18 December a letter was sent to the Prime Minister from A. J. Balfour, G. Barker, J. M. Barrie, Arnold Bennett, Edmund Gosse, Sidney Colvin, Austin Dobson, John Galsworthy, Lord Rosebery, J. S. Sargent, H. G. Wells and George Wyndham urging the award of the Order of Merit to James. Up to that time only Hardy and Meredith had received the honour for their literary careers. It was granted on 20 December 1915; James had become an English citizen earlier in the year.

1033. To Robbie Ross[1]

Leeds, ALS

Easton Glebe
Dunmow

[sometime in 1915]

Dear Ross,

Gosse 70! We age also. Herewith is my humble contribution.

Yours ever,
H.G.

[1] This manuscript letter is located in the Gosse collection in a box labelled "70th Birthday Box". Another hand has added Wells to the signature.

1034. To St John Ervine[1]

Texas, ALS

52, St. James's Court
Buckingham Gate, S.W.

[Summer 1915?]

Dear Ervine,

I forgot your visit. Since then I've gone to Essex & all sorts of things have happened. Perhaps some day when my house in Essex is finished – the war has caught me [*illegible word*] – you'll lunch with us again. Essex is a county of extravagant freedoms for Sunday afternoons. We play hockey & our Sunday lunch is open & promiscuous. But all that waits on the builders now.

Yours very sincerely,
H.G.Wells

[1] There are several letters about the dramatization of *The Wonderful Visit* and none are dated. Their location and order is a matter of conjecture.

1035. To St John Ervine

Texas, ANS

Easton Glebe
Dunmow [Summer 1915?]

Dear Mr. Ervine,

Warmest thanks for the book. I hope to read about in it again later. When the war is over, I hope you'll come here & play in our great [*illegible word*] hockey match.

Yours ever,
H. G. Wells

1036. To St John Ervine

Texas, ANS

Easton Glebe
Dunmow [Summer 1915?]

Dear St. John Ervine,

I've read your book with very great interest for many reasons. It's really good work, though not so complete & subjective as Mr. Martin's man; but it's a happy thing you've done. I'm getting more & more in love with the idea of writing with a sort of historical gesture & I'm glad to think you're moving in the same way. A lot of your characters are phantoms & adaptations of people I've known. It's interesting to see that you have changed them. I'm obliged to you – about Ireland, you as an Irishman can say things that an Englishman doesn't care to say. I hope when the war is over that we may see something of you & your belongings here.

Yours ever,
H. G. Wells

1037. To St John Ervine

Texas, ALS

Easton Glebe
Dunmow [Summer 1915?]

Dear Ervine,

Jane goes to Cornwall with my family next week & so she can't come to any dramatic reading. And I am very restive being read to. Let me know when you are quite ready.

Yours ever,
H.G. Wells

1038. To Edmund Gosse

Leeds, ALS

52, St James's Court
Buckingham Gate, S.W. [Summer 1915?]

My dear Gosse

In the matter of Gissing, the substance of my article was embodied in a very good book on Gissing by Frank Swinnerton, who is by way of being an authority on G.G. There is also an atrocious inaccurate account of Gissing by Morley Roberts. Gissing is called "Henry Maitland"(title of book). I am "Pensus" & so on. Roberts found a clue to much that is otherwise inexplicable in Gissing's life in the fact that he got syphilis from his first wife & he rushed into print with his "revelation".

Yours ever
H. G. Wells

1039. To Edmund Gosse

Leeds, ANS

Easton Glebe
Dunmow [Summer 1915?]

My dear Gosse,

The memoir was published in the Monthly Review of August 1904. There is a copy somewhere in this house but I can't put my hand on it or I would send it to you.

Very sincerely
H. G. Wells

1040. To Edmund Gosse

Leeds, ALS

52, St James's Court
Buckingham Gate, S.W. [Summer 1915?]

Dear Gosse,

The suppression of that introduction was just one of those painful incidents that abound in literary history. Miss Collett who was Gissing's literary executor & who was highly emotional at the time kicked up a fuss because it was not respectful to G's memory – mentioned his early poverty & so on. She incited the Miss Gissings to object. The introduction was withdrawn & as Constable thought the prospects of the book [*illegible word*] by the withdrawal the estate was robbed of £50. In addition she went to various people in order to prevent a person of my notorious depravity being trustee for the civil list pension which I helped get for the sons. You helped too, you will remember. Thanks to her, though I & Whale have been trustees up to the expiration of the pension, we have never set eyes on these boys since G's death. We have just paid over the money to the no doubt indignant sister of Gissing. We have never had a line from the sons who are now both of age & in the army.

Yours ever
H. G. Wells

1041. To St John Adcock

Bromley, ALS

Little Easton Rectory
Dunmow [Summer 1915]

Dear Mr. Adcock.

Thanks very much. Of course all Foul Language & so on doesn't imply anything but the warmest good will toward St Thomas.

Yours ever
H. G. Wells

1042. To Holbrook Jackson[1]

Bromley, ALS

[The Reform Club
Pall Mall] [*c.* October 1915]

Dear Jackson,

I've just seen your very kind review of my book in T.P.[2] I pretend generally to an Olympian disregard of reviews but, to tell you an intimate secret, I've been frightfully sore about the early reviews of the R.M., & your generous estimate has lifted a very disagreeable load from my mind. I thought great things of the book as I was doing it & I was really hurt & scared by (for example) Lynd's review in the Daily News.[3]

Yours ever
H.G. Wells

[1] Jackson (1874–1948) was a writer and critic and one of the founders of the *New Age*. They had met during the Fabian days.
[2] *T.P.'s Weekly.* The book was *The Research Magnificent.*
[3] Robert Lynd wrote reviews primarily for the *Daily News*.

1043. To the Editor, *The Times*[1]

PL

[London?] [*c.* 2 November 1915]

[Sir. -] Now that something like a systematic appeal is at last being made to eligible men, instead of the vague Press ravings, the ridiculous placards and street-corner insults that have hitherto figured as "recruiting", I do not doubt the readiness and sufficiency of the response. There is, I feel, little need for exhortation. Few people in England desire to shirk their proper share in the war; if many have held back hitherto, it is mainly because they have been quite unable to find out how and where they could be used to the best advantage, or because they have doubted whether they would be used to the best advantage.

[1] *The Times*, 3 November 1915, p. 5

1044. To Woodrow Wilson[1]

PLS

[London] [15 November 1915]

To the President of the United States,
White House, Washington, D.C.

Sir, -

We understand that Mrs. Margaret Sanger is in danger of criminal prosecution for circulating a pamphlet on birth-problems. We therefore beg to draw your attention to the fact that such work as that of Mrs. Sanger receives appreciation and circulation in every civilised country except the United States of America, where it is still counted as a criminal offense.

We in England passed, a generation ago, through the phase of prohibiting the expressions of serious and disinterested opinion on a subject of such great importance to humanity, and in our view to suppress any such treatment of vital subjects is detrimental to human progress.

Hence, not only for the benefit of Mrs. Sanger, but of humanity, we respectfully beg you to exert your powerful influence in the interests of free speech and the betterment of the race.

We beg to remain, sir,
Your humble servants,

Leona Ashwell	Ed. Carpenter	Dr. Percy Acres
Aylmer Maude	William Archer	Prof. Gilbert Murray
Arnold Bennett	M.C. Stopes	H.G. Wells

[1] This letter was circulated for signature by Marie Stopes, when it became clear that Margaret Sanger was likely to be jailed because of her challenge to New York State laws forbidding transport of birth control materials. It was published in the 15 November 1915 issue of the *Malthusian* (London), pp. 85–6.

1045. To the Editor, *Daily Chronicle*

PLS

London [16? December 1915]

Sir, -

I see that in your issue of December 14 Dr. Saleeby tries to make out that I am personally responsible for some pamphlet of the Malthusian League, which I have never seen, and which I understand from the secretary of the society he grossly misrepresents.[1] In common with a number of other people I am a vice-president of that league, but that, of course, is no reason why Dr. Saleeby should pick out my single name in this way. I have nothing to do with the counsels of the society, and have attended no meetings. It is becoming a habit with Dr. Saleeby to try to fasten upon me views and suggestions that are other than those I hold. One opinion of mine, however, he declines to discuss, and that is my frequently expressed and carefully demonstrated opinion that "Eugenics" is a sham science, with no stuff of any work behind it. Years ago I slew that sham in "Mankind in the Making", and Dr. Saleeby, who goes on declaring it is alive, has still to produce a reply to my exhaustive condemnation.

H.G. Wells

[1] Wells and his colleagues in the Neo-Malthusian League were under constant attack on the subject of 'eugenics' or the practice of somehow improving the quality of the species through selected breeding. This correction appeared on 18 December 1915. The Hon. Secretary of the League, Dr B. Dunlop, also responded. The pamphlet under discussion was issued in 1914, at the beginning of the war, urging people to produce fewer children, as wartime demands on food would create serious health problems among the poor.

1046. To the Editor, *Daily Chronicle*[1]

PLS

Easton Glebe
Dunmow [*c.* 25 December 1915]

Sir, -

Dr. Saleeby persists in declaring that a certain pamphlet, for which I am no more responsible than you are for the 'science' of Dr. Saleeby, "bears my name", in the manifest hope that for some obscure controversial reason he will create an impression that I am answerable for its contents. Of course it does not "bear my name" in the sense he wants your reader to take the phrase. My name, if it is on the pamphlet at all, is probably on the back cover with that of a number of other people in a list of vice-presidents and supporters of the society. I am about as responsible for its contents as a Fellow of the Royal Society is responsible for a statement in the Philosophical Transactions. Your readers, after this specimen of Dr. Saleeby's controversial methods, will be still better able to enjoy his statement that my criticisms of the so-called science of eugenics in a book published in 1903, and still very much alive, were answered and disposed of by some personalities about my scientific knowledge – no doubt quite on the lines of the present instance – in a book published in 1909, and already dead.

H.G. Wells

[1] Two days later, Dr Saleeby returned to his attack on Wells, which elicited this letter. It appeared in the *Daily Chronicle*, 27 December 1915.

1047. To Booth Austin[1]

Texas, ALS

52, St James's Court
Buckminster Gate, S.W. Saturday [?1915]

Dear Booth Austin,

Damn you! I've just got home after weeks away, illness & convalescence, & I find heaps & heaps of things to attend to & here have I been sitting the best part of an hour, reading Zu Befell & Peace & The Spy, with all the letters unwritten. I shall finish the book before long, though I haven't the time to read anything. I think what I have read is about the best stuff of yours I have seen.

Yours ever
H. G. Wells

[1] Booth Austin was a name taken by Frederick Britten Austin, (1885–1941) a writer of juvenile stories, mainly for *The Chum*, as well as some futuristic fiction. He was the author of many short stories; several, written before the war, predicted a war between Germany and England.

1048. To Fisher Unwin

Illinois, ALS

52, St James's Court
Buckingham Gate, S.W. [?1915]

Dear Fisher Unwin.

I think it is tactless to poke the sentence (in cutting enclosed) into the faces of the public & to use it in the advertisement. The title is the best selling thing you have & this really gives away what it is far better to let the reviews disclose. Also it comes near to a breach of our agreement that you should not claim me as the author.[1]

Yours very sincerely
H. G. Wells

[1] Fisher Unwin had just published Wells's parody of Henry James, *Boon*. At this time the book was being treated as the book of Bliss, even though virtually everyone knew Wells was the author.

1049. To Fisher Unwin

Illinois, ALS

Easton Glebe
Dunmow [*c*. 1915]

Dear Fisher Unwin,

Glad you liked the articles & very glad of your note. I think you take my vivid experiences too much to heart.

Yours ever
Warmly
H. G. Wells

1050. To Fisher Unwin

Illinois, ANS

Little Easton Rectory
Dunmow [*c*. 1915]

Dear Fisher Unwin.

No! I belong to the Friends of British Freedom & we leave Russia to the (Gentile) Russians.

Yours ever,
H. G.

1051. To Mrs Braley[1]

Hofstra, ALS

52, St James's Court
Buckingham Gate, S.W. [1915–16]

Dear Mrs. Braley

Many thanks for the Lynd Hossain papers & my apologies for giving you the trouble of sending them on.

Very sincerely yours,
H. G. Wells

[1] Mrs. Braley is not known

1052. To Canon Deane

Hofstra, ALS

52, St James's Court
Buckingham Gate, S.W. [1915–16]

Dear Canon Deane.

Your review of the Great Enchantress is delightful. If I were you I should publish – which is why I am an unpopular man.

I will try & get at you in a week or so for that talk.

Yours ever
H. G. Wells

1053. To Mr Pond

Hofstra, ALS

Little Easton Rectory
Dumow [1915]

Dear Mr. Pond.

No, unless I have an absolute guarantee of the sum named it isn't worth my while. It's quite true about my voice. I can't make myself heard & I should have to go into training for a big meeting. So let us consider this thing off for a time.

Yours very sincerely
H. G. Wells

1054. To Mr March

Hofstra, ALS

Little Easton Rectory
Dunmow [1915]

Dear Mr. March.

Thank you very much for your very sympathetic criticism of the Passionate Friends & for your continuing interest in my work.

Yours very sincerely,
H. G. Wells

1055. To the Editor, *Daily Chronicle*[1]

PLS

[London] [*c* . 30 January 1916]

Sir, – A week or so ago you published two articles from me, in which I discussed the probable end of the war. I suggested the war is now in a state of deadlock which will be terminated only by the exhaustion and collapse of one or the other belligerent. I threw doubts upon the possibility of "breaking through" until a stage of exhaustion, at present remote, was reached. But I thought I made clear, that so far as I could judge, it was Germany which was to be exhausted first, and Germany, which in view of French gallantry, and Russian and British toughness, was most likely to begin the squealing. At the same time, someone else – somewhere else – seems to have thrown out the idea that this war will end in a "draw". That is an altogether different proposition, to which I do not subscribe. I believe that we are going to win this war as firmly as I did on the day that war was declared – much more firmly.

I would not trouble you with this endorsement of what I wrote, if it were not that, from Press cuttings which have come to hand, that one or two journalists, who read my article lightly and carelessly, and who lack the intelligence to discriminate between deadlock and draw, are telling their readings that I have joined the "call it a draw" school of pacifism. I find on my table, for example, a long and particularly silly article from an evening paper, in which I am declared to have gone back upon the very obvious things I wrote at the outset of the war; upon the necessity of liberating various non-German territories from German control. There is a sort of chattering contrast of what I am supposed to have said and what I am supposed to say now. It would be sheer lying if it were not palpably only stupidity. This war, because of our unscientific methods, our wastefulness, our administrative pettiness, and our contempt and distrust of novelty, is going to be a vastly longer, slower, bloodier, and more distressing business than I expected it to be. Apart from that I have not changed any opinion I have ever expressed about it.

H.G. Wells

---

[1] This letter was published 1 February 1916, under the title 'No Drawn War'. This letter was written just five months before the opening of the Battle of the Somme.

1056. To Marie Butts[1]

Illinois, ALS

Easton Glebe
Dunmow [14 February 1916]

Dear Miss Butts,

Thank you for a very interesting and helpful letter. It is so friendly & sympathetic that I will at once presume on it to write to you as if we had known each other for some time. You want to join on to something. Well, I don't know anything to join on to just at present at all. The sort of things that you & I & quite a lot of other people have been thinking, has not crystallized & don't seem to crystallize into societies & churches & associations. I have been thinking a lot about what is to hold us – the others & you & me – together in some sort of coordination. I'm setting down some of that thinking. What we are getting to is God – not the bland trinity or any of that.[2] But I can't hurry the expression of that idea. I'm writing it quite differently from any other work that I have ever done, writing & rewriting it & setting it aside. I think I should have something to publish next year. And that's all that I can tell you now by way of answer to your chief question.

You ask also a lesser one about my translations into French. The trouble of getting my work done in to French has been in great confusion for some years but now it is getting into order in the hands of Mlle. Suzanne Magereau (14 Quai Jean Fouquet Laval). She's working very hard to keep pace with what I am doing at the present time. If you can see your way to getting parts of "An Englishman" etc.[3] done (in French) & published in Switzerland, I shall be glad if you would consult her.

Your position in Switzerland tempts me also to ask you to help on a matter on which I am rather at a loss. I have written a long novel representing the moods of England during the first year of the war. The chief character is an Englishman (rather in my position) who has a very charming German tutor for his younger sons. His eldest son is of military age. The last chapter of the book presents him writing a letter to the parents of the German tutor – he is returning the German boy's violin. His own son is dead in Flanders; the German is dead in Poland.[4] The letter is a sort of message from England to Germany. Well, it is a book I want to get into the hands of German readers. How is that to be done? Do you think I could get it translated into German and published in Switzerland. Can you do anything that will help me to do that?

Yours sincerely,

H.G. Wells

By an odd coincidence I met last week a Miss Mary Butts from Somerville [College]. Is she any connexion of yours?

---

[1] Marie, sometimes Mary, Butts established and ran a translation and literary agency in Geneva, with offices in France. When Wells met her is not known, but she became a good friend and correspondent of Catherine, and she was instrumental in obtaining quality translations of Wells's work, especially *The Outline of History*.

[2] The appalling death toll of the First World War led to a resurgence of religious fervour and Wells became caught up in this religious apotheosis. It is reflected in his wartime novel, *Mr Britling Sees It Through* and more explicitly in *God, the Invisible King*. Wells later repudiated

his book completely which was a sort of Deist theology. Butts had helped with the translation and the cutting of *Britling* for use in France and Germany.

[3] Wells's collection of articles, *An Englishman Looks at the World* was published early in 1914. Its American title was *Social Forces in England and America*.

[4] The German youth was based on Kurt Butow, who was a tutor to the Wells children. His letters about mobilisation, both in London and in Germany – for he left when war was declared – were used to great effect in the novel. Butow and Wells maintained contact until the early 1930s. Wells lent him money, which was repaid, and the letters from Butow (Wells's letters no longer exist apparently) are very moving, especially when Catherine Wells died in 1927. Wells's own children were not old enough to fight, and Butow survived. The accounts were so realistic that Wells received hundreds of sympathy cards, and the Chaplain's Corps put together a book of responses to *Britling* which were used to train chaplains before they went to the front lines.

1057. To the Editor, *Daily News*[1]

PLS

Easton Glebe
Dunmow

March 1, 1916

Sir, – It would be, I suppose, too good a thing for the world if our critics were sometimes critical and thought of the meaning of words, the value of contexts, and the connection of this and that in a man's writing. Mr. Lynd flings out at me an accusation that is bound to fester and rankle in the minds of his readers, that is one of the half-truths which are worse than a falsehood, when he accuses me of first adoring and then abusing Mr. Henry James.

Let me quote his words:

> Mr. Wells, who once hailed him as a
> master, recently compared him to a
> hippopotamus trying to pick up a pea.

Now there is a book called, "Boon", which Mr. Lynd chooses to ascribe to me, although as a matter of fact it is of blended origin, a discussion of Mr. James's novels and critical work by this fictitious character Boon. Obviously – even if I am responsible for this passage – it is a posed discussion, a devil's advocate statement, or why should it be so detached and "pseudonym'd". In it the tremendous mental power, the high quality of Mr. James, is insisted upon. It is a sustained lament upon the strong-mindedness of his artistic aims. The detraction is of the method, not of the man. Boon says:

It is leviathan retrieving pebbles. It is
a magnificent but painful hippopotamus.

Moreover, Boon does not say, as Mr. Lynd with his inaccurate memory would have you believe, that the hippopotamus is *trying* to pick up peas. He says it is picking up peas – "with a wealth of intellectual stuff that dwarfs Newton". Well! Is that loud praise of appreciation incompatible with the hailing of Mr. James as a master? He is a master. In "The American Scene", I hold, you may best measure his quality. At a hundred points, the work of every young man is different because of him.

H.G. Wells

---

[1] *Boon,* while published under a pseudonym, Reginald Bliss, was widely known to be Wells's book. The style was a rather cruel parody of Henry James's writing. Lynd responded to Wells in the next letter. These letters were exchanged after James's had died and were published on 3 and 4 March 1916.

1058. To the Editor, *Daily News*

PLS

[London] March 3, 1916

Sir, – I do not feel very guilty in regard to Mr. Wells. I said that Mr. Wells compared Henry James to a hippopotamus trying to pick up a pea. He retorts, that on the contrary – in so far as he is responsible for "Boon," – he compared Henry James to a hippopotamus that succeeded in picking up a pea. The misquotation is one for which I had no difficulty in forgiving myself.

Mr. Wells seems to have misunderstood the point of the quotation, which did not suggest for a moment that he had attacked Henry James as a man. I referred to him merely as an example of an intelligent person who had raised the question whether Henry James's art was worthwhile. Incidentally, I recalled as a point of some interest that Mr. Wells had at an earlier period believed that Henry James's art was very much worth while. I was thinking of the passage in "The Future In America", where Mr. Wells writes"

There exists already, of these
irresponsible American rich.
a splendid group of portraits,
some without extenuation and
without malice, in the later work
of that great master of fiction, Mr.
Henry James. I think of "The
Ambassadors", I think of "The
Golden Bowl", most spacious and
serene of novels.

Obviously, this view of Henry James is in flat contradiction of the view of Henry James expressed in "Boon". I concluded that Mr. Wells must have changed his mind. Mr. Wells, of course, has a perfect right to change his mind. And I have a perfect right to say he has changed it. I did so not as an "accusation", but as an interesting, though quite harmless, statement of fact. If I were Mr. Wells I shouldn't worry.[1]

Robert Lynd

[1] See letter 1032 for earlier items in this great literary struggle.

1059. To Romain Rolland[1]

Illinois, ADLS

[Easton Glebe
Dunmow] [5? March 1916]

My dear Romain Rolland,

There has come to me from Cambridge a translation of your book, "Above the Battle." I have been reading in it with a curious mixture of sympathy & distaste. We have in the past been correspondents; you must be assured of my profound admiration of your work & my warm assent to your general intentions.[2] I will not then dwell upon these permanent agreements, but I will proceed at once to tell you as clearly as I can why this last book of yours jars upon me and why I do not respond in the smallest measure to the complaints of martyrdom with which you preface it. You speak of those who have 'defended' you in the Parisian press, you refer to them as "comrades in the struggle". You complain, "I have been insulted". You state with a certain self-complacency, "In a year I have been rich in enemies. Let me say this to them, they can hate me, but they will not teach me to hate." And altogether your mind seems concentrated on the personal consequences of the extreme exasperation certain phrases and articles of yours, written from the security of Switzerland, have caused in France. I think your mind confuses these personal consequences with the idea of some "struggle" of which it is difficult to defend the issues. What precisely is the struggle in which you are engaged & in which you suffer these wrongs & hatreds? I have read your book very carefully and I cannot determine what it is you (& your Cambridge friends in this country) want or what you conceive you are up to. Except for a wilted aloofness from any effort or sacrifice, except for an expansion of the implications of your title, I can find no intimation of guidance. You are "Above the Battle"; you are wiser than anything that is said on either side; in a wiser world there would be no battle. That is the effect of your book upon me. Let us grant that. From the point of view of us who are in the battle, who struggle, no doubt clumsily, pitifully, & from the Swiss standpoint, with a grave loss of literary dignity, to defeat & discredit a militarist system that would not leave us alone & make a League with Russia and our other allies, for the peace of the world, your superiorities are, (forgive me), uninteresting. What are your proposals? What is the alternative in your mind that permits your systematic disengagement of them who fight against Germany?

But about these "insults" of which you write; is this really the time for us writing men to complain of the sufferings of the burked article or the uncivil or unjust repartee? I too have had my crosses. I could join grief to your grief. There have been paragraphs in the New Age, in Town Topics, rude paragraphs, disrespectful allusions in the Morning Post, a most distressing parody in the New Statesmen...The Censor also but I restrain myself.... And the Labour Leader, a paper rather affected by your Cambridge friends, published much ignorant and foolish matter about 'Tzardom' at the beginning of the war, drew me into an indignant controversy, and then not only refused to print my most crushing and conclusive comunication but paraphrased it misleadingly and abused me. You of all people will be able to undersand the acuteness of my sufferings under this – this dreadful persecution. Yet still I do not think that this is the sort of thing will constitute a serious grievance in this present time of stress and heroic effort. Passions are out. There are people not 'Above the Battle' but in it, who have undergone worse experiences even than you or I. They have suffered from terrible wounds, from gashes even worse, I am told, than the curb by editors & concussions worse than blows of the censor's stamp; they have undergone extremities of exhaustion; they have lost not merely readers, but brothers and sons; some have lost sisters and wives.

And moreover, my dear Rolland, is your conscience quite at peace upon the score either of the wisdom or the justice of all your writing? Let me quote but one sentence from the article that caused the resentment against you in France. You say: "And thus the three greatest nations of the West, the guardians of civilisation, rush headlong to their ruin, calling in to their aid Cossacks, Turks, Japanese, Cingalese, Soudanese, Senegalese, Moroccans, Egyptians, Sikhs, and Sepoys – barbarians from the poles and those of the equator, souls and bodies of all colours."

Now is this the Genuine Olympian note? To me it seems no better than the shriek of a wildly excited and intensely prejudiced mind that has got completely beyond self-control. I would not condemn you on the score of having written it. All of us odd people who write and overwork have our moments of wild expression, if this sort of thing is to damn a man there is scarcely a writer of standing who will not be damned. But it seems to me that after an accident of this sort it becomes a writer to do his utmost to suppress the consequences of it as soon as possible. Your best friends in France, whom you call your enemies, did what they could to anticipate your duty. But you, I learn, will not have that headlong passage suppressed. It is at the root of all your vast effect of grievance. You get it reprinted, you allow it to be translated and circulated here in England and America. Is this the obstinacy of an ill-advised writer or does this astonishing passage really summarize your mental attitude with the attitude of the people of the Cambridge Magazine who are responsible for its British publicity? Are you really so lost in the conceit of our western civilization that you can, after a year for reconsideration, endorse this wild & whirling passage? Is "Cossack" all you serene souls about the battle can say for Russia? Russia without whose aid & confidence no peaceful settlement can be possible! Do you really believe Egyptian, Sikh, Bengali, Cingalese and Japanese are less civilized that the Junkers & boors of west and east Prussia? And above all, what do you and your friends propose?

I come back to that question. The "Above the Battle" people in this country have recently been asking that our government should formulate our terms of peace, and continue to pretend that it has not done so, after it has done so in the plainest manner. Well, let me deal with a pacifist with pacifist weapons, and ask what are your terms of peace? What purpose lies behind all your lamentations about the universal violence, your discouragement of brave young men, your objections to our allies? Do you propose that we give way to Germany? Do you propose that each western country shall make a separate peace with Germany, getting what terms it can and leaving the "barbarians" in the lurch? Do you indeed propose anything at all? Do you indeed do anything whatever in this book of yours but make pathetic & futile gestures?

And if you do not, have you any right to complain that the general disregard of your high-toned aloofness, or the occasional suppression of some particularly mischievous statement, is an expression of "hate"? Nobody, my dear Rolland, hates you. But a great numer of those who toil and attempt down below "In the battle", who are convinced that only by sweat and agony and blundering and sacrifice & great generosities can any solution of our catastrophic problems be hammered out, do find your attitude, up there above the clouds in Switzerland, irritatingly self-important and irritatingly unhelpful.

Your constant admirer,
H.G. Wells

---

[1] This letter appears in holograph draft, in typescript with corrections and in a slightly different form in the *Daily Chronicle*, 7 March 1916 as 'Lament of a Pacifist: An Open Letter to M. Romain Rolland'. Rolland, (1866–1944) a French novelist, perhaps best remembered today for the massive *Jean Christophe*, 10 volumes, (1904–12) was awarded the Nobel Prize for Literature in 1915. He had recently written a book *Above the Battle* which prompted Wells's response to his acquaintance. Rolland lived in Switzerland from 1915 to 1938, and both here and after his return to France, mounted an intense attack on Nazi and totalitarian ideologies. The version of the letter printed here is the revised, typed version, of the holograph of this document.

[2] Further correspondence between the two men does not seem to have survived, at least in Wellsian archives.

1060. To Marie Butts

Illinois, ALS

Easton Glebe
Dunmow [19 March 1916]

Dear Miss Butts.

Very many thanks for your letter. With regard to the translation of the articles from An Englishman Looks At the World into French, I hope that Mlle Mergereau will put no difficulties in the way of your doing that. You may publish them in Switzerland upon any terms you like. When there are profits Mlle Mergereau & I share equally & I shall be very glad if you & I can do that also.

I will communicate with Pascher & Cie & I hope arrange that German edition. I am very greatly indebted to you for your help in this matter.

Of all contemporary journals the Nation is I think the most contemporary. Things are in a very black way just now in regard to criticism & discussion. We wrangle about the war & the conduct of the war. I think that there is little probability of any new beginnings until that is over.

Very sincerely yours
H. G. Wells

P.S. [*in Catherine's hand*]
In the matter of French translations of Eng. Looks at T. World please do not do anything until I can send you further particulars. Some of the essays have already been translated into French. I will send on a list of what is free for you.
Catherine Wells

1061. To Hedley Le Bas[1]

PLS

The Daily Chronicle

[London] [Late April 1916]

Dear Sir Hedley, – You did me the honour to ask me a little while ago to write exhortations about war economy for your movement. At the time I was rather entangled with some work that I thought mattered more. That is done now, but another retarding consideration still embarrasses me. On this subject, I cannot come into court, as the lawyer's say, with "clean hands." Let me give you some particulars, because they are of an instructive character. I have to confess that since this war began I have had all sorts of things done to my house and garden, and that I now perceive was wasting the national resources. The workers I employed ought to have been doing more productive work. But at the outset of the war I took counsel with the experts of the Fabian Society, and I was favoured with a printed "Memorandum of Suggestions"[2] foretelling cataclysmal unemployment, advising me to make work for as much labour as possible, exhorting local authorities to begin laying out public gardens and open spaces, and so on, and so on; and I was entirely mislead. It is well to note, therefore, that this matter of economy is by no means a simple one, that even "expert" advice, with all the wisdom of the School of Economics at its elbow, can be absolutely mischievous in these matters if it is not industriously critical and clear-headed. Moreover, I bought an American automobile at the end of 1914, in order to discontinue a hired car, and release a young man for the war. I was under the impression, which still prevails, that our primary need was men; that the conservation of national riches, was a secondary question. Of course, I should have bought an English car or none at all. With these two blunders on my conscience, blunders which have diverted some hundreds of pounds from the War Loan into which they ought to have gone, I must write, if I write at all, for your committee in a tone of considerable charity. I cannot get that nice superior feeling about the "wastefulness" of other people, of working people, for example, who have been getting extra clothes and boots, buying gramaphones, or going to the cinema, that is now so prevalent.

I find myself very clear now, at least, upon the essentials of the present situation. We have got to reduce all unnecessary consumption to a minimum, and to direct the energies of everyone not already in war service or fully busied on necessary work into the production of war material or of export goods that will serve to pay for war material. With the official and administrative side of the economy and conservation of energy your committee is not, I assume, concerned. Waste in the public service is outside your sphere and so I will not enlarge here upon the duty of everyone in or outside of the public services to watch for every sign of waste, and not to hesitate in calling attention as vigorously and effectively as possible to slackness, extravagance, and inefficiency in public or quasi-public arrangements. It is an excellent principle to mind one's own business, and at the present time, more than any previous time, public waste is everybody's business and its prevention everybody's foremost duty. But I take it you are concerned with merely (a) the question of control of one's own private expenditure, and (b) with the creation of a social atmosphere in which waste of every sort will be discouraged and discredited. Upon both of these issues, I will offer a few remarks.

It is not so very easy to determine what are permissible and advisable forms of economy at the present time. We are advised to turn off servants; but if the servants are elderly, not very competent, or otherwise unemployable, it is not a saving for the community as a whole to tumble them out upon the rate payer. It is merely shirking a personal duty. We are advised to dig up our lawns and grow vegetables, but if that involves the employment of more garden help or the retaining of possible agricultural labourers in garden work, it is a question whether our amateur and probably very wasteful horticulture is really not an injurious way of depriving the farmer of labour he could use far better off than we can. The absolute duty of turning off all indoor men servants and all able and intelligent women servants who can go into munitions making and export manufacture seems evident and straightforward. But it seems equally one's duty that they do get that other work, and to assist them to it. The case for new clothes and especially fashionable clothes seems equally made out. And here it is I come to (b) the question of social atmosphere. Modest, beautiful, inexpensive and unpretentious clothing is available for every woman who chooses to abandon the ideal of "smartness", and we can all contribute a little, even the street boy can give his help, in his own peculiar way, to the discouragement of feminine parade. A writer in the "New Statesman" has recently made a moving appeal to the ladies of society to promote this propaganda of economy, and certainly if the ladies eminent in politics and society, whose portraits, by a kind of necessity, appear from week to week in our illustrated newspapers, could be induced to utilize this unavoidable publicity in exemplifying the charm of simple and homely costume, there can be no doubt of the great influence their example would have on less distinguished and less original women of means.

We are all, I suppose, more prone to condemn extravagance in the fields of our own virtue, and so I can condemn smartness and expenditure upon fashion very readily. I dislike bedded out plants, too, and I suggest as another excellent economy for this year that there should be a truce in "bedding out" in everybody's garden. And remote from any temptation on my own account, I cannot see why we should let hunting and game preserving go on any longer. I am scandalised by the exemption of hunt servants from military service, and by the continuance of race meetings. I am told that hunting and racing keep up the breed of horses. This strikes me as a ridiculous excuse; the breed of horses is evidently kept up by breeding them, and not by tolerating an abundance of foxes and such-like vermin. If we want cavalry horses, the reasonable way to get them seems to breed and exercise them as such. One might as soon pretend that the corps de ballet keeps up the domestic servants. Nor do I see why the large areas in this country devoted to golf, a ritual which eats up grazing land and employs a vast amount of labour in order that English people should play a game only suited to definite areas of Scotland, and only fit for Scotsmen, should not now return to saner uses. Nor do I care a rap if anyone goes to the theatre as one has it in England any more for ever; I can do without it, and so here again I am ready to recommend drastic saving. When, however, I find Mrs. Sydney Webb in the same exemplary fashion renouncing the cinema and alcoholic refreshment, I find myself more nearly touched. It is a question whether a reasonable amount of alcoholic stimulant is not necessary to the digestion of many middle-aged people, and whether sudden total abstinence may not fling large numbers of influential persons between the ages of 50 and 70 into states of dyspeptic digestion injurious to our national morale. Nor do I see the cinema show as a very wasteful relaxation. For a few pence, people can get shelter, warmth and mental distraction for some hours. It is cheaper and better to sit in a "movy" palace than in a public-house or over a store of alcoholic liquor with nothing to do at home. London at present is full of straggling soldiers with nowhere to go, and the "movies" give them a welcome rest and interest. And the "movy" palaces are a real relief for many overworked mothers, who get their children out of mischief and out of the weather for long hours at a cost of 2d. and even less a head. Finally, the "movy" industry both as business and as national propaganda; Mrs. Sydney Webb has probably never thought of its possibility for the advertisement of national ways, fashions and products to foreign countries.

Another point in which I find myself in strong dissent from Mrs. Webb's recommendations is her discouragement of holidays. We are not going to win this war by working people into a state of neurosthenia. The whole of this economy may easily degenerate into a propaganda campaign of injurious and wasteful skimping, a release of that passion for miserliness that lurks in nearly everyone. It is not always economy not to spend money.

It is with grave reluctance that I lend myself to any scheme for urging "saving" upon the poor. My early home was extraordinarily poor, I know the "poor life" at close quarters, and I know only too well the loss in life, efficiency, service, and self-respect, that arises from underfeeding, bad boots, inconvenient furnishings, booklessness, uneducational employment of the very young, and dinginess. I would earnestly implore any working-class woman who reads this not to think of saving money out of the food, clothing, warmth, education and self-respect of her family. Until all her social superiors are shabby there is no need whatever for her to go shabby, she may rest assured. She can always tell what the ruling classes are doing in that matter by the illustrated papers on the station bookstall. They will advise her speedily enough when the day for dinginess dawns. Until that time there is but little sense in her going shabby. And she is an idiot if she cuts down her children's food, even by one lump of sugar, while there is a single toy-dog left in Great Britain. But it is a shameful thing for her if any of her people are not now busily employed either in getting education or doing productive work in all their available time. It is a shameful thing for any one of any class not to be educational or immediately useful now. True economy is not abstinence but use. I would say to everyone, do not starve and pinch but save. Save your minutes, save your energies for the national cause. And use them. Do not be content until you are employed. It is good, of course, not to take an extra lump of sugar in your tea, but the country needs you much more than it needs a lump of sugar. If you can only work on lump sugar, then eat lump sugar.

But what the working people of this country do need to be told is that at last there is a probability that they will have a fair and reasonable form of investment, with a Government guarantee, brought within their midst. It has never been the case up to now that a working man would invest a pound or so safely, profitably and interestingly. Strong interests have worked against that, and the Labour party has never cared enough for the popular welfare to protest. The vulgar rich have abused our people for not saving and never tried to find out what happened to workers who did save. The state has done everything in its power to prevent the working people of this country saving; it has left them a prey to financial sharks, to the betting man, and to such attractive devices as the buying of cheap pawnable articles, gramaphones, jewellery and the like, with their surplus money. The only safe investment, the post office savings bank, has offered a rate of interest that would convulse a financier with derision. The poor man's attempt to save has been earmarked as plunder for "private enterprise". The insurance of the poor is a joke – for everyone but the poor. Naturally, people cannot revolutionise their lifelong habits in a day, and one still hears of workers buying jewellery and musical instruments – as they have always been accustomed to do in times of affluence.

But now all is changed. This crisis, with its possibility of gold dethroned, has so scared the financiers, who are also the "experts" in these questions, that they are prepared to drop their former practical monopoly of money-lending; and the British state, for the first time in its history, is not only willing, but anxious, to borrow the money of the workers at a fair rate of interest. It is slowly unbending, so that quite soon one might expect people of average intelligence to understand what its popular schemes of investment propose; the method of subscribing five shillings to the War Loan that was tried last year, was altogether above my understanding. I did my utmost for a day to get some War Loan in this "popular" way, and failed. But the posters were rippers and no doubt tantalised millions. All this is being altered. There exists some ways in which a common man with a few shillings can buy Exchequer Bonds. I do not know what it is; none of the posters tell me. Most working people do not have the time to find out, even when they have the shillings to invest. But the way exists. People have to realise this. The workers have never failed in patriotism, and I think that if only your committee will devote a large portion of its energies to explaining more fully and clearly than the Government seems able to do, just how and where surplus wages may be dropped back into the national till in the quick and simple purchase of Treasury Bills and War Loans, just how that five per cent, without any fuss is to be got, you may leave the rest of the question of working-class savings to the national good sense. My best wishes to your committee in its patriotic work.

Yours very sincerely,

H. G. Wells

---

[1] Hedley Le Bas had been appointed to head The National War Savings Committee, with the mandate 'to promote economy in private expenditures during the war' and he asked Wells to write on behalf of the Committee. Wells responded with this 'Open Letter' in the *Daily Chronicle*, 2 May 1916.

[2] Wells is referring to *The War Emergency: Local Citizen's Committees in Town and Country, A Memorandum of Suggestions* (London: Fabian Society, 1914); it also appeared in the *New Statesman*, 22 August 1914, pp. 623–4.

1062. To Marie Butts

Illinois, ALS

Easton Glebe
Dunmow

30 April 1916
[*in another hand*]

Dear Miss Butts.

Mrs. Wells has written to Payot about the change in title.[1] I quite agree with your suggestion. I am following your experiments with interest. I don't think I differ much from you about the deadly "middle class". All my life I have lived exceptionally with exceptional people & I would certainly rather live in a slum than a suburb.

I shall read your introduction with keen interest.

Yours ever
H. G. Wells

[1] This may refer to the French title given to *Mr Britling Sees it Through*, which appeared in French as *Mr Britling Sees Through It*. In any event the title of the condensed version of the novel was not changed.

1063. To the Editor, *The Times*[1]

PLS

Easton Glebe
Dunmow

9 May 1916

Sir, – The composition of the Flying Corps Committee is an effectual answer to the clamour recently raised at the Linnean Society by a number of scientific men, men of letters, and such like nonentities for an increased development of scientific training in the country. Outside the legal profession, the Government can find only two men, both distinguished and highly specialised engineers, for the inquiry, and "a military officer of high rank" is still being sought. Three K.C.'s and a Judge of the High Court complete the body, and demonstrate at once the brilliant universality of a legal education and the hopeless folly of educating one's sons for any career but the bar.[2]

Very truly yours
H.G. Wells

---

[1] This letter appeared in *The Times* on 10 May 1916.

[2] Wells, R.A. Gregory, E. Ray Lankester, Sir Harry Johnston, H. A. L. Fisher and others had met on 3 May to discuss change in the Civil Service examinations. They wanted to include more science. The group took over an earlier committee, 'The Committee on the Neglect of Science', and meetings continued to be held. A number of publications ensued as well, although it was to be 1922 before the Civil Service examinations were modified to any great degree.

1064. To Victor Fisher[1]

PL

[London] [9 May 1916]

I believe this meeting will make it plain to all the world that the spirit of socialism is altogether for this war against the crime of the German monarchy. There are no men and women more resolved to give themselves fully and unreservedly to the supreme need of ending for ever the evil threat of German world rule than the Socialists of this country.

---

[1] A meeting was held at Queen's Hall on 10 May 1916, to welcome Prime Minister Hughes of Australia to England, and to mark the contributions of the Anzac forces to the Allied war effort. Although sponsored by the Labour Party, it became an all-party affair. Victor Fisher read letters from those who were unable to attend, including Wells. Wells's letter, along with Hughes's speech, appeared in *The Times* 11 May 1916.

1065. To Marie Butts[1]

Illinois, ALS

The Reform Club
Easton Glebe
Dunmow [15 May 1916]

Dear Miss Butts.

Mrs. Wells is getting you that list. It seems Davray has translated most of the Englishman articles already. This will stand in the way of your using any of them as articles but it need not prevent you doing all or any part of the book as a [*missing words*] arrange about two thirds of the Eng. Looks at World as a book in Modern English Socialism and publish it in F[rance] & S[witzerland]? As articles there is the work of a clerk with Davray. It would probably lead to trouble between Mlle. Godet & Mr. Pinot if she translated any of the materials & let Le Carre[?] have it under pretensions that it was new material

Negotiations with Rascher are still going on – but I think they will end satisfactorily. Davray, whom I met in London yesterday, sticks tight to New Worlds For Old which he declares he has translated but cannot get published.

I am very sorry indeed of your ill health. Perhaps I will see you soon. I am going to France and the Italian front & I hope to return through Switzerland.

Very sincerely yours
H.G. Wells

[1] Although this text is very corrupt, it is worth providing as much of it as possible as it throws light on the problems of translations at a time when Wells is searching for a replacement for Davray for the French translations.

1066. To the Editor, *Daily Chronicle*[1]

PLS

Buckminster Gate, S.W. [*c.* 16 May 1916]

Sir, – Mr. Robin H. Legge's uncivil letter, so far as its rudeness goes, might very well be left to itself. But there is a foolishness in it that goes beyond incivility and deserves a word of attention because it is an admirable specimen of that sort of foolishness that obstructs one at every turn in English affairs, and which is constantly blocking our way to sane and necessary developments. Mr. Legge starts off with the completest misunderstanding of the proposals he attacks and flares at once into an incontinence of rage and hostility. "What is this superhuman difficulty in the matter of the Russian alphabet of which Mr. Wells prates so glibly?" he begins – at the boiling point from the very start. Now I said nothing of any superhuman difficulty. What I said was to the great multitude of people with limited time and energy available who would like to learn Russian at the present time, the immediate presentation of Russian in Russian characters made an obstruction sufficiently serious to stop them and that a far quicker way to a working knowledge of Russian was possible if we could organise an introductory system of transliterated textbooks. That Mr. Legge should fly into a passion about that, and that there are no end of Mr. Legges in the country, is just one of those difficult facts we English have to face at the present time. Is it a sort of demented patriotism that moves him? I think it must be for he goes on to declare (what I think is quite true) that the "English are quite as good linguists as folk of any other nation". But that is no reason why they should learn Russian the clumsiest way around.

Mr. Legge is apparently hopelessly confused between learning and using an alphabet. It is quite true that any fool can learn the Russian script in half an hour just as any fool can learn all the moves of chess in ten minutes or less, but to use the script is quite another matter. What he fails to grasp is that the misleading resemblance of the two alphabets acts as a persistent drag upon the learner of the elements, and this drag is sufficiently great to make many busy people drop the attempt. I quite admit, as Mr. J. H. Shakespeare testifies, that "after a little time the alphabet presents no difficulty at all" – particularly if one can contrive to concentrate for a week or so upon it, avoiding other mental occupations. But most people cannot do that. Very few people in this country can afford more than four or five scattered hours a week to Russian. What I am asking for is the easiest and cheapest way of getting to grips with the Russian language, because it is of the utmost national importance. And the interesting thing to which my mind returns is that at once Mr. Legge is set bawling and foaming at the bare idea.

And it is quite characteristic of Mr. Legge's type and its peculiar detestation of clear ways and short ways that he suddenly resolves to crush me by authority. I am just an ordinary Englishman interested in Russia, who has been to Russia and nibbled at the language, a teacher of some fair experience, a man who has studied and written on educational method, the father of a son at a public school where Russian is being taught, and who is following in that son's work in Russian with particular attention, and it fills Mr. Legge with wrath and hatred to discover me expressing my impertinent opinions in the matter. "Has Mr. Wells", he asks, "referred to Sir Robert Blair (the L.C.C. education officer) or to other educational authorities on a large scale?" That's a smasher. But indeed Sir Robert Blair – I must offer him my apologies for discussing him in this relation – is no more of an authority on language learning than I am. He is a very able and distinguished director of scientific and technical education, and a leading student of American methods. Neither he nor any other "educational authorities on a large scale" have any special powers or any special qualifications for taking up this new and most urgent work of making Russian easily accessible. It is at present unassigned work. Now is the time for discussion, the time for a comprehensive review of the problem before us, and for the organisation of the best method. Russian teaching is being taken up now, but in a disorderly, wasteful and inefficient fashion. Three or four competing systems of transliteration perplex and confuse the public mind. At least three public schools have Russian masters – one has two Russian teachers – but these masters do not communicate with one another and there courses have nothing in common. A muddled variety of textbooks and "Russian made Easy" handbooks is being rushed upon the market, but we still need a school dictionary at a reasonable price. The amount of time and energy being spent upon "beginning Russian" is very considerable, and the net result in acheivement I believe to be preposterously small. I want to do what little I can, and I try to do it, to get things into a more efficient state. And, it is curious, it opens profounder and graver questions, to find Mr. Robin Legge, full of insult and blind hostility, tugging and hammering away at me – for what earthly reason? But I will not brood further on Mr. Legge now. The matter of real value now is that people should understand that this Russian language problem is not to be solved by sporadic "lesson" giving. There is an immediate necessity for a conference upon transliteration, method, text-books, and a syllabus of instruction. We need an initiative from some education authority, from Mr. Henderson, or the London University, for example. At present the bulk of Russian study in this country is mere undisciplined pottering.

H. G. Wells

[1] Wells had written an article for the newspaper, 'Looking Ahead: World Languages', which appeared on 13 May 1916. There were several responses to him, and he wrote this letter, which appeared on 17 May under the heading, 'Method in Russian Teaching'. He returned to the subject several times, urging Russian to be taught in school, and he repeated some of these views in 'Tidying up the Language Question: With Particular Reference to Russia', 6 June 1916.

1067. To the Editor, *The Times*[1]

PLS

Easton Glebe
Dunmow [*c.* 21 May 1916]

Sir, – Mr. Harry Roberts has addressed to the Labour Leader an Open Letter, which reinforces an attack I have already made upon the small group of people who run that paper. They and their associates who run the Weekly Herald are doing their utmost to impede this country in the prosecution of the war, to discourage patriotic efforts, and hamper the supply of munitions. They set up a clamour for peace, peace, "immediate peace". Mr. Roberts and I then challenge them. We ask, "Do you want this country to make an unconditional surrender to Germany irrespective of the Allies, and if you do not what are the minimum terms you would consider satisfactory?" To this plain challenge no honest reply is forthcoming from the group. Messrs. Jowett, Ramsay MacDonald, Trevelyan and Ponsonby, who are leading lights of the Labour Leader, are also members of the House of Commons. Not only Mr. Roberts and I but a number of other people have demanded of them just this plain reply we cannot get. The inevitable conclusion is that this peace clamour is at least intellectually dishonest. They cry "Peace", just out of contrariness; it is a way of annoying old friends in office; it is an excuse for shirking, for unhelpfulness; it is an appeal for the vote of the shirker; it is a sort of political lock-up investment against possible discontents after the war; it is a cry of distress; at any rate, except for Mr. Bertrand Russell, none of these people are prepared with any definition of peace at all. He is frankly a non-resister and so has at least an arguable position.

Yours, etc.,
H.G. Wells

---

[1] This letter, entitled 'The Evasive Pacifist', appeared on 23 May 1916.

1068. To A. G. Gardiner[1]

Gardiner, ALS

[London] [*c.* 15 July 1916]

Dear Gardiner,

My friend Haynes has written a book on The Decline of Liberty in England. It is tosh. But he wants me to review it & will not mind if I slate it. It will give me an opportunity of opening what I intend to be a thorough quarrel with the New Witness lot by whose ideals the book is obsessed. I hate the school with the idea of the Right of Every Man to belch in his neighbour's face with a growing savagery. Will you therefore propitiate Lynd & let me have the book to make a middle article of it?

Yours ever,
H.G. Wells

[1] Gardiner was editor of the *Daily News*, and a friend of Wells's. The book was duly sent and Wells wrote his review which led to the debate he wanted to see. That aspect of the debate in letters appears below in this collection. The other items of interest are: the review itself in *Daily News*, 24 July 1916; a response from Cecil Chesterton, 26 July and G. K. Chesterton, 27 July; Wells's response to the *Daily News* (letter 1070) letter; Wells to the *New Witness*, 3 August 1916 (letter 1072). Wells replied to Chesterton in *The New Witness* on 10 August while letters from others appeared there on 27 July, 3, 10, 17, August 1916. E. S. P. Haynes was a friend from the Fabian days. He served as Wells's lawyer for a long time. In the review Wells described the *New Witness* as being similar to eating spring onions, 'a present excitement with a sort of afterwards'.

1069. To the Editor, *Daily Chronicle*[1]

PLS

St James's Court
Buckingham Gate, S.W. [*c.* 24 July 1916]

Sir, – If a modest contributor may be permitted to criticise his editor, he would urge that before letters from correspondents making flat assertions of grave social importance are printed, those correspondents should be invited to produce some proof of their assertions. In your Saturday issue you let loose my friend Mr. Edwin Pugh with an assertion that since vodka was prohibited in

Russia drunkenness has increased. This will be believed and quoted. I don't believe it for a moment. Has he a scrap of evidence? There does seem to be evidence that a certain small number of incorrigible dipsomaniacs in Russia have resorted to methylated spirits, and so forth, and consequently there has been a percentage increase in the (small) number of deaths from drunkeness. But I venture to hazard the opinion that Mr. Pugh has just invented his general increase.

H. G. Wells

[1] This letter appeared 25 July 1916.

1070. To the Editor, *Daily News*[1]

PLS

[London] July 26 [1916]

Sir, – It carries one back to those happy days in the Fabian Society, so dessicatingly recorded by Mr. Pease in his "History", to have a "Reply to Mr. Wells" and Cecil Chesterton putting with an air of crushing invinceability the usual three questions beside the mark. I will not imitate his apologies for invading your space with this discussion, because it is a discussion of the fundamentals of Liberalism and because I find in the very next column to his letter the same old accusations about Mr. Chadband's daughter[2] "who would make a capital Inspector" and the spirited objection of the free spirited prosperous man to the "spectacled gentleman in seedy black, who calls on behalf of the Inland Revenue, and the pert youth in blue serge and brown boots who wants to know if the kitchen maid is insured". This imputation of ugliness and bad manners and dishonesty to whatever is publicly organised, with its implication of some strange natural beauty and perfection in the boozy, chaotic, and undisciplined, is the pith and marrow of the thing I attacked in my review of Mr. Haynes's book.

Now Mr. Chesterton puts three questions to me[3] with an air of wanting to put me down – questions going wide and far from my positions, but questions that will enable me to rub in the thesis upon which I am most concerned, the thesis that suspicion and everlasting railing can paralyze all liberal social development. First he asks, "Does Mr. Wells maintain that our politics are free from corruption?" Already I have shown that nothing is free from corruption. I instanced the twelve apostles. And a man who refused any food or drink that was a little decayed and corrupted, would die of thirst and starvation right away. Consequently, when (question 2) Mr. Chesterton asks, "Does he admit that the exposure of such corruption is among the duties of a citizen?" I say at once quite distinctly that promiscuous accusation is not a public duty but a public nuisance, that a dozen more important duties come before muckraking, that a movement or measure which is good on the whole should not be damned for incidental scandals, and that a perpetual uproar of "exposure" ends at last in an utter disregard for "exposure", so that finally really vital corruption escapes in the general confusion. The sweater bullies and sweats, but his victims get no protection because we must have no inspectors for fear of "Chadband's daughter".

The rich man shirks his taxes and sends off his ailing housemaid to starve because an efficient tax-collector is supposed to wear "seedy black", and the inquiring insurance man is "pert" and has "brown boots". "Finally", asks Mr. Chesterton, "is Mr. Wells prepared to establish a Collectivist State wherein the means of production are to be at the absolute disposal of the kind of politician we have at present?" Now we come to it.

I forgive Mr. Chesterton his "absolute". But Mr. Chesterton knows perfectly well that I have been a consistent and strenuous critic of political institutions, ready even to call in Mr. Chesterton himself to learn what he had to say about them, and that I have written abundantly upon proportional representation, which I believe will cure most of the admitted evils of the party system and political professionalism, upon the influence of electoral areas upon political quality, upon the electoral influence of lawyers, and so on. I concede the present inefficiency of the democratic and do my utmost to make it an efficient method. Meanwhile Mr. Chesterton has done little but shout "democracy", week by week. He now declares that we have not got democracy; but has he or any of his associates produced a single working suggestion of how to "get" democracy? Do they want democracy? My impression is that they want nothing but noise, obstruction and mob rule, accusers everywhere and inspectors nowhere. My whole case against them is that they darken and damn every constructive possibility in this uproar about corruption. It is a question of proportion. I do not see that the quotation of one of the many pungent criticism I have discharged at Mr. and Mrs. Webb convicts me of any inconsistency. To show that under their influence Fabian theory broke down to a point which justified the phrase "Servile State", is one thing, and to pretend that they are the organisers of a fearful conspiracy against the "European" man is quite another.

As Mr. Haynes' book shows, it is impossible to work or hope while conspiracy mania darkens the mind. If any considerable section of Liberals are infected by this habit of suspicion, then the part of Liberalism in the history of the next few decades will not be a part of the state of reconstruction, but the role of the howling gallery booing every performer in a passion of impotent and irrational hate.

H.G. Wells

---

[1] This letter, published 27 July 1916, appeared as part of an exchange of letters which derived from E. S. P. Haynes's book and Wells's review. The issue here was whether an anti-Catholic bias was contributing to a loss of understanding and liberty in England. Wells's letter was entitled, 'On the Conspiracy Mania', see letters 1068 and 1072.

[2] Chadband is a character in Charles Dickens's *Bleak House*. His name became synonymous with unctuous religious hypocrisy.

[3] Another Chesterton letter was printed directly above Wells's contribution under the title, 'Liberty and Mr. Belloc: Mr. G. K. Chesterton Replies to Mr. Wells'. E. S.P . Haynes had the last word in this venue with a brief letter supporting Cecil Chesterton, 28 July 1916.

1071. To A.G. Gardiner

Gardiner, ALS

Easton Glebe
Dunmow [July 1916]

My dear Gardiner,

You place me in a fix. I meant you to have my Italian articles & Donald to have my French. They could of course be run all in one paper because the S. Evening Post is going to run them in a series.[1] My difficulty is that I like you & Donald very equally in these matters, that you both pay the same & that I don't care to have any bidding up of the price. I don't like playing off people one against the other. I wish it could be possible for you & Donald to arrange the matter between you. There will be 3 Italian articles & 5 French & they will run in series. In addition, I intend to do some other articles (not yet fully planned) on What Men are Talking About. Talk I have had & heard (with little bits of picturesque description) will be the stuff of these & they won't go into the S.E. Post, but into other American papers. I don't know how you stand with Donald, but I'd like you to show him this letter & discuss these articles with him. I don't want friction or misunderstanding of any sort. One could have the Franco-Italian series of description articles; the other the Talks [2]

Yours ever,

H.G.Wells.

[1] These are the articles that eventually made up *War and the Future: Italy, France and Britain at War* (London, 1917). The American title was the English subtitle. In the end, the *Daily Chronicle* did the series in England, and Gardiner and the *Daily News* were unable to do any of these articles, which were also done in *The New York Times* rather than the *Saturday Evening Post* which printed another series later.

[2] This is what did happen. The second group of pieces, published originally in the *Daily News*, became, *What is Coming?* (London, 1916).

1072. To the Editor, *New Witness*

PLS

[London] August 3, 1916

Sir, – I have already dealt with Mr. Cecil Chesterton's 'Reply' fully and conclusively in the Daily News, wherein I was subjected to a massed attack of the Brothers Chesterton. The columns of The New Witness are, I feel sure, open to Mr. Cecil Chesterton for any further remarks he wishes to make.

Very sincerely yours,
H.G. Wells

1073. To Catherine Wells

Illinois, APCS

Cambon
France

Tuesday
[postmarked Aug. 16, '16]

No letter from you since I left England – I had a long excursion yesterday & saw the quiet harmless trenches at Soissons. A 77 mm shell burst 200 yards away but it wasn't very exciting & there are no symptoms of shell shock. [1]

Health is good
Bins

[1] Wells took a long tour as a war correspondent at the French and Italian fronts. The articles from this tour became *War and the Future* (London, 1917).

1074. To Anna[1]

Illinois, ALS

Easton Glebe
Dunmow

[mid August 1916]

My dear Anna,

Your box is absolutely wonderful, just wonderful. There were people here when it came & I just took & undid it in the middle of them & the effect it produced of my being the spoilt darling of Fortune was simply unanimous. I went up many inches in importance in all their estimations. And seriously it was the lovliest present & made me happy to hear it from you. The box will be lovely for hankies long after its contents have vanished & you made it.

We all eat the sweets with much gusto & one visitor has gotten a toothache through over indulgence. I said (she sits behind me now & especially wants me to thank you for sending it while <u>she</u> was here.)

Did I tell you that H.G. is going to Italian headquarters next week to be shown something of the Italian front. About three weeks of it I expect he will have & he will be melting hot, poor thing.

I shall try & get together some snapshots of our house to send you. <u>Do</u> let me know when are in London again. It <u>would</u> be nice to see you.

With very very many thanks & love from

Jane

P.S. I have taken to opening all packages in the midst of visitors. The next was sausage for breakfast!

---

[1] Anna is unknown. She may be Anna Jane Blanco-White, who was about to celebrate her 7th birthday in December.

1075. To Catherine Wells

Illinois, ALS

Hotel Continental
3, Rue Castiglione
Paris, France

Tuesday
[17? August 1916]

Dear Mummy,

The channel boats have been stopped on account of submarines for three to four days so that I have had absolutely no word or sign from anyone in England since I started. I got Deloré Radcliffe's telegram putting me off – in order I suppose that Northcliffe should go to Gintza[?] – & I have telegraphed him that I go on to Italy tonight but I have had no reply. I hate to mess about with passports & permits – Oh! it's a silly bore. I sent you a Swiss post card on Tuesday. On Monday I spent from 7 in the morning to 1 the next morning messing about in Senli's Compiègne district, inspected sections of the Somme defence, crossed the bridge the English built when they retook Soissons & went right up to the front line trenches. I was under fire, but not a considerable fire. The nearest shell, a small 77 mm, burst about as far off as the Coronation Stand is from the front door. (I saw nothing I couldn't have seen in The Illustrated London News.) Yesterday I had conversations at the HQ with Generals Castelneau, Joffre, & Pellé.[1] I doubt if it will affect history very profoundly. They are all sure & so are Generals d'Anselm & Bacqué who command at Soissons that it will all be over in six or eight months.

About letters, I shall leave instructions here, that my letters are to be sent to Italy. Tell, in your letter to Italy, what you have done on this matter. I think that on receipt of this you had better send on everything that is in hand to the Commando Supremo address, & not send anything more. My one intention is to get this silly shiftless mucking about over as soon as possible & to get back to work. It's an imbecile expedition.

Poor bored
Daddy

---

[1] Marshall Joffre (1852–1931) was commander in chief of French forces until December 1916.

1076. To Marie Butts

Illinois, ALS

Address "Not to Be Forwarded"
52, St James's Court
Buckingham Gate, S.W.
Udine — Aug. 17. 16

Dear Miss Butts.

Very many thanks for your letter. I shan't – I shall miss you – return via Switzerland. I shall return as I came, by Medane & probably go up the English front & come by Boulogne. I would very gladly come to Brittany if I had the time. I should enjoy the symphonies with M. [*illegible name*], Mr Chevrillon[?] & yourself beyond measure. That little piece of intellectual enthusiasm, Suzanne Magereau was at Plongineau & is returning now to her usual address 14 Quai Jean Fouquet Laval (Mayenne). I wish you could see her.

I'm afraid that this business of a German translation of the last novel must slide for a bit. This sort of time is incompatible with doing business. The Italians are making a very fine show on the front.

Very sincerely yours
H. G. Wells

1077. To Catherine Wells

Illinois, ALS

52, St. James's Court — Friday
Buckingham Gate, S.W. — [20? August 1916]

Dear Jane,

I got home at 1 a.m. this morning. I was in the trenches under fire at Martinperich 1 p.m. yesterday with C.E. Montague of the Manchester Guardian. Thence Amiens & a really very jolly motor ride to Boulogne. I'm dead tired this morning & being petted by Lewisham. I think I shall stay here until you come up. I've lived in transit so long that it's bliss to be in 4 or 5 rooms of one's own. These two photographs are as bad as usual. Here is a souvenir also that ought to interest the boys. Imagine a large modern railway station, originally glass cased but with all the glass on the ground, great smashed & shattered glass where shells have burst, a confusion of wild flames & guns going everywhere. The sandbagged line of trenches (near abandoned villages) cut through the slate rather obliquely. The sofas of green plush are still in the waiting room & the booking office looks as though it had been kicked by an impatient guard. The place is unhealthy & liable to German shells. On the table & floor of the booking office lie heaps of tickets & luggage labels. This has been the condition of Arras station now for long months.

Give my love to the boys. They seem to be having a good time. I shall be glad to be back with them at Easton.

Loving,
Bins

1078. To Walter Lippmann

Yale, TLS

52, St. James's Court,
Buckingham Gate, S.W.

[September-October 1916?][1]

Dear Lippmann,

With regard to the question of Wilson, I'm rather pro-Wilson. I should vote Wilson if I were an American, but I think he does lack hard decision. In my forthcoming book, "War and the Future", I suggest what I call a "Third-Party" solution of the war, i.e., a solution not from the point of view of victory, but from the point of view of Right. Why should you not try to get out in America what I might call an American Peace Idea, the peace the American mind would like which would mention Ireland and India as well as Bohemia and Belgium? Tell both sides plainly what neutral minds think is a just settlement. So far as the war goes I think I have now a fairly strong grasp of the situation. On the west and generally the Germans are beaten. The first half of 1917 will – in spite of our generals – demonstrate that. The boundaries will be drawn by a rather ascendant but not completely ascendant Western Europe.

But the big treaty, the League to Enforce the Peace, the broad general settlement, has to be made by all the world.

Yours,

H.G. Wells

---

[1] The date 1917 appears on this letter in another hand. Clearly however it was written just before the US election of 1916. Lippmann was serving on 'The Inquiry', an American group attempting to create a peace that would solve world problems. Other letters between Wells and Lippmann of this time are instructive, especially with their echoes of the Fourteen Points address made by Wilson as a guide to peace; see letters 1127 and 1144.

1079. To Mr Hudson

Hofstra, ACCS

Easton Glebe
Dunmow [date unknown]

My dear Hudson,[1]

Why is David Lubin no good for our purposes?

& why the devil couldn't Steed tell me about the memorandum when I showed it to him? It must go out to the members of the committee before the meeting. However I will come up on Monday instead of Tuesday to see him.

Yours ever

H.G. Wells

---

[1] This letter must go with the next two, even though it is undated. It is to a clerk in the War Aims office at Crewe House where Wells had assumed a role in propaganda and development of War Aims. One can deduce that Crewe House had plans to use Lubin's ideas.

1080. To David Lubin[1]

PLS

Easton Glebe
Dunmow Oct. 1916

My Dear Mr. Lubin,

I have read your Let There Be Light with great care and interest. I am now returning it to you with the two typed papers you asked me to return. I find in myself a very complete understandng of your line of thought and a very warm sympathy. You will see in my God The Invisible King I take up a more Christian attitude than yours. I am agnostic in regard to your God and I use the word "God" to express the divine in man. You will have to allow for this proper difference in terminology when you read what I have to say. We are at one in looking to a world in which mankind is unified under God as King.

I would be very interested to know more of the history of your thought and the particulars of your life. I do not think they would be satisfactory material for a novel but have in mind a book The Kingdom of God which might possibly be written round your work and the personalities of yourself and your mother.

I wish by the bye you could get me a copy of Let There Be Light to keep. I would like it by me.

Very Sincerely yours,
H. G. Wells

---

[1] This letter, as well as the next, appears in Olivia Rossetti Agresti, *David Lubin: A Study in Practical Idealism* (Boston: Little Brown, 1922, reprinted by the University of California Press, 1941). Lubin was a visionary with a particular interest in world agriculture and nutrition. He proposed an early version of the League of Nations. The letter appears in Agresti, p. 334. Lubin responded 4 November 1916, telling Wells that he liked *Britling*, apart from the theology. In May 1917 the correspondence was resumed with more discussion of *God The Invisible King*. Wells responded with letter 1173 in May 1918, but Lubin found Wells's venture in theology not very interesting. Lubin died of Spanish Influenza on 1 January 1919. The institute continued to function and is regarded as the beginning of the Food and Agriculture Agency of the U.N. See *New York Times* 23 May 1920 for an article by Agresti on the Institute and the League of Nations; the second of the Wells letters appears on p. 338 of her book.

1081. To David Lubin[1]

Bromley, Transcription

[London] [1916]

I have been interested in the International Institute of Agriculture for some years, and it was that which made me give Italy, a kind of central part in the world pacification in "World Set Free".

---

[1] This fragment appears in a file also containing a transcript of several letters from Lubin to Wells, and the two Wells letters printed in this volume. It is also in Agresti, p. 338.

1082. To Clement Shorter[1]

Leeds, ALS

52, St. James's Court
Buckingham Gate, S.W. postmarked 2 Oct 16[2]

My dear Shorter,

Are you Irish? You don't look it. My mother was a Neal and I have a kind of feeling for Ireland. I am bitterly ashamed of her. There she sulks, earning the undying contempt of the inarticulate English, while England fights the greatest war in history.[3] Her contribution to the struggle (so history will tell us – ignoring the Irish element in the Irish regiments) was a kind of cheap stab in the back, organized by a man who came to her in a German submarine.

You stick Erse letters in your paper. Do you speak Erse? Does your wife?

Ireland has dipped herself in the German blood. How can she be clean again? She is one with the Greek "reservists", shabby & dirty. Cathleen ni Houlihan is a wretched old woman indeed only fit to sell matches in the street, a public house loafer woman who leads boys to shame & death. We know her now.[4]

Yours ever,
H.G.Wells

---

[1] Shorter (1857–1926) was a writer, critic, columnist and editor before and immediately after the First World War. He had some impact on the pension grants for George Gissing's children, in his work as editor of *The Sphere*.

[2] This letter belongs to the period when Wells was in the propaganda office of Lord Northcliffe, and the time of the horrors of the Somme battles. The letter is a clear attempt to put pressure on Shorter to offer less about the Irish and more of a positive nature on the war.

[3] The number of Irish volunteers who fought and died in the cause of the Allies was actually very large indeed.

[4] Cathleen ni Houlihan is a character in Irish mythology. William Butler Yeats (1865–1939) drew on her persona in his *Countess Cathleen* plays.

1083. To Clement Shorter

Leeds, ALS

52, St. James's Court
Buckingham Gate, S.W. [postmarked 7 Oct 16]

My dear Shorter,

Thanks for your patient and reasonable letter. But England suffers from Dublin Castledom as much as Ireland (see Britling) This is no reason why Irishmen should behave like hysterical children & start in on me & my Sherwood Foresters in the midst of a big war. I just say the British governing class is nothing better than a collection of damned fools. They are wasting lives in France most appallingly. But we want some greatness of mind from the Irish, we want help in our struggle to make a saner & better England instead of all its idiotic development of a racial quarrel. You talk of how this or that affects Irish feeling. Don't you realize that England's feeling is getting savagely angry with Ireland?

Yours ever,
H.G.W.

1084. To Clement Shorter[1]

Leeds, ALS

120, Whitehall Court
S.W. 1 [1923?]

My dear Shorter,

So you too have come to the resurrection phase. I've always belonged (in theory) to the "publish & be damned" school so I can't very well object to my letters to you coming out if you want them to come out. Anyhow there are ~~some~~ more of the scandalous endearments here, that failed to restrain Mrs. Aria. But I qualify my permission with the condition that you publish this letter also. I think it is just to Ireland & myself to have it explained that these letters were written soon after some very jolly young men, very kindly civilized young men, of the Sherwood Foresters, who had just been guests in my house had been murdered in Dublin by enthusiastic patriots. And also, after an experience of controversy with Mr. Henry Arthur Jones, I would like to underline, emphasize, shout, repeat, hammer-in & insist upon the fact that the fourth sentence in my first quoted letter refers to Ireland & not to my mother. You will say that there is no one so idiotic as to suppose that it does refer to my mother. Nevertheless permit me to anticipate such an extremity of controversial vigour & nip it in the bud.

The English people are [not] angry with Ireland any more. Those bitternesses have been lost in ampler bitternesses. She is working out her destiny now in her own way. [*Another brief phrase is blacked out and is unreadable.*]

Yours ever,
H.G. Wells

[1] Although this is a signed holograph letter it is filled with emendations, and balloons, so it may, in fact, be a draft. However the original does lie in the Shorter papers. It is being printed out of chronological order because it refers so closely to the previous two letters. Shorter was preparing an autobiography, found Wells's earlier letters, and wrote asking permission to print them in his book. Wells's reply is therefore more relevant here than later.

1085. To the Editor, *Daily Record*, Glasgow

Illinois, TCC

Easton Glebe
Dunmow

Novr. 3rd, 1916.

Dear Sir.

I am enclosing a letter for publication drawing attention to the urgent necessity for recruits for the Artists Rifles.[1]

May I ask you to give special prominence to it, but not before the 6th instant. If you can supplement it with any Editorial comments I shall esteem it as a favour.

By reason of its constitution the Corps is one in which all connected with the Arts, especially literary men, must take a sympathetic interest.

Yours sincerely,
H.G. Wells

[1] The Artists' Rifles was one of the 'Pals' Battalions raised to supplement the regular army after the devastation of the Somme.

1086. To the Editor, *Daily Record*, Glasgow

PLS

Easton Glebe
Dunmow

[*c*. 5 November 1916]

Sir, – May I appeal to anyone who can join the Artists Rifles with a view of getting a commission, or assist in the recruiting, do so without delay? The corps is hard put to it to find the 500 men a month it requires.

It is zealous to preserve its distinctive character and its distinctive characteristics, and it is eager to secure every available man of its peculiar type. It is by no means restricted to "artists" as we commonly understand the word in Britain. It is true that some sixty years ago the corps was raised by Lord Leighton, Robert Edis, and Val Prinsep exclusively from artists and sculptors, among them such well-known men as Watts, Millais, Val Prinsep, Holman Hunt, William Morris, and Poynter; but from that start the corps has always been eager to secure and has secured, artists, architects, musicians, writers, and, indeed, every sort of man who could be classed under the useful Russian term, the Intelligentsia. As I run my finger down the list before me I find William Watson, Forbes Robertson, Victor Horsley, Sir Leander Starr-Jameson and so on. The corps has held out a friendly hand to the bank clerk who wrote a little poetry, to the civil engineer, the skilful photographer, or the certificated teacher. From the first until today the corps has stuck to its conception of a democratic, spirited regiment, in which intellectual and educated men whose devotion to some creative profession prevented them from taking commissions or specialising in military matters in peacetime could, nevertheless, make themselves available for the military necessities of the country.

How admirably it did that work the story of its first battalion in Flanders witnesses. It never reached the trenches as a battalion. In the first battle of Ypres there had been such serious losses that many of our shattered divisions were practically without officers at all. One brigade of the Seventh Division had eight officers left of 143, another had four. The losses in men was on nearly the same scale, but they were losses that could be replaced by drafts from England; the officers seemed irreplaceable.

In this emergency Lord French seized upon the Artists and converted 100 of them straight away into officers of the Regular Army and sent another 450 to the other regular divisions after the men had been given a short course in an "extemporised school" just behind the fighting line. These men went into the trenches to play their part as officers of almost every one of Lord French's

Regular Regiments still wearing the uniform of private soldiers of the Artists Corps, and many of them died in that uniform. This is their quality. Before the war the "Artists" were not an O.T.C., but they did actually provide more officers than any single O.T.C. before the war. And what the corps wants now is to secure for its ranks any available man of the potential officer class who has not yet joined up. It believes that it has only to be known to such men as to get them; and my immediate objective in writing this letter is to make the opportunity known and to ask everyone who is in a position to assist in the advertisement of the requirements of the Artists' Rifles to do so. The corps offers a particular atmosphere, and it appears to a particular type which is unfortunately scattered in schools, offices, studios, and the like, all over the three kingdoms, and which is, consequently, very difficult to get at. It foresees a shortage of men, and at the same time, the very men it wants may be drifting unknowingly into far less congenial units.

The address of the Artists' Rifles Association, which is very earnest in the matter, is Duke's-Road, Euston Road, W.C. To it all inquiries and offers of help should go.

H. G. Wells

1087. To Upton Sinclair

Indiana, ANS

52, St James's Court,
Buckingham Gate, S.W.

21 Nov. 1916
[*in another hand*]

Dear Upton Sinclair

Yes, but Direck isn't speaking his own faultless Boston tongue. It is explained that when he comes to England he feels obliged to behave like a stage American.

Yours ever
H.G.

1088. To the Director of the Press Bureau

Bromley, ALS

Easton Glebe
Dunmow [*c.* end 1916?]

Dear Sir,

With this is an envelope with a letter addressed to Mr. Paul Reynolds & a post card to myself. There are also two papers on the Italian campaign. I shall be glad if you will read them at your early convenience & either post on to Mr. Reynolds, my New York agent, or let me know of any delay.

Very sincerely yours,
H.G. Wells

I enclose a stamped post card which I will be glad if you will use. [1]

[1] The Press Bureau censored prospective articles from the war front, and Wells was submitting his copy with this letter.

1089. To Mr Mack[1]

Hofstra, ALS

Easton Glebe
Dunmow [1916–17]

Dear Sir,

Mr. Algernon Rose writes to me saying you have some discovery of importance to the country. I do not see where I come in except that Mr. Rose has written to me. Lord Fisher is the head of an Inventions Committee & there is also such a committee at the Ministry of Munitions. To each of these you should send a preliminary memorandum. If you think I could understand your discovery you might also send me in confidence a similar memorandum. What science I have is chiefly biological & psychological. I am scientifically speaking a first class Honours Zoological B.S. in an advanced state of decay. My physics & chemistry are indicated by the Intermediate Science Exam of 25 years ago.

Very sincerely yours
H.G. Wells

---

[1] This person is not further known.

1090. To A.G. Gardiner

Gardiner, ALS

Easton Glebe
Dunmow [1916?]

By dear A.G.G.

You know as well as I do that there is no such happiness for a writer as to be overpraised, beautifully, abundantly & conspicuously by a writer he likes and respects.

Very many thanks,
Yours sincerely,
H.G.

1091. To Enid Bagnold[1]

Illinois, ALS

52, St. James's Court
Buckingham Gate, S.W.1. [1916]

Dear Enid Bagnold,

I keep thinking of you. Which is I suppose a natural result of meeting (or as really the first meeting) a new & exciting sort of personality. I'm sorry you can't come on Wednesday because we should have a foursome with

Rebecca & a writer she has discovered called Booth Austin. I shall try to fix something next week.

Yours ever,
H.G.

---

[1] The series of letters which begins with this one continued to the end of Wells's life. They are among his most charming, and at the same time, most humorous. and flirtatious. Enid Bagnold was a Volunteer Nurse's Aide in the First World War when she was quite young. Her experiences gave rise to the classic, *Diary Without Dates* (1917). She wrote many plays and some fiction, the best known example of which is *National Velvet* (London and Toronto: Heinemann, 1935).

1092. To Enid Bagnold

Illinois, ALS

52, St. James's Court
Buckingham Gate, S.W.1. [1916]

Dear Enid Bagnold,

You wrote me a kind note with a picture & I haven't answered it for weeks & ages. The dreadful truth is that it got itself driven out of my head by a crowd of powerful disturbances. Two people whom I care for more than anyone: one had an operation & the other didn't almost die but got so ill & so distressingly ill that I was at my wits' end.[1] And a clear opportunity of doing SOMETHING (it ought to be larger letters than that to do it justice) came my way & made me very excited & busy & sleepless & afraid I couldn't pull it off. I have pulled it off & I think now everything is well & I have slept like a dog for a week. I tell you these confidences because I don't want you to get disagreeable intentions. I put your note in my pocketbook intending a <u>most</u> amoosing reply & it nudged me once or twice. . . . but a sincerely amoosing reply now I feel wouldn't do. Come & talk somewhere. Come & have lunch with me – at Romaine's – on Friday, June the 7th. And tell me all about everybody you have ever loved & I will tell you all that is suitable for your ears about my similar experiences. And let us discourse on art & life waving our knives & forks about in the excitement of the theme. And believe me always,

Yours ever,
H.G.

[1] Both Catherine and the younger Frank Wells were ill.

1093. To Enid Bagnold

Illinois, ALS

Easton Glebe [1916]

Dear Enid Bagnold,

Many thanks for the information about Tinker.

How is your soul? I saw your verses in the Nation. There is a deliberate feminism about you that I don't comprehend. Write me some novels, please.

Yours ever
H.G.

1094. To Enid Bagnold

Illinois, ALS

Easton Glebe
Dunmow Tuesday to Friday
52, St. James's Court
S.W. 1 [1916]

Dear Enid Bagnold,

I liked you very much & I hope you like me. You & I have got to have a thought for each other. I shall try & fix a lunch or dinner this week or next. As it may have to be fixed rapidly you'll forgive me if I fire a sudden telegram at you one day.

Yours ever,
H.G.

1095. To an unknown addressee

Boston, ACCS

52, St. James's Court
Buckingham Gate, S.W. [*c*. 1916]

My dear Sir,

I am a novelist & I want to get back to novel writing. (I'd be very glad to see what you have to say of my "Mr. Britling.") This war has dragged us all into journalistic outbreaks & I suppose I shall continue to write shorts at intervals until after the peace. But most of these occasional articles go into the Chronicle & News, which papers meet me very comfortably in the matter of rates & so forth & enable me to secure publication in America.[1] It would save me an enormous amount of bother if I could arrange to sell the English & American rights to specially written articles to one purchaser who would see to the simultaneous publication on both sides. The trouble of that is a very serious deterrent at the present time. If that could be arranged, I should be willing, I think, to agree for one or two [of] your articles early next year for £150 all serial rights. This year I shall turn out a number of articles of various sorts (parts of a book) on Italy, France and England at war. After that I shall hold my peace until the coming settlement or I should get too excited. The first articles are all promised for, but it is these latter publications I suggest to you.[2]

Very sincerely yours
H.G. Wells

---

[1] Wells did do very well out of this journalism. His usual fee for the *Chronicle* was 25 guineas each, and more came in from republication in books and in the United States. This letter is a bit problematical to decipher, but this seems to be what was intended.

[2] His book on these war theatres was published in both America and England in early 1917. The articles which made up the book were also published in both countries in the press, and were probably arranged by his correspondent, who may have been Meade Minnegerode, who was connected to the *New York Times* where they appeared in the US.

TELEPHONE:- KENSINGTON 588.

Private   1. Oct. 1916

41, CROMWELL ROAD,
S.W.

My dear Mr. Wells,

I passed a vy pleasant Sunday reading "Mr Britling" & I congratulate you on producing such a suggestive & moving record of these strange times.

You will have been interested to see the success with wh yr land battleship idea was at last – after many weary efforts – put into practice.

Yours vy ty,

Winston S. Churchill

1096. To Mrs Thomas Hardy[1]

Indiana, ACCS

52, St. James's Court
Buckingham Gate, S.W. 1 [1916?]

Dear Mrs. Hardy,

Jane, i.e., Mrs. H.G. Wells, before going off to her Red Cross work instructed me to telephone to you that we shall be at home to tea to-day after five o' clock. I have been pursuing you with a telephone since then. I want to tell the Master to write another Dynasts about this war but somehow we never get in one's premeditated things.

Yours ever,
H.G. Wells

[1] The envelope for this invitation is inscribed in Wells's handwriting, 'Dynasts' in the upper left corner and 'HG Wells, V.D.' in the upper right. It is addressed 'To Await Mrs. Thomas Hardy at Lady St. Helier's, 52 Portland Place' with 79 Harley Street, W. crossed out

1097. To Ezra Pound[1]

Cornell, ALS

52, St. James's Court
Buckingham Gate, S.W. [1916]

Dear Pound,

I'm no good writing the R.L.F. [Royal Literary Fund] because (1) I have hurt Gosse's feelings re "Boon". & (2) I have stopped my subscription on account of the Crossland grant. Hueffer says he could get Joyce a job at the war office (Censorship.) Also I will telephone Pinker.

Yours ever
H.G. Wells

[1] Ezra Pound (1885–1972), an American poet and critic, who by the time of this letter had moved to London where he was a significant figure in the modern literary world. After 1924 he lived in Italy and roused resentment when he supported the fascist government of Italy, and began to be pronounced anti-Semite. From 1945 to 1958 he was incarcerated in St Elizabeth's hospital for the Insane in Washington, DC. He returned to Italy after his release. His leading work, an experimental group of poems, called *The Cantos*, has had a substantial impact on modern poetry. This letter marks the beginning of the subsidy that Wells and other writers made to James Joyce (1882–1941) in order that he could carry on his work without fear of going without food and drink. Wells continued to contribute to these funds until 1927, see volume 3. There is more correspondence on the matter but most of the letters were written by Catherine Wells. In the late 1930's there is a small correspondence from Pound to Wells, but searches in all of the likely sites have produced none from Wells to Pound. I wish to thank Carroll Terrell for conducting this search for me.

1098. To James Joyce

Cornell, ALS

The Reform Club
Pall Mall [late Autumn 1916?][1]

Dear Mr. Joyce,

I don't see much chance of getting to Zurich just now. D.V. you'll come to London & then we'll celebrate our joint existence.

Yours ever,
H.G. Wells

[1] In addition to the subsidy fund, Wells also reviewed very favourably Joyce's novel, *Portrait of the Artist*. They met once or twice and the end of the subsidy in 1927 came after a famous luncheon together. Several letters about this occur in volume 3.

1099. To Miss Langham[1]

Korn, ALS

52, St. James Court
Buckingham Gate, S.W. [1916?]

Dear Miss Langham

I never write autographs for people & when they send stamped envelopes I scratch out the address & use them for some necessary correspondence.[2] (This is a war economy & will help us to beat the Germans) But as you really seem to know what is in some of my books I hope you will soon rise above this sort of collecting. And I am writing to tell you so.

Yours very sincerely
H. G. Wells

[1] She is otherwise unknown.

[2] Wells stuck to these rules until the early 1930's after he was diagnosed with diabetes and became active as a fundraiser for the Diabetes Foundation. He then began the practice of only giving his autograph when people gave him either a cheque or cash to the amount of half a crown (two shillings and sixpence) to go to the Foundation. See volume 4 for letters dealing with his new rules and his role with the Foundation.

1100. To Booth Austin

Texas, ALS

Easton Glebe
Dunmow [1916–17]

Dear Booth Austin

I've already posted one letter to you rather hinting at work. I've told you a lot of my movements. Would you care to come over here for a weekend and Monday? There is probably a chap coming from Cambridge about some scientific government scheme but otherwise there won't be many people about. Then we might plan a book. I'm likely to be [*illegible word*] about Leigh & London until Saturday.

Yours ever
H. G.

1101. To Booth Austin

Texas, ALS

52, St James's Court
Buckingham Gate, S.W. [1916–17]

Dear Austin

I don't see that story & there it is! But you ought to do it.

Yours ever,
H.G. Wells

1102. To Bernard Shaw

British Library, Typed Transcription[1]

Easton Glebe
Dunmow Jan 12. 1917

Dear Shaw,

The swine do impose a right to censor (severely) your articles on the Front but not the rest of your literary career. My book on the front is held up now by G.H.Q. on the score of the criticism of the staff work.* But if you go & see them they get timid & make concessions.[2]

Thick boots & waders. The mud is terrible. Macintosh & a furlined coat. Stick to the republican issue; it's vital.

Yours ever
H.G.

Be careful how you tip the French chauffeurs.
He is frequently a rich embusque.[3] Northcliffe
tipped the owner of the Nord Sud. Otherwise
generous normal tipping.

*But in the later part of the book which deals with the war generally & not the "front", I get it all in — uncensored.

[1] Read in Illinois

[2] Wells's collection of war dispatches appeared in the press in both the US and the UK, *War and the Future: Italy, France and Britain at War* (London: Cassell, 1917).

[3] A Wellsian word derived from the French *embusquer*, to ambush.

1103. To J. M. Dent[1]

AL

13 – 1 – 17

To J.M. Dent,

A proposal has come to hand from America for a subscription edition of my work – to be sold only in sets at 2 dollars a volume. If it is published some sets will be sold over here. I shall be glad of your consent to the inclusion of The Wonderful Visit & The Wheels of Chance in this collection. I want to make it as complete as possible & I am told that there is not the slightest interference with the normal edition.[2]

[1] This letter was offered for sale in Ferret Fantasy Catalogue Q99B, issued March, 1993

[2] This edition did not materialise, but such discussions led eventually to the collected works, called the Atlantic Edition, in twenty-eight volumes. Another short undated letter from Wells to Dent also appeared in this catalogue – 'I was at Garden City last week & much interested.' The text would date the letter to be after 1920, and perhaps came from his 1921 visit to the United States to cover the Washington Disarmament Conference.

1104. To St John Adcock[1]

Bromley, ALS

52, St. James's Court
Buckingham Gate. S.W. [early 1917]

Dear Mr. St. John Adcock,

Lucas rather infringed my copyright when he gave you those drawings. But I forgive him. So far as Public Opinion goes I'm quite willing for the

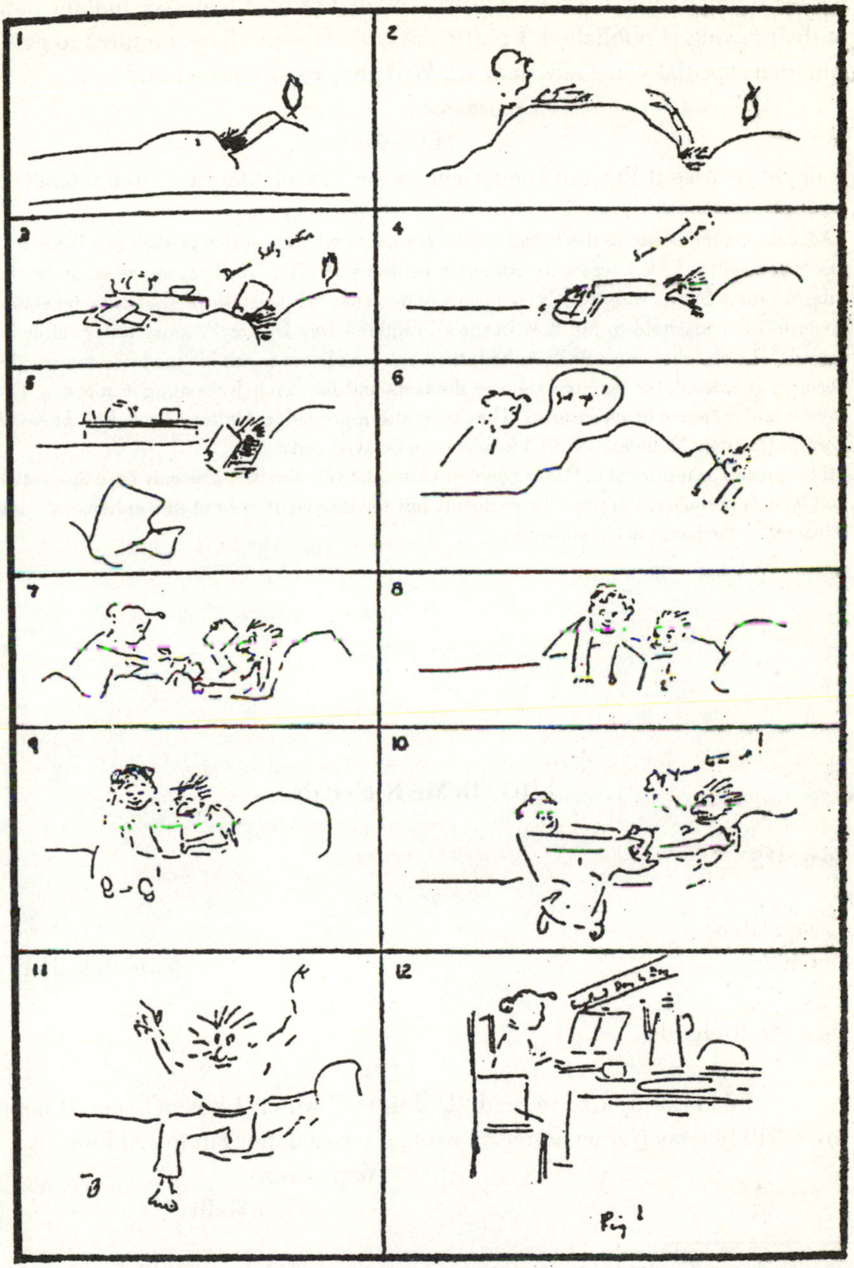

A CRUSTY DAWN

The small writing reads: 3 'Damn silly letter'; 4 'Some damned bore'; 6 'Get up!'; 10 'You'll tear it!'; 12 'England Day by Day'.

further reproduction, but there I think it ought to stop. Please see that the date of the drawing is published. I particularly don't want these pictures to go to America especially just now or at all. Will you drop Lucas a hint?

Yours ever,

H.G. Wells

It might be wise if P.O. put "copyright in the U.S. of America" in a footnote.[2]

---

[1] Adcock was the editor of the magazine the *Bookman* where a series of sketches Wells had drawn and sent to E. V. Lucas were printed in February 1917, p. 35. They appeared under the title, 'A Crusty Dawn', with Wells's comments in his letter to Lucas: 'the enthusiastic reception given in his household to Mr. E.V. Lucas's "England Day By Day", immediately after its arrival'. The sketches show Wells in bed; the book is delivered with his tea by Catherine; he becomes engrossed; the two struggle over the book and Jane ends by reading it in peace. The story is told in twelve block cartoons. They were also reprinted in Audrey Lucas, *E. V. Lucas: A Portrait* (London: Methuen, 1939). Lucas was an essayist and critic.

[2] If the piece was reprinted in *Public Opinion* I have not yet seen it. Lucas may have thought he had Wells's permission to print the cartoons, but the copyright even of this ephemeral work remained in the hands of the author.

1105. To Mr Richards

Texas, ALS

Easton Glebe
Dunmow [*c.* March, 1917]

Dear Mr. Richards,

I'd certainly like to read "Dubliners" which I haven't seen. I hope Joyce will like my <u>Nation</u> notice.[1] I wrote it not to flatter but to sell him.

Yours ever,

H.G.Wells

---

[1] Wells's review of *Portrait of an Artist* appeared in *Nation* on 24 February 1917. It continued to be quoted in the Penguin edition until into the 1980s. It was used to headline a leaflet which was handed out at theatres during the intervals, and elsewhere, and which also quoted from other reviews. Wells's was at the top of the handbill; I own a copy of this handbill.

1106. To Kathleen Pelham[1]

Milwaukee, ACCS

Little Easton Rectory
Dunmow [early 1917]

Dear Lady Drogheda,

Please let me have a proof of that preface to 52 St. James's Court, S.W.

In my haste I think I left out a sentence or so I had in mind and I wrote "polyplane" which is a thoroughly bad word for "multiplane" which it ought to be.

Yours sincerely,
H.G. Wells

[1] Kathleen Pelham, wife of the Earl of Drogheda, was a member of the Anglo-Irish aristocracy. She became very interested in aircraft and their historic development during the First World War. Her interest resulted in a major exhibition showing this development at the Grosvenor Galleries in 1917. Wells wrote the introduction to the exhibition catalogue, one of the rarest items in his bibliography. Money raised at the gallery was given to the Red Cross and to the Royal Air Corps Relief Organisation.

1107. To the Editor, *The Times*[1]

PLS

[London] [late February 1917]

Sir,— I should be glad of your permission to put before your readers certain considerations that I think should modify the present reluctance to issue some sort of premium bonds. It is too often overlooked that a difference in scale may amount in effect to a difference in kind. This is a principle entirely disregarded in our public treatment of the investments of poor people. As a consequence we are failing to attract large amounts of money to the public service, and we are allowing that money to be spent in a manner that is socially wasteful.

The point to be insisted upon is that the significance of any sum of money to a human being depends very largely upon its measurement by the human scale. £5 a year is not the same things as £500 a year reduced to the scale of one in a hundred; the latter is a possible income, the former is not a living income at all; the former is a possible tip, the latter not. The investment of £10 by a man who earns a pound a week is a proceeding differing altogether in its nature from the investment of £1000 by a man with an income of £100 a week. It is a different psychological process. It may sound paradoxical, but the former sum is less important to the investor concerned than is the latter. And the ten shillings a year of the former is infinitely more negligible to the pound a week man than is £50 a year to the hundred pounds a week man. The reason for this is that while the larger sum represents life-size things, so to speak, the smaller represents only incidental things. For £50 a year one may, for example, get the service of a gardener permanently added to one's life; one may have some full weeks of holiday; one may pay the annual rent of a week-end house, and so on and so on. There are endless such things to be done with it; things that even a millionnaire can feel as additions to life. But an annual 10 shillings buys nothing that will spread in permanent satisfaction over a year. It will scarcely cover an evening's "beano" for a working-class family; it falls short of a sound pair of boots. It is no permanent improvement whatever. It is, comparatively intangible. It is intangible because, though we have reduced the sum of money to one-hundredth, we have not reduced the size of the investor's hands, feet, and appetites. And consequently 10 shillings a year is not so attractive to the poor man as an investment inducement as an annual £50 is to a wealthy man. It is not only harder for the former to spare £10 but the reward of interest we offer him is not so attractive. It may be at the same rate, but it is not in the same ratio to the things that matter. He gets a lesser "reward" for a greater "abstinence". He wants more feel for his money; the temptation to spend his captial and not save at all is therefore altogether greater than it is for the rich man. Poor people, as any intelligent inquirer will find out do not think of investment; they think of saving – which is quite a different idea – because of this intangibility of these small annual sums. They put by money against an emergency. When they feel secure (with £20 or £30 in the savings bank, say, and a club subscription against the worst misadventures in life), then they spend all they get. Anyone not a miser would do the same. It is not a question of education or forethought. Ordinary interest for a poor man isn't worthwhile.

The savings bank at present only gets such precautionary hoarding. Given that safety hoard, then the more careful wage-earners who feel affluent but cautious, and who are making money beyond their normal expectations, either gamble or try to buy something that will be saleable again in the event of their wanting money, and which in the meantime will give that real satisfaction which a shilling or five shillings a year cannot possibly give. The surplus money that we covet now for the War Loan is spent – not because working people are extravagant, but because they are not mere mathematical machines but human beings – upon pleasant pawnable objects, upon jewellery, furs, pianos, and pianolas, concertinas, harmoniums, motor-bicycles, sideboards, and so forth. These things give real satisfaction, and are at the same time negotiable securities. Gambling gives hope, also a precious thing in life. A secure five-per-cent of £5 or £10, on the other hand, gives nothing of any real value to a poor man at all. It is a buried talent. This is the *crux* of the problem of the small investor. It is not the extravagant but the careful working people who are being so stupidly abused for "extravagance" at the present time. The really extravagant ones spend their extra gains upon food, drink, and music-halls. The sane careful ones either back horses or buy houses, pianos, gramophones, watches and so on by instalments, because these are the only sensible investments that our world offers them.

Now there is only one way in which an investment of from a few shillings up to £20 or £30 can be made really attractive to a poor man, and that is to give a chance of a tangible return for his money. You must in some way give him at least the hope or a feel, a satisfaction. For a working man to put a pound into the War Loan is pure patriotic sacrifice; if he is to be put upon a footing of fair equality with his richer fellow investor he must be given the sporting chance of a premium drawing. There is no other way. By giving him a premium bond he is given not only interest but hope. He need not be offered a money prize. Sudden spendable wealth, I admit, may "upset" a poor man. But the whole psychological process of working-class investment would be changed without that if we were to issue numbered and registered four per cent, pound bonds or five pound bonds, and if we were to convert a certain proportion of these bonds every year into five per cent bonds for a hundred pounds. Each pound bond, that is might suddenly win a prize of £99. Every bond a man could get would increase his chance of that pleasing possibility. We should then add the hope of speculative investments to the normal incentive or mere saving or patriotic self-sacrifice, which are at present the only inducements to invest the working man has. We should enormously stimulate working-class investment – at the expense of the music-halls, the bookmaker, and of the gramophone, fur-coat, and concertina industries, which at the present time suck up a huge volume of surplus earnings.

Yours very truly.
H.G. Wells

---

[1] Premium Bonds were a major topic of discussion as the cost of the war increased. The letter appeared on 3 March 1917.

1108. Israel Zangwill to H. G. Wells

Illinois, TLS

Far End
East Preston
Sussex

March 3rd, 1917

My dear Wells,

I am sending you an American Jewish paper re "Mr. Britling" which might not come your way, but which might interest you in view of your intention of writing further on religion. You must not assume, of course, that I am in agreement with the criticism whether for blame or praise. But I must say that the attitude of some sections of the British reading public towards that work has reminded me of an early epigram of my own:

> "It is only by being misunderstood that a great man can
> have any influence upon his mind."

By the way, I have not been able to avoid a couple of references to you in a forthcoming lecture (Moncure D. Conway[1] Memorial Lecture) on "The Principles of Nationalities" next Thursday evening at 6:30. I shall write to the South Place Institute people to send you a platform seat in the faint possibility of your being able to come.

With kind regards to you and Mrs. Wells.

Sincerely yours,
Israel Zangwill

P.S. I have just read your letter on Premium Bonds, which bears out my theory that a novelist member – as a scientific expert in human nature – is a necessity to every War Cabinet.[2]

---

[1] Conway (1832–1907), an American clergyman and abolitionist. He lectured in England during the US Civil War, and settled down in London where he continued as a pastor from 1864 to 1897.

[2] Although a few of Wells's letters to Zangwill have survived and appear in this volume, those from the First World War period have not been located. Since they provide another view of that period a few of Zangwill's letters to Wells do appear in this volume.

1109. To Marie Butts

Illinois, ALS

Easton Glebe
Dunmow [15 March 1917]

Dear Miss Butts,

I shall watch your experiment with interest. Perhaps you are right. I live the life of a specialist & have all sorts of devilling done for me. I travel first class to be able to read & write in the train. I have perhaps a special horror at the idea of doing things for myself. And I don't know much about the life that the bourgeoisie [live] here or in Switzerland. Perhaps it is paralyzing. My mother was a servant in a big house, my father a professional cricketer & I went to work in a shop at thirteen. My life for years was a desperate struggle to get away from wages slavery. That may unseat the idea of anyone going back to it out of peculiar terrors.

Yours ever,
H.G. Wells

1110. To the Editor, *The Times*[1]

PLS

[London] [c 15 March 1917]

Sir, – There seems to be a very general failure to grasp the importance of what is called – so unhappily – Proportional Representation in the recommendations of the Speaker's Conference. It is the only rational, honest and efficient electoral method. It is, however, in danger of being thrust on one side as a mere fad of the intellectuals. It is regarded by many ill-informed people as something difficult, "high-browed", troublesome, and of no practical value, much as science and mathematics were so regarded by the "practical" rule-of-thumb industrialists of the past. There are all too many mean interests in machine politics threatened by this reform, which are eager to seize upon this ignorant mistrust and use it to delay or burke the political cleaning-up that Proportional Representation would involve. Will you permit me to state, as compactly and clearly as I can, the real case for this urgently-needed reform – a reform which alone can make Parlimentary government anything better than a caricature of the national thought and a mocker of the national will.

The essential point to grasp is that Proportional Representation is not a novel scheme, but a carefully worked-out remedy for universally recognized ills. An election is not the simple matter it appears to be at the first blush. Methods of voting can be manipulated in various ways, and nearly every method has its own liability to falsification. Take the commonest, simplest case – that case that is the perplexity of every clear-thinking voter under British or American conditions: the case of the constituency in which every elector has one vote, and which returns one representative to Parliament. The naive theory on which we go is that all the possible candidates are put up, that each voter votes the one he likes best, and that the best man wins. The bitter experience is that hardly ever are there more than two candidates, and still more rarely is either of these the best man possible. Suppose, for example, the constituency is mainly Conservative. A little group of pot-house politicians, wire-pullers, busy-bodies, local journalists, and small lawyers, working for various monetary interests have "captured" the Conservative organization. For reasons that do not appear they put an unknown Mr. Goldbug as the official Conservative candidate. He professes a generally Conservative view of things, but few people are sure of him and few people trust him. Against him the weaker (and therefore still more venal) Liberal organization puts up a Mr. Kentshire (formerly Wurstberg) to represent the broader thought and finer generosities of the English mind. A number of Conservative gentlemen, generally too busy about their honest businesses to attend the party "smokers" and the party cave, realize suddenly that they want Goldbug hardly more than they want Wurstberg. They put up their long-admired, trusted and able friend Mr. Sanity as an Independent Conservative. Everyone knows the trouble that brings. Mr. Sanity "is going to split the party vote". The hesitating voter is told, with considerable truth, that a vote given for Mr. Sanity is a vote given for Wurstberg. At any price we do not want Wurstberg. So at the eleventh hour Mr. Sanity is induced to withdraw, and Mr.Goldbug goes into Parliament to misrepresent us. That in its simplest form is the dilemma of democracy. The problem that has confronted modern democracy since its beginning has not been the representation of organized minorities, but *the protection of the unorganized masses of busily occupied, fairly intelligent men from the tricks of the specialists who work the party machine.* We knew Mr. Sanity. We want Mr. Sanity, but we are too busy to watch the incessant intrigues to oust him in favour of the obscurely influential people, politically docile, who are favoured by the organization. We want an organizer-proof method of voting. It is an answer to this demand, as the outcome of a most careful examination of the ways in which voting may be protected from the exploitation of those who *work* elections, that the method of Proportional Representation with a single transferable vote has been evolved. It is organizer-proof. It defies the caucus. If you do not like Mr. Goldbug you can put up and vote for Mr. Sanity, giving Mr. Goldbug your second choice, in the most perfect confidence that in any case your vote cannot help to return Mr. Wurstberg.

There is the cardinal fact in the discussion of the matter. Let the reader grasp that, and he has the key to the significance of the question. With Proportional Representation with a single transferable vote (this specificaton is necessary because there are also the inferior imitations of various election-riggers figuring as proportional representation) *It is impossible to prevent the fictive candidature of independent men of the party beside the official candidate.* Without it at the next Parliament, the Parliament that will draw the broad lines of the Empire's destinies for many years, will be just the familiar gathering of old Parliamentary hands and commonplace party hacks. It will be a Parliament gravitating fatally from the very first towards the old party dualities and all the falsity and futility through which we drifted in the years before the war. Proportional Representation is the door for the outside man; the Bill that establishes it will be the charter to enfranchise the non-party Briton. Great masses of people today are utterly disgusted with "party", and an anger gathers against "the party politician" as such that he can scarcely suspect. To close that door now that it has been opened ever so slightly and to attempt the task of Imperial Reconstruction with a sham representative Parliament on the old lines, with large masses of thwarted energy and much practical ability and critical power locked out may be a more dangerous and disastrous game than those who are playing it seem to realize at the present time.

I am, etc.,

H.G. Wells

---

[1] One of the causes for which Wells campaigned for most of his life was that of Proportional Representation in Parliament. This letter, which appeared on 30 March 1917, was also reprinted in a pamphlet calling for PR.

1111. To the provisional government in Russia[1]

PL

[London] [*c.* 31 March 1917]

The news of the Russian revolution, of this giant stride from autocracy to republican democracy, astounded Western Europe. This great change in Russia, this banner of fiery hope that has been raised over Europe, was no farce or spectacle. It comes, indeed, as the call of God, too, to every liberal thinking man throughout the world. We had not dared to hope it. Even men who, like myself, have been more energetic in pleading the cause of Russia in Western Europe and America, who have been saying ever since the war began: 'You are wrong in your fear of Russia; Russians are by nature a liberal-spirited people, and their autocracy is a weakness that they will overcome' – even we who said that counted on nothing so swift and splendidly complete as this revolution. Today Russia stands a giant challenge to every vestige of the dynastic system that has darkened, betrayed and tormented Europe for unnumbered years.

British diplomatists and publicists may make their tepid acknowledgements of the cause betray perhaps a habit of sympathy with the dark forces overthrown. These are matters of form and transition, but in the hearts of the four British nations the Russian revolution burns like a fire.

---

[1] After the breakdown of the Tsarist government, a provisional government was formed. Many British people cabled their good wishes to the new government, including Lord Bryce, Bernard Shaw, Lord Crewe, John Hodge (Minister for Labour), G. N. Barnes, (Minister for Pensions), and Wells. These were printed in *The New York Times*, 1 April 1917, p. 3. Wells's comment, in a more elaborate wording, also appeared in the *Daily Chronicle* 5 April 1917. Others who appeared in this second collection of greetings under the headline, 'Democracy's Salute to Freed Russia – Striking Messages of Welcome from Well-Known Men and Women', were Arnold Bennett, the Bishop of Birmingham, Ronald Barrows, (Principal of Kings College), Hall Caine, Dr Clifford, Marie Corelli, Will Crooks, Sir Arthur Conan Doyle, Mrs J. R. Green (widow of the historian), Sir Oliver Lodge, the Lord Mayor of London, Sir William Dunn, T.P. O'Connor, Mrs. Pankhurst, and Sir Mark Sykes. The American version of Wells's letter appears first, followed by the English version as letter 1112.

1112. To the provisional government in Russia

PL

[London] [*c.* 31 March 1917]

The news of this Russian Revolution, of this giant stride from autocracy to republican democracy, has astounded Western Europe. If we have not burst forthwith into a tumult of rejoicing it is for no lack of sympathy and admiration. But a man who cheers the winner in a fencing match and laughs gleefully to see the villain of a farcical play baffled and tripped up, may sit silent for a time when he hears the call of God. And this great change in Russia, this banner of fiery hope that has been raised over Europe, was no farce nor spectacle, it comes indeed as the call of God to every liberal-thinking man throughout the world. We had not dared to hope it. Even men, like myself, who have been most energetic in pleading the cause of Russia to western Europe and America, who have been saying ever since the war began, "You are wrong in your fear of Russia. The Russians are by nature a liberal spirited people, and their autocracy is a weakness they will overcome," even as we said this, counted on nothing so swift and splendidly complete as this Revolution. Today Russia stands a gigantic challenge to every vestige of the dynastic system that has darkened, betrayed and tormented Europe for unnumbered years. "The Republic of Russia", men are saying everywhere in England, "and then the Republic of United Poland, the Republic of Greece, the Republic of Bulgaria; the end of tricky diplomacies and monarchical ambitions; the precursor of the world federation of republics that will ensure the enduring peace of the world". The British diplomatists and publicists may make their tepid acknowledgements of the change, betray perhaps a habit of sympathy with the dark forces overthrown, these are matters of form and tradition, but in the heart of the four British nations the Russian Revolution burns like a fire.

1113. To the Editor, *New Witness*[1]

PLS

[London] [*c.* 1 April 1917]

Sir, – Once more Mr. Shaw rattles his mind at me, and at last reluctantly "pauses for a reply". Once more I have that henpecked feeling ... These replies cannot go on. If only I could trust the pause to last I think I would not reply now. As it is, there is little to be done except to tell Mr. Shaw that his communication is seen and noted. He adds nothing to his former attempt to show that he has always taught that the human species changes by a change in the average and not by the projection of Supermen. His former attempt was inadequate, and a few bad analogies do not improve his case. Neither does he make things better for his plea for a sort of trade-union conspiracy of prominent writers to impose themselves on the public as important personalites, by reproaching me with want of *esprit de corps. Esprit de corps*, when it takes the form of saving the face of a gang at any cost, is the basest of gregarious impulses. There is no *corps* in the case of literature. (Which later sentence will not prevent Mr. Shaw making out that I have called writers a "gang" any more than he has been deterred from pretending that I have reproached Dante with adultery and deprecated literature as the work of immoral people.) Mr. Shaw's idea of some sort of "benefit of clergy" for writing people, is a childish claim for an unfair immunity.

For the rest his letter is just the old tiresome Shaw trick of imputing silly motives and offering foolish advice. It used to be effective in the dear old Fabian Society; it had its fighting value before that well trained audience, in leaving a serious antagonist, after a torrent of nonsensical personal talk, with nothing whatever to which he could reply, sputtering protests, "But I *didn't* say.....I *didn't* intend...." The serried spinsters tittered at the poor lost creature fumbling to recover the issue and it was all very amusing. Now that we get Mr. Shaw into the unsympathetic open the contest is less uneven. But I warn Mr. Shaw that in these busy times two replies upon the Consistency of Mr. Shaw is as much as he has any right to demand.

Yours, etc.,
H.G. Wells

---

[1] This letter was published on 5 April 1917 under the heading 'The Undamnable Mr. Shaw'.

1114. To the American People[1]

PL

[London] [3 April 1917]

Don't fight for yourselves: don't fight for us, but fight with the freed democracies of the world to make an end forever to all aggressive imperialism.

[1] The signal that the United States was about to enter the war on the side of the Allies came with Woodrow Wilson's speech of 3 April 1917. Although there was a debate in Congress, the declaration of war passed on a divided vote. Many English leaders welcomed the American intervention and sent messages of good will to the United States. Wells's cable was among those which appeared in the *New York Times* on 4 April 1917, p. 3, along with many others.

1115. To the Editor, *The Times*[1]

PLS

Easton Glebe
Dunmow, Essex [*c.* 18 April 1917]

Sir, – Will you permit me to suggest to your readers that the time is now ripe, and that it would be a thing agreeable to our friends and Allies, the Republican democracies of France, Russia, the United States, and Portugal, to give some clear expression to the great volume of Republican feeling that has always existed in the British community? Hitherto that has neither needed nor found very definite formulation. Our Monarchy is a peculiar one: the general Republican feeling has found satisfaction in the assertion that the British system is in its essence, a "crowned Republic"; and it is very doubtful whether even in Ireland there is a considerable section disposed to go beyond the implications of that phrase. But it will be an excess of civility to the less acceptable pretensions of Royalty and a grave negligence of our duty to liberal aspirations throughout the world if thinking men in the British community do not now take unambiguous steps to make it clear to the Republicans of Europe, Asia, and the American Continent that these ancient trappings of throne and sceptre are at most a mere historical inheritance of ours, and that our spirit is warmly and entirely against the dynastic-system that has so long divided, embittered, and wasted the spirit of mankind.

The need extends beyond even the reassuring establishment of a common spirit with the French, Russian, American and Portugeuse Republicans. The ending of this war involves many permanent changes in the condition of Eastern Europe and Western Asia. In particular there is the question of the future of the reunited Polish people. The time has come to say clearly that the prospect of setting up some puppet monarch, some fresh intriguing little "cousin of everybody", for a King in Poland is as disgusting to liberal thought in Great Britain as it is to liberal thought everywhere else in the world. We have had two object lessons in Bulgaria and Greece of the endless mischief these dynastic graftings cause. Bulgaria is by nature a peasant democracy as sturdy and potentially as pacific as the Swiss. A King has always been an outrage upon the ancient Republican traditions of Athens. So long as Russia chose to be repesented by a Tsar and to permit an implicit support of the Greek monarchy through him, so long were British publicists debarred from a plain expression of their minds in connexion. But now the case is altered. It is, I am convinced, a foolish libel upon a disinterested and devoted monarch to hint that the preposterous "Tino" has now a single friend at Court among the Allies. The open fraternization of the British people and the Greek Republicans is practicable, necessary and overdue.

For the demonstration of such sentiments and sympathies as these, for the advancement of the ends I have advocated, and for the encouragement of a Republican organization in Central Europe, some immediate organization is required in Great Britain. To begin with, it might take the form of a series of loosely affiliated "Republican Societies", centering in our chief towns, which could enrol members, organize meetings of sympathy with our fellow-Republicans abroad, and form the basis for more definite purposeful activities. Such activities need not conflict in any way with one's free loyalty to the occupant of the Throne of this "crowned Republic".

Very sincerely yours,
H.G. Wells

---

[1] This letter, under the heading, 'A Republican Society for Great Britain', appeared on 21 April 1917.

1116. To Captain Charles

Boston, ACCS

Easton Glebe
Dunmow [*c.* April 1917?]

Dear Capt. Charles,

Thank you for your friendly note. I didn't like the telegram though I jumped to its real significance but I think it a pity that soldiers should think their uniform stands for King rather than country. My Times letter didn't suggest the abolition of Geo V. at all. You don't perhaps know all that is going on.

The Court has been playing the fool with the Greek princes & it has been necessary to start this warning discussion.[1] Good wishes.

Yours ever
H.G. Wells

See Monday's Times

[1] See Wells's letters to *The Times*, 21 April 1917, 'A Republican Society for Great Britain', and 23 April 1917, 'Republicanism in Great Britain', 1115 and 1117, which discussed the Greek monarchy. Also see letter 1119 to the *Daily Chronicle* and his piece in *The Penny Pictorial* 19 May 1917, pp. 337, 341, 'The Future of Monarchs'.

1117. To the Editor, *The Times*[1]

PLS

52, St. James's Court
Buckingham Gate, S.W. [22 April 1917]

Sir, – I am greatly obliged to you for the publication of my letter, and equally so for your admirable statement of the case for monarchy in the British Empire. It may, however, arrest the development of a misconception if I point out that there is really no conflict whatever between your statement of the case and the opinions underlying my letter except upon the advisability of forming republican societies under that title in this country. Few people wish to see any change in the "golden link" of Empire. On the other hand there can be little dispute that very many minds are disturbed and becoming restless on account of our tepid treatment of the Greek Republicans. It is unfortunate that we should seem to encourage, however slightly, the Greek Royal family at the present time and many of us who are by no means so sure as we would like to be that the full weight of British influence will be thrown into the scale in favour of liberal institutions and the breaking up of the dynastic net in Eastern Europe. Hence this disposition to republican activity. None of these things ought to reflect upon our own Throne. The position of the British Monarchy is a special and peculiar one; we have no business bringing it into these matters, and it should be possible to profess and discuss the republican idea freely and fully without implicating the Imperial Crown.

Very sincerely yours,
H. G. Wells

[1] This appeared in the issue of 23 April 1917 under the heading 'Republicanism in Britain'.

1118. To the Editor, *Daily News*[1]

PLS

[London] [*c*. 22 April 1917]

Sir, – Mr. W.F. Barrett does neither P.R., nor myself justice, when he declares that I have recently become a convert to "P.R." I have worked steadily for "P.R." for the last ten years and more. No intelligent man who looks into the question can fail to see the enormous advantage of this method of election.

H.G. Wells

[1] This appeared in the issue of 23 April 1914. Barrett extended his thanks to Wells for his letters on 24 April 1917.

1119. To the Editor, *Daily Chronicle*[1]

PLS

[London] April 26, 1917

Sir, – A considerable discussion has broken out upon the question of republican feeling in this country. As a result of a rather hasty reading of a letter addressed by the present writer to the "Times", it has been assumed there is some movement afoot for the setting up of Republican institutions here, and Lord Montagu, the Maharajah of Bikanir, and others have been eager to express their convictions that the people of India will never tolerate a British republic. (The ties of Empire, one may note, bind both ways).

If I may, I should be glad of your help to stem the tide of this misapprehension. No such profound changes as these have been advocated. What has been suggested is, firstly, that we should have the grace to recognize freely and generously the advantages of the republican form of government in America, Russia, France and Portugal, and then to express our opinions of the manifest desirability of a republican form of government in Germany, Greece, Bulgaria, and the forthcoming new state of Poland. We do not wish to discuss the British monarchy at all. We believe we do it the best service in our power by separating it altogether in our thoughts from the outworn and altogether rotten

German dynastic system that has been so fruitful of evil in Europe. We believe that it will be able so to separate itself in fact. But if any criticism of the dynastic system on the Continent of Europe is to be treated as an attack on the British Imperial Crown, then the whole situation becomes confused and dangerous.

They do the King a poor service who would use him for a fastness from which to attack the critics of the treacherous Constantine, the Prussian monarchy, the Austro-Hungarian empire, and the obsolete Tsar, and who meet any abstract discussion of republicanism with old-fashioned Royalist blustering. They lay themselves open to the sinister retort that there is then a trade union of monarchs, and that all of them must stand or fall together.

H. G. Wells

---

[1] From the issue of 27 April 1917

1120. Israel Zangwill to H. G. Wells

Illinois, TLS

Far End
East Preston
Sussex

May 4th, 1917.

My dear Wells,

I am glad of our measure of agreement. Yes, the Jews – so far – have failed; even the Galilean Jew, backed by all the organized weight of Christendom. On God and his Englishman you seem to reproduce my very criticism from Milton. But for me the big man in the war is not the English Wilson, finely as he reproduces the Jewish prophets, but the Jewish Bloch, to whose prophecy you have yourself done homage, and who was the original inspirer of the Hague Conference. Peoples produce prophets – as the English have produced you – but a prophetic majority has never yet existed; and to try the Jews by a standard assuming such wholesale fineness is one of the fallacies that vitiate your treatment of the Jewish question, and which may make me one day enter the lists against you. As for Russia, nothing can condone the British policy which for years put back the clock of freedom. I commend to you particularly an article in to-day's Daily News, called "Free Russia and Britain". I can see nothing against the Russian people themselves in my lecture, but in my last book my prophecy stands that it is Russia that will drag us back to freedom.

Sincerely yours,
Israel Zangwill

1121. Israel Zangwill to H. G. Wells

Illinois, TLS

Far End
East Preston
Sussex

May 10th, 1917

My dear Wells,

I hasten to acknowledge your kind gift. Of course, I cannot appraise it without the careful examination its great thesis demands, nor can I hope that you have entirely triumphed over the difficulties to all theistic conceptions; but a greedy glance at your book shows it to be finely written and vehemently alive, and I rejoice to think it may revive the intellectual controversies of our youth. We have had too much physical fighting and too little spiritual and intellectual.

I have already recommended your book to the Chief Rabbi and Mr. Claude Montifiore; [1] but as I still feel it leaves me in your debt, I am instructing my publisher to forward a copy of my prohibited play, "The Next Religion", as what you say about organized religion reminded me of it.

With cordial thanks both for the book and its contents.

Sincerely yours,
Israel Zangwill

---

[1] The book is *God The Invisible King* (London: Cassel, 1917) which had just appeared (the preface is dated May 1917). Although Wells was later to repudiate his book, it created a substantial discussion in England for six months. Wells had lunch with the Chief Rabbi and Montifiore to discuss the significance of the book, and the sort of Deistic religion Wells was advocating.

1122. To the Editor, *Nature*[1]

PLS

[London]

[early May 1917]

Mr. Livingstone's letter is satisfactory so far as it goes, in promising to spare such boys as are unworthy of classical blessings, but I think many of the readers of Nature will see in its phrasing just that implicit claim to monopolise the best of the boys for the classical side of which I complain. We do not want the imbeciles, the calculating boys, the creatures all hands and no head, and so forth, for the modern side. We want boys for scientific work who may be not "unsuited", but eminently suited for Greek and Latin, in order that they may do something better and more important I write with some personal experience in this matter. I am very much concerned about the welfare of two boys who have a great "aptitude for linguistics", and who would make excellent classical scholars. I think I can do better with them than that, and that they can serve the world better with a different education. In each case I have had to interfere because they were being "muddled about with" by the classical side masters, and have got Russian substituted for the futile beginnings of Greek. The fact remains that Mr. Livingstone does, under existing conditions, wish to retain compulsory Greek.

H.G. Wells

---

[1] In the 19 April 1917 *Nature* Wells reviewed a book, *Science and the Nation*. He advocated eliminating Greek from the curriculum. R.W. Livingston, who felt that the better boys needed the classical languages, commented on the review. This letter is Wells's response to Livingstone's comment. Both letters appeared on 10 May 1917, p. 205.

1123. To S. S. Koteliansky[1]

Illinois, APCS

52, St. James's Court
S.W. 1. [May 1917]

My dear Sir,

I wish I could have half an hour's talk with you on Friday. Would it be possible for you to look in here at 5:30 on that day. There is much in the Russian situation that I cannot understand.

Yours very sincerely
H. G. Wells

---

[1] Koteliansky was one of the most interesting and yet most shadowy of the international figures in Britain in the last years of the First World War. 'Kot' or 'Koto', as he was universally known, was an editor and writer.

1124. To S. S. Koteliansky

Illinois, APCS

52, St James's Court,
S.W. 1. [postmarked 12 May 1917]

Dear Sir,

I want to send my new book to Gorky. Can you give me his exact address.

Very sincerely yours,
H.G. Wells

1125. To S. S. Koteliansky

Illinois, APCS

52, St. James's Court,
S.W. 1. [mid May? 1917]

Dear Sir,

Then I will avail myself of your kind offer and address the book I want to reach Gorky care of you. Mrs. Wells is sending an article from Easton.

Very sincerely yours,
H. G. Wells

1126. To an unknown addressee[1]

Illinois, TCC

Easton Glebe
Dunmow [postmarked May 18, '17]

Dear Sir,

I have always been the steadfast friend of Russia. At the outset of the war when the pro-German socialists here, who now belabour the Russian

Revolution with their approval, had nothing but abuse and insult for the "Russian barbarians". I stood out for the essential rightness and greatness of the Russian mind and will. The Revolution has abundantly confirmed the attitude I then took up, in the Labour Leader against Zangwill, Snowden, Morel and their associates. So now to-day I repeat my faith in the profound instincts of the Russian democracy. I know that they will spare no exertions and endure every hardship to crown this war which is to end dynastic monarchy and aggressive militarism for ever, with a triumphant victory. Long ago I wrote, 'This is a war to End War.' That I repeat to-day and no single fact has done so much to confirm this faith in me, as the Russian Revolution. I send my greetings to Gorky in this supreme hour of the struggle to liberate mankind, the German people included, from [a] net of aggressive monarchy and to establish international goodwill on a basis of international justice and respect.

H.G. Wells

---

[1] The addressee must be Maxim Gorki. Koteliansky frequently acted as a go-between to Russian sources, and certainly knew individuals on all political sides in eastern Europe, especially after the first stage of the Russian Revolution in the spring of 1917. After the Bolshevik phase, he may not have been as well placed, but he knew Gorki and found ways in which Wells and others could maintain some ties with Gorki, and with the majority wing of the Russian Revolutionary forces. The story of his life, and perhaps the story of Moura Budberg who forms part of this scene, has not yet been told completely. Wells's ties to these two persons, and to Ivan Maisky, Ivy Litvinoff (married originally to Walter Low), as well as others, may yet emerge more fully from the Kremlin archives. There are a dozen or more letters from Wells to Koteliansky, but they mainly deal with tutoring sessions for Gip Wells, before the Wells's went to Russia in 1920, and other routine matters. In fact after 1922 most of the letters to Kot came from Catherine Wells. The relationships were close however. Marjorie Wells was with Kot when he died in January, 1955. Kot, in addition, to receiving letters from Wells, also delivered several for him to a variety of addressees; three of them, 1126, 1127 and 1134, are included here as having a wide significance. The first is apparently addressed to Gorki in a very roundabout fashion. The second, written the next day, is a remarkable statement of war aims or terms for peace which parallels the fourteen points address of Woodrow Wilson. The third (6 July) is a comment on the British press in the wake of the Russian Revolutionary events. The standard book on Koteliansky and his circle is John Carswell, *Life and Letters: A. R. Orage, Katherine Mansfield, Beatrice Hastings, John Middleton Murry, S. S. Koteliansky, 1906–1957* (London: New Directions, 1978.) I have argued the importance of these documents, and the position of Walter Lippmann, Colonel House (and a dinner party at Easton during this period), as well as documents from these sources, at the end of chapter 9 of my biography of Wells; see, in particular, the documentation in footnotes 41 and 43–5.

1127. To an unknown addressee

Illinois, TCC

52, St. James's Court, S.W. [no date but Koteliansky dated it 19 May 1917]

Dear Sir,[1]

I am an Englishman who knows his countrymen to the bone and you may take my word for it that no government, no power in the world could prevent them from making peace, if they could be sure of

(1) The liberation and <u>compensation</u> of Belgium by Germany.
(2) The liberation of all the invaded and annexed regions of France, those taken in 1871 being of course included.
(3) The reunion of the Italian provinces of Austria (the Trentino and Trieste) to Italy.
(4) The liberation of the Poles (including the Poles of Posen and Galicia) from foreign oppression.
(5) The liberation of Servia and of the Servian peoples.
(N.B. no item 6)
(7) The evacuation and restoration of Rumania.
(8) The liberation of Armenia, Arabia and Palestine from Turkish misrule.
(9) The abandonment of imperialist aggressions on the part of Germany.
(10) The securing for Russia of a free access to the Mediterranean.

In addition English opinion and the national will of England is strongly in favour of

(11) home-rule or autonomy for the Tchekoslovak peoples.

All the British peoples are at one with the Americans in desiring to see some permanent League of Nations, in which of course it is hoped to include a liberated Germany, set up to keep the peace of the world, to control international shipping and to prevent the clash of commercial interests developing into international conflicts. It is for these ends the British, French and Italian peoples are fighting to-day. We fight to overcome the German war makers and end war for ever.

Yours very sincerely,
H.G. Wells

[1] To whom this was delivered, for it apparently did not go through the post, is not known. The similarity to certain speeches of Woodrow Wilson may indicate a source. Walter Lippmann, Bainbridge Colby, even Colonel House himself were all possible recipients. There are several

guarded accounts of a dinner party hosted by Countess Warwick at about this time, and it may be that the document derived from the conversation at that table. It may well have been read and seen by others in France, Russia, England and elsewhere.

1128. To the Editor, *The Times Literary Supplement*[1]

PLS

[London] [*c.* 20 May 1917]

Sir, – Your reviewer of my "God The Invisible King" makes so entertaining and attractive a description of the thesis of that book that I find it impossible to refrain a word or two of comment and correction. He is, I think, a little biased by an idea, a mistaken idea, that I am something or other called a "biologist," instead of being just an ordinary human being writing about a very universal interest. He represents me as believing that "the aim of God and of man " is the overcoming of death for *some future* generation *of man*," and on this supposition he makes great play with me. He makes such excellent play that almost apologetically I point out that it is sheer nonsense to read any such meaning into my book. To anyone not obsessed by a preconception that my ideas must be "biological" ideas, it will be plain that my conception of immortality for the individual life now and for ever is the merger of that life in the greater being of the race. As Man I may live for ever; as H. G. Wells I die and end. As long as mankind endures it will be the same story. We touch immortality now as surely as ever mankind will touch it. We are all parts of one immortality.

Your reviewer thinks not in the common language, but in a jargon in which the phrase "absolute values" plays an inordinate part. It is a phraseology with which I am unfamiliar; I may not be alone among your readers in that respect; it conveys remarkably little to my mind. "Value" comes into philosophical talk, I imagine, by way of studio slang, and originally to express relative importance. "Absolute values" seems to be merely a bad way of speaking of "fixed standards." If it is not, I miss what it is your reviewer has in mind. Through a number of paragraphs I am reduced to a state analogous to a whaler when the quarry has gone down. I should feel altogether baffled and defeated were it not that, at length when he comes up again out of the depths of his technicalities, I find him emitting indisputable nonsense. For example, he comes up in this fasion: -

> Just as we love men for what they are and not only for what they are trying to do, so we must love God for what He is and not only for what He is trying to do. God for those who are most intensely aware of him is an artist and not a philanthropist. He has but one function, namely, to conquer death for man, or perhaps for all life.

Now if your reviewer said that God was a beauty, or a "character" I could understand the spirit at least of this "*must* love"; but an artist is just exactly what God is to me, the being, that is, of a creative effort, whose material is man. "Philanthropist", like "respectable person", is in my English a mere form of abuse. It implies a petting condescension altogether alien to an acceptable idea of God. What sort of an "artist" can God be, if he is not trying to do something? And your reviewer would be quibbling were it not so plain that he is merely blundering when he declares that salvation from death is not a positive good. How can there be any continuing conquest of death that is not life and life and more life and more and everything that life implies?

It seems to me that your reviewers disposition to treat my book as if it were written from a specialized standpoint arises out of his own extreme specialization of attitude. Throughout his pose is not so much that of a common human being as of a spiritual connoisseur. He faces the spectacle catalogue and pencil in hand. He reproves my blindness because I will not see God the great artist in the stars and the lilies of the field, "which are of the same order as the stars, being, like them what we call nature". And he claims Plato to stand beside him in this crushing condemnation of my Philistine theology. But Plato sometimes laughed at himself; let me but parody a well-known dialogue, and remind your reviewer of hyaenas, cuckoos, tape-worms, offal, the incidentals of disease and the processes of corruption "which are of the same order as the stars, being, like them what we call nature". Let us take in some case other than the lilies under the stars. Let your reviewer consider himself greatly afflicted by midges and sitting in the twilight of a close and sultry day holding in his hand a recently exhumed human shoulder blade gnawed by a wolf. Does that also, which is "of the same order as the stars, being, like them, what we call nature", still sustain him in his astonishment at my agnosticism about the God of Creation?

Very truly yours,
H. G. Wells

---

[1] This letter appeared in the issue of 24 May 1917, p. 24, under the headline, 'A Desperate Hope'.

1129. To the Editor, *Daily Chronicle*[1]

PLS

[London] [*c.* 1 June 1917]

Dear Sir, – The time seems to have come for much clearer statements of outlook and intention from this country than it has hitherto been possible to make. The entry of America into the war and the banishment of autocracy and aggressive diplomacy from Russia have enormously cleared the air, and the recent great speech of General Smuts at the Savoy Hotel is probably only the first of a series of experiments in statement.

It is desireable alike to clear our own heads, to unify our efforts, and to give the nations of the world some assurance and standard for our national conduct in future that we should now define the ideas of our empire and its relationship to the world outlook much more clearly than has ever hitherto been done. Never before in the history of mankind has opinion counted for so much and persons and organizations for so little as in this war. Never before has the need for clear ideals, widely understood and consistently sustained, been so commandingly vital.

Is it not the plain lesson of this stupendous and disastrous war that there is no way to secure civilization from destruction except by impartial control and protection in the interest of the whole human race, a control representing the best intelligence of mankind, of these main causes of war: (1) the politically underdeveloped tropics, (2) shipping and international trade, and (3) small nationalities and all regions in a state of political impotence or confusion?

It is our case against the Germans that in all these three cases they have subordinated every consideration of justice and general human welfare to monstrous national egotism. That argument has a double edge. At present there is a vigorous campaign in America, Russia and neutral countries generally to represent British patriotism as equally egotistic, and our purpose in this war as a mere parallel to the German purpose. In the same manner, though perhaps with less persistence, France and Italy are also caricatured. We are supposed to be grabbing at Mesopotamia and Palestine, France at Syria. Italy is represented as pursuing a Machiavellian policy toward the unfortunate Greek republicans, with her eyes on the Greek islands and Greece in Asia.

Is it not time that these imputations were repudiated largely and conclusively by our alliance, and is it not time we began to discuss in much more frank and definite terms than hitherto has been done the nature of the international arrangement that will be needed to secure the safety of such liberated populations as those of Palestine, of the Arab regions, of the old Turkish Empire, of Armenia, of reunited Poland and the like?

I do not mean mere diplomatic discussions and understandings. I mean such full and plain statements as will be spread through the whole world and grasped and assimilated by ordinary people everywhere – statements by which we as a people will be prepared to stand or fall. Great Britain has to table her world policy. It is a thing overdue. No doubt we have already a literature of liberal imperialism and a considerable accumulation of declarations by this statesman or that; but what is needed is a formulation much more representative, official and permanent than that – something that can be put beside President Wilson's clear rendering of the American ideal. We want all our peoples to understand that our empire is not a net about the world in which the progress of mankind is entangled, but a self-conscious political system, working side by side with the other democracies of the earth, preparing the way for and prepared to sacrifice and merge itself in a world confederation of free and equal peoples.

H.G. Wells

---

[1] Wells continued his efforts to focus the British people and government on the purpose of the war. On 4 June 1917 he wrote this letter to the *Daily Chronicle* 'Wanted: A Statement of Imperial Policy: Mr. Wells and the Plain Lessons of the War". The letter was rejected by *The Times* on the grounds that it was 'too revolutionary'. It was reprinted in *The New York Times* on the same day and it appeared in his book *In The Fourth Year* (London: Chatto and Windus, 1918).

1130. To an unknown correspondent

PL

[London] 22 June 1917[1]

I agree with you that we need a concise Labour programme, but I would make it shorter rather than longer than yours. May I suggest -

1. The ultimate abolition of all hereditary privilege and the establishment of Democratic Republicanism throughout the Empire.

2. The conversion of the Empire into a League of Free Nations.

3. The concentration of foreign policy upon the establishment of a world alliance of all free nations to prevent wars and armament for wars, to control world shipping and transit, to prevent vexatious tariffs and other trading hostilities, and to protect uncivilised and politically confused countries from conquest and exploitation.

4. The nationalisation of land and natural resources, of all transit services, of the staple food trade and of the drink trade.

5. The nationalisation of banking.

6. Universal suffrage for all over 21, with, of course, proportional representation upon the lines laid down by the P.R. society.

7. Penalisation of deliberate falsehood in advertisement and the press. (This is absolutely essential to the health of democracy.)

8. Liberation of religion from state control (and subvention.)

9. Free education up to 16 for all and further education for everyone with the necessary capacity.

10. Minimum wage.

11. Motherhood and old age pensions on a computable scale.

---

[1] Wells was apparently thinking in terms of lists of goals at this time in his life. An unknown correspondent in Manchester wrote him and asked for a statement of goals for the Labour Party after the war. The recipient provided the *Manchester Guardian* with a copy of Wells's letter and his programme. They printed it on page 5, on 22 June 1917, under the heading, 'Mr. H.G. Wells's Labour Programme'.

1131. To A.T. Simmons

Illinois, ALS

52, St. James's Court
Buckingham Gate, S.W.1. [*c*. June? 1917]

Dear Tommy,

Austin wants bracing up; I mean to make every man who opposes P.R. ashamed – just as though he had been caught eating peas with his knife. You can't go soft with men who don't mean the right thing & they are much more amenable to good square trouncing than they are to history criticisms. Can't you do something to make the P.R. question <u>tell</u> in the London University election? Won't you join the P.R. Society? I ought to be put up for the L. University.

Yours ever,
H.G.

1132. To Mr Hudson

Hofstra, ANS

[Crewe House
London] July 2nd [1917]

To Philips, F.O.

Dear Hudson,

Will you put this through First a German translation. Then it must be approved by some sound authority & then sent to Dr. Mitchell[1] .

H.G.W.

[1] Note accompanying next item

1133. To Mr Hudson[1]

Hofstra, ADL

[Crewe House] [*c.* July 1917]

British War Medal

awarded

to the Kaiser

for courage and devotion to duty

The official "London Gazette" says that while the battery in which he was serving was being heavily shelled he excavated three men from a demolished dug-out & carried them to safety. He then went out & carried in a badly wounded officer. Then under heavy fire, he extinguished a fire in the gun pit caused by a German shell.

But perhaps the Kaiser we mean is not the Kaiser you are thinking of. The Kaiser we mean is Sergeant L. Kaiser. Kaiser is a good German name. He is a good German who like many good Germans in the American & Allied forces is fighting for the freedom of Germany & the League of All The Nations which will bring peace to mankind. He is in the Australian Field Artillery. There is no conscription in Australia. There are no Junkers there. A German can live better there than he can in Germany. Why fight against him?

---

[1] This is the proposed text of a letter, and a dispatch to the press, both in English and German, as part of the propaganda work at Crewe House where Wells was then working.

1134. To an unknown addressee[1]

Illinois, TCCLS

52, St. James's Court, S.W.1. [statement undated, but Koteliansky added 6 July]

The recent Russian victory has been a victory for liberalism throughout the world. In Great Britain in particular it is welcome. It is useless to disguise the fact that British opinion is not unanimously in favour of the Revolution. While the mass of British peoples welcomed it with enthusiasm, there can be no denying that a small but influential class view this birth of free people with hostility and fear. These British reactionaries, alarmed at the spread of democratic and republican sentiments, lose no opportunity of belittling and misrepresenting the renascence of Russia. Such periodicals as the Morning Post, Blackwood's Magazine and the like, quite unchecked by the censorship that has prohibited the exportation of the Nation, maintain a flow of insult and depreciation of the great liberal republics of Russia and America. They assure their readers day after day that a republican people must needs be foolish in peace and feeble in war, that free institutions mean confusion of purpose and weakness of aim. Every extravagance of even the smallest body of Russian extremists is displayed and exaggerated to the utmost; every instance of indiscipline and indecision is flung into the faces of British liberals with the taunt; "These are your republican friends!" If Russia makes good; if Russia preserves her unity and her resolution in the face of German Kaiserism, all these taunts will recoil upon the heads of those who make them. If the Revolution in Russia fails, we in Britain fail. We shall come out of this war with our freedom impaired and our hopes broken. Russia is the battleground of freedom to-day for all the world and all the world knows it. The battles we fight on the western front are just the give and take of this gigantic war, but a great victory by the new born Russian republic will be a battle decisive for the whole future of mankind.

H.G. Wells

---

[1] This may have appeared in newspapers, or it may have been circulated as a round robin letter by Koteliansky. However it was used, it does provide a new glimpse at the rather murky events of 1917 in eastern Europe. The statement was printed in Petrograd in the *Bitzhevia Vedomoeti* who provided it to the *Daily News* who published it under the heading, 'Mr. H. G. Wells's Message', in their issue of 9 July 1917.

1135. To the Editor, *The Nation*[1]

PLS

Easton Glebe,
Dunmow July 31st, 1917

Sir, – I see that Mr. Shebbeare, instead of addressing me directly, has written me a sort of open letter in the Nation, to ask for my authority for the statement that the Christian Churches are the steadfast enemies of the illegitimate, and that they regard a bastard as a child especially tainted by the sin of his origin over and above his normal share of original sin. I am afraid I can not meet his demand for citations. As a novelist I spend my time learning what I can about people's experiences and ways of thinking, rather than in documentary study, and the trend of my observations is to show the Churches in the light in which I have set them.

It is a common claim that organized Christianity is the great upholder of family life as against Atheists, Socialists, and modern tendencies generally. As a matter of fact, it seems to me , in spite of Mr. Shebbeare, that organized Christianity is the great obstacle between the illegitmate and any family life at all. Believing as I do not only that a child has its best chances for a wholesome growth of mind and body under the immediate protection of its mother, but also that the presence, help, and active participation of its father in its fortunes and education is really necessary to its well-being, and that no child should be a solitary child, I have been enormously impressed by the difficulties put in the way of an unmarried woman keeping her illegitimate family and her social comfort at the same time, and by the practical impossibility of the father openly fathering such a child. The social atmosphere tolerates any sort of seclusion and concealment and falsehood rather than "open sin" of this sort; and the social atmosphere is, I submit, created and sustained by the Christian Churches. An attempt to bring up an illegitimate family in comfort and dignity and without falsehood in such a country as ours is almost invariably opposed and defeated by the impossibility of getting servants and governesses and proper educational facilities and of sheltering the children from insult and humiliation; and the centre of that oppostion, as far as my observations go, is almost invariably the local vicarage or manse. Illegitimate children are, in practice at any rate, treated as tainted by the mere fact of illegitimacy. Directly the mother can contrive to pass herself off as a widow or pretend her child is adopted, and that the man is a cousin or a friend, the difficulties vanish. There is nothing further to trouble about then, except to keep the lie flourishing and to guard against the horrors of domestic blackmail. I may be wrong in ascribing to doctrinal Christianity what is perhaps a purely social prejudice, and I may be unjust in treating the vicarage as a centre of Christian teaching rather than as an active centre of conventional social ideas. I shall certainly welcome any declaration from Mr. Shebbeare that orthodox Christian doctrine, as opposed to current Christian practice, is on the side of the illegitimate family rather than against it, and still more shall I welcome any instance of a Christian Church which has been helpful in keeping the illegitimate family from disintegration. I know of plentiful instances to the contrary.To the ordinary vicarage the ordinary prying servant who has found a compromising letter trots off with a quite justifiable confidence. I know of no parish where an artificially sterile married couple with a gramophone would not be infintely more welcome and made infinitely more comfortable as parishoners than an unmarried woman with an admittedly illegitimate child, though she might be the best of mothers and the ablest and most dignified of women.

Yours, etc.,
H. G. Wells

---

[1] This letter appeared in the issue of 4 August 1917, p. 455 under the heading, 'The Church and the Illegitimate'. This letter has more personal significance than most of his letters to the press.

1136. To Siegfried Sassoon[1]

McMaster, ALS

Easton Glebe
Dunmow

August 20th, 1917
[*in another hand*]

My dear Sassoon,

I will try & get hold of Rivers – When your six weeks are over, I hope you'll be free to start upon your proper work in the world – which is poetry only by the way. Human muddle isn't an affair of goodness versus wickedness. It's a complicated tangle of motives that has to be analyzed. Analysis of a riddle is half its solution. We want to store passion & indignation & get the Human Problem stated. Oh! you think I'm a prissy bore but it's only by boring away at the statement of the flat broad things in human relationship that we can get any effective reform movement to work. We've got to soak the human mind with the ideas of World State, Kingdom of God, Brotherhood of Mankind, International Control of Shipping, Trade, Health & so on. – until national flags look like nursery games or the tricks of pill vendors.

I'm scribbling this much in a hurry but I think it says (as badly as possible) what I mean.

Yours ever,
H.G. Wells[2]

---

[1] Siegfried Louvain Sassoon (1886–1967), poet and novelist, best known for his poems of the horrors of war collected in *Counterattack* (1918) and *Satirical Poems* (1926).
[2] This remarkable letter sheds even more light on the campaign to bring an end to the war. Rivers was the doctor at Craiglockhart who treated Sassoon, Wilfred Owen and others.

1137. To Siegfried Sassoon

McMaster, ALS

52, St. James's Court
Buckingham Gate, S.W.1

Sept. 1917
[*in another hand*]

My dear Sassoon,

I counsel patience. Don't get locked up out of the way. Then don't do anything excessive. Do ostentatiously sober things. Take your discharge for "shock" & then let every action show that it was a mere excuse, that you are a grave & balanced man set upon the peace of the world. Don't develop into a "case".[1] Treat all that happens to you as incidental to the efforts of sane men to get this crazy world into a state of order again. Don't seem to become in any way a man with a grievance. If sensitive fine minded men allow themselves to be tormented into mere shrieks of protest then the blockheads & the blood drinkers will prevail for ever. Personally, I am concerned that if I live another twenty years I shall see the world manifestly going sure & straight to the great peace of mankind. Even I who am 51 will live to see that day. You are much more sure than I am. We are in the same line.

I shall be in London most of this week. I'd like to come & talk to you.

Yours ever,
H.G.Wells

---

[1] Sassoon had been decorated for bravery with the Military Cross. Badly wounded, he was invalided home; upon recovery he publicly criticized the conduct of the war and was threatened with a court martial. To avoid a national outcry he was discharged from the army on medical grounds and was to follow the advice in this letter.

1138. To Miles Malleson[1]

PLS

52, St. James's Court,
Buckingham Gate, S.W. [1916]

My dear Sir:

I think that a small minority of the C.O.s are sincerely honest men but I believe that unless the path of the C.O. is made difficult it will supply a stampede track for every variety of shirker. Naturally a lot of work of control falls on the hands of clumsy and rough minded men. I really don't feel very much sympathy with these "martyrs". I don't feel so sure as you do that all C.O.s base their objection on love rather than hate. I have never heard either Cannan or Norman speak lovingly of any human being. Their normal attitude has always been one of opposition – to anything. Enthusiasm makes them liverish. And the Labour Leader group I believe to be thoroughly dishonest, Ramsay MacDonald, I mean, Morel and the editor. I may be wrong but that is my slow and simple conviction.

Very sincerely yours,
H. G. Wells

---

[1] Malleson, a friend of Bertrand Russell, was married to the actress, Colette O'Neil. They were active in the No Conscription Fellowship, made up of persons who declared conscientious objection to the First World War and refused service. Wells accepted this view of C.O. status, because Russell, founder of the Fellowship, had stated his position clearly before the war. This letter to Malleson, written by Wells at the end of 1916 or the beginning of 1917, deals with conscientious objector status. It was published in Russell's, *Autobiography* Vol. II (London: Allen and Unwin, 1968), pp. 93–4. Placement of the letter is in relationship to these early letters to Sassoon. Part 1 of Vol. II of Russell's *Autobiography*, pp. 3–133 is an excellent introduction to this issue, and is filled with printed correspondence of the day on the subject.

1139. To Siegfried Sassoon

ALS

McMaster
Easton Glebe
Dunmow

Monday morning,
[date unknown][1]

My dear Siegfried,

You honour me too much in that picture. You've never yet known the fear of the New Generation & so you don't have the blessed reassurance your friendliness gives me.

[*A wonderful 'picshua' of Chronos carrying an hourglass, a scythe labelled "Extinction" while looking at Wells, who is holding a picture of Wells holding a picture, with the words, "Not yet. Look at this."*]

H.G.

---

[1] There is no indication of when this letter was written, except that it is apparently after the end of the war. Placement here is through the principle of relevance.

1140. To G. K. Chesterton

Illinois, Typed Transcription

Easton Glebe
Dunmow [early Autumn 1917]

My dear G.K.C.,

Haven't I on the whole behaved decently to you? Haven't I always shown a reasonable civility to you and your brother and Belloc? Haven't I betrayed at all times a certain affection for you? Very well, then you will understand that I don't start out to pick a needless quarrel with The New Witness crowd. But this business of the Hueffer book in the New Witness makes me sick. Some disgusting little greaser (named Prothero) has been allowed to insult old F.M.H. in a series of letters that make me ashamed of my species. Hueffer has many faults no doubt but firstly he's poor, secondly he's notoriously unhappy and in a most miserable position, thirdly, he's a better writer than any of your little crowd and fourthly, instead of pleading his age and his fat and taking refuge from service in a greasy obesity as your brother has done, he is serving his country. His book is a great book and Prothero just lies about it – I guess he's a dirty minded priest or some such unclean thing – when he says it is the story of a stallion and so forth. The whole outbreak is so envious, so base, so cat-in-the-gutter-spitting at the-passer-by, that I will never let The New Witness into the house again.

Regretfully yours,
H.G. Wells[1]

[1] This letter appeared in Maisie Ward's *Gilbert Keith Chesterton*, p. 411. Cecil Chesterton did go to France. This controversy surfaced in several other papers, and Wells was careful to support Hueffer/Ford. Maisie Ward reprints Chesterton's answer, on pp. 411–12, and Wells's response, letter 1141. She cut Prothero's name from the letter in her version. Hueffer/Ford's book was almost certainly *The Good Soldier.*

1141. To G. K. Chesterton

Illinois, Typed Transcription

Easton Glebe
Dunmow [Autumn 1917]

Dear GKC,

Also I can't quarrel with you. But the Hueffer business aroused my long dormant moral indignation and I let fly at the most sensitive part of the New Witness constellation, the only part about whose soul I care. I hate these attacks on rather miserable exceptional people like Hueffer and Masterman.[1] I know these aren't perfect men but their defects make quite sufficient hells for them without these public peltings. I suppose I ought to have written to C.C. instead of to you. One of these days I will go and have a heart to heart talk to him. Only I always get so amiable when I meet a man. He, C.C., needs it – I mean the talking to.

Yours ever
H.G.

[1] Both Hueffer and C. F. G. Masterman came from German ancestry. Both were subject to much mudslinging in the press. Masterman was unable to work in the official war effort, and Hueffer enlisted to escape the attacks and changed his name from Hueffer to Ford.

1142. To S. S. Koteliansky

Illinois, Typed Transcription

52, St James's Court,
S.W. 1. [postmarked 28 Sep. '17]

Dear Mr. Koteliansky,

How are you? I have not heard from you for some time. There is a little matter which I should very much like you to put before Gorky. I have never yet received any copy of the Russian translation of Mr Britling Sees It Through in book form. I have translations of that novel now in a great variety of languages and I should particularly value the Russian one.

Very sincerely yours,
H. G. Wells

1143. To Bernard Shaw

British Library, TCCS[1]

52, St. James's Court
Buckingham Gate, S.W. [November ?1917]

My dear Shaw.

I used the ticket and liked your lecture very much & it was amusing to see the old faithful Fabian breed still gathering to its feast. I applauded your Republicanism & endured your theology except that your phrase (Guest's I believe originally) of the "Life Force" embodies an almost encyclopaedic philosophical & biological ignorance. But you are all wrong about Russia & rather out of drawing about Germany. For the latter you need to read When Blood is Their Argument[2] by Hueffer, a book with a lot of superficial vanity & silliness & some wisdom & knowledge. As for Russia, the Russians are more like the Irish & English than any other people in the world. Petrograd, where they discuss political assassination at the dinner tables, is amazingly like Dublin. Put Castleism for Czarism. You rage at Russia as an autocracy; you might just as well rage at Ireland as a Vice-royalty. Neither is true of the people & the country; it is their misfortune, not their fault. I'm no fool, I've got eyes & ears & I assure you that the Russians belong to the North European system much more essentially than the Prussians do. They are, to use your disgusting race cant, whiter. And don't you bother about Russia's mission in China. China will see to any mission work that is needed there.

Yours ever
H.G.

---

[1] Read at Illinois

[2] Wells had reviewed Hueffer's book in the *Daily Chronicle*, 25 March 1915, under the title 'The Perversion of Germany: A Study in Educational Organisation'. Wells, Shaw and Hueffer clashed on Russia and Germany earlier when Wells wrote in the *Daily Chronicle*, with Hagberg Wright, on Russia, 22 September 1914, which Shaw responded to 23 December 1914. Hueffer chimed in on 24 December 1914, supporting Wells. Wells gave his full views on 31 December 1914 with 'Muddleheadedness and Russia, With Some Mention of Mr. Shaw'; see letter 1015.

1144. To Bainbridge Colby[1]

PL

[London] [*c.* 20 November 1917]

Dear Mr. Bainbridge Colby,

You asked me, after our conversation at the Reform Club on the evening of November the fourteenth, to set down on paper my views upon the part America might and should play in this war. It was not the military side of the matter that engaged us, though I feel very strongly that by a bold use of scientific invention the American intelligence, accustomed to a large handling of economic problems and the free scrapping of obsolescent material and methods, may yet be of enormous service and stimulus to the Allied effort; it was rather the political role of America about which we talked. I warned you that I was perhaps not to be taken as a representative Englishman, that I was scientifically trained, a republican and "pro-American". I repeat that warning now. Here are my views for what they are worth.

They are based on one fundamental conviction. There is no way out of this war process – there may be a peace of sorts but it will only lead to a recrudescence of war – except by the establishment of a new order in human affairs. This new order is adumbrated in the phrase, *A League of Nations*. It lies behind that vague, more dangerous because less definite, phrase "a Just Peace". We have, I am convinced, to set our faces towards that order, towards that just peace, *irrespective of the amount of victory that falls to us*. We may achieve it by negotiations at any point when the German mind becomes open to the abandonment of militant imperialism. If by a sudden change and storm of fortune we found Germany deserted by her allies, prostrate at our feet, our troops in Berlin, and her leaders captive, we could do no more, we should do ourselves and the whole future of mankind a wrong, if we did more, than make this same "Just Peace" or set up this League of Nations. There is, I hold, a definable *Right Thing* for most practical purposes in international relations; there are principles according to which boundaries can be drawn and rights of way and privileges of trade settled and apportioned (under the protection of the general League) as dispassionately as a cartographer makes a contour line.

This I believe is the conviction to which a scientific training leads a man. It is the conviction, *more or less* clearly developed, of rational-minded people everywhere. It is manifestly the idea of President Wilson. It is the conviction that has to be made to dominate the world.

And this conviction of a possible dispassionate settlement is one for which the world is now ready. I am convinced in no country is there even one per cent of the population anxious to prolong the war. The ninety and nine are seeking helplessly for a way out such as only a dispassionate settlement can give. But they are kept in the war by fear. And by mental habit. Few men have the courage to reach their convictions. They must be led to them or helped to them. They fear the greed of their antagonists, fresh wars, fresh outrages, and an unending series of evil consequences, if they seem to accept anything short of triumph. No one can read the newspapers of any belligerent country without realizing how the overwhelming share of fear in now prolonging the struggle. Germany as much as any country, fights on and is helpless in the hands of her military caste, *because there is no confidence in Germany in the possibility of a "Just Peace"*. There is an equal want of confidence in London and Paris and New York. To create a feeling of confidence in that possibility of a Just Peace everywhere is as necessary a part of our struggle for a right order in the world as to hold the Germans out of Calais or Paris.

It is easy to underrate the pacific impulse in men and overrate their malignity. All men are mixed in their nature and none without a certain greed, baseness, vindictiveness. After the strain and losses of such a struggle as this it is "only in human nature" to prepare to clutch and punish whenever the scales of victory seem sagging in our favour. Too much importance must not be attached to the aggressive patriotism of the Press in the belligerent countries. Let us keep a little humour in our interpretation of enemy motives and remember that though a man has still much of the ape in his composition, that does not make him an irredeemable devil. The same Germans who will read with exultation of the submarining of a British passenger ship, or pore over a map of Europe to plan a giant Germany reaching from Antwerp to Constantinople founded on blood and dreadfulness and ruling the earth, will, in his saner moments, be only too ready to accept and submit himself to a scheme of general good will, provided only that it ensures for him and his a tolerable measure of prosperity and happiness. The belligerent element is present in every man, but in most it is curable. The incurably belligerent minority in any country is extremely small. There is a rational pacifist in nearly every man's brain, and the right end of the war can come only by invoking that.

It is here that the peculiar opportunity of America and of President Wilson comes in. America is three thousand miles from the war; she has no lost provinces to regain, no enemy colonies to capture; she is, in comparison with any of the Allies, except China, a dispassionate combatant. (If China can be called a combatant.) No other combatant except America can talk of peace without relinquishing a claim or accepting an outrage. America alone can stand fearlessly and unembarrassed for that rational settlement all men desire. It is from America alone that the lead can come which will take mankind out of this war. It is to America under President Wilson that I look as the one and only medium by which we can get out of this jangling monstrosity of conflict.

What is wanted now is a statment of the Just Peace, a statement without reservations. We want something more than a phrase to bind the nations together. America has said "League of Nations" and everywhere there has been an echo to that. But now we want America to take the next step and propose the establishment of the League, to define in general terms the nature of the League, to press the logical necessity of a consultative, legislative , and executive conference, and to call together so much of the conference as exists on the Allied side. *There will never be such a conference until America demands it.* There will never be a common policy for the Allies or a firm proposal of peace conditions, unless America insists. This war may drag on for another year of needless bloodshed and end in mutual recrimination through the sheer incapacity of any Ally but America to say plainly what is in fact acceptable to all.

In addition to the moral advantage of its aloofness, America has a second advantage in having a real head, representative and expressive. Possessing that head, America can talk. Alone in our system America is capable of articulate speech. Russia is now headless, a confusion. Italy is divided against herself. In France and Britain politicians and party leaders make speeches that are welcomed here and abused there. No predominant utterance is possible. It will be no secret to an observant American such as you are, that Britain and France are divided in a quarrel between reactionary and progressive, between aggressive nationalism and modern liberalism. All the European allies are hampered by secret bargains and pacts of greediness. They have soiled their hands with schemes of annexation and exploitation in Syria, in Albania, in Mesopotamia and Asia Minor. Russia was to have had Constantinople and so forth and so forth. The ugly legacy of the old diplomacy entangles our public men hopelessly to-day. Even where they are willing to repudiate these plans to-day for themselves, they are tied by loyalty to the bright projects of their allies, and silenced. Their military operations have had no real unity because their policy, their war aims, have been diverse. The great alliance against the Central Powers has been a bargain system, and not a unification. The allied statesmen, challenged as to their war aims, repeat time after time the same valiant resolution to "end militarism", free small nations, and the like, standing all the time quite resolutely with their back to the real issues which are the control of the Tropics, the future of the Ottoman Empire, and international trade conditions. So it seems likely to go on. Any voice that is raised to demand a lucid statement of the Allied aims in these matters is drowned in a clamour of alarmed interests. In Britain and France "hush" in the interests of diplomacy is being organized with increasing violence. Only America can help us out of the tangle by asserting its own interpretation of the common war purpose, and demanding a clear unanimity on the part of the Allies. The war was begun to defeat German imperialist aggression. It is with extreme reluctance that the European powers will accept the only way to salvation, which is the abandonment of all imperialist aggression and the acceptance of a common international method. The League of Nations is a mere phrase until it is realized by a body whose authority is supreme, overriding every national flag in the following spheres, in Africa between the Sahara and the Zambezi, as a trustee in Armenia, Syria and all the regions of the earth whose political status has been destroyed by the war, and permanently upon the high seas and vital channels (such as the Dardanelles) of the world.

America in the last three years has made great strides from its traditional isolation towards a responsible share in framing the common destinies of mankind. But America has to travel farther on the same road. The future of America is now manifestly bound up with the peace of Europe for that peace cannot be secured unless these sources of contention in the supply of tropical raw material and in the transport and trading facilities of the world are so controlled as to be no longer sources of contention. It is easy to argue that America has "no business" in Central Africa or Western Asia, that these are matters for the "powers concerned" to decide. But it is just because America has no "business" in Central Africa and Western Asia that it is necessary that America should have a definite will about Africa and Western Asia. Her aloofness gives her authority. The "powers concerned" will never of their own initiative decide. They are too deeply concerned and they will haggle. It is, I fear, altogether too much to expect a generous scheme for the joint settlement of regions by powers who have for a century cultivated a scheming habit of appropriation. But none of these powers can afford to haggle against the clear will for order of America at the present time.

What is suggested here is not a surrender of sovereignty nor a direct "international control" of tropical Africa, but the setting up of an over-ruling board composed of delegates from the powers concerned: Frenchman, Englishman, Africander, Portuguese, Belgian, Italian and (ultimately) German, to which certain functions can be delegated as powers are delegated to the governments of the United States of America by those states. Among these functions would be transport control, trade control, the arms and drink trades, the revision of legislation affecting the native and his land, the maintenance of a supreme court for Central Africa, the establishment of higher education for the native, and the systematic disarmament of all the African possessions. A similar board, a protectorate board, could take charge of the transport, waterways, customs, and disarmament of the former Ottoman empire. Only by the establishing of such boards can we hope to save those regions from becoming at the end of the war fields of the bitterest international rivalry, seed-beds of still direr conflicts. It is in the creation and support of such special boards, and of other boards for disarmament, international health, produce control and financial control, that the reality of a League of Nations can come into being. But Europe is tied up into a complexity of warring and jostling interests; without an initiative from America it is doubtful whether the world now possesses sufficient creative mental energy to achieve any such synthesis, obvious though its need is and greatly as men would welcome it. In all the world there is no outstanding figure to which the world will listen, there is no man audible in all the world, in Japan as well as Germany, and Rome as well as Boston – except the President of the United States. Anyone else can be shouted down and will be shouted down by minor interests. From him, and from him alone, can come the demand for the unity without which the world perishes, and those clear indications of the just method of the League of Nations for which it waits.

There is another area, an area beyond the scope of international controls, which remains an area of incalculable chances because no clear *dominant idea* has been imposed upon the world. That is Eastern Europe from Poland to the Adriatic. The Allies have no common idea, and they never have had a common idea and do not seem to be capable of developing a common idea about this region. They do not even know whether they wish to destroy or enlarge the Austro-Hungarian system. Vague vapourings about the rights of nationality conceal a formless confusion of purposes. Yet if the Allies have no intention of rending the Austro-Hungarian empire into fragments, if they do not propose to cripple or dismember Bulgaria, it is of the extremest importance that they should say so now. There is no occasion to make the Austrian and Bulgarian fight, as if he fought for his national existence, when he is really only fighting for Germany. All liberal thought is agreed upon the desirability of a practically independent Poland, of a Hungary intact and self-respecting, of a liberated Bohemia, of a Yugoslav autonomous state. None of these four countries are so large and powerful as to stand alone, and there are many reasons for proposing to see them linked into a league of mutual protection, mutual restraint and mutual guarantees. Add only to this system, the present German states of the Austrian empire, and such a league would be practically a continuation of that empire. But the European allies lack the collective mental force, lack the mouthpiece, lack the detachment and directness of purpose necessary for the declaration of their intentions in this matter, and they will probably go into the peace conference unprepared with a decision, a divided and so an enfeebled crowd, unless America for her own good and theirs, before the end of the war, gives the lead that will necessitate a definite statement of war aims. Only President Wilson and America can get that statement. To us in Europe our statesmen have become no better than penny-in-the-slot gramophones, who at every challenge for their war aims, say "Evacuate Belgium, restore Alsace-Lorraine to France and Italia Irredenta to Italy, abandon militarism and *-Gurrrr!*" The voice stops just when it is beginning to be interesting. And because it stops the war goes on. The war goes on because nothing can be extracted from the Allies that would induce any self-respecting Bulgarian, Austrian, or democratic-minded German to regard peace as a practicable proposition. They have their backs up against the wall, therefore, side by side with the German militarist – who is the real enemy – because we will not let them have any alternative to a fight to the death.

There, my dear Mr. Bainbridge Colby, are the views you ask for. You have brought them on yourself. You see the role I believe America could play under President Wilson's guidance, the role of the elucidator, the role of advocate of a new world order. Clear speech and clear speech alone can save the world. Nothing else can. And President Wilson alone of all mankind can speak and compel the redeeming word.

---

[1] Colby was a member of the US mission in England, working on post-war planning during the First World War. He met Wells at a dinner at the Reform Club on 14 November 1917 and asked him to write to Woodrow Wilson. Philip Guedalla took the letter to Colby who turned it over to Wilson. It is a gloss on a letter printed elsewhere in this work to unknown addressees, which was 'distributed' by Wells's friend, S. S. Koteliansky. The earlier letter 1127, which was more explicit in describing a possible post-war Europe also went to Wilson, via Walter Lippmann. Both letters are important because the transmitters felt that they had influenced Wilson's thinking, the first letter on the Fourteen Points address, and the second, on the League of Nations itself. This letter appeared in Wells's *Autobiography*, ch. 6 §6.

1145. To Marie Butts

Illinois, ALS

Easton Glebe
Dunmow

Nov. 23, 1917
[*in another hand*]

Dear Miss Butts.

I can't make head or tail of your Sgt. François. But he seems to be arguing on the lines of your revolution to abandon this life so to speak & go & live in ideal purity & devotion in France. You will find it can't be done. You will still be in the existing system – there is no other system – but at a point of less advantage for changing it. The poor & oppressed & the worker & wages earner are in it just as much as the millionaire. In your present position you are probably far more able to propagate ideas of social policies than you will be when you have renounced it. You will be then so much occupied in the struggle against the discomforts of poverty as to have neither the temper nor freedom to help in the evolution of the Socialist state – which is coming sooner than you expect.

In answer to the points you raise
(1) I think it is Clough but I can not trace it. It is some minor Victorian poet.
(2) I cannot answer this. I am writing in the train & have no copy of the book to refer to. The word used is "paragraph". Do not confuse paragraph with "Section" (§).
(3) Gilbert Murray LL.D., D. Lit. etc is a great Greek scholar & English man of letters Regius Professor of Greek (Oxford). His translations of Euripides have been abundantly performed in England & America & have great narrative & poetical beauty. He has been spoken of as an English ambassador to the U.S.A.
(4) I've not the book of me & I don't know Putney Bevan of Trinity Coll.
(5) ring as in "boxing ring". "Keeping the ring" is preventing anyone interfering in a fight.
(6) Here again I do not know what is the context. I suppose "tricks of affluence" means illusions of sense or suchlike deception.

Yours ever,
H. G. Wells

1146. To the Chairman, *National Conference on War Aims*[1]

Illinois, TLS

[Easton Glebe
Dunmow]

December 26th, 1917

Dear Sir,

I regret very greatly the impossibility of using the platform ticket you send me and taking part in your conference. More and more do I drift to the conclusion that in a great Labour party, and in that alone lies the political hope of our country. Upon the Labour side alone do there seem to be general ideas and broad views of the future of the world. If Labour has one fault more conspicuous then another it is modesty. In foreign politics in particular Labour with a pathetic confidence in the bluff of education that goes on at Oxford and Cambridge still consents to see our national destinies fooled about with by narrowminded, tradition worshipping, class conceited prigs like the Cecils, genteel reactionaries like Balfour and their cousins and friends. These people in power have no ideas adequate to the needs of the present time. They dread Revolution more than German imperialism. Their idea of a war aim is to make the world safe for gentility. Their associates are more outspoken and more frankly reactionary. While a man like Carson[2] is in the government, a man who sneers at the League of Nations and at every ideal that makes this war worth while to Labour, I doubt whether this war is worth while. If I were of any influence in the Labour movement, I would use all my strength to insist that before Labour makes one single further concession to forward this war, this traitor, this mother of the Irish bloodshed, this lawyer who will do his utmost at the peace settlement to cheat the people of any good results from the war, should be banished as completely as Haldane has been banished. Down with Kaiserisim and Carsonism! They are two sides of the same evil thing and the rottenest of the two is Carsonism. While Carson is in our government our hands are not clean in this war.

The hope of the world is the League of Nations. Let us insist upon that. Not only German imperialism, but English Toryism and every class and clique, every antiquated institution, every cant of loyalty and every organised prejudice, must be sacrificed and offered up to that great idea of World Peace and a unifed mankind. Every class in Europe except the royal class, has given its sons in this war and has suffered bitter things. Let the young giant of Labour see to it that we exact equality of sacrifice. Our boys have given their lives for this war that they believed would end war. Is it a great thing then to ask that Cecils should sacrifice their self-importance, and kings offer to abdicate, that the way may be made straight for the United States of the World?

Yours very sincerely,

H.G. Wells

---

[1] Wells was convinced that a clear statement of war aims by the Allies would, would bring an end to the war once the German population understood what these aims were. He felt that a peace conference would produce a peace based on those war aims. This document is just one more in the series addressed to Woodrow Wilson, and to other leaders; see letters 1126, 1127, 1134 and 1144.

[2] Sir Edward Carson (1854–1935) an Irish Unionist who founded the Ulster Volunteer Force, threatening civil war if Home Rule became reality. The law was enacted but suspended for the duration of the war.

1147. To Philip Guedalla

Illinois, Typed Transcription

[Easton Glebe] [December ?1917]

My dear Guedalla,

Dates go wild at Christmas time & when Jane asked you here for Jan. 5th, she meant Jan 19th. I shan't be here on the former week end & I can't bear to miss your wisdom.[1]

H.G.

---

[1] After Catherine Wells had written him two further letters, they finally settled for the weekend of the 17th, when they put on a version of *A Midsummer Night's Dream*. A playbill is in the Wells papers. Guedalla played a role new to the play, Mr Montague Chutney.

1148. To Frederic Harrison[1]

Boston, ALS

Easton Glebe
Dunmow

[*c*. late 1917]

Dear Harrison,

So far from being assailed, I am being cuddled by bishops.[2]

Whether you deal with God as a living reality, or as a formula depends on the quality of your imagination. The fact remains that he is the one formula upon which humanity can be unified & which satisfies the craving for personal leadership which otherwise rests duly on bosses & kings. He is a spiritual (or if you are a materialist, an artificial) back-bone. Otherwise we are all snobs or prigs.

Yours,
H.G. Wells

[1] Probably Frederic Harrison, the well-know positivist.

[2] A reference to Wells's controversial book *God The Inivisible King* (London: Cassell, 1917). This letter also exists in a nearly complete form in Wells's more casual handwriting.

1149. To Hugh Walpole

Texas, Typed Transcription

52, St. James's Court
Buckingham Gate, S.W.

[late 1917]

My dear Walpole,

I quite forgot the cursing and reviling when I met you – and it was very pleasant to meet you – but I had heard about it. One doesn't attach much importance to that sort of thing either way when one is 51 and whatever I may have said of you – well I hope it was neat. I think the fuss a lot of you made about the James parody in Boon was a little unjust. The old man was a little treacherous to me in a very natural sort of way, and the James cult has been overdone. Anyhow nothing I've ever written or said or anything anyone has ever written or said about James can balance the extravagant dirtiness of Lubbock and his friends in boycotting Rebecca West's book on him in the Times Literary Supplement. My blood still boils at the thought of those pretentious academic greasers conspiring to down a friendless girl (who can write any of them out of sight) in the name of loyalty to literature. It makes the name of James stink in my memory.[1]

Yours ever,
H.G. Wells

[1] Walpole had said in his diary and in public that he was angry over *Boon*, but how he could not remain angry at Wells.

1150. To Mr Murray[1]

Illinois, ALS

52, St James's Court,
Buckingham Gate, S.W. [1917?]

Dear Mr. Murray,

I just don't grasp the matter. I'm all for the Central Clearing House as you know – but I have not the time, brains nor special knowledge to estimate whether the existing honest demand is merely a nuisance among nuisances or the tragic final obstruction you say it is.

Very sincerely yours
H. G. Wells

[1] Murray is not further identified. He urged Wells to take over the scientific clearing house which Wells had proposed, as Murray felt that it was failing to achieve its purpose in the mobilisation of invention.

1151. To Edgar Jepson

Hofstra, ANS

Easton Glebe
Dunmow [1917?]

My dear Jepson,

No rationing makes my head swim. Give me simple little subjects like P. R. & I'm all right. But the bare thought of Food makes my head go into my stomach.[1]

Yours ever
H.G.

[1] A system of food rationing had been put in place to conserve the food supply in Great Britain. It was supplemented by a voluntary abstention on certain days of the week of certain foods, meat, sugar, and others. Wells had trouble with this latter, forgetting which day was dedicated to which abstention.

1152. To Dr Clarke[1]

Hofstra, ALS

Easton Glebe
Dunmow [late 1917-early 1918]

Dear Dr. Clarke,

Thanks for the cutting & the kind things you say of me. I shall be worrying you later for some information for a big League of Nations book we are compiling. I want instances of the Thirty Years War profiteers being the dominant families in Germany. Could you some time give me a compact memorandum (names & occupations) upon this subject? It is for the authoritative (I hope) book of the League of Nations Association.

Yours ever
H.G. Wells

[1] Dr. Clarke was another colleague at Crewe House. Wells spells his name occasionally without the 'e'. Possibilities for his identity include Austin Clarke (1896–1974) a poet and journalist who lived in England at this time, but he was better known in Ireland, or Sir Frederick Clarke (1880–1952) who studied modern history and was a Professor of Education at Cape Town during this period, 1911–52. He might well have spent the war in London, however; see letters 1164–5 and 53.

1153. To Dr Clarke

Hofstra, ALS

52, St. James's Court
Buckingham Gate, S.W. [1917–18?]

Dear Dr. Clarke,

Very many thanks for the book you are lending. Will you let Grew have the Document & my ideas & what I want of him when he returns to Crewe House. I know he can do the thing we want better than anyone else. Gilbert Murray has done a first rate note on Roman war profiteers.

Would you care to join the League of Free Nations Assn? I am sending applicant forms anyhow.

Yours ever
H.G. Wells

1154. To A. G. Gardiner

Gardiner, ALS

52, St James's Court
Buckingham Gate, S.W. [1917–18?]

Dear Gardiner.

I was busy doing up the article for the Chronicle & then it occurred to me that as it follows on after Harold Spender & touches on your current correspondence, it ought to come to you.

Yours ever,
H. G. Wells

1155. To an unknown correspondent

Illinois, ACCS

52, St James's Court
Buckingham Gate, S.W. [1917–18]

Dear Sir,

I know nothing of the treatment of mental cases.

Very sincerely yours,
H. G. Wells

1156 . To Frank Swinnerton

Reading, ALS

Easton Glebe, Dunmow [early 1918]

Dear Swinnerton.

I hope In the Fourth Year[1] will be out soon. Would Messrs. C & W care for me to inscribe 20 to 30 copies to leading statesmen & men of affairs? I have found that a good advertisement for such books in the past. If so I will come along & do it & C & W can pack & send them off. I mean people like Buckmaster, Ponsonby, Winston, A.J.B., the Bishop of London & so on.

—

I hope you will have a long press list. Don't forget such papers as The League of N. Society Monthly Report (1 Central Building S.W.) The Humanitarian, the Herald & The Labour Leader & also the religious papers, Guardian, Tablet, British Weekly &c. It is a book that will thrive on quotation and discussion.

—

Meanwhile the Labour Party press man wants to reprint the Labour & the African Problem article & also the recent Chronicle article as a pamphlet.[2] I have told him to ask you. I think that if he reprints these chapters with a full acknowledgement to the book – giving its title, price & publisher, you will find it quite good advertisement. But Messrs. C & W must decide upon that point.

Yours,
H. G.

[1] This book is a statement of Wells's beliefs in a world government and especially a League of Nations. Its sub-title was *Anticipations of a World Peace* and Chatto and Windus who published the book, also published an abridgement, both in 1918, titled *Anticipations of a World Peace.*
[2] Whether the Labour Party pamphlet was published is not known. The condensed version of the main book probably superceded the idea. The Wells articles he mentioned are 'The African Riddle: My View of the Labour View', in the *Daily Mail* 30 January 1918 and 'A League of Nations,' in the *Daily Chronicle* 20 April 1918. Both of these pieces were also published in the United States. The League of Nation idea is a feature of at least six of his articles in the first half of 1918.

1157. To Frank Swinnerton

Reading, ALS

52. St. James's Court
Buckingham Gate, S.W. [1918]

Dear Swinnerton.

Oh! P.S. I'd like to stipulate that C & W should undertake to set up the book as soon as M.S. is in hand & to let me have 4 sets of proofs – I can then send corrected proofs to America.

Yours ever,
H.G. Wells

1158. To Enid Bagnold

Illinois, ALS

Easton Glebe
Dunmow Rec'd 4th Feb. 1918
[*in another hand*]

Dear Miss Bagnold,

Your book[1] I've read appropriately in bed. I go to bed occasionally for a day or so, partly on account of colds & partly of disgust I take with my fellow creatures. It's such a bloody mess of a world & you can't get the idiots to do things that must [need] planning & certainly help to clean it up a little. They like the bloody mess. But you are a dear sister & a great comfort. You've got a clear, clean sure mind that makes me feel there is learning in the world that will save it. And your book is beautifully done. Thank you very much for it & for writing such friendly words in it & for sending it just when I needed it.

Yours ever,

H.G.Wells

[*On a separate sheet of paper appears in Wells's handwriting:*]

She's a modest creature & doesn't understand the swim she creates.

Has she never heard of poor old gentlemen who have to pin up over the shaving glasses, "I must not fall in love again."?

He is like that.

[1] This book was her famous account of First World War nursing, *Diary Without Dates*. The 1918 date is added by Bagnold, I believe.

1159. To Mr Marlowe[1]

Hofstra, ALS

Easton Glebe
Dunmow

[probably late February 1918]

My dear Marlowe,

I never asked to write for the Daily Mail[2]. You asked me. If you don't like that article send it back. There is no harm to me that I can see. I've written one more but it is on the same lines so I won't trouble you with it.

Yours ever,

H.G.Wells

[1] An editor with the *Daily Mail*.

[2] The articles in question were printed on February 20, 28, and March 1, 1918 under the title 'The League of Free Nations: Some Independent Opinions'.

1160. To Walter Lippmann

Yale, TTYS

Buckingham Gate — March 13, 1918

Lippmann
Bentham
Maybury Road
Woking — Reply Paid

Have urgent engagement five tomorrow. Can you come twelve fifteen Friday or twelve forty five Saturday.

Wells
St. James's Court[1]

[1] Wells was introduced to Lippmann by Graham Wallas, who had acted as a mentor to Lippmann. Lippmann was active in The Inquiry, a semi-official group of advisors to Woodrow Wilson researching the possibilities of peace after the war. Wells could be considered as an adjunct member, as his advice was widely sought by Lippmann and others. Letters of introduction from Lippmann provided easy access to Wells. Such letters on behalf of William Allen White, S. H. Wolfe, Professor Henry S. Canby, and others are in the Lippmann archives at Yale. The telegram relates to these visits.

1161. To Enid Bagnold

Illinois, ALS

52, St. James's Court
Buckingham Gate, S.W. — Monday [1918]

Dear Enid Bagnold,[1]

Will you lunch on Wednesday (day after tomorrow) at the Criterion at 1:30? I will try & bring Rebecca. If so please send a wire here to H.G. Wells. Then I will watch you two clever humans surveying each other. You ought to love each other but one never knows. If I can find a mitigating man I will.

You are still exercised by the remarkable left[?], but that about the soldiers making kissing sounds is really quite right. Every man & particularly me is a rather horrid boy of 14 + something else. If somebody did a surgical operation to my brain & removed certain small parts of it, I should become a lascivious urchin – & extremely happy. If you were a man I wouldn't have the urgent desire to get friends with you that I have now. It's quite irrational. I don't write coy letters to Swinnerton, whose work I think fully equal to yours. My attitude & intentions towards you are honourable & respectful but don't think that they are strictly honourable. They are h & r by an effort & under constraint. There is a lot of constraint in my life. I am working myself ill & I have been for months. I know I am doing quite considerable things. Possibly the particular part I am playing doesn't admit of an understudy. But, oh!, I am bored & tired. Other people when they die want to go on to a Higher Plane. If God is merciful to me & wants to reward me, he will put me down in a Lower Plane, he will send me to the Moslem paradise & Rebecca (whom I adore) won't want me to keep faith & there will be a variety of people like you only less critical & very easy. A lot of sailing about in boats -sunshine sunshine sunshine -some tennis – good talk, inexhaustible appetite & no shame.

What nonsense!

H.G.

[1] The letters to Enid Bagnold have very few clues as to dates. They could be any time between 1916 and 1919, but the 1918 dates are most likely. After the war Bagnold wrote plays, and fiction and is most famous today for her novel, *National Velvet*. Bagnold told Wells once that he had muffed his chance in this letter by not pursuing her in a more animated way.

1162. To Enid Bagnold[1]

Illinois, ALS

Easton Glebe
Dunmow

[April 1918]

Dear Enid,

I can't draw for Exhibitions. I can only be artlessly merry with pictuas in private. Don't let Furst make my pen self-conscious. Besides I am already too brilliant. If I draw it will only annoy people more.

Love

H. G.

[1] This letter was enclosed with a letter from Herbert Furst asking Bagnold to ask Wells if he would do some caricatures for a project involving the art work of writers and others to be shown in an 'Author-Artist' exhibition. Bagnold wrote a note across the bottom asking Wells to do something. Wells responded with the letter, but also illustrated the original note.

1163. To Enid Bagnold

Illinois, ALS

The Reform Club [early 1918]

I snatch a moment to write to the poor brave sufferer.

"Love, H.G." means Love = that state of gracious feeling in which all sweet & starry souls regard one another. See D. Clarke on "Charity" in the Commentary on the New Testament.- I forget the page

H.G. = me.

Why, if you want that delightful country house, (with cream) don't you get it? You are as clever as I am at least & I have got a country house with things on a tray & all that sort of thing, by doing things that any woman could do. Why do you insist on the male as a medium to comfort?

There is something very unsound about your sex. I don't insist upon a large touring car, a yacht & a permanency before I – urchin.

Love,

H.G.

You write to me. You have more time. You have endless time & I am dead. Now I ought to be doing things at Crewe House that you could do just as well if you weren't a demoralized female.

1164. To Dr Clarke

Hofstra, ALS

Easton Glebe
Dunmow [early 1918]

Dear Dr. Clarke,

Translators always intrigue against each other & though no one has raised anything about you "one never knows." I'm leaving Crewe House on account of the Anti-German stunts[?] , but here is a letter you ought to keep by you.

Yours ever

H.G. Wells

Encl.[1]

[1] What the enclosure was is unknown, perhaps a testimonial to his work by Wells?

1165. To Dr Clarke

Hofstra, ALS

52, St. James's Court,
Buckingham Gate, S..W. 1 [date unknown 1918]

Dear Dr. Clarke,

Your proper mark in these matters is the Overseas Society at 22 Burleigh Gate with whose activities I have little connexion.

Good Luck!
Yours
H.G. Wells

1166. To Frank Swinnerton

Reading, APCS

National Liberal Club
Victoria Street, S.W.1. [Spring 1918]

Excuse the post card. No envelopes at this ~~damn~~ (ssh!) club. Ernest Rhys (address in Who's Who) has been asked to review In The Fourth Year by Major Donald Davies for some Welsh monthly he owns. Please send him a copy.[1]

H.G.

[*in another hand*] – Ernest Rhys Esq. 48 West Heath Drive, Hampstead, N.W.

---

[1] Davies was a colleague on the War Aims Board at Crewe House. Rhys (1859–1946) began his professional life as a mining engineer. By this time he was the chief editor of the Everyman Classics series. Swinnerton was also connected with this series, acting as a commissioning editor and they knew each other well.

1167. To Siegfried Sassoon

McMaster, ALS

52, St. James's Court
Buckingham Gate, S.W. [*c.* early 1918]

Dear Siegfried Sassoon,

I am yours & all my time is yours barring that I have got a damned sub-committee of the C.A. Transport Ctte dinner (letters always). That I am on a committee that ought to have existed three years ago on trench warfare transport (endless letters & visits to experimental grounds) that I am trying to teach the Daily Mail the elements of political science & that I have the most beautiful novel in the world spoiling because my mind is distracted & I'm all at sixes & sevens.[1] It's a glorious scheme rotting to pieces under my nose. I am ill with neurasthenia so I keep on trying to go on with everything when I might break & the only soul in the world who can give me rest is worried to death by a domestic complication & her house the only haven where there is happy peace, has been hit by shrapnel & the cat killed.

I take you this extensively into my confidence because I don't want you to think that my not contributing to your journal is mere shoddy & callousness. When will you be able to come to stay for a long week end at Easton ?

Yours ever,
H.G.Wells

---

[1] Wells invented a device he called 'telpherage', designed to carry supplies and messages to the front lines via a series of collapsible poles which held the communication lines. The plans, dated 26 November 1917 are at Illinois. The novel he was writing was *Joan and Peter* (London, 1918). The haven must have been Rebecca's home, although when it was hit by shrapnel is not known. The letter must be early in 1918.

1168. To. W. Baxter

Boston, ALS

52, St. James's Court
Buckingham Gate. S.W. [probably early 1918]

[*The letter is marked at the top, in Wells's hand:*]
Private. Source of information not to be divulgded.

My dear Baxter,

Your questions are rather a lot for a busy man. I left Bromley at the age of 13. I went into a drapers shop at Windsor on (unsuccessful) trial. Then to a Midhurst chemist, then to Midhurst Grammar School, then to a Southsea draper for (2 years [indentures cancelled at my request]), then back to Midhurst as junior master (cp. Mr. Lewisham) then W. London as a teacher in botany at the R. C. Science (3 years) (cp. Mr. L – only I didn't marry,) then a year of scholastic teaching, then at University Correspondence College for 2 years (2 or 3 years), then journalism, books. B. Sc.1st class honours. Mother died at 82 in 1905. Father shot his thumb off when rabbit shooting. He played good cricket. Built house at Sandgate. Am still a J.P. on the Folkestone bench. Father broke his leg while pruning vines. Any[?] things stay [*in another hand*] – style no good at all.

I have to pay subscriptions to all sorts of things in Essex where I live but I'll go a guinea for the Gymnastic Club enclosed. [*in the margin, in single parenthesis*] – No objection to be a V.P.
Recent addresses as above & Little Easton Rectory, Dunmow.

I belong to no literary club, only The Reform, & Automobile & National Liberal, but the Author's is a good club, I believe.

I think I'm very nice to answer all this so carefully,

Yours ever,
H.G. Wells

1169. To the Editor, *The Times*[1]

PLS

52, St. James's Court
Buckingham Gate, S.W. [*c.* 12 March 1918]

Sir, – It is with something like dismay that many of us here have read Mr. Lloyd George's utterances upon the only possible unifying idea of our Alliance, the League of Free Nations. What is there to hold us together if that idea is not strenuously supported and developed? Hostility to German imperialism – and when we can claim a victory over that; disintegration? In which case we may reckon securely on the world being dominated by a German Emperor within the next half century. Mr. Lloyd George declared that the Bolshevists talked of a League of Nations. Upon that point I would like to challenge him. Like most men who have had the leisure to do so, I have tried to understand these strange movements in Russia so far as the Press would permit, and I cannot remember a single mention, much less any advocacy, of the League of Nations in the published utterances of any Bolshevist leader at all. And be it noted the possibly kindred extremist Press in France, the Press which may quite conceivably be German paid, is already issuing pamphlets against the League of Nations as being an idea of the *bourgeoisie*. Those I have seen advocated a vague "brotherhood" of labour and deprecated any "organization" of the league, which I should think would be quite the Bolshevik idea. The head and leader of the League of Free Nations movement is our great Ally, President Wilson, who has been denounced again and again as a "capitalist" and so forth by Bolshevik speakers. The great mass of those who support the idea of the League is to be found in France, the English- speaking countries, and Scandinavia.

Yours, etc.,
H.G. Wells

---

[1] This letter, published 15 March 1918, was headlined 'The Bolsheviks and the League of Nations'.

1170. To an unknown addressee

Hofstra, ALS

Easton Glebe
Dunmow [early 1918]

Dear Sirs,

I will be glad if you will send the M.S. of Joan & Peter (Part1) to Mr. Brett of Macmillan & Co. & ask him to acknowledge receipt to me.[1]

Very sincerely yours
H.G. Wells

[1] I do not know to whom this letter is addressed. Perhaps another publisher, an agent, or a stenographic firm. The latter seems more plausible. The book was serialized in *The School World* (*Journal of Education*) and *The New Republic*, so it may be directed to their editors.

1171. To Philip Guedalla

Illinois, Typed Transcription

[Easton Glebe] [Spring 1918]

Dear Philip,

I shall try & get you on the telephone one day for tea with you. Life is more crowded than ever since I have taken to advising Northcliffe on Foreign Affairs. Oh I wish I were back in 1911 when Politics didn't matter a damn.

H.G.

1172. To Edgar Jepson

Hofstra, ALS

Easton Glebe
Dunmow

Private [late Spring 1918]

My dear Jepson,

I would have jumped at your offer three weeks ago. But now I am an ex-official. I resigned[1] the conduct of the German section of the E.P.C. after a long, dignified (on my part) & fundamental dispute with Northcliffe on the anti alien campaign of the Northcliffe press.

Yours ever,
H.G.

[1] This allows us to date this letter in the late spring of 1918.

1173. To David Lubin

Illinois, ALS

Easton Glebe
Dunmow

May, 1918

My dear Lubin:

A Noumenon cannot "act upon" Phenomena. Phenomena are the aspects of Noumena in the time-space system of conscious life. This matter affects your general argument. And as for the mission of the Jewish race, that is manifestly an affair for that race which is not mine.

Except for your race restriction you speak of "Israel" very much as I speak of God. What's in a name? Your God of negatives, the God of Maimonides and Spinoza, I define not by negatives but by polite doubts and call the Veiled Being. My "God" is the Israel of all mankind.

Unless you translate these terms you will keep at loggerheads with my work. Really there is a close parallelism between "God" as I understand him, your "Israel" and (except for the association with the man Jesus) the "Spirit-Christ" of Pauline Christianity.

Yours ever,
H.G. Wells

1174. To Graham Wallas

LSE, TLS

Crewe House
Curzon Street, W.1. 11th June, 1918

Dear Wallas,

Very many thanks for your letter about Gregory, which quite answers my own impression of the man. I think he is just the sort of German that we want here, and I shall do my best to get hold of him. I am told that unfortunately he has already had a disagreeable experience as a result of attempts to dig him out. Steele Maitland, it appears, tried to get him to the Foreign Trade Department, the only result being that the ancestral "Guggenheim" washed up into the negociations, and stopped the whole enterprise and caused the gravest suspicion.

Yours very sincerely,
H.G. Wells

[*In Wells hand under his signature is the following:*]
Sir Sidney Low is <u>on the committee</u> here. His father's name was Loëwe & his position in England is <u>exactly</u> that of Gregory.[1] Oh, England! Oh, my country!

Graham Wallas, Esq.
56, Southwood Lane
Highgate, N.

[1] I do not know who this Gregory was. Foreign nationals were accorded very bad treatment in the UK and in the USA during the First World War.

1175. To Chatto & Windus

Reading, APCS

Easton Glebe
Dunmow [date stamped 20 June 1918]

Dear Sirs,

The League of Nations seems to be getting a boom. I wish you would try a special advertisement of my book next. 'The clearest & best discussion of the League of Nations & Democracy,' I suggest very l...

[*Remainder of letter is smudged with ink and is not legible*]

Yours very sincerely,
H.G. Wells

1168. To the Editor, *The Times*[1]

PLS

52, St. James's Court
S.W. 1. June 28, 1918

Sir, – I have been following with the keenest interest the public discussion of the League of Nations project in the House of Lords, the Press, and elsewhere. There seems to be a disposition in many quarters to regard the proposal as a premature and hasty one. We are being counselled to go slowly in this matter, to look before we leap, to try experimental half-measures, to sit down quietly in front of the manifest difficulties of the proposal, and, in fact, to let it ripen for a time – as we have let the problem of Ireland ripen for a century, and as we are now letting India get ripe. These are, I know, thoroughly sage and British methods; they are methods that have done much to make Great Britain what she is at the present time; they have received the public endorsement of many of our elder statesmen, and I would be the last to run counter in most matters to the tradition in which I have been born and bred, but the peculiar conditions of the present struggle call, I think, for a certain unusual energy, even, indeed, for haste, and call so strongly as to justify a complete departure from that discreet dilatoriness which is so frequent a characteristic of British statecraft.

The war becomes more and more manifestly a war unlike preceding wars, a war differing in nature from them. It is more and more clearly the half-conscious effort of humanity to adjust its habits and its ideas of nationalism and loyalty and its old political forms and methods to the new scale which has been created by the increased range of the means of human communication, of all means of communication from railways and wireless to pamphlets and guns, during the last 100 years. These things have destroyed territorial autonomies, and made the world one system physically, while mentally and politically it remains many. While this process of adjustment continues it seems bound to be an increasingly wasteful and, in its acuter phases, an increasingly cruel and bloody process, until a new equilibrium is attained. It is a process, therefore, that should be shortened in every possible way, and that the only final adjustment that the wit of man has so far been able to discern is this scheme of a federal League of Nations overriding "sovereignty" in such matters of universal concern as trade and armament and tropical control. To such a League we must come if we are to come to anything out of this welter of blood and destruction. Let me set down very briefly some chief reasons for urgency in this question, urgency that may even seem undignified to those accustomed to the slow gestures of public life. They are -

(1) The increasing destructiveness of modern scientific war – of which this war, make no mistake about it, is only an improvised sample.

(2) The impossibility of controlling armaments and securing a world disarmament without a properly empowered supernational authority.

(3) The impossibility of relieving the economic struggle in the world by a mere network of treaties, tariffs, and dealings without a world authority.

(4) The impossibility of achieving any satisfactory settlement of the problems of tropical and derelict countries – Africa and Mesopotamia, *e.g.* – without a world authority.

(5) The impossiblity of developing the rich and splendid promise of air traffic in anything but a belligerent direction without a world authority.

No doubt the constitutional and sentimental difficulties in the way of establishing a federal League of Nations are colossal and intricate. But they must be overcome, because there is no way out for humanity except to overcome them. People do not seem to realize how far the consuming of the world has already gone and at what a pace it is now proceeding. The world now is not like an old unsatisfactory house that we have plenty of time to rebuild, that it would be a pity to rebuild too hastily; it is like a house on fire; and the time to get to work if we want to save it is now.

Yours, etc.,

H.G. Wells

[1] This letter was published on 29 June 1918. Wells also published pieces on the League and Britain, the League and Italy and general pieces on the League in half a dozen other places.

1177. To Lord Northcliffe[1]

Illinois, TCCD

To The Chairman of the Enemy Propaganda Committee.

[London, Crewe House?] July 17th, 1918

Dear Sir,

In relinquishing my position as the Organizer and Conductor of the German propaganda under your committee, I would like to put on record a brief outline of the work I have done and an explanation of my resignation.

My membership of the Enemy Propaganda Committee dates from February 8th of this year when I was invited to join it by Lord Northcliffe.

On May 12th Lord Northcliffe wrote to me as follows – "I would be very grateful to you if you would undertake the organization of propaganda work against Germany. I know of no one who could do it better, and I have arranged, if you should desire it, to have the assistance of Mr. J.W. Headlam, the chief of the German section of the Foreign Office, should you accept this post....Mr. H.K. Hudson, secretary to the Committee will be at your disposal as Secretary of the German section; and office accommodations and staff will be provided for you at Crewe House."

Acting on this little instruction I came to Crewe House and set to work, as far as the still unorganized condition of the staff permitted. It was at once evident to me that no sort of general plan of operations existed and that it was impossible to conduct any effective propaganda without one. I set to work with Mr. Headlam, with the concurrence of Sir William Tyrell, Mr. Philips and Mr. Wickham Steed, to prepare a memorandum upon the Allied aims which our propaganda was to subserve. This memorandum has already been printed in our minutes. Since it was endorsed by Lord Northcliffe and not unfavourably received by Mr. Balfour, I have taken it as the directing plan of the activities of the German Propaganda.[2]

In accordance with this memorandum and a shorter memorandum which does not appear on our minutes, but which is accessible on the files upstairs, I have engaged in the following activities.

In concert with Mr. Wickham Steed I have mingled in the office of the League of Nations society, and we have been largely instrumental in drawing up and getting accepted a re-statement of the aims of that Society more in accordance with the terms of our directive memorandum. Arising out of that we have assisted in the formation of a new and more efficient League of ~~Nations Association for propaganda and the study of the problems arising out of the league proposal~~ and this association is already well forward with the preparation of that authoritative book upon the League which was originally proposed by Mr. Wickham Steed as a counter-blast to Naumann's "Mittel Europa". This book will be produced under the auspices of a special committee, consisting at present of Viscount Gray, Mr. Steed, Mr. Spender of "The Westminster Gazette", Professor Gilbert Murray and myself. Without any charge upon the resources of the E.C. propaganda Mr. William Archer has been engaged as the salaried editor of the enterprise, and he will be assisted by an adequate staff.[3]

I have also done all that lies in my power to establish a liason with the French League of Nations Movement, ~~but my work has been much impeded by that entire lack of cooperation which seems to exist between different Government departments. The Censorship seems to have a foreign policy diametrically opposed to that which our Propaganda is supporting. For example, six copies of Lloyd's News containing an article by Mr. Arnold Bennett, specially written at my request, and directed to various residents in France have been held up. In the direction of Italy our efforts have not been as greatly impeded and~~ After a number of attempts, involving much correpondence, a vigorous League of Nations movement is now afoot in Italy in which Dr. Mario Borsa of "Il Secolo" promises to play a leading part.

The disorganised state of affairs in Russia had prevented our developing a League of Nations movement upon the Russian side, but unless some violent change in the policy of Crewe House occurs, this development should now be practicable. By these operations we may hope to keep the League of Nations movement well before the German mind, both as a threat and as an invitation.

A second line of propaganda has been the appeal to the German worker. In this matter the British Labour War Aims necessarily play an important part. In its original form the statement of these aims was decidedly unwieldy and I have arranged with the Executive of the Labour Party to accept and issue a shorter and much more negotiable summary prepared by me. Its compactness adapts to leaflet use and brings it within the compass of a newspaper article.

Meanwhile, upon the economic side I found the information available at Crewe House was imperfect and of very irregular value. Before we could undertake a propaganda of economic discouragement and persuasion in Germany, it was necessary that we ourselves should be more fully informed upon the facts of the case, and after a very burdensome correspondence with a considerable number of specialists a file of expert reports has been made, and a complete summary of the scientific, technical and industrial situation is now available for our use. I have already prepared and issued two articles and could have sent out many more had I had adequate secretarial assistance. The digested material is, however, available for my successor and will not, I feel sure, be wasted in the hands of Mr. Grew to whom I have entrusted it.[4]

In relation to this economic campaign, I have also interviewed Mr. Havelock Wilson and used the material of the interview in propaganda.

I would like at this point to commend to the Committee the work of the British Scientific Products Exhibition, through the kindness of the organisers of which the making of this Scientific and Technical Summary has been possible. This exhibition itself is a work of real and efficient economic propaganda.

For deterrent propaganda I have also made careful investigation into the hardships of the U-Boat crews. I have prepared an account of the deaths of U-boat men which is not only very horrible, but strictly true. This has been translated by Dr. Clark, and handed to Mr. Guest for dissemination among the classes and districts in Germany from which the U-boat crews are drawn. He, however, declines to make use of it, having views of his own as to what constitutes efficient propaganda. The material is available for my successor.

A considerable amount of preliminary enquiry has been directed to developing the Russian Route into Germany. This should be specially useful in connection with the economic and League of Nations side of our propaganda. It is in the hands of Mr. Talbot who will, I feel sure, carry it through to the operative stage.

The question of leaflet distribution as an integral part of the propaganda work of bombing raids in the interior of Germany has been constantly before our sub-Committee. At the request of Lord Northcliffe I have interviewed Lord Milner, who has referred me to the Air Board. Sir Charles Nicholson has interviewed Major Baird, who has referred him to the War Cabinet. I have also had a conversation with Lord Weir on the subject but his views in the matter appear to be against distribution. I leave this complication to the ingenuity of my successor.

Pursuing the idea of our guiding memorandum and the express utterances of our statesmen, I have directed our propaganda in the direction of making it clear to the Germans that a democratized, de-militarized Germany has nothing to fear from us or our allies. Through Mr. C. E. Russell I have tried to get in touch with several German-American Societies advocating the conception of a republican Germany. As I thought it inadvisable to deal with these societies as a propaganda agent, I have communicated with them over my own signature and from my own address, and I do not know how far the intelligence of our postal censorship will give to the situations and put me in possession of their replies.

Dr. Clark and Mr. Bechhofer have been engaged to prepare a pamphlet to be called, "The True Germany", exalting the more liberal elements of German culture as against militant militarism. I have also taken into consideration a project from Mr. Will Dyson, which I hope will be developed, for a series of quasi-German caricatures attacking imperialist militarism from the standpoint of German Minority socialists.[5] Unfortunately, as a result of the indiscriminate agitation against people of German origin in this country, I have been deprived of the services of Mr. Bechhofer. His exceptional intelligence and ability would have made him invaluable at Crewe House as a watch of the German and Russian Press, and for the preparation of propaganda material. It is perhaps irrelevant to point out that as the British born and educated son of a naturalized Central European parent, his position in England is exactly that of Sir Sidney Low, who is still our valued colleague upon the Enemy Propaganda Committee.

Throughout my tenure of responsibility the organization of the staff has been a task of very great difficulty, due very larglely to the absence of any clearer conception of what our work was and of any preliminary definition of the country's war aims and purposes. In Dr. Clark, Mr. Gerhardis, and Mr. Grew we have at last, I think, got the nucleus of an efficient producing organization.

It is in connection with this campaign in favour of the True Germany that the conflict has arisen which has led to my resignation. While I have been trying to develop a campaign of reassurance to all republican, pacific and liberal minded Germans, various of the newspapers owned by Lord Northcliffe have been conducting a violent campaign in the contrary sense, a campaign of indiscriminate and irrational denunciation of all things German. The position of Lord Northcliffe at Crewe House is to [my] mind incompatible with the activities of Lord Northcliffe in Carmelite Street. The activities of "The Evening

News", of "The Daily Mail", more particularly, seem to me entirely mischievous and injurious to the interests of the Allies. I have corresponded with Lord Northcliffe at some length on these matters and his last reply is to this effect:

"I entirely agree with the policy adopted by my newspapers which I do not propose to discuss with anyone."

I hold that Lord Northcliffe in taking office as a director of Propaganda has brought his responsibility as newspaper proprietor within the purview of this Committee. Unless the Committee can see its way to agree with me on this point I must place my resignation as Organizer and Director of the German Propaganda in its hands.

Before concluding I would like to urge the very great inconvenience and difficulty in the working of the Enemy Propaganda Committee arising out of its location in an inaccessible part of Mayfair. The work of the Committee could be conducted with far more efficiency if it were carried on within a minute's walk or so of the rest of the Ministry of Information. I would suggest to the Committee the advisability of such a removal before its organization develops farther.

I may add that, in resigning my task of organizing and conducting the German Propaganda, I do not resign my membership of the Enemy Propaganda Commitee as I feel that my criticism and comments may still be of use to the Country. I hope, therefore, that the minutes of meetings of the General Committee for Enemy Propaganda will continue to be sent to me.[6]

Yours faithfully,

---

[1]Northcliffe was the functional head of the German propaganda unit. The date is later than the actual resignation; it may be that he asked for a formal statement for use in the War Cabinet. This is a carbon, and a late draft. The words cancelled by Wells may nevertheless be useful to readers. Wells remained on the Crewe House staff for a time, working on League of Nations affairs.

[2] This document can be found today in Sir Campbell Stuart, *Secrets of Crewe House*, (London, 1920) and H. G. Wells, *The Common Sense of War and Peace* (Harmondsworth, 1940).

[3] A major publication effort was mounted, but the war ended sooner than expected, and, in the event only two short items were published, H. G. Wells, *et al*, *The Idea of a League of Nations*, and H.G. Wells, *et al*, *The Way to a League of Nations* (both Oxford, 1919). The first of these also appeared in the United States published by Little Brown. Those lines which are cancelled were done so by Wells prior to the final document. This draft circulated fairly widely, however, and so the interlineations remain because of their importance.

[4] Much of Wells's prolific journalism during the war can be traced now to his work at Crewe House. He was a valuable member in this post, and editors sought his byline. In addition, it is now possible to see clearly why he pursued a personal road toward world peace, as he felt the League had broken down before it began.

[5] This followed logically from Will Dyson (with a foreword by Wells), *Kultur Kartoons* (London, 1915).
[6] Wells remained on the committee and participated in some of its meetings directly. He continued to write material for the press which reflected the views of the committee, although his disillusionment about what was possible through traditional government methods intensified.

1178. To the Editor, *Saturday Evening Post*[1]

Texas, TCCS

[London] Friday, 23/8/18

Dear Sir,

I think you know something of the work of my friend and neighbour, Major Britton Austin. The other day we had a conversation that may perhaps interest you. We are both very keen on the League of Nations idea and inclined to doubt whether people realize the urgent necessity of some effectual guarantee of the peace of the world. Bad as this war has been, we believe it is child's play to the sort of war that will have to be waged, if people still insist on waging war, in twenty years time. We have thought therefore of collaborating in a serial story of the "Next War", and working out to their full possibility the various new ideas and devices this war has produced. Air War, Tank War, Undersea War are all things in their tender infancy; as we want to show what they will be like if they grow up and get loose. Does this appeal to you as a serial?

Yours very sincerely,
H.G. Wells

[*at the bottom:*]

This is the duplicate of a magnificent piece of typewriting I have just done & sent to the Saturday Evening Post.

[1] At the time of writing, I know of no SEP article . Wells had used a typewriter before, but not often, nor would he again. This letter is written in about 7 point type, smaller than newsprint.

1179. To Frank Swinnerton

Arkansas, TLS

Easton Glebe
Dunmow [October 1918?]

Please reply to 52, St. James's Court, Buckingham Gate, S.W.
[*in Catherine's hand*]

Dear Swinny,

What of next week end?

I've got a M.S. of Johnston's I want you to read & tell me about (unbeknownst to him)[1] and in the present shortage of paper (& time for writing). I want to talk about Woman (what I have read) & the novel (which I shall have read by next Saty.)

Your adoring,
H.G.

P.S. This would be the 26th. On Nov. 2nd I shall very likely go to Oundle.
C.W.

---

[1] Very probably *The Gay-Dombeys* which Chatto and Windus, Swinnerton's employers, published, see letter 1190. The post script is by Catherine Wells. A copy of this letter is also in Illinois.

1180. To the Editor, *The Times*[1]

PLS

52, St. James's Court
Buckingham Gate, S.W.1. [*c.* 28 November 1918]

. Sir, – For many of us this coming election – or, rather, this nomination for Parliament by Mr. Lloyd George of his wealthy, influential, and useful associates – will have only a spectacular interest. We feel we have to go through with the business and clean up the mess afterwards. We shall probably vote "Coalition" in most cases, for we neither want Mr. Asquith back nor an experiment by Ramsay MacDonald, Mr. Philip Snowden, and Mr. Sidney Webb, but we shall not forget that Mr. Lloyd George, instead of being the nation's choice, has preferred to be its *pis-aller*.[2] The real political work before intelligent and public-spirited men now is the selection and organization of a reserve Government, a Salvage Government, against the inevitable smash-up of this adventure of rich men, unsupported as it is either by Labour or by any general understanding on the part of the public of what reconstruction is needed.

The election, however, though it has very little political significance for anyone outside the worlds of finance, of business, and of "Old Parliamentary hands", is very valuable as a crowning demonstration of the hopeless inefficiency of our present electoral methods. As your columns have testified again and again, the only sane, logical and practicable method of democracy is the method of election known as P.R. This method, and this method alone, allows of the candidature of men of similar opinions side by side without any risk of splitting the party vote, letting in the Opposition man or the like. It would permit of a Coalitionist Liberal standing against a Coalitionist Tory in a soundly Coalitionist constituency, without the slightest danger of that constituency falling to a non-Coalitionist. It has always been anathema, therefore, to the local busy-bodies, who rig our constituencies and sell us to some Tory gold-bug or Liberal carpet-bagger, according to our particular shade of conviction. Under its rule they would have nothing to sell. It was bitterly opposed by the gentry who work the National Liberal Federation. The numerous obscure Liberals who sat for London almost trampled on one another in their zeal to vote against it. God is patient, but just, and I note with a mild satisfaction how far from happy they are now. The wail of Liberalism betrayed. Liberalism was betrayed when P.R. was rejected, and it was betrayed by the party-hack Liberals. But the Belfast Unionists are equally unhappy, and my subtle friend, Mr. Sidney Webb, who has always been so scornful towards P.R, may now, with a Coalitionist in front of him, and a medical candidate and a schoolmasters' candidate to share the Labour vote of London University, find that something is to be said after all for honest methods of voting. This coming election is only a particularly bad instance of a long-standing evil. Now it is Mr. Lloyd George alone dictating to the ordinary elector; hitherto it has been a dictation of alternatives. Parliament has always been a joke at the expense of the democracy, and now the joke has become extravagant. Everybody will see it. Nobody will feel represented by the packed Parliament ahead. And having no confidence left in the Parliamentary medium of expression, people will express themselves by sulking, passive resistance, strikes and sabotage.

Very sincerely yours

H.G. Wells

[1] By the end of the war it was clear that whatever political reforms might be achieved, proportional representation in Parliament was not to be one of them. Earlier in the war, it seemed possible; a parliamentary commission had even called for its implemention. This letter was published 30 November 1918, under the headline, 'Who Killed P.R.?'
[2] Make-shift, sometimes also as 'worst course'

1181. To Citizens of the United States[1]

PL

[London] [*c.* 6 December 1918]

Greetings to the great English-speaking Republic which has solved itself, and now must help the world solve its problems of diversity and unity and republican freedom with order and stability. European crowns flicker and fall like candles burned to the socket. Let there be no more of these false flares, but let star after star be added to your pioneer star until the whole human sky gleams with liberty, equality, and brotherhood.

[1] On 8 December 1918, a huge meeting was convened to give thanks to the United States for its participation in the war. Messages of grateful thanks were read out, and spoken. Wells sent his to the meeting to be read, and it was printed in *The Times*, 9 December 1918, along with many of the other sentiments.

1182. Jan Smuts to H. G. Wells[1]

Illinois, ALS

Savoy Hotel 28 Dec 1918

Dear Mr. Wells,

Your letter gave me the greatest pleasure. I thank you very much for it. I know you have given a great deal of thinking and active interest to the subject. and I therefore especially value your opinion.[2] The next stage is to move the political big wigs forward, and that can only be done by the formation of a powerful and impudent public opinion.

Yours very sincerely

J.C. Smuts

[1] On 23 December 1918, General Jan Smuts,(1870–1950) the South African statesman, sent Wells, via his secretary, an advance print of a pamphlet on the League of Nations. He said the reason for sending it to Wells was "The subject is of the greatest importance, in view of the coming Peace, and he wishes to be helpful in the formulation of public opinion and stirring the public interest in the League." In a letter which we apparently do not have, Wells responded very favourably to Smuts. However, Smuts's return letter to Wells, from the Savoy Hotel, dated 28 December 1918, is probably important enough to publish as an indication of the work which Wells and others gave to the establishment of a working peace at the end of the First World War.
[2] Wells was Secretary of the League of Free Nations Association. The group, which was promoted by both Crewe House and private individuals, published *The Idea of the League of Nations* and *The Way to a League of Nations* (London: Oxford and Boston, 1919).

1183. To Frank Swinnerton

Arkansas, ALS[1]

Easton Glebe
Dunmow

Dec. 1918.

Dear Swinny,

I am in bed with a congested chest. These are the days when one demands a book to read. I've always held off Shops & Houses doubting if it could possibly be as good as Nocturne. Well, for the first 2/3rds of it I am amazed. It is the same hand & I apologize profusely to you for doubting. The three Hughes girls wonderful! You have done something of the kind before but never any better & Dorothy wonderful too. Alive & right. Up to the concert my Son. And then! What happened Swinny? The writing became automatic. The lamentable Charles Dickens became the control. The story is "wound up" brutally. Dorothy herself becomes a member of the Punch family. I can't understand it.

I know this isn't the nicest sort of letter to get but it is the most wholesome. You really are a First Rater. The first part of the book proves it. Nocturne might have been a kind of flash of splendour but this book shows you can do it again. But you've jilted the book after leading it on.

Yours ever,
H.G.

[1] A typed copy of this letter is in Illinois also.

1184. To Herbert Read[1]

Victoria, ALS

Easton Glebe
Dunmow [end 1918-early 1919?]

Dear Captain Read,

This is dreadful reading & wonderfully well done. It is a piece of unity that ought to be kept always. But I don't know much about publishing it. I think if you were to send it to G.H. Mair of the Cross Atlantic News Service, 184 Fleet Street, E.C. 4., with this letter, he will probably give you the best possible advice. An American magazine rather than an English one paying about half as much or less seems the most likely destination. Then if you can do two or three other things of this sort, you will have a great and memorable book.

Yours ever,
H.G. Wells

---

[1] Herbert Read, (1893–1968) was Professor of Art in Edinburgh, a poet and student of aesthetics. This letter may possibly refer to Read's efforts to collect and publish the papers of the imagist poet, T. E. Hulme (1883–1917) who was killed in France. The papers were published as *Speculations* (1924) and *More Speculations* (1956). Read's best known books are *The Meaning of Art* (1931) and his *Collected Poems* (1946). I attribute the date to this letter from the use of Captain Read by Wells in his salutation. The letter may concern some of Read's own poetry, as well, see letter 1185.

1185. To Herbert Read

Victoria, ALS

Easton Glebe
Dunmow [date unknown]

Dear Mr. Read,

Your Naked Warriors is frightful & very fine. But why are all you chaps putting it down in vers libre & a generally artificial manner. What is wanted for the next generation & what you could do before you forget it (you will forget a lot of it) is to set down in plain English, without any setting as fiction or poetry, a lot of things that you know have happened. What war is. It would be much more impressive than even your verses to tell how Cornelius Vane or the biggest man in Kneeshire was shot in a dispassionate way with an open minded discussion of its necessity – under the conditions. The night before last I heard a young general talking about Passhendael (was it – I have a frighttful cold in me & cannot spell?) in 1917. He was just facty – but it was tremendous.

Yours very sincerely,
H.G. Wells

1186. To C. K. Ogden[1]

Boston, ALS

Easton Glebe
Dunmow [date unknown , *c.* 1918]

Dear Ogden,

I've read your article & am very pleased with it. I don't take it seriously. Language has always seemed to me a comic (but the only) way of counting & holding down & getting on with thought. Grotesque – like the sexual act for example – but all we have. I used to find Lady Welby a frightful bore because she was really serious in her idea that something else was practicable now. You aren't like that.

Yours,
H.G. Wells

[1] Ogden developed Basic English, a modified version of English based on simplified spelling. He and Wells had discussed the possibility of using Basic for propaganda purposes. They became friends and their correspondence continued until Wells's death.

1187. To C. K. Ogden

Boston, ALS

Easton Glebe
Dunmow [late October 1918]

Dear Ogden,

I was deeply hurt by your silence but now I understand. We do want the population question tackled. It is the "theatrical" weak point of the League of Nations.

I am on the phone at St. James's Court, S.W. Victoria 2360 (then after much bitterness you get me) Could you lunch with me Nov 5th at the Royal Automobile (the Reform is still closed to visitors)? Or would you care to come to Easton for a week end — a flat restful offer usually except for a certain ball game. There is a train from Bps. Stortford that gets you to the Lodge station about 6 & a back train to Cambridge on the Monday morning.

Yours ever,
H. G. Wells

1188. To C. K. Ogden

Boston, ALS

52, St. James's Court
Buckingham Gate, S.W.1 [*c.* 1918]

Dear Mr. Ogden,

I am sending you some particulars of the L. of Nations Research Ctte. You will see from the account of the work of that Research Ctte,that we have a biological sub-ctte which has to prepare what will ultimately become a chapter in a textbook of the L of N's. Now, one part of that chapter, a part standing alone, must be a dissertation on the population question. The L of N's will give peace to the earth & some sort of economic unit control. But the Bengali & the Chinese (?) will then breed like rabbits – then what? (I put these things in compact brevity – customary between really great minds). I am told you are the man are to handle the question & show that the remedy & necessity is raising the standard of life. Would you care to become a member of the biological subcommittee of the Research Ctte of the L of N's.Union (forgetting the L of N's Associates) with the set intent of writing that part of our chapter for us? I serve as the chairman of the said Research Ctte.

Yours very sincerely,
H.G. Wells

1189. To C. K. Ogden

Boston, APCS

52, St. James's Court
Buckingham Gate, S.W. 1 [November ?1918]

Dear Ogden,

I waited half an hour for you at the Reform on Friday. What happened to you?

H.G. Wells

1190. To Frank Swinnerton

Reading, ALS

Easton Glebe
Dunmow [late 1918]

Dear Swinnerton,

As Sir Harry's agent[1] I don't like the agreement sent to him. If your people don't like the prospect of the book, I wish they would say so and have done with it. [*in Swinnerton's hand*, 'But we do.'] I know perfectly well that it is a good saleable book & when I proposed it to your people I meant it as a great thing for them. But if so there must be a fair agreement. Your people have tried to sneak the U.S.A. rights [*F.S. note*, 'essentially these to be authors'] – & Canada which is greedy & ridiculous. They've started a haggle about (chapter 1) the length. They've imposed vexatious terms about the correction of proofs

[*F.S.*, 'merely formal to keep costs down'] ; they've put in an iniquitous remainder clause, they burke presentation copies (thoroughly bad publishing) by clause 9 & they give the author no relief if they let the book go out of print.

I ask you, is this business? Will you let me have a fresh agreement cutting out USA & Canada & specifying 'no longer than 150,000 or shorter than 80,000 as the length, omitting 2 & 4, the last three lines of 5 / 6 & 8/ altering 6 to 25 in Clause 9, & inserting the usual clause providing for the return of plates & all rights to the author if the publisher declines to reprint when out of print, after due request from the author.

I have been ill in bed or I would have attended to the damn business before. I've now got all the m.s. in hand & Jane has been checking on it. It is a great lark & I will write it a selling preface as soon as I am bright enough. If you people are really under the impression that this is a dud book, you had better see it. But I'm not pleased with your people. I meant nothing but kindness to them.

Yours ever,
H.G.

---

[1] Sir Harry Hamilton Johnston (1858–1927) was an explorer, anthropologist, and later a novelist. He led the Royal Society's expedition to Mount Kilimanjaro in 1884. He and Wells had met at the 1916 meetings of the Committee on the Neglect of Science. They became good friends, and Johnston worked assiduously on the early portions of the *Outline of History*. Wells acted as his agent in producing his first novel, *The Gay-Dombeys* (1919), which tells the story of the Dombey family in Australia. Wells wrote an introduction to the book, and read it in its various stages, as did Catherine Wells. Johnston lived a good part of the year 1918 at Easton Glebe. Wells suffered from symptoms of Spanish influenza for much of 1919.

1191. To Maurice Baring

Illinois, ANS

Easton Glebe,
Dunmow [1918?]

Dear Maurice,

I was very sorry not to meet you at Mrs. Pedley's. Will you lunch with me at the Reform at one on Friday?

Yours ever,
H.G.

1192. To Marie Butts

Illinois, ALS

Easton Glebe
Dunmow [Date unknown, 1918?]

Dear Miss Butts,

Unless you think strongly otherwise I don't think I shall obey the Divine summons & write to Madame D. I feel that if she is encouraged she may become very tiresome. But you have made a delightful account of her & I will write rather than desolate her. I feel however if I don't write God will simply reject me & all will go on happily with some other agent in my place. I hope Sir Oliver L.[1] I suppose you couldn't suggest that?

Yours ever,
H. G. Wells

Don't you think that – all things considered – we are getting much more League of Nations than we had any right to hope for?

[1] Lodge (1851–1940) was a physicist. He was the first president of the newly founded University of Birmingham. He was a pioneer in radio-telegraphy and made several important discoveries concerning the properties of radio waves.

1193. Ezra Pound to H. G. Wells

Illinois, TLS

[London?] 6 Sept. 1918

Dear Mr Wells:

Can you give me half an hour, some time this week or next? I think there is just a chance of getting rid of the American import duty on books, and of getting a decent American copyright law. For two dozen reasons both personal and national, the job is very much worth doing.

Nothing but Armageddon would make it possible, but the circumstances should be used now that they are standing about.

Sincerely yours,
Ezra Pound

[*In Pound's hand*] I have not written to anyone else on the subject & should like to talk with you before I do so.

1194. To Frank Swinnerton

Reading, ALS

Easton Glebe,
Dunmow [1918]

Dear Swinny [1]

Certainly. What do you say to 15% – the first 3000 & 20% to 6000 & then 25%? Or anything else you like to suggest. I leave it to you. But I want a clause from you either to publish an edition at 25 pence or less or to relinquish the cheap rights, two years after publication. I want to get the stuff to the elementary teacher.

Yours ever,
H. G.

? Colonial and India. Tauchnitz rights reserved.

[1] This letter has to do with the final negotiations of *In The Fourth Year*.

1195. To Marie Stopes

Illinois, TCCS

52, St. James's Court,
Buckingham Gate, S.W.1. [1918]

Dear Dr. Stopes,

I am reading (I really am) the Constitution of Coal* But most of my time is taken up with the Constitution of the League of Nations. I certainly want some more talk with you and I hope soon when I can find a white spot in my tangle of committees that coincides with a white spot in your tangle we may have some more talk.

Yours,
H. G. Wells

[*In Stopes's hand:*] * This was the memoir published by the Government – written by myself and Dr. R. V. Wheeler of the Home Office.

1196. To Marie Stopes

Illinois, TCCS

52, St. James's Court,
Buckingham Gate, S.W.1 [1918]

Dear Dr. Stopes,

I'm so sorry about Thursday evening. I had told my wife to make a dinner engagement on Wednesday or Thursday. I made no note of it in my engagement book. Hence the clash. The other engagement would have been difficult to break because (1) A, the hostess wasn't in her own house but in the house of another lady, B, we didn't know, so that A would have have had to explain to B after B had planned out a dinner of her own and A's guests. (2) A isn't "one of us" and would have misunderstood our explanation. (3) A was in transit through London. But it shows how much I have to learn from Bennett who never does things like this.

I would [say] to you "Wednesday next preferably or Thursday". You have arranged Thursday, so Thursday it shall be at 7: 30 at the Lyceum for meeting.

Yours sincerely,

H.G. Wells

1197. To Marie Stopes

Illinois, TCCS

52, St. James's Court,
Buckingham Gate, S.W.1. [1918]

(Later than June when I married)[1]

Dear Doctor Stopes,

I will try to get you on Tuesday but – The situation is like this. I have a very bad cold and cough. I have to run about London and make a speech also in this week. I may get so knocked out that I can't come on Tuesday. On the other hand the chances are that I shall come. As, I take it, your dinner happens anyhow, may I accept provisionally? I have sent on your invitation to Miss West, who will reply. I have no doubt she will be as eager to come as I am.

I shall be at Easton Glebe, Easton Dunmow until Tuesday morning. Would it trouble you to let me have a card to say when and where at that address and also to this address "not to be forwarded".

I shall look forward with great interest to meeting Mr. ——————!? Do you realize I don't know your husband's name?

Yours,

H. G. Wells

[1] These words are Marie Stopes's later emendations, probably made when she was sorting her correspondence for a researcher.

1198. To Edward Garnett

Illinois, TLS

[London] [1918–19?]

Dear Garnett

I like your paper very much. We want a new thing in the place of the present L of N – whether we call it a revised L of N or experiment No. 2 is really a question of detail. We can't go on with what we have.

Yours ever,
H.G.

1199. To Leonard Woolf

Texas, ALS

Easton Glebe
Dunmow [late 1918]

Dear Woolf,

You see I am yours to command & I really shall read the International.

When would you like to have a serial in the Int'l Review? I am writing by this post to Massingham of a blunderingly brilliant opportunity for the Nation which might equally well be offered to the International. I have done a remarkable and beautiful (but in places & by the older standard slightly blasphemous) version of the book of Job. It is really a dissertation on good or evil in the world & education in relation to that. Job is a schoolmaster. God & Satan look at times nothing like the Absolute & the Relative. Elihu is a young doctor. Sir Eliphaz Burrows is the patentee of the Temanite hutments. Bildad has become Mr. William Dad & is a loving portrait of an honest county aeroplane builder. Zophar is Mr. Joseph Farr, a teacher of technical chemistry. The story is 40,000 words. It will divide into pieces of 10,000 and quite easily. It is finished & you can see it. The price for the Nation is £200, but the Int'l Review can have it for £100. It will probably also run in The New Republic.[1]

Yours ever,
H.G.Wells

N.B. Book publication not later than May 20th.

[1] This is the novel, *The Undying Fire.* (London: Cassell, 1919). It appeared in the *International Review*, March–June 1919. The first portion of the book also appeared in *The Nation*, 8 March 1919, and it was serialized in *The New Republic* from 29 March to 10 May 1919.

1200. To St John Ervine

Texas, ALS

Easton Glebe,
Dunmow. Sunday [1918]

Dear St. John Ervine,

I've been wanting to get your address for weeks. I heard about your leg & wanted to know how you were. We've been anxious to get you here sometime for a talk. I have a little job (unpaid) that I want to put upon your shoulders coincident with the L. of F. Nations movement.[1]

There is no one I would sooner have at 22 [*an illegible address*] than yourself. I shall make it my business on the executive to secure you if I can. It's not much of a job for you & it's no great kindness to entangle you in it, but you are the very man we ought to have. And it can, in good hands, be a great work. It will be very pleasing to me to have your there because I'm very much in & out & I shall then have a chance of getting to know & speak with you.

Yours ever,
H. G. Wells

[1] Wells was very active in the League of Free Nations movement. This private group, along with other groups acted as a promotional agency for a form of world government. Wells was probably recruiting St John Ervine to one of their committees, researching, writing, and giving speeches.